More Praise
LEVON
From Down in the D...
Birth of the Band and Beyond by ...a B. Tooze

"Sandra B. Tooze . . . brings a man and a musical era to life. . . . [She] interviewed Helm in 1996 for her Muddy Waters biography. She draws on that material as well as on rigorous research and numerous other interviews with key figures to depict Levon Helm both as a consummate musician and somebody it'd be a lot of fun to have a beer or three with. . . . Ms. Tooze relates . . . the cradle-to-grave sweetness of his personality (with the occasional flare of red-hot anger, to be sure) and the subtle, understated nature of a technique that influences drummers to this day."

—*The Wall Street Journal*

"This is a book about one of the great characters I have ever been privileged to know. Levon Helm was a brilliant actor, a wildly gifted musician, a hilarious and charming raconteur and, like me, an Arkansan with a mama named Nell. This book beautifully celebrates his exuberant and remarkable life."

—Mary Steenburgen, Academy Award–winning actress

"Sandra Tooze has not only written the definitive biography of Levon Helm, but she's also written an outstanding life-story of modern American music, encompassing all of the colorful characters that Levon Helm met along the way. Levon embodied the evolution of blues, rockabilly, country and folk that meant so much to so many, defined the soundtrack of my life, and inspired a generation. . . . A must-read musical odyssey of a true hero of rock and roll."

—Steve Katz, founding member of Blood, Sweat, and Tears; author of *Blood, Sweat, and My Rock 'n' Roll Years*

"Sandra B. Tooze offers a brilliant road map covering how [Levon Helm] became one of the towering figures in 20th century music. Ride shotgun as she follows Helm's wild exploits—from early Sixties cult hero with the Hawks to playing stadiums with Bob Dylan and the Band. This is the story of rock and roll."

—Brad Tolinski, author of *Play It Loud: An Epic History of the Style, Sound and Revolution of the Electric Guitar* and *Light & Shade: Conversations with Jimmy Page*

"Tooze has done us a significant service—*Levon* is a judicious, tender and remarkably thorough biography of an American icon, a definitive biography of Levon Helm."

—Arkansas Democrat-Gazette

"Levon Helm went from Turkey Scratch, Arkansas, to Bob Dylan's first electric tour, Woodstock, and the Last Waltz. And that's only scratching the surface of where author Sandra Tooze takes us as she deftly tells the story of a modern music icon. *Levon* brilliantly puts readers behind the scenes of many of the most important moments in rock 'n' roll history with a man whose influence on them was immense."

—John Glatt, author of *Live at the Fillmore East and West: Getting Backstage and Personal with Rock's Greatest Legends*

"I thought I knew a lot about my old friend Levon Helm, but Sandra Tooze has captured all the nitty-gritty details of the life and times of the man who was, arguably, the most soulful and beloved drummer/singer in the history of rock 'n' roll. . . . A wild journey that is exhilarating and heartbreaking in equal measure."

—Happy Traum, folk musician, Woodstock, New York

"The Band's drummer Levon Helm always insisted he had 'the best seat in the house' and his views from that perch are recounted here. Tooze is a no-frills scribe—she's done her homework and she straightforwardly tells Helm's story. Kicking off with a vivid description of his youth, she reminds us that he came from the South that he brought to life in song."

—MOJO

"I just finished the book and you really nailed him. Your writing is awesome because I couldn't put it down."

—David Fishof, former manager of the Band and founder of the Rock and Roll Fantasy Camp

"[Pulling] no punches, Sandra Tooze's *Levon* is a love letter to one of the signature drummers and dynamic vocalists in rock history. . . . Not forgetting what is important, Tooze fills the book with observations and firsthand accounts of what made Helm worth writing and reading about, pointedly his preternatural musical talents that he never abandoned and continued to celebrate until his last breath."

—The Aquarian Weekly: 50 Years of Rock

"Thank you for writing this book. I could see Levon on every page—feel his happiness, frustrations and his journey from Marvell to Woodstock. As I read, I remembered the many happy times we enjoyed. He was my friend through thick and thin—good and bad. I miss him."

—Mary Vaiden, lifelong friend of Levon

LEVON

From Down in the Delta to the Birth of THE BAND and Beyond

SANDRA B. TOOZE

DIVERSION
BOOKS

For
Mary and Anna Lee,
whose love for Levon
still burns bright

For more information, email info@diversionbooks.com

Diversion Books
A Division of Diversion Publishing Corp.
www.DiversionBooks.com

First Diversion Books edition June 2019.
First Diversion Books trade paperback edition August 2021
Hardcover ISBN: 978-1-63576-704-9
Trade Paperback ISBN: 978-1-63576-913-5
eBook ISBN: 978-1-63576-702-5

Printed in The United States of America

Library of Congress cataloging-in-publication data is available on file.

CONTENTS

1

Best Seat in the House

Levon Helm always said of the Arkansas Delta, "It's where blues, country, and gospel hit in a head-on collision, which became rock 'n' roll."

Round about cotton-picking time each fall while Levon was growing up in the 1940s and '50s, tent shows would stop off in Marvell—a bustling little town near his home in Turkey Scratch. For Levon, a precocious, fun-loving child, there was nothing better. Across the road from the fairgrounds, troupes such as Silas Green from New Orleans or Levon's favorite, the F.S. Walcott Rabbit's Foot Minstrels, would pitch a large four- or five-pole tent around a couple of flatbed trucks, positioned side by side to create the stage. Smaller tents served as dressing rooms and refreshment stands. A master of ceremonies, dressed in a top hat and twirling a cane, introduced the performers: singers, black-face comedians, a chorus line of beautiful dancers, and a nine- or twelve-piece band with horns and a full rhythm section that included—most crucially—a drummer.

"It was the only time that country people like us could see a real staged show with costumes and lights and music and everything," Levon remarked. "So that was high rollin' back in the cotton country...And we always went, of course. You couldn't beat that show."

"In those days," Helm noted, "the audience was segregated: People with red hair and freckles would be on one side, and darker complexions on the other. I'd be sitting there right in front of the drummer, just staring at him all night."

To young Levon, the drum stool looked like the best seat in the house.

The main program ended at about 10:30 or 11:00, when most families with children went home, but Levon's father would let him stick around. For an extra dollar or so, the late-night show—called the midnight ramble—continued until twelve. "That's when the jokes would get spicier, and the girls would do a little hoochie-coochie dance," Levon often said, with a twinkle in his eye. "Back then, to get down to a bikini was like, 'Goddamn!'"

Looking back on a career that coincided with the evolution of modern music, Helm cited those tent shows as seminal to the development of rock 'n' roll: "Today when folks ask me where rock 'n' roll came from, I always think of our Southern medicine shows and that wild midnight ramble. Chuck Berry's duckwalk, Elvis Presley's rockabilly gyrations, Little Richard's dancing on the piano, Jerry Lee Lewis's antics and Ronnie Hawkins's camel walk could have come right off F.S. Walcott's stage."

MARK LAVON HELM[*] was born in Elaine, Arkansas, on May 26, 1940, to Nell and Diamond Helm, the second of four surviving children. It was a tiny town—population 634—situated in the heart of the Arkansas Delta, the alluvial plain of the Mississippi River, twenty-five miles southwest of Helena and ninety miles southwest of Memphis. His parents were sharecroppers, both with their roots in the area.

Bubba Sullivan, the same age as Levon, was also born in Elaine, and he recalls it as a lively town when he was growing up. It did, however, have an infamous past. Back in 1919, Phillips County was a hotbed of racial unrest, with black citizens protesting unfair sharecropping practices, trying to organize a farmers' union, while white planters were quaking in fear of a Communist revolution. Terrified that a black insurrection was at hand, white women and children were evacuated to Helena while those who stayed behind were barricaded in heavily guarded buildings.

---

[*] Lavon (accent on the second syllable) would be largely known as Levon by the time he was seventeen and had joined Ronnie Hawkins and the Hawks. For consistency, he will be referred to as Levon throughout.

When shots were fired at a black church meeting, authorities claimed a riot was underway. The Helm family heeded the warnings, armed with guns to defend themselves and their property, but the unrest never reached them. Some whites rampaged through the countryside, killing all the blacks they encountered. Troops were sent in, and all blacks in the area were thrown into a stockade. Those who supported unionization were charged with murder and tortured to elicit confessions.

Morse Gist—who became the proprietor of a Helena music store—remembered his mother telling him that his father, an ex-trooper, was called back into service. His dad was sent to Elaine where, Gist said, "I got the impression he was not very proud of what took place down there."

Levon was born into a state that had never fully recovered from the Civil War. The economy had been devastated, and slavery was replaced by sharecropping, which was still a form of peonage for blacks and poor whites. Following a feeble recovery in the 1920s, the Great Flood, Great Drought, then Great Depression brought more disaster to Arkansas. Of the 1930s in the Arkansas Delta, English novelist Naomi Mitchinson wrote, "I have travelled over most of Europe and part of Africa, but I have never seen such terrible sights as I saw yesterday among the sharecroppers of Arkansas."

Elaine is situated only a couple of miles from the Mississippi River, and when Nell and Diamond lived there with their first baby, Modena, before Levon was born, there were gangs of itinerant laborers working on the nearby levee. Some of these drifters were ruthless criminals, and on one occasion, the Helm family found their country cabin surrounded. As Levon heard it,

> One night, they were having supper. They heard a rattling at the door. They heard a rattle at the window. They knew there was somebody out there. A rattle at the back door. They knew there were a *lot* of people out there...[My dad] makes a big show of taking up his shotgun, loading it up, getting behind my mom. Mom picks up the baby, picks up the lamp, they walk out the door. Nobody bothers 'em. They knew they gotta keep walking, and

there was nothing to look back for. The food on the table was what it was all about.

When Levon was a baby, more than half of all Arkansans were farmers, and the state was limping out of the Depression. Residents had poor access to health care, and a survey of the state's schoolchildren found that 90 percent displayed some physical ailment, including rickets and undernourishment. The quality of education was well below the national average, with only 70,000 of the 170,000 youths of high-school age enrolled in school. Only 8.7 percent of those age twenty-five and over had completed four years of high school. When the draft for World War II was instituted in September 1940, there was a problem recruiting in Arkansas because so many men were not up to military standards—a rejection rate of 43 percent due to poor health and low education levels.

As the war ended, mechanized agriculture was displacing laborers, and many returning veterans dismissed farming outright. Combined with a lack of jobs in other sectors, it all led to a population decrease in 1940s Arkansas.

Then there was the stain of segregation, a reality of the South while Levon was growing up. The first school district in Arkansas's Delta region to integrate was Hoxie in 1955, but in 1957, Governor Orval Faubus used the Arkansas National Guard to prevent integration at Little Rock's Central High School.

LEVON'S FATHER, JASPER Diamond Helm, was born in 1910 in Holly Grove, directly west of Phillips County. Tall and lean with limited education, he was resolute in his opinions and as equally unshakeable in his support of Levon. Levon's mother, Emma "Nell" Helm, born in 1916, was pretty and blonde, a sweet woman who nevertheless was the disciplinarian of the family. "They were gregarious," Levon's close friend Paul Berry recalls, "both of them extroverts in their own way, totally unselfconscious about their background. Levon's personality is very, very reflective of his mom and daddy."

Nell married Diamond in Elaine in 1933, and their first daughter, Modena, was born the following year. Linda was born two years after

Levon, followed by a baby who died, then the birth of Levon's brother, Wheeler. As a child, Levon was especially close with his sisters and very protective of them. Throughout the years, he became especially devoted to Modena.

While Levon was an infant, the family moved about thirty miles north to the small settlement of Turkey Scratch, Arkansas, on the western edge of Big Creek. The region saw conflict in the Civil War after Unionists freed the slaves in the Helena area. During the Battle of Big Creek, Confederate soldiers raided plantations that had been confiscated by the Unionists, intending to re-enslave the workers. On July 27, 1864, approximately fifteen miles south of where Turkey Scratch came to be located, about four hundred colored Unionist infantry and artillerymen held off almost twice as many Confederate soldiers until the Illinois cavalry arrived and repelled the Confederates—although they continued to stage raids in the area.

In the early days before there was a township of Turkey Scratch, only a few settlers had cleared small farms in that vicinity. Most of the territory west of Big Creek was undeveloped timberland, with low wetlands punctuated with sand ridges. The hunting was excellent and varied, with one exception: there were few wild turkeys. One group of hunters brought a flock there to establish themselves. As the turkeys scrounged for insects to eat, they clawed the leaves off the sand ridges, thus the name of the hunting grounds became Turkey Scratch. Robert Lockwood Jr., the great bluesman who considered himself the stepson of Robert Johnson, was born here in 1915. After drainage canals were dug around 1923, more land could be cleared, roads were built, and new farmers settled. A.B. Thompson Sr. and his wife, Jessie, moved to the area in 1929. He built a general store and post office, and called the corner where it was situated Turkey Scratch.

Until Levon was three or four years old, his family lived in a shack not far from A.B. Thompson's shop, on the opposite side of the road. Like most sharecroppers' homes it was elevated somewhat by pyramid-shaped concrete blocks as a guard against flooding, although this house was a substantial distance from Big Creek. It was an unpainted shotgun shack, but turned sideways, so the longest sides faced front and back. It had a small living room, two bedrooms, and at the back, a kitchen with a wood stove. A potbelly stove probably supplied heat for the front room. A long front porch extended the width of the house, and a smaller porch was outside the kitchen. There was a water pump in the yard, as well as an outhouse.

Like Elaine, this was cotton country, flat as a drum head, the cultivated fields interspersed with stands of oaks, gums, ash, and cypress. During the long summers when it was time to chop cotton, the average temperature rose to 95 degrees and could climb much higher. "Boy, that sun would rip your hide right off," Levon said, remembering the oppressive heat in the shadeless fields.

Diamond, as a typical sharecropper, likely farmed about twenty acres of cotton on land owned by A.B. Thompson Sr., who also owned their house. Devised after slavery to keep workers tied to the land in service to the planter, the sharecropping system usually designated half the profits from the crop at harvest time to the owner, with the sharecropper keeping the rest. This type of farming was a family occupation; as soon as children were old enough, they helped. By the age of seven, Levon had a summer job as a waterboy for the families and hired hands working in the fields.

IT WAS A happy childhood, abounding in laughs and mischief. Levon was an attractive, clean-cut youngster, with blond, neatly combed hair, typically dressed in freshly laundered shirt and jeans. Brimming with hijinks and jokes, he was quick to coax a chuckle out of most situations. Irreverent, yet kind and thoughtful, he possessed a magnetic charm that drew people to him and allowed him to sidestep situations he wanted to avoid. Levon had a laid-back personality, but despite that, was the leader of the pack. He was not reluctant to tell his friends what to do and how to do it; they loved him anyway.

The residence the Helms moved to next—still on A.B. Thompson's land—was farther from the store, tucked back on a dirt road on land adjoining Big Creek, and near the Cavette family. Longtime neighbors, the Helms and Cavettes were also the best of friends. Clyde and Arlena Cavette had one son and three girls, Mary, Tiny, and Jessie Mae, whom everyone called Sister. Levon's mother, Nell, and Arlena had grown up together in Elaine, and most Sundays the two families got together for dinner. In fact, they had relatives in common—one of Mary's aunts married Levon's uncle, and another aunt married Nell's cousin. Often Levon just called Mary his sister.

"I don't remember ever *not* knowing him," another neighbor, Anna Lee Amsden (née Williams), declares. "We went to…grade school, high school, graduated together. We'd just always been friends." She was born the same year as Levon, and her sister, Peggy, and Levon's sister Linda were the same age, so they all spent a lot of time together as kids.

"We'd go to each other's house," Anna Lee says. "Our parents would play cards together—and … if the kids went to sleep, that's where they left them until the next morning. So there might be four or five kids piled up on one bed, and that's where we'd wake up the next morning, and our parents would come get us. We were just like brother and sister forever."

Another of Levon's closest friends was Charles "Mutt" Cagle, whose family lived about a mile away from the Helms. In fact, before Levon's sister Modena finished high school, she married Mutt's brother Ralph, and their son Terry—Levon's nephew—would follow a musical path like his uncle.

The Helm household was full of fun. Both Nell and Diamond had a good sense of humor. "It was like a carnival every time you went over there," Anna Lee recollects, chuckling, "because Levon would do something that Nell would get so upset with him [over], and she'd want to kill him, but she wound up laughing."

It didn't matter that economically they were impoverished. Anna Lee continues,

> We were probably in the fourth or fifth grade before any of us had electricity, if we had it that early…Mutt Cagle's dad had the first television in the [area]. I remember Wednesday nights we would all go over there and watch the fights…Eventually, we all got television and fans. We were all dirt poor, but we didn't know it, you know, because everybody was the same…We didn't know there was any other way. It didn't bother us not having electricity or an indoor bathroom because nobody else had one.

Mary Vaiden (née Cavette) laughs when she thinks of Diamond: "Oh, my Lord, Diamond always knew the answer to everything. Sometimes it wasn't correct, but he was adamant about it. He was a strong supporter of Levon, and if Levon said, 'Let's walk down this ditch naked,' he'd say, 'Well, okay, son.' He was very outgoing." Mary doesn't recall him doing much farm work; he hired out a lot of it. He had a job as deputy sheriff for the Marvell police force in the late 1940s or early 1950s. Levon's uncle Alan Cooper was deputy sheriff there in the 1960s.

Nell was a God-fearing woman who taught her children that despite the segregated society they lived in, all races were equal. She was strict with them—as well as with her extended family and the neighbors' kids. Both Levon and her grandson Terry Cagle remember her digging her fingernails into their scalp when they misbehaved. Mary admits, "She'd spank me as quick as she'd spank Levon. She was a special person. She was the one in the family who kept a hand on him; it wasn't Diamond." Keeping her children clean and tidy on a dirt farm wasn't easy. "Nell washed [laundry] in a wash pot," Mary says, "and hung the clothes on a line with starch, and they were as stiff as a board, and she would iron them with a flatiron. Levon could never get out of that house and onto that school bus without starched and ironed blue jeans with a crease in them."

LEVON HAD SOME Chickasaw blood through his father's mother, Dollie. After Diamond's father died and left her with seven or eight children, Dollie married a Pentecostal preacher named Luther Crawford. "Miss Dollie, oh, she was a mess!" Mary recalls with a laugh. "We'd go down to her house in West Helena, and she lived in a shotgun house, and you could just run straight through. And we'd run and play, running back and forth, and she'd say [of Levon], 'That child is going to be in prison before he's grown'…She just could not make him behave."

After her second husband died, Dollie moved in with the Helms. When Nell called her for dinner, she'd reply, "'Well, if the Lord's willing, I'll make it,'" Mary says. "And she would carry this spittoon with her wherever she went—it was a Maxwell House can, a coffee can—and she carried it everywhere. And she'd be talking to you and spitting. I always thought she looked like a little bird. She was so cute, and she was always immaculately dressed, very clean, starched and ironed, and she would put her hair up in a bun…She still was in charge, she thought."

Levon adored his grandfather Wheeler Wilson, Nell's father, who lived in nearby Marvell. Mary remembers him as kind and sweet. Nell's parents separated when she was a child, and Wheeler married Agnes, whom Nell thought of as her mother. Later in life, Levon bought them a house. Agnes had only one earlobe as the result of a contentious partnership her grandfather had regarding a corn crop. When Wheeler's disgruntled partner burst into their house, a gunfight ensued, and a bullet sheared off part of Agnes's ear.

Levon was nurtured in an incredibly tight, loving community. Many people in Turkey Scratch were, at the very least, distant kin, and even those who weren't—black or white—were often called aunt or uncle by the children. One example was Sam Tillman, a black man who worked for Anna Lee's uncle and lived with his family just down the road from the Helms. "We all loved him, but he would get on to us just like he would one of his kids," Anna Lee points out. "And Levon made the remark one time that he'd always go see Sam every time that he came home, and he said, 'You know, Babe, I believe Sam would still spank me if I did something wrong.' He was part of the community, and we loved him to death."

Every year on the Fourth of July, the residents of Turkey Scratch got together for a fish-fry picnic. The men went hogging for catfish in Big Creek, then the women fried the catch in lard and served it with fried potatoes and watermelon. For Halloween, the adults would throw a wiener-roast party for the kids. On other occasions, families got together for house parties, pie suppers, or bonfires.

Nearly all the white people in the community attended County Line Missionary Baptist Church on County Line Road outside Turkey Scratch. One Sunday every June, the congregation held a southern church custom called "all-day singing and dinner on the ground." "Daddy would hook the horses to the wagon, and Mama would have a wagonful of food," Mary reminisces. "I don't know why they cooked so much. People would bring a sheet, and they would line them up, end to end, all around one side of the church. They'd lay it out, and people would eat all day long, and they would sing [hymns]…Levon loved that because he could eat all day."

Levon said, "Everybody would make picnic baskets and bring them to the church. They'd get out a big meal at dinner time. They'd lay out bed sheets and put the food out … all lined up, a row of bed sheets and a big tub of lemon-aide down at the end. It was great." It was spiritual but also fun. "You know, music is supposed to have that kind of effect," he said. "It's supposed to take you out of these troubles and misfortunate times."

"Levon loved those things," Anna Lee confirms. "He couldn't wait…People would bring potato salad and they'd bring block ice for tea…To the day he died, he always wanted to have something like that in Marvell…He talked to me about that so many times."

MUSIC WAS A significant part of life in Turkey Scratch, especially in the Helm household. Mary attributes most of Levon's prodigious musical talent to his mother. Nell and Modena had beautiful alto voices, and they also sang in church, although there wasn't yet a church choir. Diamond, a musician with a good bass voice, had a deep repertoire of folk and country songs that he passed on to Levon.

"Sitting on Top of the World" was one of Diamond's favorites, and several tracks on Levon's 2007 recording, *Dirt Farmer*, were songs the family sang at home. As Levon pointed out,

> Songs like "The Girl I Left Behind," "Blind Child," and "Little Birds" are the first songs that I ever learned. My mom and my older sister were good singers, and my dad played guitar and sang for Saturday-night house dances out in the country. We all came from that participation generation, you know. If you wanted to hear music back then you had to sing it yourself, and play for each other.

It was from singing with his family that Levon developed his understanding of vocal harmony. He credited "Little Birds" for providing him with his first awareness of where to place harmonies and how they support each other.

Before he had a guitar or drums, Levon was singing while beating out a rhythm in hambone dances, a holdover from minstrel shows, where the performers stomp and pat their arms, chest, and legs in time with the music. He remembered a house party one night at his uncle Pudge's when he was a young child. They moved the furniture aside and the music was supplied by a guitarist, a fiddle player, and likely someone on mandolin. "I had a big grocery box, pasteboard box," Levon said, "and I beat that thing to death that night...I volunteered to play percussion."

Before the Helm house had electricity, they had a battery-operated radio, or if the battery failed, Diamond extended a cable from the tractor battery to the radio in order to tune in to stations as far away as Shreveport, Oklahoma City, or Nashville. Nashville's WLAC was known for its R&B shows, and that city's WSM broadcast of the *Grand Ole Opry* with Bill Monroe and His Bluegrass Boys was a family favorite. As Levon got older, WDIA Memphis had disc jockeys B.B. King and Rufus Thomas; a host of blues stars played on West Memphis station KWEM; and Ike Turner had a show on Clarksdale, Mississippi's WROX. And throughout it all, Helena had KFFA.

Levon's musical tastes were significantly shaped by a steady diet of blues on Helena's Radio KFFA, which was inaugurated in 1941 upstairs in the Floyd Truck Lines building on Cherry Street. Beginning in November that year, every day from noon until 12:15—and later 12:15 to 12:30—the station aired the first regular radio show to feature blues, *King Biscuit Time*.

When Max Moore, owner of the Interstate Grocery Company, got stuck with a load of flour he couldn't move, he had a brilliant idea how to advertise it. Bubba Sullivan got the story from *King Biscuit Time*'s longest-serving host, Sonny Payne:

> Sonny Boy [Williamson] and them wanted to play on the radio, and Sonny [Payne] said that Mr. Max Moore was smart enough to know that there was like 142 grocery stores in Phillips County then...so he got King Biscuit Flour [as a sponsor], and he gave

them fifteen minutes on the radio. You think, now here it is 1941, and you hear blacks on the radio. Shit, that was the first [station] that ever let blacks play—a big deal.

The longest-running radio show in history first featured live performances by harmonica player and singer Sonny Boy Williamson II (a.k.a. Rice Miller) and electric guitarist Robert Lockwood—both vocalists as well—then soon included James "Peck" Curtis on drums and pianist Robert "Dudlow" Taylor. It was a huge success. Throughout its long run, the show's band comprised different musicians, all blues masters, such as Robert Nighthawk, Pinetop Perkins, Willie Love, and Houston Stackhouse. The show also featured guest performers—Little Walter, Jimmy Rogers, and Muddy Waters, to name a few—who used it as a way to advertise their upcoming gigs in the area.

"These were working musicians," Levon said of the King Biscuit Entertainers. "People like Sonny Boy, Robert 'Dudlow' Taylor, Peck Curtis, and Pinetop Perkins had it in their blood. For them it was a calling; there was no other choice. I like to think one of the reasons they achieved greatness was that they were pretty much left alone to develop their own musical styles."

If a music show was in the vicinity, the Helm family were there, and Diamond thought nothing of driving to Memphis to see a performer. Looking back at the genesis of his musical career, Levon attributed it to the first live show he remembered attending—Bill Monroe and His Bluegrass Boys—when he was six years old. "That night changed my life," Levon stated, "and I had no doubt what I wanted to do from then on." Music was now his mission. Before he had an instrument, he'd sing and pretend to play guitar on a broom. Cowboys and Indians had lost its appeal.

2

From Turkey Scratch to the Hawk

Although he was bright, Levon cared little about academics. At school, he played the clown—his constant, distinctive laugh carried throughout the classroom. He tried to find a joke in every situation and frustrated his teacher without end.

For his first three grades, Levon attended the County Line School, housed in the County Line Missionary Baptist Church. Every morning, he walked along the dirt road in front of his cabin out to the main gravel road to meet Anna Lee, and they'd walk to school together.

Miss Stella Harris taught all eight grades—about sixteen students altogether—in the church's Sunday-school room. Modena was in the eighth grade when Levon started there. There was no running water, so the bathrooms were dry toilets behind the school. For fun in the schoolyard, the kids would play softball or dodgeball or run races.

As Anna Lee recalls, "Everything was funny to him, and he would aggravate the heck out of you," particularly one girl, Linda Lou, whom Levon drove crazy. "She wasn't a pretty girl, but she thought she was. She had a bad temper, and she'd get in trouble, and Miss Harris would lock her in what we called the cloakroom—all it was was a small closet [where] we kept our lunches and coats...and she ate everybody's lunch!"

When it came time for vaccinations, a big, rough Italian nurse the students were afraid of traveled to the County Line School to administer the needles. "We had a pump house," Anna Lee relates, "and we'd go in there one at a time and get a shot. Levon always hid in the woodshed, which was back a piece from the school...He didn't want a shot. They'd have to go drag him out every time."

But Helm would step up to take care of his friends. "There were some boys that lived down close to me," says Anna Lee. "I got a bicycle when I guess I was seven years old, and I rode it to school one morning, and they threw rocks at my bicycle. So Levon and another friend—a good friend of his named…Mutt Cagle—both walked me home that afternoon, beat the boys up. Got in a fight with them. They never threw rocks at my bicycle again."

SIX MILES SOUTH of Turkey Scratch, about seventy miles southwest of Memphis, lies the small town of Marvell, named after Marvell M. Corruth, who moved there with his slaves from Lamar, Mississippi, shortly before the Civil War and established a large plantation. It was also the birthplace, in 1926, of blues drummer Sam Carr, son of guitarist Robert Nighthawk. By the time Levon was born, 830 people resided in Marvell, and the population stayed at about a thousand all during the 1940s. A busy railroad line ran through town transporting freight—especially cotton—as well as passengers. The "doodlebug" was a small train that took people back and forth to Helena, and the Delta Eagle connected Helena with Memphis.

Starting in fourth grade, Levon and Anna Lee went to school in Marvell. "We were really uptown then," Anna Lee observes. "We were going to the *big* school." Mary, who was two years older, was already there. When Helm first attended it, the building housed all grades up to twelfth; later on, another structure was constructed on the property for the lower grades. Also on school grounds, there was a brick building for the teen club. It was a segregated school; Marvell public schools didn't integrate until 1965.

It was here that Levon met Edward "Fireball" Carter, who became a lifelong friend. He'd had some medical challenges since birth, and because he was so slow on the football field, the coach chided him by sarcastically calling him Fireball. He was the conscientious one of Levon's group of male friends.

Levon always joked around on the ride to and from school. "There was this one little girl on the school bus," says Anna Lee. "Her name was Daisy Mae, and he just worried the heck out of her. And she'd get off the bus, and he'd [call out,] 'I love you, Daisy Mae!' and she'd just shake her head and keep running. This went on forever. He just loved to aggravate people." Yet it was all done in a friendly way, never mean. Anything he could think to do for a laugh, he'd do. He was always popular; everyone liked him. In seventh grade, he and Molly Molitor were chosen king and queen of their class, and through the years, he won several popularity contests.

Fourth grade was also the year Helm got his first guitar, a Silvertone. Their mailman, Ralph DeJohnette, was the best guitar player in the area, and Levon would meet him at their mailbox in order for Ralph to show him how to tune his guitar or go to his house to practice.

EVERYBODY WENT TO town on Saturday afternoons, especially after the harvest was in and farmers had extra money to spend. The main street of Marvell was bustling. Levon and Anna Lee would buy a Coke float and a bag of peanuts at Anderson's Drug Store for fifteen cents. The Hirsch and Davidson's department stores faced each other on opposing corners, and nearby was a building housing the pool hall and the Capitol Theatre.

Levon loved the movies. He and his friends would go to the Capitol, where African-American patrons were segregated in the balcony, to see the latest film. His friends would leave after the feature was finished, but Levon stayed on to watch the same show over and over. Finally, at eleven o'clock, "We'd be waiting for him to come out," Mary explains. "We were sleepy. And Nell would say, 'Diamond, go in there and get Levon.' And Levon would be sitting in the front row... On Saturday night that was the big deal. We knew we had to wait for him. And nobody said a word; we just waited."

In addition to movies and music, two of Helm's other preferred activities were eating and sleeping. Anna Lee remembers late one morning when Levon was still in bed: "Somebody said, 'Well, why don't you fry some bacon? That'll wake him up.' [Nell] said, 'Hell, I could cook a whole hog, and he wouldn't turn over.'"

Nell was an excellent cook. "If you got invited to eat with Nell and Diamond, you didn't turn it down," Paul Berry notes. "She could do fried okra...in an iron skillet, cornbread, minute steak, fried chicken, pie, cobblers—what we call good ol' home cookin'. It's soul food...It was just good, and there was going to be plenty of it." Levon loved her lemon icebox pie. As he grew older, she'd have to make an extra one just for him as he'd eat a whole pie in one sitting. Anna Lee laughs as she recounts one incident in which Levon had no shame in pursuit of one of his favorite foods:

> They went to the store one time, the Safeway in Helena. That was a big trip, to go to Helena then. And watermelons had just come out. And he's ten or eleven years old, maybe older...and he wanted a watermelon. And [Nell] said, "I'm not buying a watermelon now because they're too high. Wait 'til the price goes down." [Levon said,] "I want a watermelon!" She says, "Well, you might as well hush, you're not getting one." All of a sudden he falls to the floor, and he starts screaming and beating the floor and kicking his feet: "I want a watermelon! I want a watermelon!" Poor Nell was so embarrassed. She said, "Oh, hell, if you'll get up, I'll buy you a damn watermelon," and she bought him a watermelon.

If there was an unpleasant situation he wanted to avoid, Levon wasn't shy about doing so. When it came time each summer for a dose of Grove's Tasteless Chill Tonic—a concoction of quinine suspended in syrup used as a preventative for malaria—Helm would run away and hide. One day when Levon, Linda, Anna Lee, and Peggy were playing at the Williams house, they were particularly naughty, and after repeated warnings, Mrs. Williams spanked the three girls, but then Levon was nowhere to be found.

> Our house sat on concrete stilts, [Anna Lee reports,] and he was under the house! And he would just laugh his head off. And my mum told him, "You got to come out sooner or later. When you do, you're going to get a spanking." Well, he just laughed. So finally he wore her down, and she got to laughing because his laugh was infectious. And when he came out, he was the one that didn't get a spanking. She'd forgotten about it, and it was over with.

Levon's laugh was something no one forgot—very unusual—and he laughed a lot. He could find something humorous in most situations, and if nothing funny was happening, he'd create it with his jokes and by playing tricks on people. But it would end with a hug. He was kind and never shied away from making fun of himself.

He was curious and began his smoking habit early. Mary remembers him trying to smoke before he had access to tobacco: "One day [Levon] said, 'We're gonna smoke,' and I said, 'No, we're not gonna smoke'…Anyway, it was a muscadine vine [a type of grape]…He broke [the thick vine] off, and he lit it, and we puffed on it…like a cigarette… About ten minutes into it, my whole mouth started swelling up, and I start crying, 'Oh, Mama Nell's gonna be so mad!'"

ON SATURDAYS, THE King Biscuit Entertainers traveled around Phillips County playing live shows at country grocery stores and gas stations in such places as Elaine, Marvell, and Wabash, and sometimes across the river in towns on the Mississippi-state side.

From about age nine, Levon tried to get to Marvell on any Saturday afternoon the King Biscuit Entertainers were playing there. The musicians came out on a small bus, which had "King Biscuit Time" and ads for the flour and Sonny Boy Meal painted on its sides. They'd spread out a tarp and open the back of the bus to reveal Dudlow Taylor's piano. Peck Curtis would set up his kit, and the rest of the band would put out their mics and amps and then plug in. They'd play for about an hour to large, enthusiastic crowds, then head off to another town. Levon loved it. And when Diamond took him to Helena, thirty-six miles from home, Levon could witness the radio show in person:

> My main piece of business was to make it to the radio station,
> [Levon said,] and they didn't care. I'm just a kid come in off the
> street…I would go in, get over in the corner and watch Sonny Boy
> and the King Biscuit band do their radio show. I'd stop by Abby's
> Cafe usually and grab myself three donuts for a quarter and have
> my lunch right there in the radio station. I guess that really put
> me over into the blues side of music as far as what I still favor.

Helena is the seat of Phillips County, which includes Elaine, Marvell, and Turkey Scratch. The town was incorporated in 1833 and named after the daughter of Sylvanus Phillips, considered to be the first white person to settle there in 1797. Unlike those other towns, Helena is on the shore of the Mississippi River, protected from its sometimes-devastating floods by a levee. It would become a prosperous steamboat port.

Right after World War II, when Levon was a child, "Helena was like a little Chicago," Robert Lockwood told Bubba Sullivan. "It was businesses everywhere…There wasn't a lot of money around, but see, they worked in the fields every day, but they [got] *paid* every day. You might not make much money, but you know when money's in circulation, you know, everybody's gettin' a little piece of the pie." As Helm grew up, Helena still had vestiges of its frontier heritage. There was gambling, bootlegging, and prostitution, and most of the blues icons had played there, such as Muddy Waters, Howlin' Wolf, and Robert Johnson. By 1950, Helena's population was just over eleven thousand.

As he grew up, some of Helm's favorite musicians, in addition to the King Biscuit Entertainers, were his early influence Bill Monroe and other country artists such as Patsy Cline, the Carlisles, Ernest Tubb, George Jones, and especially Lefty Frizzell. In the blues genre, it was Jimmy Reed and Muddy Waters. He declared, "Right there in the Mississippi Delta region around Helena and Clarksdale, Mississippi, and West Memphis, Arkansas, in that area, Muddy was one of the big record sellers. Muddy was a big radio star and Muddy was a big jukebox star also. You couldn't miss Muddy Waters's music, it was that strong, and it was on the good radio stations, and you could find it on those big Wurlitzer jukeboxes. It was great." Whenever Muddy came to play nearby, Levon would go out to hear him. "You knew that the Muddy Waters Band was going to be one of the best you'd hear all year."

THE SPRING THAT Levon was nine, Diamond taught him to drive a tractor, plowing fields then planting cotton seeds. To add more interest to a day on the tractor, "He liked to clown with it. He liked to pop wheelies and turn circles and all that stuff," Anna Lee remarks.

"He would enter tractor-driving contests and win at the [state] fair... Anything he set his mind to do, he could do."

Like so many in the Delta, "the sound of the blues, rhythm and blues, and country music is what we lived for, black and white alike," Helm said. "It gave you strength to sit on one of those throbbing Allis-Chalmers tractors all day if you knew you were going to hear something on the radio or maybe see a show that evening." Levon always had a battery-operated radio with him on the tractor, so he could sing along with the songs he heard on KFFA or on KXJK in Forrest City. One time when Diamond hauled him out of bed to work on the tractor when he'd been out too late the night before, Levon fell asleep at the wheel. "Grandpa got him for that!" his nephew Terry says.

"Levon, he just never took anything too seriously, you know," Mary points out, "but he hated the farm, I can tell you that. Both of us did." Nevertheless, "He always loved the smell of new ground being turned over in the spring," Anna Lee adds. "[In later years,] he loved to come home in the spring of the year and just be around it."

Helm described the cycle of work on the farm: "You get out of school in May, and that's when you've already started planting cotton. You work from there right through 'til September, and the only break in there is the Fourth of July. I found out at about the age of twelve that the way to get off that stinking tractor, out of that 105-degree heat, was to get on that guitar." In that environment, "Music was a way to get a lot of things that you couldn't get otherwise," says Bubba Sullivan.

In about sixth grade, Levon joined the 4-H Club, but he had an ulterior motive: "On the farm, the 4-H Club was how country kids got to go to town," he said. "If it was that or a hog-calling contest... whatever it was going down, I was game for it...just to get out of work!" He even managed to avoid a lot of the drudgery of raising a calf each year for the state fair competition. Anna Lee laughs when she remembers Levon's tactics: "That's where he talked Mary and me into feeding, carrying water for that calf, grooming it, 'cause he could talk us into anything. And he'd take it to the fair and win first place and get all the money. We never got a dime!"

Levon, Mary, and Anna Lee worked in the summers chopping

cotton—hoeing the cotton rows to thin out the plants and turn over weeds and grass. The fields of the Helms and Cavettes extended as far as Big Creek. "We would race like crazy to get to the end [of the rows] so we could go jump in the creek before the rest of the hands got there," Anna Lee says. It was sweltering, hard work, but also, "It was fun," she insists, "because he'd keep us laughing all the time. He'd pretend a snake was there [in the water]…It was never a dull moment. We had a ball."

One of Helm's cherished memories was at harvest time, starting in September, when he would get in the back of a wagon "with two mules pullin' it, full of cotton and layin' up on the top of it, just as soft as a mattress, and layin' there and watchin' the sky go by…and that harness jinglin' and rattlin', going to…gin that cotton."

"I was a terrible cotton farmer," Levon conceded. "You know, I was a pretty good tractor driver. But I just didn't have the heart for it. And, you know, I would look up and see a plane going across and wonder if it was going to New York or somewhere."

Levon had other jobs as well. He adored A.B. Thompson and helped him in the general store. When Mary Phipps's shop on County Line Road was being renovated, Levon did a lot of the work, and hired a hot local band, Harold Jenkins and the Rock Housers, to play at the grand opening. Jenkins, who later changed his name and gained worldwide fame as country star Conway Twitty, was born just across the Mississippi River and moved to Helena when he was ten. Levon also worked at Vic Thompson's grocery store in Marvell, and for a short time, he had his dream job in the movie theater, but he was let go for consuming too much popcorn and too many Cokes.

WEATHER IN TURKEY Scratch could be dangerous. The worst flood occurred in 1937, when the water from Big Creek extended as far as County Line Church. While Levon was growing up, the Helm farmland was occasionally inundated. One year, he and his friends went water skiing over some fields. Another time water flooded the road in both directions from the Helm house, so the whole family moved in with the Cavettes for a week. Levon was always especially kind to Mary's sister, Jessie Mae—nicknamed Sister—who was disabled; he made sure to include her in everything. Sister, Mary, and Levon were out together in a rowboat overtop a flooded cotton field when somehow Sister fell out. Levon leapt up, ready to dive in and rescue her, heroically proclaiming, "If I die, you all tell Mama that I died saving Sister!" He jumped in and discovered, with some disappointment, that the water was only up to his knees.

More common than floods were mud holes in the roads. They'd get so bad that the Helms would use either a tractor, boat, or mule to get the kids across one to catch the school bus. At times, the bus itself had to be pulled though the mire by a tractor.

Tornadoes could be deadly in this part of the country. In fact, before Levon was born, the Helm house was torn off its foundation by one. The Cavettes had a storm cellar—dug by Clyde Cavette and Diamond—that they shared with the Helms. Those without a safe place to go might shelter under Big Creek Bridge. Mary remembers how everyone hated the storm cellar, except her daddy, Clyde, and Diamond. At the slightest hint of a squall, they'd insist that the two families go into the cellar. "It could sprinkle rain in Little Rock," says Mary, "and we had to go to the storm cellar."

In March 1952, severe weather descended on the South, spawning eleven lethal tornados, causing 209 deaths, 112 in Arkansas alone. In Judsonia, a town about 60 miles northwest of Turkey Scratch, 365 homes were destroyed and 30 people killed. That time Diamond and Clyde insisted that the two families stay in the shelter for three days. Terry Cagle was there, a little boy standing up to his knees in water. "It was horrible," Mary maintains. "Can you imagine? His family and our family in this little bitty storm cellar?…When Daddy and Diamond finally decided we could get out, Nell said, 'I am never coming down here again!' We never went again. Diamond and Daddy would go, and we'd stay in the house."

AT ABOUT AGE ten, Levon reprised the hambone act he'd been doing at home with his family to win a talent show at school. Then a couple of years later, he fashioned a standup bass from a washtub, broom handle, and clothesline for his younger sister, Linda. With himself on his Silvertone guitar, harmonica, and Jew's harp—and playing hambone on his thigh—they became the musical duo Lavon and Linda.

For Levon especially it was an ideal way to get out of doing chores and some schoolwork, plus an opportunity to hone his music and performing skills. They played songs they'd learned at home and hits from the radio. Both siblings were outgoing and very personable. With Linda looking demure in a pretty dress and Levon wearing starched and pressed jeans, their blond, all-American good looks and talent gained them ever-widening audiences. "We played at the high school anytime they would ask us," Levon said. "Lions Clubs, Rotaries, 4-H Clubs."

Paul Berry had a part-time job serving food and washing dishes at the University of Arkansas in Fayetteville, in the northwest corner of the state, when he first saw Lavon and Linda perform there at the annual 4-H Club statewide final competition. A thousand to fifteen hundred winners from local districts in such diverse skills as chicken and cattle rearing, parliamentary procedure, cooking, tractor driving, and music came to Fayetteville in hopes of being proclaimed the best in the state. During a break, Paul snuck a look at the music performances in which Lavon and Linda were competing:

> They started with "Dance with me, Henry, all right, baby," and they did a Carlisle family thing, "No Help Wanted." It was a call-and-response kind of thing: "Do you need any help?" "No help wanted"…It had a little turnaround there on the gut bucket that was really clever. I just sat up straight in my seat. I don't want to get too hyperbolic about it, but they were rocking. We didn't have the term *rock 'n' roll*. This is 1952 or '3—something like that—and rock 'n' roll wasn't in the lexicon in my neighborhood.

Berry was impressed with their vocal harmonies and the way Levon connected with the audience. "He had personality," he says. "You could tell that when he was performing there was nothing self-conscious about him, and he was that way about his music the rest of his life. He did what he did, and it never was about lights or costumes; it was about whether he could rock you or not—and he could." Not only did Lavon and Linda win that competition, Helm also came first in the statewide tractor-driving contest.

Helena businessman Charlie Halbert drove them to different performance venues. So, too, did Bob Evans—the big-time promoter for the Miss Arkansas and Miss Louisiana pageants and the songwriter of "Phillips County Blues"—who took the duo under his wing. They played at pageants and political rallies. As Lavon and Linda became well known around the state, they performed on Helena's KFFA Radio and on *Dance Party*, a WHBQ-TV production out of Memphis. Evans also managed a majorette, and Levon played behind her while she twirled her baton.

Levon got his first good guitar, a three-quarter-size Martin, when he was fourteen. The Gist Music Company, a store on Helena's Cherry Street, was opened in 1953 by Morse Gist's father, who ran a jukebox business out of the back with his music store in front. "He bought his first Martin guitar here," Morse Gist said of Helm. "His daddy brought him in, and he picked it out…I remember that Levon paid it off fifty cents a week, an agreement with his father." For the rest of his life, Levon would drop in the store to see Mr. Gist anytime he was in Helena.

Another guitar player joined the duo on occasion. Thurlow Brown, a guitar and upright-bass player, was at least a couple of years older than Levon and was an amazing musician. He'd been out to California and played guitar with Roy Nichols and James Burton, and he brought their influences back to Helena. He had the first Telecaster in Phillips County—Mr. Gist ordered it for him—and his playing was different, hot. He could have gone on the road with a band, but he wouldn't leave his farm. He was a character, and Levon loved to laugh about his exploits. At one point, Thurlow got a mail-order monkey as a pet, and when the two of them had had a few beers, they got into aggressive wrestling matches. Thurlow was a tough guy, but as the monkey grew, Thurlow was increasingly outmatched and finally realized he had to get rid of his pet.

As Linda became a teenager, her mother concluded it was improper for her to have her leg up on top of the washtub. Nell finally pronounced, "No more, 'cause I can see up your dress." And that was the end of Lavon and Linda.

ELVIS PRESLEY STARTED attracting attention in 1954 with his Sun Records hits "That's All Right," "Blue Moon of Kentucky," and "Good Rockin' Tonight," and his appearances on *Louisiana Hayride*. On December 2 that year, with Helm in raptures, he sang and played acoustic rhythm guitar at Helena's Catholic Club with Scotty Moore on electric guitar and Bill Black slapping the upright bass while spinning it around. There were no drums, and, "The nuns wouldn't allow him to do his gyratin'," Levon remembered. Nevertheless, he described it as one of the most astounding shows of his life. Bubba Sullivan was also there and recollects Elvis performing "Tutti Frutti" as he shook his leg to the screams of all the girls.

On January 14, 1955, Elvis was back in the area, and Levon and his friends caught the show in the high school auditorium in Marianna, just a few miles north of Turkey Scratch. This time Bill was playing an electric bass, and Elvis had a drummer—D.J. Fontana, the former house drummer for the *Louisiana Hayride* radio show. The impact the performance had on young Helm was monumental. He observed, "D.J.'s drum parts changed Elvis, Scotty, and Bill's good rockin' trio into one of the top-notch rock 'n' roll bands in the Memphis area. Now the show was truly electrifying." He saw that Fontana was "doubling everything that Elvis is doing. He's doubling part of what Bill Black is doing. He's answering Scotty Moore's riffs and just knocking the lights out with them drums…It was one of the best bands you ever heard."

> When D.J. Fontana showed up on the scene, boy, was that something! [Helm said] He would just plant those drums! It'd always been that the rockabilly stuff was real bouncy, driving fours on the bass drum, almost like a jazz feel at times. Circling, just continuously circling. But when D.J. came in, all of a sudden he would plant that thing down and he would start stacking verses against each other with his fills, building up to the solos, and riding the solos in and riding them out. It was great because D.J. gave the music some foundation, some architecture. He was a hell of a drummer, and his technique was great. He had fast hands and could do them Buddy Rich kind of press rolls if he wanted to. He played like a big band drummer—full throttle.

Levon recalled the impact that "Money Honey" had on the crowd: "Then D.J. would put that triplicate on you: rat tat tat, rat tat tat, WHAM! People didn't know what they were supposed to do or not do—they were up on their chairs." Anna Lee was there with Levon and some other friends, and she saw how overwhelmed Helm was with Fontana. An older, red-headed boy named Max Hill, nicknamed Swivel Hips, was also in attendance. "And Elvis was singing and dancing," Anna Lee says, "and Max jumped up… in the aisle and started dancing…Elvis just took the microphone and said, 'Take it, Red!' and just kind of stood back and watched him go."

Other musicians who were Levon's favorites included Huey "Piano" Smith and rockabilly bands such as Billy Lee Riley and the Little Green Men, and Jerry Lee Lewis. Locally, he enjoyed Ralph DeJohnette, drummer Bubba Stewart, and their electric-mandolin player, who performed most Saturday afternoons in Marvell's pool hall.

By the time he was fifteen, Helm was going as far as Memphis to hear musicians or to sneak into Helena's notorious Delta Supper Club, the Rebel Club in Osceola, and Newport's Silver Moon. Levon had a high-school friend he'd go to hear bands with. "B.L. Reed was the one who first started taking Levon to shows because he had a car and nobody else had one," Mary reveals. "B.L. said, 'Do you smoke?' and Levon said no. He said, 'Now you do,' and gave him a cigarette. And later on, he said, 'Do you drink beer?' and Levon said no, and he said, 'Well, now you do.' So B.L. was his teacher."

If live music wasn't on offer, Helm went to Chapel Silas's grocery store in Trenton, just south of Marvell, where, as Levon says, "Mr. Silas had one of the best jukeboxes in Phillips County, and I would settle there and feed that jukebox and he would feed me, you know, bologna and cheese."

Mary remembers one night when Levon was about fifteen and everyone was at a high school basketball game watching him play. The police appeared with some devastating news for the Helm family. Their house had burned to the ground; they lost everything. It was likely caused by an intruder who had broken in to steal their hams. "In a situation like that," Mary says, "the community comes together and helps them refurnish their home." From here, the Helms moved down the dirt road to an old structure that previously housed the Gotze store and installed a kitchen so it was suitable to live in.

BUBBA SULLIVAN GOT to know Helm when they were both in high school—Bubba in Elaine and Levon in Marvell—because their schools competed in athletics. "He wasn't worth a shit in sports," Bubba comments, although everyone was encouraged to try. Levon played softball, junior basketball, and football.

He started playing football in the seventh grade—he was number 54—but Levon admitted that wasn't where his talents lay. Even though he was fit and quick, he said, "Hell, I didn't know what to do when we had the ball." When he was in high school, he played right guard for the Marvell Mustangs. "The coach was Ervin 'Whale' Crown," he recalled. "That bastard weighed 350 to 360 pounds…He'd been an offensive tackle at Southern Mississippi, then he came back to us and he tortured us…He'd scream, 'You little idiot…Get on the end of the bench so I don't have to look at you!'"

ALTHOUGH HE WAS a guitarist, Levon continued to be fascinated by drums. "I thought [F.S.] Walcott had the best band," he concluded, "and between their left-handed drummer and James 'Peck' Curtis, Sonny Boy Williamson's drummer, I knew exactly where I wanted to sit when I got to play with a band."

Peck Curtis was a profound influence. Born in 1912 in Benoit, Mississippi, and raised in Arkansas, Peck was a well-rounded entertainer—a musician, tap dancer, and blues singer—who'd toured in the 1930s with medicine shows, and had played washboard and drums with the likes of Memphis Slim, the Memphis Jug Band, Howlin' Wolf, and Robert Johnson. It's been said that Peck made the drums sound like an orchestra, darting in and out of a song, sometimes sparse, other times deep and dense, never a slave to strict 4/4 time. He played with homemade blast sticks—or hot-rod sticks—bundled lengths of piano wire fitted into a wooden handle. "He'd have a stick in his left hand," Helm explained, "and carry that hot rod in his right: Rap, bap, bap,

bap! Then he'd go to the cymbals for the crash with the piano strings, and it was a wild damn sound." Looking back at the times he saw the King Biscuit Entertainers, Levon said,

> As good as the band sounded, it seemed that [Peck] was definitely having the most fun. I locked into the drums at that point. Later, I heard Jack Nance, Conway Twitty's drummer, and all the great drummers in Memphis—Jimmy Van Eaton, Al Jackson and Willie Hall—the Chicago boys (Fred Below and Clifton James) and the people at Sun Records and Vee-Jay, but most of my style was based on Peck and Sonny Boy—the Delta blues style with the shuffle. Through the years, I've quickened the pace to a more rock-and-roll meter and time frame, but it still bases itself back to Peck, Sonny Boy Williamson, and the King Biscuit Boys.

The other notable drummer who came out of Phillips County was Sam Carr, although by the time Levon was growing up, Carr had moved on. Perhaps the strongest impetus for Helm to concentrate on drumming was supplied by Jimmy Van Eaton, who'd played drums with Billy Lee Riley and the Little Green Men, and Harold Jenkins. He was a session musician at Sun Records for the likes of Charlie Rich, Roy Orbison, Johnny Cash, and perhaps most notably for Jerry Lee Lewis.

D.J. Fontana, the Louisiana-born drummer who'd rocked Levon's world when he first toured with Elvis, was another major influence. Fontana played with the King for fourteen years, supplying the back-beat for such standards as "Blue Suede Shoes," "Heartbreak Hotel," "Jailhouse Rock," and "Hound Dog."

In the blues world, Levon was impressed with Fred Below from Chicago, who played with many of the giants at Chess Records, including Muddy Waters, Howlin' Wolf, Little Walter, and Chuck Berry. Another Chicago blues drummer, Clifton James, inspired Levon with his distinctive beat on Bo Diddley's hits. Helm also loved big-band drummers, such as those who played behind Junior Parker. Another favorite was Earl Palmer, a New Orleans R&B drummer who displayed his innovative style on numerous Fats Domino and Little

Richard hits. He played no more and no less than the song required, a philosophy that Levon followed throughout his own career.

In order to perform in clubs, Helm taught himself to play a shuffle. He describes the night in Forrest City, Arkansas, when he first sat in as a drummer:

> I was fourteen or fifteen when I started going up to Memphis and seeing the players. But when I got a little older, I was one of those people who had to stay out all night, who couldn't go home. Eventually, I had a couple too many and sat in with somebody one night. The drummer got ill or didn't show up, so I just sat in. I watched a few of the drummers, and it looked so easy. So I ended up playing at a dance one night.

Levon joined the school drum corps when he was in tenth grade, the first year the school had a band, although at one point, he was temporarily kicked out. An influence for him in this type of drumming was the Grambling State Marching Band out of Louisiana. Levon could already play drums when he started with the band, and the school didn't offer any music training. "I would have enjoyed school a lot more if we'd had some real music classes," Helm maintained. "There were talent shows and school plays and we would encourage each other to sing and act, but it was more of a social thing." Terry Cagle, Levon's young nephew, attended elementary school then, and one of his fondest memories was when the band came out to call all classes to assembly. He could hear, above the rest, Levon beating his drum—and cutting through even that, Levon's unique laugh as he played.

Helm usually carried a small radio with him on the school bus. He'd play along on a Jew's harp or practice drums, as Anna Lee describes: "On the bus, when he got into the band at Marvell playing the drums, he would take two pencils and put his books in his lap, and he would play the drums. And the rim of the back of the bus was his cymbals. And he did that day after day after day."

When he was in Marvell on Saturday afternoons, Levon would often stop off to see Ralph DeJohnette and Bubba Stewart play at the pool hall while he'd study Stewart's drumming technique. He'd also spend a lot of time in another part of Marvell. "Behind the downtown area is an alley," Terry Cagle says, "and that alley is where the black club is, and they would rock 'n' roll until you didn't let 'em rock 'n' roll anymore."

AS FAR AS learning the school curriculum, Levon hadn't changed as a teenager. Anna Lee remembers the run-ins Helm had with a minister who was also the math teacher, Brother Steiner—a strict disciplinarian who was frequently exasperated by Levon's antics and academic laxness:

> [Levon] was such a clown, and the math teacher was too smart to be a teacher in a public school—Brother Steiner. He had written a book; he was just very, very smart. He'd caught his hand in a hay baler when he was a kid, and he had a steel plate in his hand... and he'd come up behind Levon, and he'd poke him on the head: "Helm, if a book falls from heaven and hits you in the head, don't think the good Lord sent it." Because he was just a clown. And I really think Brother Steiner...passed Levon and me, Bobby Watkins, Fireball and a few others just to get rid of us...[Levon] and Watkins always sat close together in class until they would be separated because they couldn't keep from talking. They'd talk or they'd make noise or he'd be sitting there tapping out music. We drove the teachers crazy. [laughs] But I guess they all liked us.

Levon had first-hand experience with the corporal punishment dealt out at Marvell School. "We had a paddle, and they'd tell you to bend over and grab your ankles," Helm noted. "You'd bend over in them tight jeans and *BAM*, four or five good ones." Anna Lee says,

> The rules were no running in the hall, no running to the lunchroom because we had to go from one school over to the elementary school to the lunchroom. And [Levon] and Fireball Carter, Bobby Watkins and Ray Foran were all running a race. The door had a half-glass door at the top, and they ran into the door and broke it. Had to go to the principal's office. Of course, they got a spanking.

Levon thinks, "Well, I'm gonna wait until last so it won't hurt so bad. He'll be tired." Well, they got Fireball first…[When it was Levon's turn,] he said Mr. Oaker, the principal, he actually picked him up off the floor when he come down with that paddle…He said [the principal] wasn't wore out.

[Levon hurt] so bad that he went to the boys' bathroom. He said, "I thought I was bleeding"…And he said he climbed up on the counter in the bathroom, pulled his pants down and was looking at his rear end [in the mirror] when the math teacher walks in. [laughs] He was German, and he said, "Helm, can I help you with anything?" [laughs] He said, "I was so embarrassed!" But the day we graduated, [Levon] stole that paddle, and it's floating in Big Creek somewhere. He said, "No other kid will be spanked with that paddle."

When Helm got his driver's license, Anna Lee remarks,

On Sunday afternoon, we'd go to Helena and drive Cherry Street, round and round and round…and wave at all the kids because all the kids from the surrounding communities would do that. Or we would go to the swimming pool and go swimming, in Helena over by the levee. Sometimes on Friday nights, if we didn't have football practice or basketball games…we would go to the drive-in movie in West Helena.

And just before they turned into the drive-in, in order to save on admission, they'd cram as many kids as they could into the trunk of the car.

Girls were naturally part of Helm's high school years. "Levon was very starch-and-iron crewcut, perfectly put together. Always had lots of girlfriends," Mary mentions, "but they changed probably about every two weeks. He always had the prettiest girlfriends, always the best ones." Dating was usually done in groups. One place they'd go was the gravel pit—a spot their parents said was off limits—and they'd climb the fire tower there. "Our parents never worried about us getting pregnant or anything like that. They worried about us getting *killed* because we'd do all this stupid stuff. But we did it in droves; we wouldn't have died by ourselves," says Anna Lee, laughing.

One of Mary's favorite stories was about the time Levon and his best friend, Mutt Cagle, set up a double date with two girls from Helena. "That was big time," she reveals.

> So they told [the girls] they were going to take them out to dinner, but they stopped at the grocery store and got some bologna and sliced white bread—Wonder Bread. They picked them up in a truck. They turned down the road to go to the country club, so the girls think they're going to the country club, but they parked under a tree and got out, put a blanket out. One of the girls, Levon said, would not get out of the car. [laughs] He was always pulling tricks on people.

It's been said that Levon cheated his way through school. It wasn't because he lacked intelligence—he was more focused on joking around and on music. He used to copy from Henry Sootoo, a Chinese-American friend. Another target for his eagle eye was Anna Lee's cousin Pat Wooten, a very good student. "She was left-handed," Anna Lee says, "and Levon always managed to get across the seat from her because she turned her paper upside down when she'd write. He always sat on the left-hand side of her and he copied off of her all the time. And he made the remark many a time, 'If it weren't for Pat Wooten, I would have never graduated.'"

WHEN LEVON WAS in high school he formed a band he called the Jungle Bush Beaters. Although his interest in drumming was growing, as well as his ability, he remained a guitarist with this group. Thurlow joined him on guitar, Jennings Strother was on an amplified standup bass, and a younger schoolmate, likely Tommy Hewlett, played a snare drum, with Mary Vaiden's cousin Jimmie Lee Harpole as an added attraction. "Tall, blonde, a very curvaceous girl," Mary states, "and all she did was stand up there and wiggle...She was decoration, but she enjoyed it, and they had a good time...Everybody thought they were good. Whenever they played, everybody came to see them."

> The Jungle Bush Beaters had perhaps the best guitar man any-where [Levon wrote]. Ask any music fan from the Delta about Thurlow Brown and the way he played that Fender Esquire. Thurlow was bending strings and stretching notes before I ever got to hear Fred Carter Jr. and Roy "the Werewolf" Buchanan. Thurlow Brown meant the musical world to me and filled my life with the knowledge of a master musician.
>
> As quiet and introverted as Thurlow was, he surprised some people when he met and immediately bonded with bottleneck guitarist Robert Nighthawk. They became lifelong friends... Thurlow was one of the few musicians that Nighthawk would even play with, that's how great he was.

Thurlow went on to back Mack Self in his recordings of "Easy to Love" and "Mad at You."

One of Helm's lifelong credos was, 'If they aren't up dancing, you haven't done your job as a musician,' and that started with the Jungle Bush Beaters. They performed the current hits of the day. "One of the first things we had to learn was how to play a dance," he said. "And if you didn't know how to play 'Let the Good Times Roll' by Louis Jordan, you know, you weren't going to play too good of a dance. And if you couldn't get the people on the dance floor, you know, your return engagements were going to suffer. That's what it's really all about to me." Their gigs were limited, however, because they were too young to play in local clubs.

C.W. Gatlin—future Rockabilly Hall of Fame guitarist—and Bubba Sullivan remember seeing Levon play at Albert Vogel's place near Wabash, just south of Marvell. When Vogel got out of the navy, he bought a set of drums from Morse Gist, set up a kitchen in his tractor shed and turned his shack into a juke joint. A relative of KFFA's Sonny Payne, Vogel was a strong supporter of music. He had some prominent blues artists at his juke, and black musicians could play there if they were good enough.

Bubba would get a ride out there with the farm hands who worked for his father. "One of these old rough, tough guys," is how Bubba describes Albert. "He had a black guy that worked for him called Big Jim...some of the King Biscuit Entertainers and C.W. Gatlin and some of those guys would all go out there and play." It was self-segregated—blacks danced on one side of the room, the whites on the other. The Mexican cotton pickers were served beer, but they had to stay outside. "If a fight started, Mr. Albert...and Jim would get back to back and they'd just clean house, man," Sullivan relates. Vogel fought at the drop of a hat, and there would be no interference from the law. Out where his shack was, he *was* the law.

"I remember the first time I went out there," Bubba says. "Thurlow's sitting there playing the guitar—had that damn cigarette stuck in the end of the guitar...He was just an ol' country guy. He'd be just as happy out there at Mr. Vogel's smoking a cigarette, playing a guitar and drinking a beer as he would have if he was playing the damn biggest hall in America." And if there were no other musicians around, he'd play along with the jukebox.

LOOKING BACK ON his early development as a drummer, Helm commented, "You had to imitate before you could possibly originate. You had to play like Earl Palmer and D.J. Fontana and be able to bring exactly what the song needs. Anything more than that, you may be working on a great style, but you're doing the music a disservice."

Lavon and Linda had opened for Harold Jenkins at the launch party for Mary Phipps's store. Impressed with the young man, Jenkins allowed him to sit in several times as a drummer and singer with his band, the Rock Housers. Anna Lee recalls Helm playing drums with the group when they performed at Marvell High School as a fundraiser for their class trip to Washington, D.C. Levon did a fine job with the more experienced musicians. "He could play anything, anyway, anyhow," she says.

Bubba Stewart, the Marvell drummer with Ralph DeJohnette, coached Helm for a while. Then Levon picked up more pointers from Jack Nance and Tommy "Porkchop" Markham, who played in the Rock Housers—Nance teaching him how to twirl his sticks. He also learned from watching W.S. Holland, Carl Perkins's left-handed drummer, whenever he performed in the area. As for stage presence, C.W. Gatlin says there was already none better; Helm had charisma.

"I've always thought that my snare drum should sound a lot like J.M. Van Eaton's snare drum on Jerry Lee's 'Whole Lotta Shakin',"' Levon observed. "That's usually the way I try to fix it. I like that sort of a dull 'thud' sound with lots of wood, using the snare for the beat. I like the bass drum kind of toned down, and I usually muffle the toms down quite a bit more than is usual. I think that's mainly my personal taste." That Memphis drum sound was born out of necessity. When recording in a small space, such as Sun Records, Helm said,

> Playin' in such confined quarters makes you cut back, tone down, and blend yourself more into the sound. A drummer has to be really careful because his instrument sounds the worst of the bunch if he's not. You know, it sounds like somebody dropped the kitchen stove if you don't watch out. So growin' up around Memphis, that's what we were taught to do—get that snare drum tuned down so that the louder you played it, the better it would sound. And the louder you played it, the more thud, bump, and feel you could put on the bottom of the music.

IT WAS THE end of 1957, and billowing yellow dust mixed with the exhaust of a car speeding up the dirt road leading to the Helms' shack. Seventeen-year-old Levon was heading home after doing his chores as Ronnie Hawkins—the outrageous, gutter-mouthed singer from up in Fayetteville who considered himself the second coming of Elvis—and his guitarist, Jimmy Ray "Luke" Paulman, introduced themselves. Ronnie was the image of unbridled rockabilly raunch with his pointed-toe shoes, tight pants, and hair fashioned into a pompadour that cascaded down his forehead in what he told Levon was his big-dick look.

What the Hawk was after was a drummer for his band.

3

"The Wildest, Fiercest, Speed-Driven Bar Band in America"

It's every teenaged boy's dream, offered to Levon Helm by the self-promoting rockabilly-star-in-his-own-mind Ronnie Hawkins—join my band, tour the continent, and get "more pussy than Frank Sinatra."

Ronald Cornett Hawkins—the Hawk—was born in 1935 in Huntsville, Arkansas, just west of Fayetteville in Ozark country—the son of a barber and school teacher. The family had already tasted success in the music business before Ronnie launched his career. His uncle Delmar Hawkins made a name for himself in California as a country fiddler when Ronnie was still quite young, and in 1957, his cousin Dale scored big with his rockabilly hit "Susie-Q."

A cocky youth, Hawkins had a car and a license when he was twelve, and he started running whiskey from Missouri into Oklahoma at fourteen. He made great money, and although he was too young to own a nightclub, he bought a couple of bars with his friend Dayton Stratton, an adult who acted as their frontman. Hawkins went to high school in Fayetteville, and one of his summer jobs was as a clown diver advertising Esther Williams swimming pools. Encouraged by his mother, he attended the University of Arkansas, majoring in physical education. But music got in the way.

He sang as a child and sat in with various acts that passed through Fayetteville, such as Harold Jenkins's and Roy Orbison's bands. He formed his first group, the Hawks, when he was in university. They played rockabilly, a hard-driving hybrid of blues and country. "We were trying to play black music," Ronnie says, "but it was coming out differently because we couldn't do it right. It was coming out like country rock. We were taking the old rhythm 'n' blues songs and playing them country style with a back beat." Dash Goff knew Hawkins when he was in high school and used to listen to the Hawks play at a gas station on Dickson Street. "They'd go over there on a Saturday night," he recalls, "and unplug the Coke machine and plug in a guitar amp, and they'd all play."

Ronnie had a shot at stardom when he was asked to cut some demos at Memphis's famed Sun Records, but the timing was off. Owner Sam Phillips was already overwhelmed with the success of Elvis Presley and Jerry Lee Lewis, and there wasn't room for Hawkins. Ronnie enlisted in the U.S. Army, and during his service, he joined four black musicians to form a band called the Blackhawks. After they broke up and Hawkins left the army, he got a call from Jimmy Ray Paulman, who Ronnie says had the reputation of being the best session guitar player in Memphis. Paulman told him some Sun musicians had put a band together, and they wanted Hawkins to front it. Ronnie was sure this was his ticket to fame, but by the time he arrived, the group had already disbanded. Only guitar player Jimmy Ray and Ronnie were interested in starting another band.

The Hawk had a problem. After hyping his sure-fire success in Memphis, he was too ashamed to go home. Jimmy Ray had a cousin in West Helena who played piano, so they headed there with the intention of hiring him and finding a drummer to form a new band.

Paulman was born in 1935 into a sharecropping family in Bearden, central Arkansas, and they moved to Marianna when he was six. His father bought him a cheap guitar, and a cousin taught him the basics. Jimmy Ray briefly joined a country band, the Hill County Playboys, then teamed up with Harold Jenkins and his Rock Housers on lead guitar. Then Jenkins was reborn as Conway Twitty, and their fortunes abruptly changed. In 1957, they had a minor hit with "Need Your Lovin'," written by Paulman and Twitty, and became the first rockabilly act booked in Canada. Paulman left the band later that year to back another Arkansan, Billy Riley, until that band broke up.

Paulman's cousin Willard "Pop" Jones had been playing piano for two or three years, assailing his keyboard with an unrestrained attack reminiscent of Jerry Lee Lewis, when Jimmy Ray and Ronnie hit town. He played so hard, he could almost obliterate a piano. C.W. Gatlin remembers playing with Willard one night in Osceola when they didn't have an amplifier. "Willard called up to get one," C.W. recollects. "The word was, '*Do not* lend Willard Jones an amplifier,' 'cause he'd tear it up...He talked them out of a brand-new Fender Showman, the biggest amp made then. I plugged in it, he plugged in it, we took off. When he brought it back, it looked like it was about ten years old—cigarette burns all over it, whiskey all over it."

Jimmy Ray's brother George played standup bass, and coincidentally when Levon first sat in with a band on drums, George had been in that Forrest City group. George had a drinking problem, was belligerent with the audience, and didn't get along with his brother, so he only played occasionally with this group that was known as the Hawks.

The Hawks started rehearsing without a drummer. As Levon put it, "We were drum poor right there in my part of Arkansas. Bubba [Stewart] and Peck [Curtis] were the only two people I knew that had a set of drums." It wasn't going to be easy for Hawkins to find a drummer.

There are several versions of how Levon came to Ronnie's attention. In one, Ed Burks, who knew Ronnie from the University of Arkansas, ran into him in Helena and offered him a room to rent at his grandmother's house. Ed had a music background in concert and marching bands, singing and playing the clarinet, piano, and harmonica, and had played a show with Levon in Memphis in the paraplegic ward at the veterans' hospital. Hawkins offered to get Burks a kit so he could try his hand at drumming. As Ed remembered it, "I said, 'Well, man, I'd love to, but as you know I'm certainly not a drummer. I can keep a beat, but that's about it. We're talking about a new form of music to me, you know.' I said, 'Now let me think a minute. I keep hearing about this guy from Marvell.' [Levon] was just a kid in high school then, sixteen or seventeen years old. So I got them together."

Levon understood that it was George Paulman who told Hawkins about him because he'd sat in with George a few times in Forrest City, although Levon's pal C.W. reveals a different story: "Hawk wanted a drummer, and him and Mack [Self] were big buddies, and Mack said, 'I don't know a drummer, but I know a boy's got rhythm; he can do hambone. I believe he can play drums.'" Anna Lee thinks it was likely Thurlow Brown who told Ronnie about Levon.

As Hawkins tells it, "Jones was the one that knew Levon. [Levon] sat in with him in Will 'Pop' Jones's little band. So he played a few times, and [Willard] said he was real good, good rhythm and everything. So we auditioned him, and he passed the test. And then we started practicing."

Levon couldn't wait to begin. Ronnie and Jimmy Ray joined Levon and his parents at their kitchen table to discuss Levon's future. Jimmy Ray had played the Ontario, Canada, circuit with local musician Harold Jenkins and knew that audiences up north were starved for good southern rockabilly, plus the money was far better than they could get at home. The Hawks intended to head for Canada.

Both Diamond and Nell were insistent that their son be the first in the family to graduate from high school. Modena had dropped out to get married, and they wanted Levon to have a diploma so he could get a decent job if music didn't pan out. Hawkins proposed that Levon rehearse with the band and play gigs with them only on weekends until he graduated in May, then they'd set off on the road.

Diamond and Nell eventually agreed to Ronnie's terms, although, "If Dad and Mom could have had their preference," Levon maintained, "they probably would have preferred that I be a doctor, a lawyer, a scientist, or a great humanitarian." On the other hand, Levon was overjoyed. Not only would he be a professional musician and get to see the world, it was a chance to escape what he hated most—slogging in the dust and sweltering heat on the farm.

Diamond remained concerned, however. He'd never been far from his part of Arkansas, but he thought he knew all about what he called Canadia: "Those goddamn Canadians up there in Canadia...They'll stick a goddamn knife in ya for a nickel, never mind a dime." According to Hawkins, all Diamond had seen of that country were pictures of nineteenth-century Western Canadian mountain men and calendars of the Ontario-born Dionne quintuplets—the Depression-era miracle babies.

THERE WAS ONE more obstacle: Levon didn't have a drum kit, and he couldn't afford to buy one. He began by using a set from Peck

Curtis while also borrowing Bubba Stewart's white oyster-pearl Slingerland kit.

In 1957, Ronnie was staying at Charlie Halbert's Rainbow Inn Motel in West Helena in exchange for working around the property. Halbert was a former UCLA football player and a flamboyant entrepreneur who had made his money in a California trucking business. He'd been a stand-in for movie star Buster Crabbe. He was also the proprietor of Helena's Delta Supper Club and the Cleburne Hotel. Halbert owned the ferry service that connected Helena with the Mississippi-state side of the river before there was a bridge, and Conway Twitty's father, Floyd Jenkins, worked for him as a captain on *The Belle of Chester*. Slot machines were not allowed onshore, so Charlie installed them on his ferries. Halbert became a legend in the area after killing a passenger with his bare hands for not paying the fare.

Charlie had an affinity for musicians and had booked Elvis Presley into Helena's Catholic Club when the singer was struggling. He also helped Carl Perkins and Harold Jenkins when they were starting out. Halbert knew the guys at KFFA and arranged for Ronnie's new band to rehearse there and to borrow the equipment of the King Biscuit Entertainers.

Hawkins was always a tough taskmaster, and it was no different back then. The group had to be able to play for a three-hour dance. With him fronting the Hawks on vocals, he rehearsed his bandmates relentlessly: Levon on guitar and drums with some vocals, pianist Pop Jones, lead guitarist Luke Paulman, and sporadically his brother George on bass. They learned such rockabilly standards as Roy Orbison's "Ooby Dooby" and "Go Go Go," "Flyin' Saucers Rock 'n' Roll" by Billy Lee Riley, Billy "the Kid" Emerson's "Red Hot," and other numbers by Warren Smith and Sonny Burgess.

Jimmy Ray was one of the best rockabilly guitar players in Memphis, and he taught the band a lot. Helm's deep knowledge of blues blended with the Hawk's country raunch to bring a new flavor to Ronnie's sound. Also, as part of his musical education, Levon was sent by Hawkins to watch Jimmy Van Eaton play whenever he was in the area, as Van Eaton confirms: "[Levon] used to hang around and try to steal my licks."

Hawkins recognized Helm's natural talent for playing drums. "He couldn't use all the stuff properly yet," Ronnie says, "but he had the rhythm, and that's all we needed…He learned everything on his own eventually." Even at seventeen, Levon was able to get drunk and still keep time. Hawkins knew that he had the chops: "Right from the start, Levon played more drums with less licks than any drummer in the world. And he could make it sound right."

As Helm practiced, he aimed for the Memphis drum sound—a flat, wooden thump with not much ring. The bass drum, too, was muffled down to a bump. He attached a piece of leather to the rim of his snare, and when he wanted a particularly warm, thick sound, he'd flick it with his stick to bring it over the top of the drum and play on that. He'd also tape a towel or even a Kotex pad to the underside of the snare. "It was more of a feel than a sound," Levon noted. "It would just kind of split that music apart for a second. But what you would hear most was that backbeat. It would be coming in right on the rim shot, just crackin' and knockin'." He used light sticks and played with a traditional grip—holding the right stick overhand and the left stick underhand. Ronnie said, "Levon went through sticks. Oh, man! You couldn't find any sticks that could take that abuse."

Of course, Helm was also a talented guitar player: "Hell, he might have been the best guitar player I ever had, too," the Hawk declares. "He was better than Robbie Robertson was early on."

THE FIRST GIG Levon played with Ronnie and the band was on a Friday night in 1957 at the Rebel Club in Osceola, in northeast Arkansas. The clientele had an unruly and sometimes violent reputation. "You had to show a razor and puke twice before they'd let you in," Hawkins warned the novice drummer, using a phrase that would become well worn describing the venues they played in those early years. Ronnie reminded the towheaded teen that he had to look twenty-one.

"Levon Helm had a drum solo the first time we ever played together… We didn't practice any drum solos," says Hawkins, laughing. "All of a sudden, I said, 'Hit it, Levon!' He got up and started that Stepin Fetchit bit, where he goes around tapping on tables and glasses. [laughter] Those old, drunk rednecks loved that shit. We outdrew everyone."

Hawkins had already honed his gymnastic chops diving into Ester Williams's swimming pools, and he brought those skills to his stage show, electrifying the crowd with his front flips off the stage, double back flips, splits, and his signature camel walk (a forward version of the moonwalk). If there was a wall at the side of the stage, he'd run right up it and do a back flip while still holding the mic. He had the charisma and crassness to ignite an audience. Jimmy Ray, sounding like Carl Perkins, dominated his instrument, fingerpicking, bending strings, creating a reverb sound, all to a pulsing rhythm. Pop Jones, with one leg kicked high, maniacally attacked the piano. "God, that rhythm was awesome!" Levon remembered. "I didn't really know what I was doing on the drums, so I just kept time. People danced, so I figured everything was on target. After the show Ronnie gave me fifteen bucks, and I was in heaven."

LEVON GOT THE downpayment for his own drum kit, a red-sparkled Gretsch, from Charlie Halbert. "Charlie took us up to Memphis a little later on, up to Hauch Music Company," he said, "and we pulled down that bright red set of Gretsches off the wall with the Zildjian cymbals, and Charlie co-signed the note with me." But Helm didn't have those drums long. A few gigs were cancelled so money was short, and he couldn't keep up the payments. He had to trade his new drums for old ones—with worn-out snares and loose skins—that Jack Nance had been playing in Harold Jenkins's group.

Even then, the Hawks knew they had talent and were hankering for recognition. In fact, according to Hawkins, "Every one of us had dreams of having Elvis Presley as our roadie! That's dreamin' pretty good, ain't it?…We thought we were going to be up there with the big boys in no time because we were young and very ignorant, but we thought we were mental giants."

Although Turkey Scratch is less than thirty miles from Helena, the location of the Helm homestead presented some challenges. Especially in the spring, a rainstorm could wash out the road and the only way one could get to the Helms' place was by boat or tractor. If it looked like rain was coming on a weekend, Levon packed his band suit on Thursday night and Ronnie drove out to pick him up so he could spend the night at Charlie Halbert's motel in town.

On weekends, they played up and down the Mississippi River on the Arkansas side, and in Memphis in brass-knuckle dives and for fraternity parties and dances, with Levon singing the occasional song. Even then, Helm had the amazing ability to vocalize independent of his drumming, as if he were two separate people.

The crowds they played for were tough, mostly white. At twelve years old, Mike Beebe, a future Arkansas governor, would heave himself up to a window at the Silver Moon Club in Newport to watch and listen to the group. "They say that girls actually have gotten pregnant on the dance floor," Hawkins says of that bar. "That's the big rumor about that place. It was pretty wild, but they loved their music." One time while the band was playing in West Helena, a seemingly straight-laced youth was losing a brawl with some rednecks, so he came back to the bar with a chain saw. Ronnie claims, "He sawed the bar in half, [cut up] a few chairs and even got at the rednecks' car. Folks never did things halfheartedly at the places we played."

There'd also be matchups with the local musicians. "Being a musician in that part of the country is like being a prizefighter," Levon said. "If you're a new band in town, you make the last set an open session or else. Everybody's there, they all know music, and the local guitarists will come up, plug into your amplifier and try to run you off the stage."

They had to scramble for work, which was booked under Levon's name, as he was the only band member who joined the musicians' union. If they were lucky, they'd earn ten dollars a night. "Musicians nowadays don't know what it's like to have rough times," Hawkins insists. "Back in the fifties, rough times were when you didn't have a damn thing to put in your mouth but a woman's tit." Sometimes they didn't have enough money for gas, so Hawkins employed what he called the Arkansas credit card—a rubber hose and his mouth. "I tell you, I was the only rock 'n' roll singer in the South who had chapped lips for three years. I was belching up ethyl and regular, and even a bit of diesel now and again."

Nevertheless, Hawkins remembers those as mostly good times. "Boy, it was fun. Christ, you wouldn't believe it. We had parties that Nero would have been ashamed to attend." Ronnie was convinced that

Helm "had an extra chromosome or something. Samson couldn't have screwed that many girls in one day." A favorite diversion for Levon was to visit Odessa, a black madam in her fifties who ran a whore house on Yazoo Street in the red-light district of Helena—she was later memorialized in song by the Hawks. Anna Lee recalls a story that Levon told her about initiating a boyhood pal into the den of iniquity that was Odessa's place of business:

> They carried [a friend] down there one night…and fixed him up
> with one of the girls on Yazoo Street. And Levon and [probably
> Bobby Watkins] were waiting outside, and they start yelling,
> "Cops, cops!" and [the friend] is trying to get out of the place, out
> the window, and they're out there just laughing their heads off.
> And so they wrote this song about Odessa, one of the madams…
> and everybody in Helena knew who Odessa was. They did some
> crazy things.

For two dollars, Odessa prepared a big meal for Helm and Hawkins, then "Levon would go first," Ronnie reveals, "and then I'd go in and Odessa would say, 'Mr. Ronnie, you can go ahead, but I think that Mr. Levon has gone and taken it all. That Mr. Levon has a strip of meat on him like a horse,' she would say…Yes, sir, Odessa was a good gal, and, boy, she could cook up a storm."

Of course, during the week, Levon was still in high school. Terry Cagle, who was seven, already knew he wanted to play drums like his uncle. While they waited for the school bus, Levon got him to practice drumming on a washtub. He was very protective of Terry, somewhat of a father figure. "In the second grade, he entered me in the Little Mr. Marvell Talent Show," Terry remarks. "He played guitar behind me…and I sang 'Bony Moronie.' One of his high school friends played bass, upright bass. And I was Little Mr. Marvell—I won!"

Wanting to give his nephew a good grounding in music before he left town with the Hawks, Helm would educate Terry at the pool hall. "[He'd] take the old pickup truck," Terry says, "and he'd play pool with his friends, or he'd sit me on the bar stool, buy me some peanuts and some Cokes, and put a bunch of money into the jukebox, and we'd sit there and listen to Chuck Berry."

It was not long before graduation when Levon helped present a musical revue to raise money for the senior-class trip to Washington, D.C. A train picked up students from different schools along the way as Helm and his pal Fireball Carter raised hell. The kids were reclining in their seats as Levon ran by and flipped them up. "We wanted to kill him," says Anna Lee. "You'd hear him all over the train laughing."

The boys gambled and smuggled beer into their Washington hotel. They tricked one girl who was beyond suspicion into bringing up ice for them so they could cool their beer in a sink. Levon's friend Bobby Watkins got drunk, fell off the hotel diving board, and broke his arm. The boys snuck off on their own and got lost, then caused more trouble on the way home. Thanks to them, all future school travel to the nation's capital was cancelled.

Nevertheless, Helm was a popular youth, and throughout his school years was voted the most talented, friendliest, wittiest, most versatile, the biggest flirt, the best dancer, and Mr. Personality. "Everybody around here, at school and all that, said they knew he was going to be some kind of big deal," C.W. Gatlin comments.

"I was in high school, but I was trying to get out of high school," Levon said. "The only thing slowing me up was grades." Helm laughed at the memory. "I really had rambling on my mind. I wanted to go. One of the prettiest sights in the world was a big Cadillac rolling down the road with a big doghouse bass tied to the top of it. That looked like the car I wanted to be in." As Hawkins recollects, "Levon and I now were on a mission—a mission to put together a bitch of a band."

"HE WAS READY for the world, that boy," Ronnie says of Levon. "Seventeen years old, and he was a rocker." As soon as Helm finished high school in May 1958, Hawkins borrowed his sister Winifred's '55 Chevy, the band loaded up a U-Haul trailer with all their equipment, and they headed north for Canada. Levon was excited. Going downhill, the car could only reach fifty miles an hour; uphill, they were lucky to make twenty-five. "It was a great experience," Jimmy Ray declared. "Ron was the type of guy who would sit in the back seat and let us chauffeur him while he told us which way to go." Sometimes Paulman took the wheel, but because Levon loved to drive, he usually took over.

Thanks to Conway Twitty, their destination was the Golden Rail in Hamilton, Ontario, an industrial city about seventy miles southwest of Toronto. Booker Harold Kudlets—who had brought to Canada such venerable artists as Duke Ellington, Stan Kenton, Tommy Dorsey, Jack Teagarden, and Louis Armstrong—was also responsible for introducing Twitty to Canadian audiences, who were hungry for rockabilly. He was known as an honest businessman who never needed a contract. "When I brought Conway Twitty up," Kudlets recalled, "I asked Conway, 'Is there any groups back home in Arkansas that can work up here?' and he recommended Ronnie Hawkins."

They arrived in Canada in the summer of 1958 as the Ron Hawkins Quartet. Bassist George Paulman "was drinkin' too much, messin' up, takin' pills," so Ronnie left him behind, and they played without a bass for their first tour in Ontario.

Their weeklong appearance at the Golden Rail began with a rehearsal Monday afternoon. "All the bartenders threatened to quit when they heard what they were playing—and saw what Ronnie was doing," Kudlets says. "He was into all those back flips at the time. Really wild." That night, Hawkins claims there were only about seven people in the audience: "We started playing, and *all* of 'em got up and left the tables, left their drinks. So that means they're mad. Anyway, the club owner told Harold Kudlets, 'Get these hillbillies outta here.'"

Kudlets persuaded the owner to give the band another chance, and in the meantime, Ronnie called his pal Dallas Harms—a Hamiltonian who had played in Arkansas with Conway in one of Hawkins's clubs— and asked him to bring as many people as he could to the Golden Rail, "or we'll be gone like a July snow. Well, hell, he brought in about sixty, seventy people. There hadn't been that many people in there since World War II. Then it started. The next day, it was lined up, and it was lined up for the next ten years." Harms had pressured his co-workers at a local steel mill to catch the band's gig: "When I got to the club it was already pretty well full with my friends...and I'm darned if Levon didn't have Jack Nance's old drums. I just remember how young he looked."

For Kudlets, Helm's appearance was a problem. Levon was eighteen but looked much younger, and band members had to be twenty-one to work in a cabaret. "I said the liquor inspectors will close us up," Harold confessed, "so what we did was make Levon wear sunglasses and on the breaks keep him at a distance from everybody." Hawkins explains: "You see, he had a brush haircut, and he looked like he was fifteen years old. He let his hair grow out. It made him look a little older. By the time we got him lookin' twenty-one, he *was* twenty-one."

While Ronnie was amazing the crowds with his gymnastic antics, Levon was proving himself a showman in his own right. "He used to do things like throw up his drumsticks in the air while they're playing and never miss a beat," Kudlets observed. Helm was singing while he played drums, and in his exuberance, his laugh could often be heard above the music. No dancing was allowed in a cabaret where food was served, so the band had to be highly entertaining to hold the audience's attention.

Harold Kudlets came to think of Levon as a son and commented, "He was the type of guy who'd give you the shirt off his back. He was very good-hearted in a lot of ways. He was a typical Southerner." Hawkins describes Helm as "the easiest one to get along with. He was always laughing and joking and cutting up. He was the funniest kid you ever saw; he'd laugh about everything." Levon said of those days with Ronnie, "It was probably the most amount of belly laughs per day that anyone's ever enjoyed."

Kudlets paid the band $450 a week, although Hawkins recalls that Helm didn't save his share: "Levon and Willard spent their whole fuckin' paychecks on whores the first week they were in Hamilton. Fifty or sixty dollars on whores. Levon had the clap at least four times a week…He finally learned how to shoot himself in the ass with penicillin. He became Dr. Helm for a while and gave everybody shots because you could save money on doctors."

The band played out the week at the Golden Rail, but before moving on to Kudlets's next bookings in London, Ontario, then Toronto, they had to smarten up their image. Their Southern accents and charm wouldn't cut it. According to Dallas Harms, "The gabardine pants on their old stage clothes had gone shiny and were kinda wore out." Kudlets took them to a Hamilton tailor who made each member two stage suits. The tailor pronounced with disdain, "Those boys were right from the country. They didn't have any underwear." Nevertheless, by the time they left Steeltown, the band looked like professional musicians.

After being held over for three successful weeks at the Brass Rail in London, the Hawkins band moved on for a month-long stand at the Le Coq d'Or Tavern in Toronto. Down on the Yonge Street strip, the city was contradicting its moniker of "Toronto the Good" by attracting a seedy collection of rounders, hustlers, strippers, pimps, and hookers—plus some adventurous suburbanites exploring the dark side. Teetotalers called the bars "hatcheries of hell." Delinquents and thugs congregated at the Brown Derby, and along Toronto's neon-lit underbelly, whores flaunted their wares amid the revving engines of greasers drag racing down the street. After the bars and hotels closed, patrons could keep rocking at the Upstairs club or at the Blue Note, where working musicians would gather after their gigs and sit in with the house band until three or four o'clock in the morning.

Until the Ron Hawkins Quartet shook things up, jazz was the predominant music offered in the city's venues, such as the Colonial Tavern, the Concord Hotel, and the Edison Hotel. Oscar Peterson performed and recorded at the Town Tavern that summer, Glenn Gould was a regular at the Eaton Auditorium, Sarah Vaughan had appeared at Maple Leaf Gardens, and Woody Herman was playing at the Palace Pier on the waterfront. But Toronto audiences also had access to other genres: the flamboyant cross-dresser Jackie Shane was an R&B sensation at the Zanzibar Tavern, and the Le Coq d'Or was originally a country-and-western bar. Big name rockers Chuck Berry, Bo Diddley, and Bill Haley and His Comets had appeared at Maple Leaf Gardens back in 1956, and Elvis performed there the following year.

From its location in the midst of the Yonge Street action, the Le Coq d'Or afforded Levon an introduction to new musical influences. During a break, he went down the street to soak up some inspiration from a jazz legend. "I remember the first time I heard the Cannonball Adderley band with Louis Hayes on drums," Helm said. "What a touch Hayes had. He didn't play hard and frantic. He left plenty of room on top for dynamics. He had more control over his instrument and a more musical touch than any drummer I'd heard. It made me want to learn how to really play drums." Another influence in the jazz world was Dave Brubeck's drummer, Joe Morello. "That's what's uncanny about Levon," Paul Berry points out. "Here's this essentially uneducated kid from Turkey Scratch, Arkansas, who just was a sponge…and his ear led him to the great musicians from the jazz world to rock 'n' roll."

Hawkins and his band caused a furor at the Le Coq d'Or, attracting the rough crowd that roamed the strip. The club was jammed. The stage was small, with Levon on one side and the piano on the other. Jimmy Ray had a little amp for his guitar, and a mic was set inside Willard's piano. There was no mic for Levon's drums. When Ronnie did his acrobatics, Jimmy Ray had to get out of the way.

One patron impressed with their sound was Dan Bass, the A&R scout for Toronto's Quality Records, who offered to cut a single with the quartet. Levon and the others were ecstatic. "It was like dreamin'," Hawkins remembers. With Gordon Josie, the manager of the Le Coq d'Or, as their bassist, the band was taken to "a place that looked like a big ol' parkin' lot or something underground," in late summer 1958, which served as the label's recording studio on Kingston Road. The band recorded two songs that were staples of their live shows: "Hey Bo Diddley," an updated version of the 1955 rhythmic hit by Bo Diddley, and Chuck Berry's "Thirty Days." They also cut a couple of Ronnie Hawkins originals: the Buddy Holly–inspired "Love Me Like You Can" and the frantic falsetto rocker "Horace."

"It sped up," Hawkins says of their recording of "Hey Bo Diddley," "and you could hear trucks runnin' outside on that one! That was our first attempt. We didn't want anybody hearin' it, but somebody slipped a tape out…It sounded like chipmunks playing." Quality Records had increased the speed of the recording, whether by accident or to accentuate Levon's son clave rhythm—a Cuban beat—that's led by the guitar part. Nevertheless, it was considered the first true rock 'n' roll recording in Canada. The saccharine ballad "Love Me Like You Can," a 12/8 shuffle, is a more predictable fifties offering. "Horace," suffused with

Hawkins's shrieks, is an energetic exercise perhaps better forgotten. The standout recording of the session is "Thirty Days," with Levon's dynamic drumming on full display. Throughout the four cuts, Paulman's stinging guitar is a standout.

With a tentative pressing of five hundred singles, the 45 with "Hey Bo Diddley" on the A-side and "Love Me Like You Can" on the flip was released in 1959 in Canada only. Even though the disc received a fair amount of airplay, it did not sell well. It took more than thirty years for the superior "Thirty Days" to be released.

AFTER CLOSE TO three months in Canada, Levon and the band returned South, basing themselves in Hawkins's home territory of Fayetteville. Dayton Stratton, Ronnie's partner in his Arkansas and Oklahoma clubs, managed, booked, and promoted the Hawks in their Southern circuit from Fayetteville across the state line to Tulsa and the University of Oklahoma in Norman. As the group gained momentum, Dayton sent them as far afield as Memphis, Dallas, and New Orleans.

Well respected in the music business, Dayton managed Fayetteville's Rockwood Club, which was still owned by Hawkins. When Levon's sister Modena and her husband moved to the area in the late fifties, they both worked at the club, as did the future president and CEO of Tyson Foods, Don Tyson. Stratton brought to the venue such artists as Carl Perkins, Jerry Lee Lewis, Roy Buchanan, Harold Jenkins, Roy Orbison, and Russell Bridges—later known as Leon Russell.

Kirby Penick was about Levon's age and worked at the Rockwood while he attended the University of Arkansas and got to know Helm when the Hawks practiced at the club. "That was the hardest working [band]," says Penick. "For all the foolishness and fun and rowdiness of it…those guys rehearsed all the time…and that's how they got good…They worked hard at it…They had good ears. They listened. They picked up other things from other venues and other bands and things, and incorporated it into what they were playing…I think they loved doing it."

Even though Levon was performing rockabilly with the Hawks, his first love was always blues. "He is grounded so completely in the blues," Kirby explains, "and…growing up down there in the Delta with all those old black guys. That was probably as strong an influence on him as anything else that he had come by, although he'd heard a lot of country music and a lot of other styles, but [he gravitated toward] the simplicity and the reality of the blues."

"He and I were just immediately very good friends," Penick says of Helm, "because we both loved to laugh and saw the humor in almost everything…We just fell into a kind of comfort level and enjoyed talking about music and especially…the blues or Ray Charles or these things that were really knocking you out at that point."

Right from the start, Levon sang harmony, and sometimes lead, in the Hawks. "He was a better singer than almost anybody I ever saw, maybe ever, for his phrasing and just a unique, great ear, great timing," Kirby maintains. And of music in general, he adds, "Levon was a savant almost. He was really a gifted guy…He was born to do it, I guess."

The Rockwood was the place to go for college kids, including the Razorback football players. "And there was always a fight," local musician Earl Cate says. "Always a fight." Dayton Stratton was a Southern gentleman who first tried to diffuse a potentially violent situation, but if that failed, he was more than capable of handling it physically. He was fearless. Hawkins says of Stratton, "He had the hardest left I knew. He never lost a fight." When asked years later about the clientele at the Rockwood in the late fifties, Dayton claimed, "[They] were the worst crowds I ever saw…I'd have so many fights by the end of the night, of throwin' people out of there and everything, I was exhausted. It was all I could do to get the door shut."

Down there in the South, the bars were rougher, the owners more treacherous, the pay worse, and the clientele ofttimes violent. Hawkins says, "People on crack cocaine would be afraid to go in some of those places we played." And there were other challenges, like the time they followed R&B group Hank Ballard and the Midnighters—known for their lurid stunts—who, for an extra thousand bucks, played naked or wore only gold jockstraps.

C.W. Gatlin heard the Hawks at Helena's Delta Supper Club: "When Ronnie and them were playing there, that was the best band anybody around here had ever heard, and the Supper Club, they had a lot of bands." Whenever the group was in Oklahoma City, young musicians Jesse Ed Davis and drummer John Ware were there. Jimmy Karstein—who would become a renowned drummer as a long-time member of J.J. Cale's band—saw Levon play in Tulsa, at the Fondalite Club and Cain's Ballroom: "I can remember the way he set up his kit, at an angle [at the side] rather than in line or behind the band, so he could better hear and see the rest of the group. They were tight, with simple but powerful arrangements and a tremendous amount of energy." Karstein and another Tulsa drummer, David Teegarden, credit Helm as being the most important rock 'n' roll drummer that they saw in the late 1950s. Jimmy says Levon played with

> a marvelous simplicity. He's probably one of the prime examples of when they say less is more…He's what I call a backbeat drummer…He came out of the South, and [there was] a huge blues influence on his style. That's not a flashy style of drumming by any means. That's why I say less is more. He concentrated on the feel of the music…He played just what was needed. He didn't try to prove anything with his drumming…He was the king of understatement. It's just a reflection of his personality because he was understated, easy-going, a laid-back kind of a character.

The band's Southern gigs were typically one-night stands or short runs in Arkansas, Texas, Oklahoma, and Tennessee with Levon driving the band two or three hundred miles to the next dance, unlike in Canada, where they could settle at each venue for up to a month. Fortunately, the sluggish Chevy was replaced by a Cadillac and trailer. The long hauls could be grueling, so Hawkins called on the services of a doctor friend to give Helm a boost when needed: "They had these little five-milligram hearts, they called 'em—truck drivers used them a little bit. It's like drinking about five cups of coffee real quick, and so you take one of them and…[it] keeps you awake pretty good for four or five hours. So anybody who got to drive got a pill, and then they got in a fistfight over who's gonna drive!"

One time, Levon had been driving for three days without sleep, and then had to go to a town about twenty miles from where the band was staying, so Ronnie gave him three pills to keep him awake so he could get back that night.

> Three days later the truck pulled up outside, steaming and about to fall apart [Hawkins recalls the tall tale]. Levon was glued to the wheel, his eyes fixed to the windshield. He said to me, "Man, those five pills were out of this world. I just didn't want to stop drivin'." And I said to him, "What five pills? I only gave you three." When we looked in the glove compartment where we'd put them, he'd eaten two ten-amp fuses out of the amplifiers. Any man who can get high on fuses is a good man to have in your band.

"I always enjoyed it; I like traveling," Helm said. "I certainly didn't see myself sticking around one place very long if I could go somewhere else. Anyway, with Hawkins we'd go down home and head out to the local Cadillac place. He'd sign for me, and I'd drive a new Cadillac out of there every now and then. Sort of a sport, you might say."

Levon was always looking for—and finding—the fun in life: "My attitude at the time was the same that it was in high school: the goofier and funnier it is, the happier it is. At all costs, let's laugh. That's why life on the road was anything from aggravating the desk clerk in the hotel to throwin' a cherry bomb in a car where someone was sleeping. I always aimed for the laughs."

AFTER THE CIRCUIT down South, the band returned to Canada before the end of 1958. Already Toronto's music scene was changing. "When all we could play was in bottle clubs down South on the weekends, we knew one place we could go was here," Levon said of Toronto. "Ray Charles, Joe Williams, Carl Perkins, they all came here. Toronto and Memphis, they were the motherlode for me."

Helm was glad to return to where the pay was higher, the closing time was earlier, the clubs were better run, and the engagements at every venue lasted longer. That way, he could settle in at each town and hang out with friends, and not have to hit the road so often. Gordon Josie of the Le Coq d'Or said, "I think that in Hamilton they had got about $450 a week. I paid them $700. That was a lot of money back in those days. Within the year, we were paying $2000." Because it was an expense to bring the band up from Arkansas, Gordon made a deal with Jack Fisher at the Concord Hotel, farther west on Bloor Street, wherein Josie booked them for a month, then the band would move to the Concord for another month.

This time when the band came to Canada, they brought a bass player. Jimmy "Lefty" Evans, from Marianna, Arkansas, had played with Willard and Jimmy Ray in the Hill County Playboys, and had sat in with the Hawks a few times before they went north. He was a session player at Sun, then joined Conway Twitty's band in 1956 and played the Ontario circuit with him. He wrote Conway's "Why Can't I Get Through to You," which they recorded for the Mercury label. Evans briefly tried a solo career after leaving Twitty, he played bass for Mack Self's Sun recording "Easy to Love," and then joined the Hawks on an electric Fender bass in 1958.

The Toronto home for the band was the shabby Warwick Hotel, three short blocks east of the Yonge Street strip. "Downstairs they had entertainment…and hookers, everybody hustling down there at the bottom," Ronnie relates. "At the top was rooms. Twenty dollars a week for a home away from home…It was exciting because you could see all those young pimps hustling the girls around, you know. Boy, some of those girls from Quebec were beautiful. Absolutely movie stars."

It was also the setting for several of Levon's practical jokes, like the time he and a minor hustler—and the band's first roadie—Colin "Bony" McQueen had a water-gun fight, except Helm wasn't using water. "Then [Bony] smells it and realizes it's lighter fluid," Ronnie recalls. "He sees that Levon has a book of matches and he can imagine himself roasting real quick. Now, Levon wasn't going to hit him with the matches, but Bony wasn't sure." On another occasion, Helm got Bony so drunk he collapsed, then Levon stripped him naked, slicked down his hair, parted it in the middle, and drew a mustache and sideburns on him. The guys then set him on top of the elevator ashtray and pushed the lobby button.

Bill Avis first met Levon when the Hawks were at the Concord Tavern, and Bill was living kitty-corner from the club. "We weren't old enough to get in but we got to know the doorman," Avis recalls. "I couldn't get enough of the music. It was hard-driving, good ol' rocka-billy. I was there almost every frigging night." Right from the start, Bill and Levon—only two months apart in age—formed a lifelong bond.

Levon was also friendly with Freddie McNulty, a mentally chal-lenged young man from a wealthy family who lived with his grandmother in Downsview, just north of Toronto. Freddie would walk to the Le Coq d'Or—at least ten miles—stand outside and keep rhythm with the beat. Levon gravitated toward him, taking Freddie to the movies during the week, and in turn, Freddie ran errands for him.

THE TYPICAL CANADIAN circuit for the band was Windsor, London, Kitchener, Hamilton, Toronto, Kingston, Montreal, and Quebec City, playing a week or two to a month in each place twice a year. Helm remembered, "We played six and seven nights a week. We had a good booking agent, and we wanted to work all the time. Me being so young and loving good music, that's all I needed."

On top of their busy playing schedule, Ronnie demanded that the band keep rehearsing—usually in the early morning, following a gig—always striving to get better. "There was no fooling around in a Hawkins band," Levon reminisced. "A lot of guys joined thinking it would be one big orgy. He worked your ass off. He had fines for booze, drugs, and you weren't allowed to have your girlfriends around. Nothing could interfere with learning and putting out good music. We cursed him then but, boy, we wouldn't be here today if it wasn't for him. I love that man." In addition to band rehearsals, every member was expected to practice a couple of hours on his own.

Hawkins insisted that everyone be on time for their gigs. He'd get frustrated with Willard, who didn't always fit the regimented look that Hawkins demanded. Jones loved to chew gum—at ninety miles an hour, according to C.W. Gatlin—and was likely to wear mismatched socks. There was a no-smoking rule in the car, but as soon as Ronnie dozed off, everyone lit up. By this time, Levon was a chain smoker who ignored Kudlets's well-intentioned warnings to stop.

Harold Kudlets—whom the Hawks affectionately called the

Colonel so they could emulate Elvis—saw the impact the band was having and believed they were ready for bigger opportunities. In spring 1959, he contacted his friend Larry Bennett who worked in New York City with Associated Booking Corporation, owned by the mafia-connected Joe Glaser. The company handled some of the biggest stars of that era. Bennett billed Ronnie Hawkins and the Hawks as "the newest rock 'n' roll sensation" and booked them for a series of dates along the Jersey Shore. Although the band had to share a gig with the Fabulous Billy Hope Orchestra, which featured a turbaned Hope and a midget vocalist, artists such as Bobby Rydell and James Brown were also playing this circuit. Within a week in Wildwood, on the southern tip of New Jersey, the Hawks outdrew even Sammy Davis Jr., Teresa Brewer, and Frankie Laine. As Levon declared, "Ronnie Hawkins had molded us into the wildest, fiercest, speed-driven bar band in America."

This piqued the interest of Columbia Records' A&R head Mitch Miller, but because rock 'n' roll wasn't the label's focus, Hawkins wasn't sure a recording deal with them was a good fit. It's suspected that a single of "Kansas City" and "Cuttin' Out" recorded that spring by Rockin' Ronald and the Rebels on End Records is actually a demo by Ronnie and the Hawks, although the Hawk denies it. End Records was distributed by New York's notorious Roulette Records and owned by George Goldner, an original partner in Roulette.

In April 1959, Larry Bennett arranged for the band to audition for his friend Morris Levy, president of Roulette. Tall, handsome, charismatic, and dangerous, thirty-one-year-old Levy was a gangster with ties to the Genovese crime family. After his brother was murdered, he was heard threatening a client, saying, "Do you know what I did to the bum who killed my brother? I fucking took a knife and stuck it in his fucking stomach—and I *twisted* it. I stuck it in his fucking stomach until his guts fell out." Levy owned some of New York's premier jazz and bebop nightspots—Birdland, the Roundtable, the Down Beat, the Embers—befriending the likes of Dinah Washington and Count Basie. Levy teamed up with the most prominent deejay in the world, the infamous Alan Freed, starting out as his manager and backing Freed's highly profitable rock 'n' roll shows at the Brooklyn and New York Paramount theaters. During one period—until 1957—Freed owned 25 percent of Roulette. Together they unsuccessfully attempted to copyright the term *rock 'n' roll*.

Levy had established Roulette in 1956 in order to get in on the lucrative music-publishing business. Many Roulette tracks credited the songwriter as Magill, a pseudonym for Levy himself, who had nothing to do with their creation (at one point, he tried to get royalties from "Silent Night"). He took over an interest in the Gee label that same year and scored a foothold on the charts with Frankie Lymon's "Why Do Fools Fall in Love?" Jimmy Bowen's "I'm Stickin' with You," and "Party Doll" by Buddy Knox. Levy reveled in his tough-guy reputation, was usually accompanied by two bodyguards, and openly carried a gun while enticing radio deejays to play Roulette's records through payola, the practice of under-the-table payment for radio airtime. Levy might start with a fifty-dollar handshake—and escalate to the threat of violence. It was said that Levy controlled Dick Clark— the host of North America's biggest TV show for teens, *American Bandstand*—and therefore influenced his program lineup after paying off some of Clark's heavy gambling debts.

Joey Dee and the Starlighters were one of Levy's most profitable acts in the late 1950s. As Joey reveals,

> I'd get in the limo with George Goldner, an employee [of Rou-lette]. He'd drive. It would be a couple ladies of the evening, hookers, in the back of the limo and we'd drive to these towns. They'd meet with the deejays, give them an envelope with cash in it, allow them their way with the girls in the car, and then go on to the next town. And the next town. And the next town. Our records were played. God forbid they took the money and *didn't* play the records. That's when the baseball bats came out...and worse.

As for how Roulette treated its recording artists, Dee adds, "These people can open doors for you or they can put you in a box. Simple as that."

At their Roulette audition, "[The Hawks] were rehearsing at four o'clock in the afternoon when Morris Levy came in," Kudlets said. "He flipped, never heard anything like it. Six o'clock that night he says we're going to start recording an album." With Elvis in the army, Levy figured Hawkins and his band could take over that market. Ronnie and Levon knew they were dealing with a treacherous criminal, but they needed Levy's clout.

After Hawkins signed the recording contract, Levon asked him, "How long did you have to sign for?"

Ronnie's response: "Life with an option."

4

Gambling on Roulette

awkins and Helm knew the score with Roulette Records and its president. "[Morris Levy] was the biggest Jewish gangster in New York," Ronnie declares. "We learned so much from watching that man…He was like a fantasy. And everybody in his office looked like gangsters." One of Levy's friends was an original member of Al Capone's gang. The band wrote a song for him called "Uncle Charlie Mobster."

"We saw those heavies, and they were *heavies*. Bad friggin' dudes," Bill Avis emphasizes, remembering a stream of shady characters with envelopes of protection money filing through Levy's office. But even though the Hawks had heard stories of Levy cheating other acts, he took a liking to this group. Whenever he went to Roulette, Ronnie would keep Morris sweet with a case of Crown Royal Canadian whiskey, something unavailable in New York at the time. "He'd take us to his clubs and invite all the chorus girls home for breakfast," the Hawk says. And according to Avis, "Morris Levy loved Levon. Anyone that came in contact with Levon and spent any time with him, loved him." Even years later when Helm was established in Woodstock, Morris invited him to his home.

Beginning at six o'clock on April 13, 1959, at Bell Studios, Ronnie Hawkins and the Hawks—comprising Levon, Jimmy Ray Paulman, and Willard Jones, with Levy adding jazz bass player George Duvivier and four drunk background vocalists—began recording for Roulette. In that first session they cut three versions of "Ruby Baby"—a cover of the Drifters song—and two of "Forty Days" on a two-track recorder.

"The bass man passed out," Ronnie recalls, "and they had to stick his head in a commode and flush it three or four times to freshen him up a little bit."

Helm's trademark wooden sound is evident on "Ruby Baby," as he plays a Chicago shuffle—challenging at that speed—with four on the floor with the bass drum. For their next song, Chuck Berry's "Thirty Days," they gave the lyrics a twist. Hawkins claims that instead of waiting a month for the girl to return, "Morris Levy says, 'What if she don't come back, she's such a beautiful girl?' I said, 'You're right. I'd better give her ten more days.' So we called it 'Forty Days.'" Levon plays a classic 1950s drumbeat at a breakneck pace with double snare hits and fills. "He was playing the hell out of the drums," C.W. Gatlin says. "You think he's gonna quit at any minute, and he just keeps on going."

Two days later, the band recorded "Horace" and "One of These Days." Amid Hawkins's falsetto wails on "Horace"—and a tasty solo by popular session saxman Sam "the Man" Taylor—Levon again lays down a high-speed fifties groove. He uses a Latin influence in "One of These Days," similar to a Bo Diddley beat, but dresses it up behind Ronnie's suave vocals.

Their first single on Roulette—released on May 4—paired "Forty Days" on side one, with "One of These Days" on the reverse. Levy promoted it with a full-page ad in *Billboard*. Even so, it wasn't the hit he expected, peaking at a disappointing number 45.

On April 29, the band was back, with Sam Taylor again on tenor sax, to record eight more songs. "Odessa"—a nod to Levon's and Ronnie's friend from the Helena brothel—"Need Your Lovin'," "Oh Sugar," "Wild Little Willie," "Whatcha Gonna Do (When the Creek Runs Dry)"—with songwriting attributed to Hawkins, Magill, and Helm— "My Gal Is Red Hot," and "Dizzy Miss Lizzie." "Mary Lou"—credited to Hawkins and Magill, but actually written by Obediah Donnell Jessie—is the standout track from this session and would be Hawkins's biggest career success. Levon's woody hits, sounding like cross-stick, form a shuffle version of a classic fifties groove. When "Mary Lou" was released as a 45, with the slower "Need Your Lovin'" on side B, it spent four months on *Billboard*'s Top 100 and cracked the top 30 at number 26.

Levy invested heavily on ads to promote the Hawks and their records. He bought another full-page ad in *Billboard* for "Mary Lou" and sent postcards to deejays claiming Roulette had shipped 200,000 copies in the first week, although it wasn't likely. Ronnie never saw a royalty check, but he estimates that Levy spent more on the band than they would have earned. When Hawkins did try to get royalties, the person he sent to collect for him was offered two ways to leave Levy's office: through the door or out the window.

THE HEADLINE IN the *Miami Herald* read "BOOZE, BROADS AND BRIBES" and *Variety* described it as a drunken orgy, with the help of hookers bussed in from Miami. They were apt descriptions of the May 1959 annual Pop Music Disk Jockey Convention in Miami Beach, which helped trigger a U.S. Congressional probe into payola—and Ronnie Hawkins and the Hawks were in the thick of it. Levy flew them down to perform at an all-night barbecue, along with another of his acts, Count Basie, and the two bands played until breakfast was served. Levy contributed fifteen thousand dollars to the event, which included two thousand bottles of bourbon. "All kinds of women down there were for the disc jockeys. I started to act like *I* was a disc jockey," Ronnie jokes.

That month, thanks to Levy's leverage with Dick Clark, the Hawks made their first national-television appearance on *The Dick Clark Beech-Nut Show*, sharing the bill with the Skyliners, Jesse Belvin, Johnny Horton, and Paul Anka. The program had a Western theme with Dick Clark in a fringe jacket and cowboy hat. Introduced as a "wild and fantastic experience," the Hawks looked like agitators from the Last Chance Saloon as they lip-synched "Mary Lou" and "Forty Days"—Hawkins in a cowboy outfit and the rest of the band with big aprons and garters on their sleeves. Helm reckoned they looked like waiters. "We thought we were in the big time," Ronnie maintains. "That was the time when everybody in Arkansas saw us. We went back to play, and then Levon and me, we thought we were somebody then."

Also in May, Ronnie recorded some demos without the Hawks, and then on the twenty-sixth, Ronnie, Jimmy Ray, Willard, and Levon were all back in the studio. Trying another path to success, Hawkins took a shot at being a folk balladeer, grabbing onto the coattails of such bestselling artists as the Weavers, the Kingston Trio, and the Highwaymen. The band cut three tracks for *The Folk Ballads of Ronnie Hawkins*—"One Out of a Hundred," "Virginia Bride," and "Love from Afar"—plus "The Tale of Floyd Collins."

Although it didn't lead to a booking, the Hawks tried out for the popular television program the *Steve Allen Show* while Allen, his wife, Jayne Meadows, comedian Don Knotts, and some other guests were in the studio. Ronnie did his double back flips, and "Willard got on that piano," says Hawkins, "and started on that wild stuff...They'd never heard anything like that. Everybody turned around and came back to listen to us audition. [Our music] was so different, but these boys were super-good at what they did—Willard and Levon and Jimmy Ray."

Dick Clark booked the Hawks again in August, this time on his *American Bandstand* show, where they once again played "Mary Lou" and "Forty Days." Singers Jerry Wallace and Freddy Cannon also performed. Joni James was awarded a gold record, and actor Chuck Connors made a guest appearance.

During the promotional tour for "Mary Lou," the Hawks supported such acts as Anita Bryant, Bo Diddley, the Isley Brothers, and Benny Goodman. Thanks to Morris Levy's influence, that September they performed "Mary Lou" and "Forty Days" on Alan Freed's Fifth Anniversary Show at Brooklyn's Paramount, sharing the bill with Jackie Wilson, Lloyd Price, Dion and the Belmonts, and Bo Diddley. Lip-synching again, the Hawk considered it "a total mess...Kids were screaming so loud I couldn't hear the record." On another occasion, the Hawks played at Levy's posh Roundtable club, while, according to Bill Avis, Hollywood film goddess Jane Russell "was in there with John Wayne, right up on a table, drunk out of their minds, dancing."

Hawkins says,

> We thought at the time with Morris Levy doing what he did, we were going definitely to hit the big time because he knew how to maneuver. But after the disc jockey convention got busted in Florida, the government was all over the record companies for

payola…Of course, Roulette Records was one of the biggest there was because [Levy] knew how to handle that payola stuff. He was under surveillance for everything, so he couldn't do what he was doing to make us stars.

THERE WAS DISSATISFACTION in the ranks. Willard Jones was the first to leave. He yearned to get back South, plus he thought Ronnie underpaid the band. While he stayed until the end of 1959, Jimmy Ray felt much the same, complaining, "[The Hawk] made all the money, and we were paid very little."

Fred Carter Jr. was a seasoned musician before he ever met the Hawks. Born in Louisiana in 1933, he started playing mandolin and fiddle, and didn't focus on guitar until his twenties. He had led USO band tours across Europe, attended music college, was a mainstay on the *Louisiana Hayride* show, and played with Roy Orbison. When Hawkins met him, Carter was the guitarist for Dale Hawkins, Ronnie's cousin who'd made the big time with "Susie-Q." The Hawk thought Fred was a better fit for his band with his R&B feel than Paulman with his country sound. "[Hawkins] made Dad an offer he couldn't refuse, and Dad…he just loved the whole idea," his son, Jeff Carter, says. "I think the main thing they all had in common was rock 'n' roll. It was all just brand new, and they were kind of out there making up the rules as they went along. My best recollection from all of [Dad's] stories…is that they were just having a blast, enjoying the shit out of themselves."

Carter's first gig with the band was at the Alan Freed show in Brooklyn on Labor Day 1959. Jeff remembers his father telling him, "When I started first playing with Levon, son, it was just amazing. He was the greatest drummer I ever heard." Theirs would become a life-long friendship:

He loved [Levon], but first and foremost, he loved his drumming [Jeff says]…Levon's drumming is something that rock 'n' roll players and blues and all kinds of players of all genres they've tried to imitate over the years. But he had such a feel, and that's why Dad first and foremost fell in love with him was that he couldn't believe what an incredible drummer he was, but also that he played all these other instruments, he sang, and he was a ton of fun— always laughing and pulling jokes. And Dad just loved him…He saw him as his brother.

Fred Carter with Jimmy Evans on bass joined the Hawks for their September 16 recording session for Roulette, with Jimmy Ray Paulman now relegated to rhythm guitar. They cut eight tracks—all demos— including "Hayride," which credited Hawkins, Magill, and Helm as songwriters. At this session, Carter recorded a single with the Hawks as his backup band—"My Heart Cries" on side one, with "Love It Up" on the reverse.

By the beginning of October, the group was back in Toronto for an extended run. Fred Carter loved to tell stories about the fun the Hawks had onstage, but it was also grueling. "[Hawkins] rehearsed the devil out of them before and after the shows," says Jeff Carter, "made them wear tuxedos that they had to pay for, and had to have cleaned and pressed every week…There was definitely really a hard-work ethic there too because they'd play five or six hours a night and then rehearse on top of that."

WATCHING IT ALL unfold was an aspiring fifteen-year-old guitarist. For him the experience was a revelation.

"This guy on drums—Levon—his sticks were twirling, he was standing up, he was beating those drums. And they played the most powerful rock 'n' roll that I had ever heard live up to this stage," declares Robbie Robertson, remembering his first impressions of Helm and the incendiary Hawks. "There was this little kid playing drums. He looked like a little kid—you couldn't believe this guy was the drummer. And he was terrific. Terrific to look at and great to hear."

"Every bone in his body was musical," he says of Levon, "and he just lit up the room."

I thought Levon was the most talented person that I'd ever met. I was maybe fourteen or fifteen years old when I met him, and I looked up to him tremendously. Ronnie Hawkins was terrific and a great showman and a great character and all of that, but Levon was the ace in the hole…He had music running through his veins, you know. He was the real deal.

Robbie was born in Toronto in 1943 to a mother who was a mix of Mohawk, Cayuga, and Irish, and growing up, he embraced his First Nations cultural heritage. As a teen, he discovered that his biological father was not the man who raised him. Instead, his dad, who died before Robbie was born, had been Jewish, which then opened up new horizons of cultural exploration.

Robertson first became fascinated by the guitar at age eight, and after learning on an acoustic, he got his first electric instrument when he was thirteen. Soon after, he was playing in a local band called the Rhythm Chords, then Thumper and the Trambones, Robbie and the Robots, and Little Caesar and the Consuls. He was fifteen when as a member of the Suedes—which included future Hawk Scott Cushnie on piano—he opened for the Hawks. "It was the most violent, dynamic, primitive rock'n'roll I had ever witnessed," Robbie proclaims, "and it was addictive."

Enraptured by their music and fascinated by their Southern heritage, he hung around the band, helping out if needed. A fledgling songwriter, he penned two tunes for Ronnie—"Hey Boba Lou" and "Someone Like You"—who recorded them as part of his *Mr. Dynamo* album, although the credits read Hawkins, Magill, and Robertson. Ronnie wagered that this teenager would have insight into the mindset of the youth market, so with Levon at the wheel, they drove to New York in search of new music. At the legendary Brill Building, ground zero for songwriters, such pop composers as Leiber and Stoller, Pomus and Shuman, Otis Blackwell, and Titus Turner auditioned their songs for the starry-eyed Robertson.

On October 26, Hawkins and the Hawks were back at Roulette to record their first album, *Mr. Dynamo*, with Ronnie's friend from Helena, Ed Burks, on percussion and an unknown organist who filled the spot left by Willard's departure. They recut "Hayride" and "Love Me Like You Can," which had been the B-side of their single on the Quality label, and recorded six additional songs, including two more that listed Hawkins, Magill, and Helm as composers—"Baby Jean" and "Southern Love." The single, "Southern Love" with "Love Me Like You Can" on the flip side, never made the *Billboard* charts. Levon was given sole songwriting credit for "You Cheated You Lied," even though it had been released by the Slades, the Shields, and the Del Vikings the previous year.

Ronnie says,

> "Hey Boba Lou" and "Someone Like You" was two songs that [Robbie had] written that I liked, and we had a little time after the session, so I thought, Well, I'm just gonna put 'em down and see what happens. And they were released. Robbie was the song-writer for words, and Levon was good for arranging, making things fit in and all that stuff. He knew what to do, but he didn't write anything.

Scott Cushnie claimed that those two songs were actually from the repertoire of the Suedes, and Cushnie had helped Robertson write them.

In November, the same contingent was back at Levy's studio to lay down "Lonely Hours" and "Clara," which were issued on another unsuccessful 45, plus "Honey Don't" and "Sick and Tired." And at the University of Arkansas in Fayetteville, Ronnie—without any of the Hawks—recorded some unreleased tracks.

In contrast to the gangsters who ran Roulette, Fred told his son that the musicians "were all just kind of young and almost country bumpkins compared to those guys, and we were just glad to be there and didn't want to rock the boat for sure." Jeff says, "I think [the Hawks] were kind of afraid of them in a sense. I don't say that lightly. My dad was not a man to be afraid of anybody...He was a pretty tough guy, but he knew if somebody was maybe crazier than he was."

By the end of 1959, Jimmy Ray Paulman had left the Hawks, and about this time pianist Stan Szelest phoned Ronnie asking if there was a vacancy for him in the band. Levon and Ronnie went to Burlington, Ontario, to hear him play and recognized that Stan's keyboards could fill the void left by Paulman's rhythm guitar. Born in Buffalo in

1942, Stan started playing classical piano at age six, but as his tastes turned toward rock 'n' roll, he joined the Four Knights, then moved to Hamilton and played for Jerry Warren and the Tremblers. He'd come to be known as the dean of rock 'n' roll; Hawkins called him the greatest rock 'n' roll piano player on the planet. "Stan learned some of his rock 'n' roll from Willard, his style, you know," Bubba Sullivan notes. "Stan could play better than anybody I *ever* heard."

When the band went South again to play their circuit, Szelest decided not to accompany them, so Scott Cushnie—the first Canadian Hawk—took his place on the piano stool. Born in 1938 and raised in Oakville, just west of Toronto, Cushnie started taking piano lessons from his mother, a conservatory-trained pianist, at age three, and grew up playing piano and alto sax. When Robbie Robertson performed in Oakville with Little Caesar and the Consuls, Cushnie sat in on piano. Robbie was so impressed that when a new band, the Suedes, was being formed, Robertson invited him to join.

When Jimmy Evans declined to go back to Canada with the Hawks, Cushnie suggested that Robertson join the band as a bass player. Helm was skeptical. "Levon was the boss in my band," Ronnie reveals. "He was the musical director, he was everything…I had to talk him into lettin' Robbie in! [laughs]" So when Hawkins summoned Robertson down to Arkansas to learn to play bass, Robbie was determined not to let the opportunity of a lifetime slip away.

"Every time I'd bring in new musicians," Ronnie says, "Levon would work 'em, you know, show 'em the rhythms, show 'em this and that. Because Levon played a little bass, and he played a little guitar…But he was good enough to show some young fucker how he wants the rhythm goin' and chord changes and all that stuff…He was the leader."

IN JANUARY 1960, promoter Norm Riley, who briefly managed Hank Snow and Hank Williams, booked Ronnie and Levon in England to promote "Southern Love." Levon told of a very inebriated Sarah Vaughan on their Constellation flight across the Atlantic; she was starting a British tour with the Johnny Dankworth Orchestra. The Hawk and Helm jammed with Eddie Cochran and met Gene Vincent, who were both touring Britain at the time. The Arkansas duo appeared on two episodes of the ITV show *Boy Meets Girl*, which also included Adam Faith, Billy Fury, Davy Jones, and Otis Blackwell. Joe Brown, the lead guitarist for the show's orchestra, which played behind Levon and Ronnie, so impressed Hawkins that he asked Brown to come to North America and join the Hawks. Brown turned them down to stay with his British girlfriend, a move he later regretted.

By the time Hawkins and Helm were back in Helena with the rest of the Hawks, Robertson proved he had the chops to be their bass player and joined the band for their Canadian circuit. "He was younger, and he kinda depended on Levon," Kirby Penick says. "Levon was kind of the driving wheel, and Robbie was a young kid that was hanging with him, looking to him to learn how the wheels go around."

Levon and Robbie, whom Helm nicknamed Duke, became like brothers.

"Their friendship was so tight," Paul Berry remarks. "They had a way of communicating without words. They could signal each other and know where each other's mind was. Not musically; I'm just talking about chatting it up, sitting around in a motel room. They could go into all kinds of routines. They could have made it as a comedy act in my opinion if they hadn't had musical talent."

"Levon and I became really close," says Robertson. "I thought he was the best guy to me in the world. He had music coming out of his fingertips. He was fun to be with. We were experimenting with life." Ronnie explains, "[Levon] and Robbie became like Siamese twins there for a long time. It was a good combination because Levon set all the music and timing, and Robbie could write the lyrics and stuff. I thought it was going to be a real great combination."

MORRIS LEVY STILL had huge plans for Ronnie. He saw him as the next mega rock 'n' roll star. But the Hawk, ever the canny businessman, knew he could earn good, steady money in Canada. What Levy had in mind had no guarantees. Helm remembered Levy exclaiming to Hawkins, "You can't go back to Canada! You've got it all to yourself. Elvis is in the fuckin' army, and you're better than him anyway, now. Buddy Holly, Eddie Cochran—dead. There's a vacuum here, and you're the only one around who can take advantage of it. You're on the goddamn verge! You can't just vanish on me."

In Levy's eyes, Hawkins was letting stardom slip through his hands. "Ronnie wouldn't come home," Morris lamented. "He loved Canada. It broke my heart." Helm felt the way Hawkins did about maintaining Canada as a home base. He enjoyed the circuit there, and like the Hawk, he wanted an income he could rely on, especially as he sent part of it home to his parents.

The rockabilly wave had already crested, and Roulette was charged in the payola scandal, but through it all Morris Levy believed in Hawkins. Following Ronnie's foray into folk, Hawkins and Carter recorded "The Ballad of Caryl Chessman" for Roulette on February 22. A long-time criminal who'd been sentenced to death for robbery, rape, and kidnapping, Chessman was the focus of a campaign to spare his life. Levon was credited as the drummer, although there's no drum track on the song. It was paired with the earlier recording "The Tale of Floyd Collins" as the B-side. Again, no success.

Levy tried yet another tack with Ronnie that April when he sent the band down to Nashville's Bradley Studios to record *The Folk Ballads of Ronnie Hawkins* with Carter, Robertson, Szelest, and Helm; Nashville session players filled in on guitar, piano, and bass. Downstairs in studio A, Bobby "Blue" Bland and the Joe Scott Orchestra—with the great Jabo Starks on drums—were working on Bland's future hit "Turn on Your Love Light," and Levon kept running downstairs to watch and listen. Hawkins cut eight songs and Levy added three the band had recorded in May 1959 to complete the album. The resultant single was "Summertime"—with Levon playing a Latin beat—with "Mister and Mississippi" on the reverse, but the divergence from rockabilly didn't sit well with Hawkins's fans.

During this session, Fred Carter decided to leave the Hawks. As Jeff Carter tells it,

> Dad had discovered the session musicians there. He had no idea
> that you could play and make a living playing in studios and sleep
> in your own bed every night. By that point in his life, he'd already
> been gone from home and constantly on the road and in the

service playing music for ten years so that appealed to him greatly. And Levon asked him, he said, "If you're gonna leave, Fred, I'd like you to get young Robbie over here up to speed on guitar"... [Robbie] got kind of aggravated with him—and Dad didn't say this with any malice—but by the end of that week, or whatever it was, Robbie made some kind of comment about "One day I'm gonna cut you." And Dad said, "Well, if that's how you think about it, the lessons are over." And from then on, [Fred] turned his back to him onstage.

Ronnie had to scramble to get a new guitar player and temporarily hired another of Dale Hawkins's musicians, Roy Buchanan, an Arkansan with demonic Fender chops. Ronnie explains the evolution of the band:

> Robbie was on rhythm guitar at that time, and then we put him on lead for a little while, but he wasn't quite cuttin' it...so we put him back on rhythm, and we put Levon on lead. At that time, he played better lead than anybody. But we couldn't find a drummer. We flew in Conway Twitty's drummer—we flew in four or five drummers—but they didn't have that feel that Levon had. Finally, I called in a special guitar player to come in for the summer—Roy Buchanan...an unbelievable guitar player. He came up with stuff I'd never heard before. He taught Robbie a lot of stuff. He stayed the summer. That's also him playing bass on "Hey Bo Diddley."

Granted, Buchanan's playing was otherworldly, but as frighteningly talented as he was, he lacked showmanship, and he was too enigmatic for the Hawk. Believing he was a werewolf destined to marry a nun was a step too far. Robertson was ready to take over on lead guitar, and Rebel Payne was hired on bass, a young player from Alabama via Tonawanda, New York, who had played in the Tremblers with Stan Szelest.

That summer of 1960, the Hawks performed around Ontario, and in September, Bill Avis introduced Ronnie to Wanda Nagurski at a matinee at Toronto's Concord Tavern. She was more straight-laced than Hawkins's usual girlfriends, which only encouraged Helm, in a good-natured way, to embarrass her. "Levon would get deliberately fresh with girls just to shock me," Wanda says. "He'd go up a girl's skirt or down her blouse...There was lots of laughter back then. Lots. Levon and Ron were hysterical in those days."

Still searching for a successful niche, Hawkins went to Nashville in October to record *Ronnie Hawkins Sings the Songs of Hank Williams*. Although Ronnie wanted to use his own band, Levon pointed out, "The two worst things a musician can say to his producer in Nashville are 'I've been thinking,' and 'I'd like my band to play on the record.'" Helm was the only Hawk permitted to play, joined by some of Nashville's A-team session musicians: Harold Bradley and Hank Garland on guitar, pianists Floyd Cramer and Owen Bradley, Bob Moore on bass, and the Anita Kerr Singers. The single "Cold Cold Heart" had some success in Canada, but the album itself flopped.

IT WAS EARLY 1961 when Bill Avis joined the Hawks as their road manager, meaning he did most everything except perform. He was "Bizz" or "Business Bill," as Levon called him.

Although it was part of Bill's job to drive, Levon loved doing it so they switched back and forth. At first the band had only one vehicle, a Cadillac, that Ronnie rented to own. When they started making more money, Hawkins bought a cube van, so they had that and the Cadillac.

Bill was struck by the racism in the South. Their audiences were usually white; sometimes, especially in Oklahoma, they would be mixed. In the Fayetteville area, Bill noted that during the day the black population was in town doing menial tasks, but come sundown, they had to be out:

> When I first went into Arkansas...on Highway 71...there were signs—and I saw them with these old eyes—right on the side of the highway, "Nigger, don't be up here when the sun sets on your ass." In other words, be down in your holler. And that's where they lived...We'd go down there Sunday mornings and park that big white Cadillac outside the [African-American] church and put

the windows down so we could listen to them singing in the church.

The Hawks toured through Arkansas, Oklahoma, and Missouri, confronting the challenges of those rowdy southern clubs. One venue near Helena was surrounded by a car-salvage yard, and menacing guard dogs prowled around the club's parking lot at night. Inside, chicken wire shielded the stage from flying beer bottles. The walls of another venue were peppered with bullet holes. Robbie says, "We played places where the people didn't come to hear you, they came to mess with you. They'd flick cigarette butts at you, throw coins at you, steal your things, and if you get past that, *then* they'd listen to you."

Avis recalls one university gig in Oklahoma where some patrons, very drunk on moonshine, were itching to start a fight. "There was one, and he kept mouthing off, and Levon took that one drumstick, and he just eyed him right up and let it go. Oh, shit, the band had it then." The Hawks and Bill were engulfed in a barroom brawl. In one Tulsa club, the promoter ducked out with all the money from the door, leaving the band with nothing. "What did we do to retaliate?" Avis asks. "We loaded up the jukebox and the cigarette machine into our equipment trailer. We smoked Oklahoma cigarettes for the longest time! I think we sold the jukebox."

Sometimes the band gave as good as it took. After a weeklong gig at the Canadian Club in Tulsa with the house band, Leon Russell's Starlighters, the disreputable bar owner gave them a useless check. Levon and the boys returned to the club after closing, safely stowed Russell's equipment out in the parking lot, then proceeded to wreck the place. Copying what he'd seen in the movies, Hawkins poured gallons of gas inside the club and out the door. Helm lit a match and touched the line of gas. There was no delay. It all blew up at once, propelling Ronnie through the back door of the bar, temporarily blinding him, and burning off his eyebrows. All that remained of the club was smoking rubble. Everyone was so stunned they were still there when the police arrived. Because the authorities had experienced nothing but trouble from the nefarious club owner, they said, "Hell, boys, you done us a favor," and let them off.

Despite the perils of performing in the South, Ronnie was eager to expand their territory, so Dayton booked them for a couple of nights at Jack Ruby's club at the Skyline Hotel in Fort Worth, which featured a one-armed go-go dancer. The manager warned them to guard their gear all night or it would be gone in the morning, so the band members took turns—Levon and Bill on one shift. "We had to wear guns…" says Robbie. "One night the police came bursting in with dogs. The dogs nearly got us, we nearly got them. The next night somebody shot off a tear-gas bomb. It stunk up the place for four days. People would come in and start crying."

As protection on the road, they kept blackjacks under the seats of their vehicles. They'd saw the thick end off a pool cue, drill a hole and thread it with a strip of rawhide or heavy string. The band was especially vulnerable at the end of the night, carrying their 60 percent of the door admission to the parking lot. Ronnie could get mouthy if they were approached, and fights would ensue. Toronto tailor Lou Myles started making their suit jackets with a small inside pocket to hold a blackjack.

Money was tight; sometimes they didn't have enough for food. Bill confesses, "We'd go into a grocery store, and we had long raincoats on with big pockets, and we'd scoop up some bologna and make musicians steak." The Hawks stayed in cheap motels where they'd pull the sheets back to check for bedbugs. And to save more money, Levon and Bill usually shared the same bed.

Helm and Hawkins had some influential friends who helped substantially. Don Tyson, of Tyson Foods, headquartered in Springdale, Arkansas, just north of Fayetteville, was always generous. He'd treat the boys to a night at the back of the Elks Club, where the power brokers of northwest Arkansas drank and gambled, comping the band to drinks and steak dinners, and rolls of coins for the slot machines. If someone's boots looked shabby, Tyson would take them shopping. If they needed a lift, he'd fly them in his private plane. "He was just struck like a teenager," Kirby Penick says.

Back before [Tyson] got to be this big businessman as he was, he would have people coming in here—salesmen and people he was trying [to persuade] to buy his stuff…He would get Ronnie and get all the guys—the band and everybody—[to] come over and party with these buyers and whatnot…[The buyers] fell in love with it too. They couldn't wait to come back and have fun. [Tyson] knew every hairdresser in northwest Arkansas and wound up with parties full of cosmetologists and musicians and, you know, just party, party, party…He was a big supporter and kind of an angel, in a theatrical sense, to Ronnie and all the bands that he had. He was always financing that sort of thing…whether it was advancing money to buy equipment or cars or whatever.

The Hawks would drive straight through from Arkansas to Toronto. More than fifty years later, Bill still remembers the distance: "1,707 miles from Fayetteville, Arkansas, to the Frontenac Arms Hotel on Jarvis Street. [It took] a night and a day because we never stopped… How did we do that? Well, truckers have those things called black mariahs. You pop one of those and you could drive all the way to Los Angeles and then turn around and drive halfway back before it wore off. All you did was chew gum and smoke cigarettes."

In Toronto, Helm and Avis sometimes stayed just east of downtown at 193 First Avenue, at the home of Robbie's mother—Mama Kosh, as she was affectionately known to the band. Other times, Levon, Ronnie, and Bill lived in suite 902 at the Frontenac Arms Hotel. It had two bedrooms—Ronnie in one, Levon and Bill sharing the other. Tobin Rote, a quarterback for the Toronto Argonauts, also stayed there with a few other football players and, according to Bill, "would party with us on the weekends and would go out Sunday and play football, still drunk."

Levon loved the rice pudding at Bassel's on Yonge Street, and often he and Bill ate it at nighttime and for breakfast. Or sometimes Little Freddie McNulty came by to wake them up, and Bill would send him out with money to get them two fried-egg sandwiches. Change was not forthcoming as Fred didn't know the difference between a five-dollar bill and a fifty. "Levon, oh, did he look after Little Freddie," Bill says. "Bought him a Lou Myles suit and dressed him all up—and he wore that suit and got mustard all over it."

HELM MET IDENTICAL twin brothers Ernie and Earl Cate when the Hawks were in Fayetteville. Both were singers—Ernie played keyboards, Earl on guitar. Originally, their band was called the Del-Reys, and they performed Everly Brothers–style harmonies. They were also influenced by the music of Carl Perkins, Roy Orbison, Jerry Lee Lewis, Harold Jenkins, and, of course, Ronnie Hawkins and the Hawks. At first, they were too young to get into the Rockwood Club, so they'd park outside and just listen.

As members were leaving, the Hawks were in flux. They almost dodged history and remained an Arkansas band. Earl Cate remembers a white Cadillac with a teardrop trailer parking in front of their house on Maple Street:

> Levon comes out and Ronnie, you know. They got on these black silk-skin pants, you know, [laughs] and pointed-toed shoes. And I said, "Never seen anything like that before."
>
> Fact, Robbie and Levon took Ernie and I down to the D-Lux and ate one day, and they tried to talk us into goin'…back to Canada with 'em, and he wanted me to play bass and Ernie to play the keys and sing, you know. But we didn't wanna go. [laughter] We were about nineteen, eighteen or nineteen…We're afraid. [laughter]

Nevertheless, Ronnie did find a bass player who came to define the band's sound. Rick Danko—whom Levon called Pan—was a country boy born in 1943 on a farm in Greens Corner near Simcoe, Ontario. His family was musical, and Rick began playing string instruments— violin, banjo and mandolin—at five. By the time he was seven, Rick was learning guitar. Although the Danko house didn't have electricity until Rick was ten, he listened to records on a wind-up Victrola, and with a crystal set or battery-operated radio, he tuned into the great music broadcast from as far away as Nashville, West Virginia, and even Mexico. All this helped shape his wide range of musical interests, including R&B, blues, and especially country. Rick had been playing in bands since he was twelve.

He first heard the Hawks in 1960, and the sheer force of their performance—with Levon laughing throughout—was overwhelming.

He made a point of booking his band wherever they would be opening for the Hawks, until one night after a Port Dover gig, Ronnie offered him a job. Danko would start off playing rhythm guitar, then switch to bass after Rebel Payne's expected departure. Although he'd never played rhythm guitar or bass, he jumped in Hawk's Cadillac and never looked back.

In the face of Ronnie's uncanny knack of spotting raw talent, Levon and Robbie were at first unconvinced about this new recruit, but regardless, they helped him learn bass, and he picked up the bass patterns Stan played on piano with his left hand. The Hawk says, "He practiced so much that his arms swoll up. He was hurting."

Rebel Payne had been drinking too much, and his wife was encouraging him to return to Buffalo. When he left in the summer of 1961, Danko was ready to take over on bass. "Rick Danko was so musical and good-natured that he made everybody around him feel great and play at their best," Helm said. "His joyfully loose bass playing fit my drumming like a glove and completed our loosey-goosey rhythm section."

At about this time, the Hawk hired baritone saxophone player Jerry Penfound to enhance the R&B flavor of their music. Known as Ish to his bandmates, the London, Ontario, native was an army veteran who had played in Toronto for dance bands.

Danko's and Penfound's first recording session with the Hawks was in September 1961, almost a year since the last time the band recorded for Roulette. Another significant addition to this New York session was acclaimed producer, songwriter, trumpet player—and all-around recording talent—Henry Glover. As Levon expressed it, Henry was a

> great producer and songwriter who helped Syd Nathan build King Records…Henry was responsible for some of the greatest recordings of all time, like "Fever" by Little Willie John, "Blues Stay Away from Me" by the Delmore Brothers, and the early hits of Hank Ballard and the Midnighters. He composed "Drown in My Own Tears," "California Sun," "The Peppermint Twist," and countless others. And that's not all: Henry played first-chair trumpet in Lucky Millinder's band in the 1940s. You could fill a book with his accomplishments.

Also an Arkansan, Glover came to enjoy a lifelong working and personal relationship with Helm. "Levon and I struck up a pretty nice friendship, very close," Henry said. "He could play back in those days. He was considered a very, very good drummer in my estimation."

With Robbie on guitar, Rick playing bass, Jerry on saxophone, and Levon playing drums, Ronnie cut six tracks on September 13 for their album *Ronnie Hawkins: The Best of Roulette*. "Come Love," a shuffle with prominent guitar work and Hawkins's vocals backed by a chorus that likely included Dionne Warwick, Dee Dee Warwick, and Cissy Houston, was the single. "I Feel Good," the other side of the 45, was recorded five days later, along with four tracks for Ronnie's *Mojo Man* LP.

Glover was amazed at the Hawks' caliber of musicianship. "I was the A&R director for Roulette Records when Ronnie Hawkins was playing there," he said, "and in between the tracks on his sessions, [the Hawks without Ronnie] asked me to do some things on them. Actually, that was the first time I'd ever heard [a] white [band] play the blues like they did." Levon and Henry wrote "What a Party" about an imaginary assemblage of R&B greats. The Hawks recorded it on September 15, with Helm, full of bravado, bawling out lead vocals—his first time on record—while playing a swinging eighth-note groove embellished with drags on the snare.

On September 18, acclaimed saxman King Curtis joined Jerry Penfound and the band to cut "I Feel Good" and four numbers for *Ronnie Hawkins: Mojo Man*. Ronnie keeps it in the family with Dale Hawkins's "Susie-Q," and the band rocks out in "Matchbox," with a fifties beat and a profusion of fills from Levon. Two of the tracks were cut when there was still time left in the session, and Glover let the Hawks record without Hawkins. As Helm tells it,

> We would finish recording with Hawk and maybe have twenty minutes on the clock, and Henry would have us go ahead and record a couple of songs right quick. So that was some of the first times that we ever got to play in a recording situation [without Hawkins]...We did "Further on up the Road"—that

was one of our big favorites at the time. And we couldn't resist it. We just liked playing it, you know. It was fun to play, especially at dances like we were playing. We always played a lot of R&B and a lot of blues stuff.

Helm rips it up singing lead on the blues classic "Further on Up the Road" while playing a shuffle, his drums less woody than on many of his other recordings. On Muddy Waters's "Nineteen Years Old," Levon's ferocious, predatory vocals are supported by his relaxed 12/8 shuffle, slightly behind the beat, with searing guitar from Robertson. "That was the first time that we had ever recorded under any kind of professional circumstances, and it was just as exciting as it could be, and disappointing as hell too, when we heard the playback," Levon observed with a laugh.

THE ROCKIN' REVOLS, out of Stratford, Ontario, enjoyed an enthusiastic following, and in spring 1960, the Revols and the Hawks went head to head in a battle of the bands on the Revols' home turf. Put in the unenviable position of following the Hawks, the Revols dazzled the crowd when their vocalist and piano player, Richard Manuel—known as Beak—launched into "Georgia on My Mind." That was all Hawkins needed to hear. He booked all the Revols at his Rockwood Club in Fayetteville.

Born in 1944 in Stratford, Ontario, the son of a car mechanic and a teacher, Richard grew up listening to blues and country on the radio, and learned vocal harmonies in the church choir. He started piano lessons at age nine before singing and playing in his first band at fifteen. His vocals were transcendent—ranging from soulful baritone to soaring falsetto—drawing comparisons with Ray Charles. When Stan Szelest left the Hawks to get married, Ronnie convinced Richard to meet the band in Tulsa and join them on their fall 1961 tour. With that addition, Levon said, "I always just felt real confident with Richard in the band. I knew that nobody had a better singer in their band than what we had." Although the Hawks could boast two other excellent vocalists with Levon and Rick, in Helm's view, as long as Richard was there, Manuel was their lead singer.

REGARDING THE NEW lineup of the Hawks, Levon stated, "The one that was the big reward for us, though, was Garth. To get Garth Hudson, that was a big day because nobody could play like Garth anywhere. He could play horns, he could play keyboards, he could play anything and play it better than anybody you knew." Although they already had a keyboard player, Levon and Robbie believed if they could get Garth, he would propel the band to an entirely new level.

Born in London, Ontario, in 1937, Hudson was closer in age to Ronnie than the rest of the band. Raised in a musical family, he started piano lessons at five and learned accordion. He took private lessons in music theory, counterpoint, and harmony with Thomas Chattoe, an organist, choirmaster, and music director at the Metropolitan United Church in London. John Cooke, the organist and choirmaster at that city's St. Paul's Cathedral, schooled him in composition, and he took piano classes from Clifford von Kuster, who'd performed as a soloist in London, England, and in New York. Garth's parents sent him to study classical piano at the world-renowned Ontario Conservatory of Music, yet he was also influenced by R&B and early rock 'n' roll on the radio. Hudson first performed in public at his uncle's funeral parlor, where he played hymns on the organ, then when he was twelve, he was the accordionist in a country band. He belonged to a couple of jazz bands, then joined the rockabilly group the Silhouettes on piano and saxophone, which after a move to the Windsor–Detroit area and with the addition of a singer became Paul London and the Kapers.

Garth—nicknamed Honey Hudson by Helm—first met Levon and Robbie when the Hawks performed at London's Brass Rail. They started pestering him to join their band, but Garth declined. His inclination was to play more sophisticated music. He remained with the Kapers, and they cut a single—"Sugar Baby" and "Big Bad Twist"—that had modest success. Eventually, having determined that the Kapers had reached their musical limit, Garth reconsidered joining the Hawks. But his parents disapproved. Ronnie persuaded them by agreeing to hire Garth as primarily an organist and as a teacher for the other band members, offering him an extra ten dollars a week. Assured that their son's music education would not go to waste, the Hudsons finally acquiesced at the end of 1961.

The combination of Richard's rhythm piano with Garth's Lowery Festival organ brought a new richness and complexity to the sound. Robertson says,

> At that time, Garth was far and away the most advanced musician in rock 'n' roll. He could just as easily play with John Coltrane as he could play with the New York Symphony Orchestra as he could play with us as he could play with Minnie Pearl. He was just remarkable. He could listen to a song and tell us the chords to the song as it went along, I mean, songs with complicated chord structures. It widened our scope, and it was just a lot more fun.

Levon added, "Once we had a musician of Garth's caliber, we started sounding professional. You might say Garth spread the icing on the cake."

Ronnie was pleased to have a young, good-looking band—it was great for business. "In a bar, it's a different gig," he says. "You gotta go out and mix with people and shake hands and thank 'em and have 'em come back, you know. That's what you gotta do...and they were really good at it. And women really went for this band. And once you got two hundred women coming in to see the band, you got four hundred guys coming in to hustle the women."

This version of the Hawks was tight, both musically and personally. Paul Berry enjoyed hanging out with the band when they were in the South. "They were just fabulous company," he recollects. "Forget their musical prowess and how great they were, they were just a lot of fun to be with."

Aspiring musicians flocked to their gigs, hoping to pick up some pointers. Young David Clayton-Thomas—the future powerhouse vocalist for Blood, Sweat & Tears—first heard the Hawks in Toronto when he left prison in 1962. "To this day," he declares, "I believe they were the greatest rock 'n' roll band ever." David's closest friend in the Hawks was Levon, whom he describes as

> just a very easy-going, relaxed guy...Immediately, him and I hit it off...I think it was very obvious from the first time I saw him...

this guy is special. We'd never seen anybody play drums with a groove like that and sing. And as I got to know him, I realized he played damned good guitar, too…I actually saw him take over from Robbie on lead some nights. Mandolin, blues harp—he was multitalented. That became obvious right away. He liked the way I sang, and I liked the way he sang. I was a fan, more like an idolizer. [laughs] We young musicians would sit there by the bar at the Le Coq d'Or and just hang on every note.

Boisterous and ofttimes scandalous, the Le Coq d'Or was at the hub of the Yonge Street strip, and the Hawks, dressed in mohair suits with razor-cut haircuts, were its kings. Bar fights erupted nearly every night, but the band usually stayed out of it. Flying beer bottles were their main concern. Impassioned rock 'n' rollers studied their every move. When the Hawks played a new number, every other band had to learn it. If Levon added a cymbal to his kit, it would sell out in every music store on Yonge. Clayton-Thomas recalls the time a truck ran over Levon's crash cymbal when he was unloading it behind the club, and he had to play with it broken. Then, in order to get the "Levon sound," aspiring drummers drove over their cymbals.

A lot of the music was left to the band, while Hawkins socialized:

It was a total team effort, that band [says Clayton-Thomas]. I often wondered who the leader was…Ronnie's main talent is he's a lovable character, and he likes to go out and circulate and hit on the babes and schmooze up the guys. As long as he sang "Bo Diddley" and "Forty Days," the audience was happy, and he could go out and schmooze and go from table to table and let the band play, so most often—and of course at the matinees—there would be other musicians come up, jam some blues, some Jimmy Reed, some Bo Diddley, whatever, Ray Charles—a lot of Ray Charles in those days. So Ronnie was kind of the genial master of ceremonies… He's a showman.

The band made sure the back door of the Le Coq d'Or was open a crack so all the underage musicians could listen from outside.

Young patrons, such as David and guitarist Freddie Keeler, could legally attend the liquor-free Saturday afternoon matinees at most Toronto clubs. Because the Hawks played five shows a night on top of the matinee, they were relaxed about letting other musicians sit in during the afternoons. "That's when a lot of us got our start," David reveals.

> Ronnie Hawkins…took a liking to me, and I remember it was coming down near Christmas, and I didn't have a band, I didn't have a gig, and so Ronnie said, "Come and sing with my band. I'll pay you over the holidays." So I went and did two weeks at the Le Coq d'Or over the holidays [with Levon, Robbie, Garth, Richard and Rick]. I'd have done it for nothing. It was a dream come true. It was my first paid gig. I actually realized I could make a living at this.

After playing six nights a week, plus a Saturday matinee—whether in Toronto, Hamilton, or Grand Bend, Ontario—the Hawk got the Colonel to book them for Sunday gigs at Don Ivey's dance hall in Port Dover, south of Hamilton on Lake Erie. "Everybody needed an extra twenty-five dollars," Bill Avis says, "and Ronnie would take a lot more, believe me." One Sunday, Freddie McNulty made his way to Port Dover and was hoping to get a ride back to Toronto with the band. This day, however, they had some girls with them, so there wasn't room in the cars. Rather than leave Freddie stranded, Helm came up with a solution. According to Bill,

> Levon says, "We're going to put him in the [teardrop] trailer." And believe me, we did. In the trailer, besides the amps and guitars and Levon's drums, there's also Garth's organ, so we laid Freddie on top of the organ…Garth had bought moving blankets and they all went around it with straps…So we put a strap over Freddie… all the way back to Toronto…Opened the door, and there's Little Fred…If we ever got stopped or had an accident—oh, my God, I'd still be in jail!

TORONTO CONTINUED TO attract the best popular music in North America, heavily influencing local musicians. David Clayton-Thomas explains:

> Those bars—not just Ronnie's band—[led to] the formation of what we now call the Toronto sound, and there really is a distinct Toronto sound. It came about because all of those bars on Yonge Street attracted the black artists from the States, from Detroit and Chicago. In the 1960s, of course, there was a severe color ban, a black ban, in the States, no matter if they had the number-one record in the world, they played in black clubs on the black side of town. These black musicians, all the way from Marvin Gaye to B.B. King to the Muddy Waters Band, they found out they could come up to Toronto and there was no color bar up here. It attracted them the way London, England, attracted a lot of them, or Paris...
>
> Us young musicians, sitting at the bar nursing our Cokes, we would be exposed to seeing James Brown, the Ike and Tina Turner Revue, B.B. King, Albert King, the Muddy Waters Band—the greatest blues band in the world from Chicago—they played at the Edison Hotel. It was a strange kind of mix of music. You would see...the Muddy Waters Band at the Edison...and then the next band coming in would be Johnny Cash or Waylon Jennings. All of that music kind of germinated right there, and that heavy R&B Detroit, Motown, funk aspect to the Canadian, Toronto, sound was really born right there.
>
> Even moreso, there was a little after-hours club across the street, the Bluenote. There were two important places in Toronto to us musicians: there was Fran's Restaurant on the corner of Yonge and Dundas, which is gone now, and the Bluenote. Doing five shows a night, we'd basically sleep all day...then all the bands would gather at Fran's Restaurant for breakfast [at night]. Now the bars are closed...They served a twenty-four-hour-a-day breakfast, so we would all get together there: the Hawks, my band—I was playing at the Friars at the time—and these other artists. You might end up at Fran's Restaurant at two o'clock in the morning with Diana Ross. I remember having breakfast there with the Righteous Brothers.

After we had breakfast at two o'clock in the morning, we'd go to a club, which didn't open until one o'clock in the morning, and it was called the Bluenote. It was an after-hours club. It featured the hottest musicians in town in the house band. There was Doug Riley and Steve Kennedy and Kenny Marco—just heavyweights—Diane Brooks. They'd do a couple of shows, then at three o'clock in the morning, they cleared the floor, and they would have a floor show. You might see Marvin Gaye in that show, you might see B.B. King or you might see one of the top Toronto bands, because that's where we hung out until dawn. Then what did we do when the club closed? We went and found a place to party.

With so much competition, the Hawk made sure his band stayed on top. His strict rehearsal schedule for them is well known, but Ronnie rarely attended them himself, as Avis recalls:

I don't have a lot of respect for Hawkins…but I will say this: He did make the fellas rehearse because I had to be there to make sure that they were rehearsing. We'd finish up at the Concord or the Le Coq d'Or in Toronto, then I would drive him home to Wanda on High Park [Avenue], then I'd have to go right back to the hotel, wherever we were working, and sit with the guys and listen to them rehearse…Very, very seldom [was Ronnie there] unless he wanted to learn a new song.

Hawkins had a strict code of behavior for his band. There was no drinking or smoking during a performance, no smoking in the car, and, fearful they'd get arrested, no dope-smoking at any time. Girlfriends of band members weren't allowed at their gigs in case they dashed the hopes of other female patrons, reasoning that if girls stayed away, so would the guys. When the band started making more money, Ronnie imposed fines for rule violations. Avis says,

If you weren't dressed just the way he wanted, well, you'd get fined twenty-five dollars…I kept that book, and I collected the money, naturally, at the end of the week, and I'd pay everyone and have to deduct that if they had a twenty-five-dollar fine if their shoes weren't shined properly or whatever. He was very regimental, Ronnie...[Levon] kind of went with it for a little bit, but he was always a redneck. His feathers would get up.

Ronnie was meticulous about his car and strictly upheld the no-smoking rule in the vehicle. He rode shotgun in the front passenger seat, and whenever he dozed off, everyone cracked the windows and lit up. One time when Richard snuck a cigarette in the back, the Hawk woke up and smelled tobacco. In a panic—or possibly on purpose—Richard extinguished his smoke on Ronnie's hand. On another occasion, using money as a positive inducement, Hawkins offered Helm fifty dollars to quit smoking. As he tried to kick the habit, Levon ate raisins instead, but when some of them got mashed into the car's carpet, the Hawk offered him a hundred dollars to stop eating *them*.

ON FEBRUARY 2, 1962, the Hawks recorded again for Roulette, cutting "Arkansas" and "Mojo Man," which would later be released as part of *The Best of Ronnie Hawkins*. Notably, the session was produced by songwriters Jerry Leiber and Mike Stoller, with composer Mort Shuman sitting in on piano, bluesman Sonny Terry playing harmonica, and on "Arkansas," Jerry Penfound taking over on drums. It was also the first time that the new Canadian Hawks—Robertson, Danko, Manuel, and Hudson—all played together on a recording.

IN 1962, IN addition to sending home money, Helm bought a laundromat and a house on Hinshaw Drive in Springdale, northwest Arkansas, for his parents. "He'd look after Diamond and Nell," Dayton Stratton's son Randy recalls, "and make sure they were taken care of... He loved his family and wanted to get together as much as possible." Levon's sister Modena had already moved to Springdale with her family, and Linda had recently graduated and worked at Tyson Foods, a big employer in that area. When she married, Linda kept her day job and worked nights in nearby Tontitown at the Venesian Inn, a restaurant owned by her husband's family.

On March 16, Ronnie married his girlfriend Wanda Nagurski, but attempted to hush it up to preserve his image as a sexy bachelor. Though the Hawk had resisted, when Wanda was offered a job in California, he took the plunge in desperation. It was a last-minute affair—Wanda introduced her mother to Ronnie on the steps of the church. The only other band member Hawkins told was his best man, Levon. A young singer with hopes of joining the Hawks happened to walk by as the couple was leaving the church. Astonished, he asked Ronnie if he'd just gotten married. The Hawk replied, "Me? Naw, it's him," pointing to Helm. Actually, it wouldn't be long before that was true.

Levon had been periodically called down to Helena to report to the U.S. government draft office. He'd always successfully received a deferral due to a back injury. Bill Avis explains, "That's from riding so many years on a tractor...He had a metal back brace that he could put on, and it serviced for a long time in regards to the draft." But as troop levels in the Vietnam War surged under President Kennedy, the military was accepting some candidates it had previously overlooked, and Helm was facing boot camp. The Hawk was in a panic. This was his key player.

The solution was Connie Orr, whom Bill describes as "a sweet, beautiful woman," who had been married a couple of times before. A little older than Levon, "She was just a good street person. You could trust her." Connie was a Concord Tavern rounder, and that community looked after the Hawks. She agreed to a platonic marriage of convenience to keep Helm out of the grip of the U.S. military. One night, not telling any of the others, Levon and Connie crossed the border to Detroit and got married. Bill admits, "They couldn't really do it here because she was already married here." With that, Levon became a landed immigrant in Canada.

IN JANUARY 1963, Ronnie and the Hawks were back at Roulette with producer Henry Glover, and Roy Buchanan returned on this occasion to play bass. Penfound and Hudson were not included. The songs were taken from the Hawks' club repertoire—"Bo Diddley" and "Who Do You Love"—surefire crowd-pleasers on their circuit. It had been almost five years since the band recorded "Hey Bo Diddley" for Quality Records. Hawkins's vocals on "Who Do You Love" are feral. With "Hey Bo Diddley" on the A-side, the single was released that March, but with little airplay, its sales were mediocre, reaching only number 117 on the *Billboard* chart.

Eager to have them lay down more tracks before their contract expired, Levy brought the full band—minus Buchanan—back to New York on May 7 with Glover again producing. "Bossman," "High Blood Pressure," "There's a Screw Loose," and its instrumental introduction were recorded that day, with "High Blood Pressure" chosen for the 45, backed by Ronnie's cackling through "There's a Screw Loose," reminiscent of the earlier "Horace."

Bruce Bruno, an Italian kid from New Rochelle, New York, with a voice like Johnny Mathis, had already cut a couple of 45s for Morris Levy. The Hawks met him during this trip at their gig at Levy's Roundtable club. Ronnie was impressed. By that summer, Bruno was a Hawk and the band expanded to seven.

One reason for hiring Bruno was that since Ronnie's marriage, and especially after Ron Junior was born, Hawkins's interests diverged from the Hawks. Helm acknowledged that sometimes at a weeklong stand, the Hawk would appear only at the end of a set on their last night. Without Ronnie, the band started to work on their harmonies, with Manuel on top, and Rick and Levon supplying the middle and bottom.

With Hawkins so often away, a simple question came to mind: Did they even need a frontman?

5

The Hawks Take Wing

"They were boys when they started, but they were men when they finished," Hawkins says of his band in 1963. "They'd seen damn near everythin' there is to see. They practiced, played and fucked in every town you care to name. Real dudes, man."

It was late that year when the Hawks took Ronnie to the basement of the Le Coq d'Or and told him they were leaving. Hawkins had a feeling it was coming. One reason was marijuana. "I wouldn't allow any dope smoking in my band," Hawkins asserts. "I had caught them a few times and told them, 'Goddamn. If I can catch you, well you know the Mounties are smarter than me.'" The Hawks railed against the rules and fines, but Ronnie didn't want trouble with the law.

Music itself played a big part, as well. "They were the best white rhythm and blues band probably in the world at that time...They were too musical for me," the Hawk admits. "They got too good." Bruce Bruno saw a band impatient to extend its musical horizons. Levon said, "Ronnie was set in his ways and we were young and bursting with energy. We wanted to try some Cannonball Adderley stuff, and some Louis Jordan songs and for sure more Sonny Boy [Williamson], Muddy [Waters] and J.B. Lenoir." Robbie concurs, "The whole reason behind it was this: the band was becoming more knowledgeable about music and the old stuff we were doing was getting on our nerves. We were young and adventurous. We were on a musical journey, and this was the only way to explore it. It may have been partly for business reasons, too, but we really outgrew what we were doing."

The Hawks were making up to a thousand dollars per week at the

Le Coq d'Or—the highest-earning Canadian band—yet Hawkins paid each band member only seventy-five. Even with the group expanding to seven, that left more than half for Ronnie, minus Avis's cut and other expenses. In Jerry Penfound's opinion, "The split was instigated by Robbie and Levon. They said they'd had enough and wanted more money. Ronnie wouldn't have it…The way I saw it, it was strictly about money. It wasn't anything to do with music or personalities."

One night when Hawkins was supposed to be away, he caught Danko's girlfriend in the audience, breaking a strict rule. Levon backed Rick, and Helm's resentment mounted against Ronnie's authority and what he saw as the unfair split of earnings. Four months later, when Rick had still not paid his fifty-dollar fine and Hawkins caught the girl again, the Hawk fired Danko. It was the final straw.

Harold Kudlets, who had recently been let go as Hawkins's manager, was surprised one morning as he arrived at his office in Hamilton's Royal Connaught Hotel to see Helm and Danko waiting for him in the lobby. "I wondered what the hell they were doing at nine o'clock in the morning there. So they came up to the office and they told me they'd left Hawkins, and they wanted me to come back and book them," Kudlets said. "They just asked me to get the money that they were earning with Ronnie, and when they told me how much, I nearly shit. He was paying them peanuts, so I told them I'd have no trouble booking them for that figure."

The Hawks' first gig without Hawkins was at the Friar's Tavern in Toronto, followed by the Brass Rail in London, the Grange Tavern in Hamilton, then back to Toronto for a two-week stand at the Concord.

Bill Avis had also left Hawkins and was working for the Female Beatles. He was on tour with them in Detroit when he got the call from Helm to come back as their road manager. He gave them two weeks' notice and returned to Toronto and the Hawks.

Initially billed as the Levon Helm Sextet, they retained sax player Jerry Penfound or if Jerry was away, Bruce Bruno on vocals. Levon was considered the leader, only because he'd been with the band the longest and the Colonel thought he had more name recognition than the other members. Decisions were made democratically, and their income was shared equally. Because he enjoyed it, Levon did most of the driving. By May, Penfound had left, and the band name became Levon and the Hawks.

By the time the Hawks left Ronnie, "We went from being as good as anyone on the circuit," Helm declared, "to being the best band around...We sounded better than anybody but maybe the Bobby Bland band." Free from Hawkins's restraints, they played what they loved—as Levon put it, "lowdown R&B, gut-bucket blues and blazing rock 'n' roll." In the blues genre, they leaned heavily on Bobby "Blue" Bland material such as "Share Your Love with Me" and "Turn on Your Love Light"—complemented by the two saxes of Hudson and Penfound—and songs by Muddy Waters, Howlin' Wolf, and T-Bone Walker. Their rock 'n' roll standbys—usually sung by Helm—included Little Richard's "Lucille," Buddy Holly's "Not Fade Away," the Beatles' "Twist and Shout" and "Money," Chuck Berry's "No Particular Place to Go," Larry Williams's "Short Fat Fanny," and "Smack Dab in the Middle," originally recorded by Charlie Calhoun. Manuel's impassioned vocals were a stand-out in soul covers such as Ray Charles's "Georgia on My Mind," Danko sang Sam Cooke numbers, and Bruno—who would stay with the band until early 1965—was also a vocalist. Robertson worked out an outstanding guitar arrangement for "Theme from a Summer Place," which they performed as an instrumental. They played their own R&B arrangements of James Brown's "Please Please Please" and the Isley Brothers' "Shout." And they explored other genres, going through phases of immersion in gospel and jazz.

"They were respected, and most of us had an aspect of awe about them," Paul Berry says of the Hawks.

> We knew early on this was some hellacious band...[Berry continues.] We thought they were better than anything we're hearing on the jukebox. Levon once said to me...they would play on some big shows where they were the only group on the bill that didn't have a radio hit and a contract with somebody. But Levon said, "I never worried." He said, "I always had lots of confidence. We knew we had the best singer—Richard Manuel."

And, of course, they also had a first-rate drummer, one who masterfully tapped into and expressed the feel of a song, that mysterious element that eludes definition. Levon had great projection with his drums, yet he had a surprisingly gentle touch.

> I got to see Louie Hayes with Cannonball Adderley [Helm said]. I got to see some great musicians over the years, and you see somebody like that play and you can tell, y' know, that the thing *not* to do is to just get it down on the floor and stomp the hell out of it! [laughs] You're supposed to kind of dance the beat along. The way the really great players work is not frantic and out of control. But, you know, sometimes I get a kick bearin' down on it, just flesh against wood. It gives you a certain kind of satisfaction, burning one of them press rolls up. It might sting a little, but it's worth it.

He gave his backbeat heft by playing the butt end of the drumstick on the rim of the snare, striving to get the same sound he'd heard from rock 'n' roll players such as Clifton James and Al Jackson. And like a lot of Southern drummers, he often laid down his groove at the far end of a beat. "Some songs just want to lay on the back end," he said. "You get there at the last possible moment. If the song will allow for that kind of a backbeat, it seems to feel better. It makes the music more danceable." His playing typically had a slight swing, inhabiting a sweet spot somewhere between a shuffle and straight groove, a technique influenced by Earl Palmer. And he never overplayed or was flashy. It was Helm's belief that the most important factor in his approach to music was not what he played, but what he left out.

Levon never thought it was wrong to vary the tempo within a song. Of the view that a drummer should be a metronome, he pointed out, "That's not the way J.M. Van Eaton ever played. I never heard Al Jackson or Willie Hall or W.S. Holland—anybody that I ever thought was a drummer—ever play like that." In his opinion, different components in a song—an instrumental solo, a vocal part—could require minor variations in tempo. He said, "Sometimes the dynamics will make the song feel as though maybe it's slowing down. And if you put a metronome or if you have a click track in your headphones it might actually slow down, but that's the least of my worries. I don't care. I think that's what the music should do."

His advice to drummers was, "Most importantly, have fun. Laugh a lot and learn to play other instruments." Levon could switch to harmonica, mandolin, guitar, or bass whenever it was called for. He approached these instruments the way he did the drums. "Rhythmically I just find my little contribution, the pattern, the pulse and the rhythm of the song," he said.

THE MUSICIANSHIP WAS stunning, and Levon and the band were having a blast. Though Hawkins's strict rules no longer held the day, there were other restrictions. "For musicians then, you had to wear a suit and tie," Helm remarked. "It was a union rule that you can't smoke or drink on the bandstand."

Their audiences, however, had few restraints. Levon recalled bars "where you sit down, and the next thing you're slam-assin' around because you got to protect your honor or something. My neck can get as red as anybody's, but when you're 5'9" and 140 pounds, you can't jump on just anybody you see." Levon fondly recalled getting into scrapes alongside Robbie: "I still remember the Duke, my brother, who was funny as hell and always had my back should push come to shove and we had to scratch gravel getting out of town."

The guys were always joking around, and Helm and Robertson had a routine that invariably got everyone laughing:

> At parties, the Duke would wink back at me, then cleverly slip his hand in before I landed one of my hungriest kisses smack on his lips. When he'd leave (parties are always in the drummer or bass player's room), he'd stand in the doorway until all the ladies I'd been talking to and everyone else in the room would stop and look back at him. Then he'd throw me a glare like, "You hussy, don't you dare keep me waiting" and slam the door. This always brought down the house and added more fuel to the fired-up fun…We all laughed our way through the hard times.

Those times were lean. Kudlets booked them throughout southern Ontario and into Quebec, New York, and New Jersey. On the road, they "shared the same bedroom and bed on different occasions," Levon said. "There had certainly been times when maybe we could afford two rooms, and after a few flips of the old coin, we found out who was going to get the couch and who might get an extra pillow and take the floor."

Helm stuck up for what he saw as right. In spring 1964, well before he became a celebrated funk musician, sixteen-year-old Rick James, a U.S. naval reservist, was placed on active duty, but he overslept and missed the registration in Rochester, New York. Technically AWOL, he fled by bus to Toronto to avoid punishment. As he walked through Yorkville, still in uniform, the young black man was taunted with racist slurs by three white Americans who threatened to assault him. But when Levon, Garth, and a friend, Pat McGraw, showed up, they frightened off the thugs. Befriending Rick, the four went out for coffee. "Garth and Levon were beautiful cats, deep into music," James says. "We talked about Muddy Waters and Cannonball Adderley."

Even though they had to struggle for recognition, the Hawks, in Helm's opinion, were "the undisputed champions of Canadian rock and roll." Folk musician Stan Thomas agreed. He persuaded John Hammond Jr., a blues folk artist who had a gig at Toronto's Purple Onion, to come with him to the Concord Tavern to see Levon and the Hawks. "I heard this band, which was just phenomenal," Hammond recalls. "They were just so in touch and in tune. I mean, strictly blues and R&B. I was introduced to the guys, they called me up, I did a song with them that night, and we became really good friends." John describes the Hawks as "easy to get along with. Rick Danko and Levon were as effortlessly friendly as anyone you could ever meet. Very likeable people. We hung out and partied and talked about blues endlessly and plans for the future."

Hammond was the son of the respected A&R man for Columbia Records—John Hammond Sr.—who discovered extraordinary artists in popular music and blues. Part of the burgeoning folk-music scene in Greenwich Village, the junior Hammond was a friend of rising folk hero Bob Dylan. The son brought Dylan to the attention of his father, leading to Bob's contract with Columbia. As for the Hawks, their friendship with John Jr. would be an important break.

The band hooked up with Hammond again when they were booked at the Peppermint Lounge in New York City's Times Square, a mob-owned nightspot famous as ground zero for the newest dance craze. One night, when John sat in, their genre of music pushed management too far. Helm was told, "This blues shit will never get you anywhere. It's a twist joint—play the twist."

Describing his impressions of Levon, John says, "Oh, he was wonderful on drums even way back then. He was a lyrical drummer, very imaginative, and could be outrageous in his ideas. He knew all the country blues, being from that part of the South…He played very sophisticatedly when the Hawks did James Brown or Bobby Blue Bland tunes, and he could really drive songs like Little Junior Parker material." And as a vocalist, John observed, "Levon would sing his ass off."

MARY MARTIN, A young Toronto woman, who had worked as a receptionist at the New York office of music manager Albert Grossman, was back in town sprucing up her secretarial skills at the Shaw Business School—and hanging out at the Le Coq d'Or with her pal Toni Trow, listening to their favorite band, Levon and the Hawks. She remembers how the Hawks interacted when they played: "They had conversations with themselves that were so deeply musical that if you listened, you got to go along. They were the best band that we had ever, ever heard, and they took you to dreamland." She considered them to be "a really mature and loving and dedicated bunch of boys who loved the music they were doing. They executed with passion…At one point, we got to go with them one day to their hotel, and we…taught them about Bob Dylan…They taught us the real value of the Abbysinian Baptist Choir. And that seemed like really good sharing of music."

Another fan and sometime girlfriend of Helm's was Delores Robinson, who had been Miss Toronto in 1960. And then there was teenaged Cathy Smith from nearby Burlington, who had more than great music on her mind—she fell for Levon's Southern drawl and good looks. She first heard the Hawks at the Grange in Hamilton and began to follow the band from gig to gig, but being shy, she'd cower in a corner. Ever vigilant for beautiful girls, Levon spotted the striking young woman and as an ongoing joke played "Short Fat Fanny" whenever he saw her in the audience.

Eventually, one night at the Seahorse Motel on Toronto's Lakeshore strip, she had sex with Rick, although when she told him she wasn't on birth control, he kicked her out. Just then, however, Levon appeared. He had no such strictures, so she went off with him. "He was always hard to get to know," she says, "but I could feel close to him in bed."

DUFF ROMAN, A radio deejay at Toronto's CHUM Radio, formed Roman Records, and in autumn 1964, he got the Hawks into Hallmark Studios to lay down some tracks. They began with a cover of James Brown's "Please Please Please," then recorded three original tunes: "Robbie's Blues," "Biscuits and Taters," and "Bacon Fat," a song written by Robbie and Garth as an ode to the salad Mama Kosh made for Levon. These recordings would not be released until 2005 on the Band's *A Musical History*.

That fall, the Hawks continued their sweep around the club circuit, with a month-long gig at Toronto's Embassy Club and dates at Quebec City's La Baril d'Huitres, Montreal's Café de l'Est, London's Brass Rail, Hamilton's Grange, and Pop Ivey's Ballroom in Port Dover. David Clayton-Thomas, John Kay—soon to be with Steppenwolf—Domenic Troiano, and Robbie Lane—vocalist for the Disciples who later joined Ronnie Hawkins—were avid fans of the Hawks. After one of their tours, the band was back at the Friar's, and Troiano, Lane, and the Disciples were astonished at how tight the Hawks had become—they'd discovered their own sound. "I was still blown away by their musicianship," Lane recounts, "but they'd undergone an amazing transformation. They were playing for themselves, not even looking at the audience most of the time."

JOHN HAMMOND—WHO was about to start recording his third album—asked Levon, Robbie, and Garth to back him in the studio, along with aspiring harmonica player Charlie Musselwhite, Jimmy

Lewis on bass, and guitar player Michael Bloomfield, who switched to piano for this session.

So Many Roads was Hammond's second LP that combined his country blues with the electric kick of a backup band. Although the result is more notable for its youthful exuberance than precise musicianship—it was recorded in only one day at New York's Vanguard studios—it would spark important future innovations.

In "Who Do You Love," Helm borrows the rhythm from "Hey Bo Diddley," a familiar groove for Ronnie Hawkins and the Hawks. His drumming is very loose—some might say sloppy—in "I Want You to Love Me," then he redeems himself in "O Yea!" Levon plays a behind-the-beat shuffle—in stark contrast with the songs he played with Ronnie—on "Gambling Blues." *So Many Roads* is a down-and-dirty blues album that stands on its own merit but is most noteworthy for being one element that influenced Bob Dylan's future direction.

As 1964 was drawing to a close, Levon and the Hawks embarked on their first Southern tour since leaving Hawkins. It was a risky proposition. Dayton Stratton, who booked the circuit, took out a lengthy ad to convince Hawkins's fans to give this new incarnation a break. In part it read:

> This will be the first time the Hawks have toured this area without their former leader and no doubt many will be hesitant to attend some of the dances for which they will be playing because of the absence of Ronnie Hawkins. For those of you who do not let skepticism stand in the way, however, there is, I believe, a real treat in store. Once you have witnessed the Hawks in action I'm sure any doubt as to the capability of the Hawks presenting a successful performance on their own will be quickly erased from your minds.
>
> The quality of the Hawks' newly developed show material and the superb musical talent possessed by each member promises to make their debut tour a real swinger.
>
> The show and music presented by the Hawks is of the type most appealing to the student set and in view of this fact we ask your support. I realize, as do the Hawks, that your attendance will determine the outcome of this tour.

It was an experiment beginning on December 22 and tentatively lasting a week and a half. Based in Fayetteville at the Iris Motel on College Street, the Hawks were booked in Arkansas at the Rockwood Club, the 1170 Club in Hazen, the Silver Moon in Newport, and the TAC House in El Dorado. Dayton followed this with two prestigious gigs for them on New Year's Eve and January 1 at the Memorial Auditorium in Dallas—especially significant for Helm as it coincided with the Cotton Bowl game in Dallas in which his beloved Razorbacks defeated the Nebraska Cornhuskers. It was an example of Dayton promoting performances for the Hawks that would enhance their exposure with college students.

"They sounded great," Earl Cate says. "A lot of people didn't quite know what to think because they didn't have Ronnie." The switch from Hawkins-style rockabilly to R&B and blues was a hit with most, although "some people didn't dig it," his brother Earl remembers. "They thought they were a little bit too laid back…They was just playin' music, good music."

IT WAS FRIDAY, January 29, 1965, and the jealous boyfriend of a girl Rick was seeing in Simcoe, Ontario, got his revenge. He was a cop, and the girl let it slip that the Hawks were bringing a load of drugs back from a trip to New York City. The details of subsequent events were filled in afterward when, according to Bill Avis, "We became very, very good friends with some of those RCMP constables because we got them some pussy."

Levon and Robbie had gone to the States in Bill's car, while the rest of the Hawks left a white station wagon at the Toronto International Airport and flew down. Coming back, all the Hawks were in Bill's black Pontiac station wagon. "Now we're coming home," Avis says, "and we're all getting buzzed, having one [joint] before we crossed the border. But Robbie then takes the dope what's left and puts it inside his pocket." Unnoticed, eight unmarked police and RCMP vehicles trailed them to the airport, where the band intended to pick up the other car they'd left there. Levon was driving when suddenly they were surrounded by police with guns drawn, shouting, "Put your hands up! Get out of the car! You're all under arrest!" Helm had a pipe in his mouth—which they mistakenly assumed was hash—and was dragged out of the car. Bill was taken to the basement of the airport. "They literally took my station wagon [apart]," he recalls. "They stripped it because they're looking for all this marijuana, but they can't find anything…They've got my attaché case. They open that up and see all these Zig-Zag papers. 'Oh, that's for rolling dope…All of you are going to jail!'" Eventually they found the marijuana that Robertson was carrying; nevertheless, everyone was arrested as accessories and put in a holding cell in the adjacent town of Brampton.

Avis was able to get in touch with the Colonel. He called Jack Fisher, the owner of Friar's Tavern, who got them a lawyer, a retired judge and the father of the premier of Ontario. They were each released on two thousand dollars bail, with a court date scheduled for February 3.

Humiliation followed when the next Monday, the *Toronto Daily Star* and *The Globe and Mail* published the story, listing their names. Levon was relieved that it took a while before the news filtered down to his parents in Arkansas. But the cops were also embarrassed. "They got egg all over themselves," Avis continues. "They'd figured we had a bale of goddamn hash or whatever, but we didn't." He maintains that Robertson didn't even have enough weed for five joints. Rick decided to take the blame as it was his girlfriend who set the arrests in motion, so he claimed Robbie was wearing his jacket.

After the Hawks secured a number of court delays in Canada, their trial got underway in April. Danko pleaded guilty; the others not guilty. *The Globe and Mail* published a follow-up under the heading, "Drug Case: 6 to Face the Music But Later":

> "Well, that's showbiz," said Magistrate H.T.G. Andrews as he granted a 5-month remand to Levon and the Hawks. The trial heard only part of the evidence and were going to continue next week, but Levon Helm said they were about to start a 3-month US tour and had already turned down one engagement to be in court.
>
> "Have you been on Ed Sullivan's show yet?" the magistrate asked.
>
> "No," replied Helm, "but we're hoping we might some day."

The trial was held over until September. Cathy Smith—who Bill says, "was doing a few of us"—was still sweet on Levon, so when he asked her to "look after" one of the RCMP officers who was a primary witness, she agreed. The band was hoping that after her tryst with him at the West Point Motel on Toronto's Lakeshore Boulevard and her subsequent claim that she was only sixteen, he'd develop amnesia. "Ridiculous as it sounds," Smith writes, "it seemed logical at the time, and I didn't see how I was being used until later."

Shortly afterward, Smith discovered she was pregnant. In love with Levon and convinced the child was his, she confronted him with the news. He was far from pleased, believing anyone in the Hawks could be the father of what they dubbed the "band baby." Richard showed compassion and offered to marry her, but it was Helm she wanted.

Eventually the trial resumed. The Hawks' aged lawyer was bent over and crippled, often seen to be napping. When it was time for him to present their case, Bill recalls, "He goes to get out of the chair—and it's quiet in the courtroom—and he *farts*." Everyone except Rick was exonerated; he received a one-year suspended sentence.

WHILE THEIR DRUG trial was in abeyance, the Hawks were granted court permission to travel to the United States to pursue their careers. In the South, Dayton Stratton booked them at the University of Oklahoma in Norman, throughout Arkansas and into Texas, to Fort Worth and Dallas. Sometimes with not enough funds for food, one guy would divert a store clerk by buying something cheap, while the others filled their pockets with whatever sustenance they could grab. Other times, in cahoots with the checkout girls at the local Piggly Wiggly, they absconded with groceries. In one desperate attempt for cash, Levon and Robbie planned to hold up a big-stakes poker game, figuring the police wouldn't be called to an illegal gambling operation. Scared to death, they both had masks on, carrying a gun and a sack for the money when they discovered the game had been cancelled.

Helm and Bill Avis remained roommates on the road. When the Hawks played their Southern circuit, the band always stopped in Springdale, near Fayetteville, where Levon's family was now living. Avis has fond memories of staying at the Helm home with Levon, his parents, and his younger brother, Wheeler. Diamond would sing and tell stories of being a deputy sheriff in Marvell. Because they had only two bedrooms, Wheeler was moved to a pallet in the living room, and Levon and Bill shared Wheeler's room. On different occasions, the band rented a house on Maple Street in Fayetteville, stayed at the Iris Motel, and lived in a trailer in the parking lot of the Rockwood Club. The trailer didn't have a stove, however, so Richard tried to cook minute steaks with a clothes iron.

IT WAS MAY 1965, the first time Levon's childhood friend Anna Lee Williams had met the Canadian Hawks. The band dipped down to the Helena area to do some gigs, including one at Marvell's junior–senior prom. Always happy to see Levon, Anna Lee, with Mary and Sister Cavette, went to hear him play, then joined the band and Avis the next afternoon at Charlie Halbert's Rainbow Inn, where the group was staying a few extra days so Helm could catch up with old friends.

They decided to track down Sonny Boy Williamson, and Mr. Gist at the music store set them off in the right direction. The legendary harmonica player was impossible to miss—at well over six feet, resplendent in the two-tone suit and bowler that he'd brought back from his recent tour of England, carrying a valise full of harmonicas, he was an imposing figure, known to be deadly if crossed. Levon politely asked if they could jam with him. Anna Lee remembers it this way:

> That's when the police ran [Levon] and Sonny Boy Williamson off because we were all down at the hotel that Sunday afternoon when Sonny Boy and them were playing outside...We were all just sitting around, had some chairs, and [Sonny Boy] was sitting on a bucket playing harmonica, and Levon was playing...guitar, I think...We were all sitting out there, wasn't bothering anybody, and the cops come by. And because we had a black and it was an all-white motel, they made him leave. So Sonny Boy said, "Well, that's all right. I know a place over in Helena we can go to." So we went over to Walnut Street, to one of the black clubs over there...and the cops came over there and made him leave. And Levon was so upset about it because he never had a color picture

in his mind. If he liked you, he didn't care...white, black, yellow, pink, whatever. And he was so upset. He couldn't believe that it was still so backward down here, which he never did understand that. To him there was no color line anywhere. It was hard being from the South to know that so many Southerners were against blacks.

Sonny Boy amazed the whole gang. Cradled in his huge hands or poking out between his lips like a stogie, his harp had the rich sound of an orchestra, sometimes disappearing inside his mouth as he continued to play the down-home blues they all loved. "He was really beautiful," Robbie says. "He made some great records, but they were nowhere as good as the music he could play in just a little room. He really dug us, we really dug him." While knocking back a prodigious amount of bootleg whiskey and spitting into a can, Williamson told them stories that brought blues folklore alive. He was impressed with their chops, and the Hawks began to hope they could work with him in the future.

Still, the cops wouldn't leave them alone. Levon tried mollifying them by saying his uncle Alan Cooper was the deputy sheriff in Marvell, to no avail. Helm explained, "The plan was, when we shook hands goodbye with Sonny Boy, was that we would be back in touch and we'd try and get him fixed up so he'd come up to New Jersey and join us before the summer was out. We didn't know how the hell to pull that off, but we had some big plans." As they were leaving, Robertson looked inside Williamson's makeshift spittoon and saw that he'd been spitting blood. Before the month was out, the great bluesman was dead.

THE HAWKS HEADED up to New York, and with Henry Glover producing, they cut two of Robbie's songs—"Leave Me Alone" and "Uh-Uh-Uh"—at Bell Studios for Glover's new label, Ware Records, and for Apex in Canada. In "Leave Me Alone," Levon and Richard belt out pugilistic lyrics to Helm's quarter-note shuffle with a periodic Bo Diddley beat. "Uh-Uh-Uh" is reminiscent in spots of Eddie Cochran's 1958 "Summertime Blues." The disc identified them as the

Canadian Squires, surprising even the band itself. Calling them *Canadian* was a kiss of death for U.S. radio, and the record went nowhere.

BILL AVIS HAD previously booked a gig for his Female Beatles at one of the largest teenage nightclubs on the Eastern Seaboard—Tony Mart's—and was instrumental in facilitating a booking there for the Hawks. Conway Twitty, who also played there, vouched for the group, too. Situated in Somers Point, New Jersey, about a half-hour's drive southwest of Atlantic City, the club was owned by Anthony Marotta, a tough Sicilian American with a knack for tapping into the youth market. His son Carmen turned nine that summer, a season imprinted in his mind: "I lived in the club. When we were little kids, our life was enveloped in the club…It was a big playground for us as children."

Tony Mart's was acclaimed for its continuous music. When the Hawks played there—still dressed in suits—there were two large stages with up to three bands accompanied by go-go dancers. As one group ended its set, the next band on the other stage would take up the tune—a favorite break song was "Green Onions"—then continue into its own show. Officially, the club held 1,300, although in reality it was often crammed with 1,500 to 2,000 patrons.

Levon and the Hawks caused a sensation. "I think one thing that needs to be underscored is just how phenomenal they were," Carmen Marotta says. "They were rockabilly. We didn't have rockabilly. We had influences of rockabilly, but we were Jersey Shore. They would play things like 'Little Liza Jane,' you know, in a rockabilly style, and they were rockin' the house with it." He also observed the band—with Danko still on rhythm guitar—arranging covers of rock 'n' roll hits and James Brown songs. One memory is of Hudson poised atop the bar blowing his saxophone, playing "Shotgun" like Junior Walker. The way they blended their vocals impressed young Carmen, who would lean against the railing beside Manuel's keyboard until closing time. "Their four-part harmonies were hugely entertaining and phenomenal even then," Marotta recalls. "The vocals were a huge, huge part of it." Levon was the band leader offstage, but Robbie was the front man onstage. "There was always a ying and yang there," Carmen says.

"My father loved Levon, and Levon loved my father," he points out.

"You have to understand that these guys were so great. We had a lot of great bands, you know…A lot of great musicians played there, but nobody was ever better than Levon and the Hawks." The band continued to thrill crowds that summer at Tony Mart's. A poster advertising them as headliners announced, "Over 110,000 fans have acclaimed them the greatest."

The Hawks continued their push for another record deal following the disappointing release of their Ware/Apex single and returned to Toronto to cut some demos. New York producer Aaron Schroeder—who had been a prolific songwriter for the likes of Rosemary Clooney, Nat King Cole, Sammy Davis Jr., Pat Boone, and Elvis Presley—discussed signing Helm and Robertson as songwriters, and the Hawks as a band. Schroeder was the music publisher for multi-instrumentalist and songwriter Al Kooper. "They came up to the office," Kooper says, "and I met them there—and we all remember that. Robbie was already a songwriter but so was Levon." When Henry Glover reviewed Schroeder's contract, however, he considered it not much better than a con, with virtually all of the Hawks' earnings going to Schroeder. Somewhat deflated, they turned it down.

Back at Tony Mart's for the remainder of the summer, the band and Bill Avis needed more space than was afforded by the four-bedroom apartment above the club. "You can imagine the amount of women that were moving through," Carmen remarks. "What they did was they rented the little house next to my house, which was… right down the street…in addition to the apartment over top of the Mart…I think Levon stayed in the apartment above the club, and I think some of the other guys…were at the other house. That was kind of a party house, too. There were a lot of female invitees staying overnight at that establishment…My sister used to watch for them because of her crush on Robbie." It was what Carmen calls "open sexuality…It was the Jersey Shore in the summertime—don't ask, don't tell."

The band liked to hang out across from the club at a restaurant owned by a well-known football coach. Marotta declares, "One of [Levon's] famous lines was, 'We were having a good time down there, Carmen. The roast beef sandwiches were good in Coach's Corner, and the coach's daughters, they were pretty good too!'"

Six months pregnant, Cathy Smith followed the group to Somers Point, still pining for Levon, but she found him uninterested, especially after he eyed the attractive, affluent Bonita Diamond. Helm adamantly refused to take responsibility for Smith's pregnancy. Bill Avis says that no one in the band believed Cathy. Increasingly desperate in the face of Levon's indifference, she told Rick that if the band didn't force Levon to take care of her, she'd get them busted again for weed. Her threats were ignored.

When her blonde-haired daughter was born six weeks premature, Smith named her Tracy Lee—Lee for Levon. She phoned him with the news; still, Helm didn't care. According to Cathy, Levon's parents offered to bring up the child. Initially, she decided to raise the baby herself, but later gave her up for adoption. The following year, as a waitress at Toronto's Riverboat, she began an affair with Gordon Lightfoot while still smarting from Levon's rejection.

During the day, the musicians sometimes played softball. Conway Twitty appeared at the Mart a few times that summer, and he was great at the game. Levon took time, however, to review his musical chops. He had practice pads, Carmen says, "and Levon would go lock himself into an air conditioning room up on the roof and practice. And when we were running around as kids, he was always very generous and benevolent with his time…He would hang out with us kids and show us the drum pads and let us play with the sticks."

At night, Carmen recalls the Hawks playing tirelessly:

> There certainly were a number of illicit substances involved. They became entranced on that stage, and one night at ten minutes after two—there was a strict no-live-music curfew at two o'clock—the cops were at the door, screaming and yelling and saying, "We're going to have to start arresting people if the music doesn't stop." We couldn't get them to stop! We couldn't get their attention on the stage. They were so into it…Finally, Dad got a bouncer…to go up and shake Levon—grab him by the arms and shake him and say, "You gotta stop, you gotta stop!"…That's how intense it was.

That summer, Helm got the Colonel to book the Cate Brothers for a two-week gig at Tony Mart's—their first time on the road. Earl Cate remembers how tight the Hawks were, how great they sounded. In addition to playing two new songs Robertson had written—"He Don't Love You (and He'll Break Your Heart)" and "The Stones I Throw"—Earl says, "They did 'Shotgun,' you know. Junior Walker. 'It's Not Unusual' by Tom Jones, [laughs] believe it or not. And 'A Summer Place.' Garth played it on the keyboard. [laughs] I mean, songs you would never think about them playin'. 'Walkin' the Dog.' Well, and then, of course, Richard did the Ray Charles stuff."

MEANWHILE, BOB DYLAN had gone electric. In early 1964, he proclaimed in song that times were changing, and by that summer in *Another Side of Bob Dylan*, he was rebelling against being typecast as a protest folkie. Although that album was not electric, Dylan was clearly exploring new directions. Influenced by *So Many Roads*—the electric blues album the Hawks had recorded with John Hammond—and having heard the Byrds on an electric version of his composition "Mr. Tambourine Man" at their January 1965 recording session, Dylan began to experiment in that vein the same month when he recorded *Bringing It All Back Home*—one side acoustic, the other, rocking electric. He further explored rock-tinged possibilities when he recorded with John Mayall's Bluesbreakers—including their young guitarist Eric Clapton—that May in England. The transformation was well underway by July when he released the rock anthem "Like a Rolling Stone," then enraged folk purists with an electric set at the Newport Folk Festival.

Mary Martin was back in New York in the office of Albert Grossman, Bob Dylan's manager, after a stint at Toronto's Shaw Business School to improve her secretarial skills. The Hawks sent her a demo tape, which she played for Grossman associate John Court. His response: "Miss Martin, we aren't interested in talent of that caliber."

She had witnessed Bob's electric conversion at Newport, and immediately thought that Levon and the Hawks could provide the perfect backing for his new sound. She never tired of touting the band to Bob—who describes her as "a rather persevering soul"—whenever he was in the office. She also sent Rick Danko an advance copy of Dylan's newest album, *Highway 61 Revisited*, in which he used a backing band of rock musicians on all except one track. Rick loved a couple of the songs, although it made no impact on the rest of the group. "When I turned the band onto Bob Dylan," Danko recalled, "we were going through a jazz period. Art Blakey and the Jazz Messengers, Mose Allison, stuff like that."

There had been rumors at the Mart that a character looking suspiciously like Dylan had been seen hanging around, scoping out Levon and the Hawks, but Carmen Marotta doesn't give it much credence. Another report claimed that Albert Grossman sent a scout, Dan Weiner, to check on the band. On the other hand, Carmen says, "We know for a fact that it was John Hammond Jr.—the great bluesman—who was dispatched by the Grossman organization to verify that this was in fact the band that was the Hawks."

The phone call came in mid-August on a Monday or Tuesday, as Carmen was told, then someone went upstairs to get Levon. Near the rear entrance of Tony Mart's—by the snack bar and near the stairs to the band apartment—there was an old wooden phone booth, and the call was transferred there. Bob Dylan was on the line. His offer was for Helm and Robertson to back him—with bassist Harvey Brooks and Al Kooper on organ—at a concert at Forest Hills, New York, and at the Hollywood Bowl. Levon said he'd speak to the rest of the Hawks and get back to Bob the following day.

While he was aware of the song "Like a Rolling Stone," Levon didn't immediately connect it with the person on the phone. He asked Harold Kudlets if Dylan could even fill the Hollywood Bowl since they would be the only band. The Colonel assured Helm that he could. Levon also wanted Tony Marotta's opinion. According to Carmen,

> After Levon talked to Dylan, he went to my father and said, "Tony, this is the situation"…and the first thing my father said, in his gruff English-Sicilian accent is, "Okay, I'll make a few calls." In other words, he was going to call his top guys in New York, 'cause he dealt with MCA and other agencies, and find out for Levon if [the offer] was real. They were making thirteen hundred dollars a week for six nights, four sets a night, and Dylan offered them

five thousand…It was a major situation for them, and Dad did verify that it was quite legitimate and that the Grossman organization and Dylan were very real, and that they could rely on these representations. So Dad agreed to let them go, very magnanimously. They didn't really have a written contract anyway, but Dad loved them.

"We were scheduled to finish out at Tony Mart's [on] Labor Day weekend," Bill Avis says. "I had to let Tony know that we're leaving a week beforehand, and they had a big party for us—all the locals that we befriended in Somers Point, New Jersey, and then Tony and all his staff. They were sorry to see us go, but they knew we were going onwards and upwards."

For Levon, that trajectory would be not be smooth.

6

Dylan Plugs In and Helm Checks Out

As their stand at the Mart on the Jersey Shore wound down, Levon and Robbie drove into Manhattan for two weeks of rehearsals with Bob Dylan at the Carroll Music rehearsal studio. There at 625 West 55th Street, they met bassist Harvey Brooks and keyboard player Al Kooper, the remaining musicians from Dylan's studio band, and the inimitable music manager Albert Grossman.

The canny thirty-nine-year-old Grossman was a marketer par excellence, with a degree in economics and a background in operating clubs before starting his management career with Odetta. Although, as one client Nick Gravenites puts it, "He didn't know music from dog shit," and Pete Seeger commented, "I pitied the people who had to work with him," Albert had the ability to wrangle great commercial success for his artists, including Bob Dylan.

Although they'd listened to Dylan's current chart-climber, *Highway 61 Revisited*, Helm and Robertson were not overly familiar with his music. As Mary Martin notes, "The root of the [Hawks] was Levon, and the root of Levon was R&B. Folk music was diametrically opposite." When they started to rehearse, the two Hawks thought the band sounded terrible, although Dylan was pleased. It reminded Levon of country music, although the songs were rather long.

"Where Bobby Gregg was a solid drummer right in the pocket," Harvey Brooks says about Dylan's drummer on *Bringing It All Back Home* and *Highway 61 Revisited*, "Levon was always on the edge. It's always 'Oh, oh, are we gonna make it? Yeah!' You always made it. But there was always a natural tension with everything Levon did. It's a style that helped to create the sound of the Band later on. Dylan really related to it." Al Kooper observed that Levon "breathes in his playing… [and] kept us together like an enormous iron metronome."

Gradually, the musicians coalesced into a cohesive group, and Levon and Harvey hung out together in Greenwich Village after rehearsals, according to Brooks "just talking about what was going on in our lives at that time—the women, the complications, the opportunities, getting high and Dylan's music, which neither of us knew much about except that we both liked it."

The evening of August 28, 1965, was uncharacteristically cool for New York City—but the reception for Dylan and his band in Forest Hills, Queens, was even chillier. Fifteen thousand skeptical fans crowded into the tennis stadium, the largest audience Levon and Robbie had ever played for. After the hostility shown to Bob at Newport, the musicians knew this audience might be difficult.

Dylan performed an acoustic set alone, then gathered his band in preparation for their appearance. "I don't know what it will be like out there," Bob told them. "It's going to be some kind of carnival and I want you to all know that up front. So go out there and keep playing no matter how weird it gets!"

The booing started as Helm and Bill Avis came onstage to set up the drum kit for the electric portion of the concert. *The Village Voice* described it as a confrontation between the mods—folk purists—and the rockers as contemporary music came of age.

While the wind picked up and the temperature dipped, there were raucous jeers from the traditionalists as fruit was aimed at the musicians; Kooper was knocked off his stool. Rockers cheered as they stormed the stage. A fight erupted between opposing camps. Amid shouted insults—"traitor," "scum bag," "Where's Ringo?"—and calls for the old Dylan, the band played on, Bob reveling in his contrariness. For Grossman, all the attention—good and bad—was valuable publicity. Levon's response was to "drop 'em a finger off the side for a little self-satisfaction."

Helm, Robertson, and Harvey Brooks headed off to Los Angeles in Grossman's World War II–era Lockheed Lodestar, a small, short-haul plane that took twelve hours to reach the West Coast. On

September 3, Dylan and his band braved another packed house at the Hollywood Bowl. "I was standing next to Bob," Brooks recounts, "about to play for a mix of movie stars, folkies and hippies…I could make out the faces of the first two or three rows, spotting the likes of Gregory Peck, Mel Brooks, Peter Fonda, and Johnny Cash watching from below." As Harvey remembers it, the show was a major success. To him, this crowd was laid back, more progressive—they accepted Dylan's new direction and had none of the rigid constraints of his East Coast fans. Helm saw it the same way. Robertson, however, recollects a cacophony of boos and jeers that had almost become a sport.

BACK IN NEW York that September, the Hawks—with Danko now on bass—recorded "The Stones I Throw," "He Don't Love You," and their accelerated adaptation of "Little Liza Jane," called "Go Go Liza Jane," a crowd favorite at Tony Mart's that showcased Levon's breakneck swinging quarter-note groove. Atlantic Record's Atco label released the first two songs as a 45 (with their name, Levon and the Hawks, restored). "The Stones I Throw" on side A suggests the Hawks' gospel influence, and "He Don't Love You" includes a rare six-bar drum break in Helm's eighth-note groove. Frustratingly, the record went nowhere.

AS DYLAN WAS getting ready to embark on a North American tour—one of the biggest rock extravaganzas of 1965 and arguably the most controversial—he asked Levon and Robbie if they would stay on in his backup band. Kirby Penick maintains it was Robertson who wanted to continue, and that Helm just acquiesced. At any rate, Dylan was told he'd have to take all the Hawks or none. Bill Avis believes that due to Levon's loyalty to the Hawks, it was Helm, not Robertson, who issued the ultimatum. Mary Martin says, "I think that the wonderful and the splendid heart of the band, if you will, was Levon, and I think he really sort of said, 'If it's just myself as drummer and Robbie…we're out. We don't want that. It's either us, the band, or nothing.' And you know what? Good for him."

As of yet, Dylan had not heard the Hawks for himself. Levon and the band returned to Toronto for a two-week stand at the Friar's Tavern while their drug trial resumed. It was good to see old friends. David Clayton-Thomas sat in with the Hawks, and the Cate Brothers were playing near Niagara Falls, so they drove into Toronto to visit Levon. Earl Cate remarked that the band was dressed quite casually, no longer in matching suits and ties.

The audition that led to an upheaval in popular music took place in the wee hours of Thursday, September 16. Dylan had arrived in Toronto the previous afternoon on a private plane, then just after midnight headed to the Friar's Tavern to hear for himself what John Hammond and Mary Martin had been raving about. He agreed. That night after the club closed, they began rehearsals. As the Hawks worked on learning Bob's songs, they thought they sounded rough, but Dylan liked what he heard. "I know my thing now…" he told the *Toronto Star*. "It's hard to describe. I don't know what to call it because I've never heard it before." He was so convinced that the Hawks provided the right vehicle for his new direction, that he signed a deposition for their drug trial, stating they were an essential part of his artistic livelihood.

Just a week after first rehearsing with Dylan, the Hawks with Bill Avis flew to Texas in the Lodestar for a couple of warm-up shows with Bob at Austin's Municipal Auditorium, then at Southern Methodist University in Dallas. Much to Levon's relief, the South didn't let them down, and they appreciated Dylan's fusion of folk lyricism with hard-driving rock, delivered at maximum volume.

As a rule throughout the tour, Dylan didn't introduce his band, and they mostly kept out of the spotlight, but on October 1, in Bob's Manhattan debut as a rocker, the program at the venerable Carnegie Hall read, "Levon & the Hawks," with each band member named. The electric portion of the show was generally well received, although a few folk stalwarts left before the Hawks' set. Helm remembered that "a couple of hundred people rushed the stage at the end, shouting for more. I could see Bob standing at the microphone. He was exhausted, spaced out, but really beaming."

On October 5, the Hawks accompanied Dylan as he began recording his next album, *Blonde on Blonde*. Although they worked on four songs, none from this session made it to the final LP. Onstage or off, it wasn't easy for Dylan to adapt to a band situation. "It was a hell of a challenge," Levon admitted, "because he was still learning about a band. He would suddenly stop and break the beat, and we'd get confused and not know where we were. We'd look at one another and try to figure out if we were playing great music or total bullshit."

Nevertheless, Helm appreciated Dylan's relaxed attitude toward playing after the strict regimentation of Ronnie Hawkins. Never one who wanted to spend much time on rehearsals himself, Levon exclaimed, "Nice and loose. Let's not overprepare…I'm with you, Bobby! You could just about throw away the game plan for a show, which makes a lot of people nervous, but it tickles me…You've got to stay on your toes. I like it. It's skating in the fast lane all right."

In many venues, folk purists were incensed at Dylan's new direction, and a large portion of that fury was directed against Dylan's plugged-in backing band—Levon and the Hawks. Yet in some places where Dylan's folk music wasn't seen as sacrosanct and audiences were more flexible—such as in the South—Helm happily noted that "people would dance, clap their hands, and have a good [time]. They'd talk to you, invite you to have a drink with them. You know, that's why we were playing music—to get to meet people and enjoy their fellowship."

Wherever they were, the band took advantage of their newfound circumstances and indulged in excesses of drugs, drink, and women. Traveling in the Lodestar sure beat all-night drives in a couple of station wagons, but Levon didn't like to fly, especially after a few frightening incidents in the air in what the Hawks called the "Volkswagen of the Sky."

Playing with Bob was an invaluable experience—life-altering, as it turned out. Levon commented that "it was certainly one of the highlights of my musical career to play with Bob, tour with him, and go through some of the times we had a chance to go through together. He's a great musician and a lot of fun to make music with…Most of the times we played together, it just really suited my style because I like walking on the edge."

However, the booing continued, mostly in cities with an entrenched folk scene. For someone to whom music should be fun, Helm called it "a dose of medicine. A lot of places on that tour, there would be more booing after a song than applause…They were on us hot and heavy, boy. Them beatniks was tough!" He said, "It started wearing on me, and I got to the point where I couldn't find enough funny things to laugh about it. I didn't feel like joking around all the time like I usually do." There just weren't enough perks to make up for the downside. "It wasn't that much fun, ridin' around havin' people starin' at ya, booin' your ass off, nobody wantin' to be with ya, nothin' funny happening," he lamented. "It wasn't like people were comin' up and puttin' money in my pockets and makin' me rich, or like I had girls all over me. It was a drag, a pain in the ass."

As soon as Helm's red-sparkle Gretsch drum kit was brought out, Dylan's folkies would boo. "A lot of those folk places in those days, the drummer was the worst offender of all," he said, "next to the electric guitar player. But even guitarists could go get an acoustic, you could save them; but drummers, put a rope around them! When they were booing, that's what they were booing, that rock 'n' roll beat. They'd shout, 'Twist and shout!' 'Shake it up, baby!' stuff like that." More than once, Levon's kit bore the stains of splattered fruit.

Dylan refused to be cowed. Garth noted that "after the first two or three concerts where they booed, they didn't seem to be throwing anything dangerous and they didn't threaten us out in the hall, or in the alley, so we kept doing it." Still, doubts crept in. The Hawks listened to tapes of their shows, wondering if maybe their playing was to blame. It wasn't. The hallowed ground of traditional folk music was quaking, and some of Dylan's fans were clutching onto the past.

The Dylan tour traveled throughout the eastern states, then swung north on November 14 and 15 to play at Toronto's Massey Hall. It was good to see a lot of the band's old friends and their families again. Levon got in touch with Freddie McNulty and brought him backstage. But instead of the band returning as rock stars, they received a mixed and, at times, cruel reception in the town they considered a home. Although a lot of fans loved the loud rock, some left, while others threw pennies at the stage during the electric set. In an interview with the *Toronto Star*, Bob didn't give an inch. "If they like it or don't like it, that's their business. You can't tell people what to do at a concert." Nevertheless, when *The Star*'s Antony Ferry decried Dylan's rock direction, calling his backing musicians "a third-rate Yonge Street rock 'n' roll band," Levon was deeply hurt. "That was hateful as hell," he confessed, "and we tried to laugh while our insides wept at that stinging slur."

The whole thing was making less and less sense to Helm. "The audiences kept booing…" he said. "The more Bob heard this stuff, the more he wanted to drill these songs into the audiences…We didn't mean to play that loud, but Bob told the sound people to turn it up full force…I began to think it was a ridiculous way to make a living: flying to concerts in Bob's thirteen-seat Lodestar, jumping in and out of limousines, and then getting booed." For Levon, those gigs were "another shitty day in paradise," and "it cut me all the way to the bone…I couldn't take it. I really couldn't."

As Robertson grew closer to Dylan, and Helm remained uninvolved in the new cultural experiences Bob was offering, the interests of Robbie and Levon began to diverge. In addition, Helm was not a big fan of Albert Grossman.

Levon knew that many of Dylan's fans were advising him to dump the Hawks: "It would have been real easy for him to say, 'Hell, yeah, you're right. I'm gonna get rid of the band.' Everybody was telling him, 'You don't need these guys. Listen to the crowd. They don't want them either'…Bob stuck with us all the way through."

As Bill Avis saw it, the harsh reception was hard on everybody, but it especially affected Levon. Dylan's music had little to do with Helm's love of R&B and blues. "Levon couldn't really buy into Dylan's thing," says Jonathan Taplin, who was working for Grossman. "Even though he could see that it would be good money and big crowds, it wasn't his kind of music." Anna Lee agrees: "People weren't getting up to dance, and that was his thing. He thought that if people didn't get up to dance, he wasn't making good music." Besides, the Hawks had left Ronnie to make it on their own. Levon wasn't content to be a sideman in another backing band.

After their gig at Washington, D.C.'s Coliseum on November 28, 1965—just before the tour was leaving for the West Coast—the band flew back to their home base at New York's Irving Hotel. Helm decided he'd had enough. Unless he was giving pleasure to the audience, there was no reason to continue. Back at the hotel while the rest of the Hawks were sleeping, he told Robbie he was quitting. "I figured I'd go home, play some dances, and wait for the times to catch up," he explained. He packed his bag and headed out to catch the next bus to Arkansas, asking Robbie to give the musicians his best wishes for the rest of the tour. Robbie was heartbroken.

LEVON FOUND REFUGE on a beach in Mexico. Eventually, he needed more money, so he hooked up with Kirby Penick, his pal from Fayetteville, and as Kirby remembers it, they first went to Los Angeles, where they rented an apartment at the Villa Carlotta, on Franklin Avenue in Hollywood. It was a residence geared to musicians. Living in the same building was saxophone player Bobby Keys, a Texan who would gain future fame as an unofficial member of the Rolling Stones. "Levon was just one of those kind of guys, so friendly and so open as a person," Keys said. "We kind of just struck up a friendship. The way we really got to know each other was arguing about Texas–Arkansas football games."

Helm had a good collection of blues recordings, and he turned Keys on to such harmonica players as Little Walter Jacobs and Sonny Boy Williamson, which had a lasting impact on Keys's playing. "Actually, I learned a lot from Levon," Bobby remarked. "He's the one who suggested that, instead of playing like a saxophone player in a big band, maybe I should play like a harmonica player. And I took him at his word. A good piece of advice he gave me there. Thank you, Levon."

A contingent of Oklahoma musicians was in L.A. at the time, congregating at Leon Russell's home studio in the Hollywood Hills. Helm hung out there with players such as J.J. Cale, John Ware, Jesse Ed Davis, Jimmy Markham, Bill Boatman, Gordon Shryock, Carl Radle, Roger Tillison, and Jimmy Karstein, several he'd already met when the Hawks gigged in their home state. "That was just musicians central," Jimmy Karstein says. "I mean, the front door was never locked. They came and went twenty-four seven, you know. I'd run into [Levon] up there."

Helm recalled, "Leon and Johnnie Cale kind of big-brothered the rest of us, and kept us from getting into any more trouble than we did."

John Ware says, "So Levon and Eddie [Davis] decided they wanted to do a band. And Eddie called me up and said, 'Do you want to be in a band with Levon?' My answer is, 'Are you kidding me?'" The hitch was that drummer Ware had to play bass. A harmonica player let them rehearse in a house in Santa Monica, which he shared with a teenaged singer who cooked them dinner. Soon after, that girl—Linda Ronstadt—became a sensation with the Stone Poneys.

"So we tried it," Ware says. "We rehearsed, and we had a great time eating and drinkin' beer and playin' old blues songs…We did go one night finally down to a bar in Santa Monica to audition…and played four or five blues songs…The bartender's yelling over at us, 'Hey, y'all know "Monday, Monday"? [Ware laughs] And Levon said, 'No, we don't.'" They didn't make the cut, and Ware reluctantly concluded he wasn't meant to be a bass player.

Helm and Jimmy Markham—a singer and harmonica player—would browse in L.A. record stores for blues and R&B discs, and they went together to the Ash Grove folk-music club to see Albert King and Howlin' Wolf. Levon introduced Markham to Oklahoma guitar player Jesse Ed Davis, whom he'd first met working for Conway Twitty, and together with Bobby Keys, Gary Gilmore—and for a while, J.J. Cale—they formed a band.

Looking back, Bobby Keys observed,

> I've had the good fortune to play with some really good drummers: Jim Gordon, Jim Keltner, Charlie Watts, Levon. The thing is, with Levon, when we first started playing together we played these little joints in California, in Los Angeles. We were just playing blues stuff, just shuffles, but Levon I've noticed—and this is true for southern drummers, man—they're always laid back. I love that feel! It's never on top of the beat, always sucking it down just a little bit.

They played at Snoopy's Opera House in North Hollywood, some places in the San Fernando Valley, a few flower-power events, and at Peacock Alley, a 1940s-style lounge across Wilshire Boulevard from the infamous Ambassador Hotel. They headlined that club's blues and fried-chicken night every Sunday. They'd leave with about ten dollars each. The proprietor, whom Helm nicknamed Old Spice, billed himself as George DeCarlo and his Whispering Trumpet. He'd sometimes sit in with the group, along with Leon Russell. And when the Dylan tour hit Los Angeles in March 1966, Danko sat in and tried to convince Levon to come back to the Hawks.

Another time the band got a gig in the black section of town, in Watts, where devastating race riots had erupted the previous summer. They should have known better. Some patrons were angry that the band wouldn't share their pot, so after the gig when the group was packing up in the dark alley beside the club, they were attacked and barely escaped with their lives. "Levon was furious about getting run out," Jimmy Markham said, "and the whole way home, he just kept yelling he was going back with a pistol and 'straighten things out.'" Markham was surprised because he described Helm as "such a level-headed guy." The only other time he'd seen Levon lose his temper was when Jimmy cut his hair and accidentally sliced a piece of his scalp.

"It was a very formative time," Bobby Keys said of his stint with Levon. "There was a lot of music goin' on, a lotta pot, a lotta LSD. And lots of women…We used to take LSD every damn day together." Bobby invited Bill Boatman—a multi-instrumentalist who became best known for his guitar work with Taj Mahal and J.J. Cale—over to Villa Carlotta to partake of this new experience:

> I went over to [Keys's] apartment and took this LSD, and then we had something to eat [Boatman says]…Then I got real sick, and I stepped out into the hall, and I was getting into this LSD trip, and I was getting real nervous and shook up, you know, so Bobby Keys, he came out, and he says, "Okay, let's go up and see Levon"…So we went over there and Levon, he could see the distress I was in. So just me and Levon and Bobby Keys sat down, and Levon got his acoustic guitar out and started real softly singing some blues songs that he knew for quite a while, and that really calmed me down.

"[Helm] had the smallest Harley-Davidson motorcycle ever manufactured—not quite what you'd see clowns ride around on at the circus but suspiciously similar," Keys said, "and we used to get on that thing just *blazin'* and go down Sunset Boulevard." Or when he needed a car, Levon drove his girlfriend Bonnie's Corvette.

One time, Helm and Roger Tillison—singer, songwriter, guitarist, and trumpet player—took their dates to see El Cordobés, the theatrical Spanish matador who was performing in Tijuana. After the bull was dispatched, "Someone came up with the idea of trying to find the legendary and much-rumored cabaret show featuring 'the Woman and the Donkey,'" Tillison related. "[Bonnie] really put her foot down on the idea and started saying that we sure as hell weren't going to be using her car for anything weird like that. I think that's about the time that Levon suggested that she take the Greyhound bus back to Hollywood, and we would take her car and meet her back at the Villa Carlotta as soon as the show was over." But Bonnie won out, and they all headed home to L.A. with Helm playing harmonica and singing blues tunes along the way.

LEVON ALSO SPENT time in Fayetteville during his hiatus, joining the Cate Brothers Band for their gigs around Arkansas. "He had that special thing…charisma," Earl Cate recalls. Helm never met a stranger. When he walked into a room, he filled it with positive energy and his sense of fun. Ernie Cate says, "You'd introduce him to a person, and it's automatically like he'd known them for years."

"I think he was a little bit burned out with the band [on the Dylan tour]—the whole scene—even though he loved the guys," Earl points out. Dylan had Paul Berry's phone number in Fayetteville, and Paul recollects Bob calling to discuss the possibility of Helm's return to the tour. "I was certainly lonesome for the band," Levon conceded. "I guess I believed that at some point we would get back together. I didn't figure that they would give up their dreams just to be Bob's backup band." In Berry's opinion, Helm's refusal to go back wasn't primarily about booing; he was tougher than that. There had been some criticism of Garth, which greatly annoyed Levon, and in addition, as he told Paul, "We're going somewhere as the Hawks. Why do we want to get back with somebody fronting the show?" Even though Helm was foregoing a big payday, Berry says, "Levon could be happy with money or happy without a dime."

When Helm left town, he recommended a new drummer to the Cate Brothers, his fifteen-year-old nephew. And Terry Cagle—looking, playing, and sounding exactly like his uncle—took up the drum stool.

Levon and Kirby Penick drifted over to Memphis, where Mary Cavette and Anna Lee Williams were sharing an apartment. Mary cajoled Helm into cutting his hair, so she says, he got "the worst haircut you have ever seen in your life." Persuading him to get a nine-to-five job was hopeless. Helm mostly slept through the day and watched a lot of TV, hoping to get his career back on track, though doing little to make it happen.

In fact, Levon and Kirby had hoped to get jobs at Stax Records—Helm loved the music the label was producing—but that wasn't forthcoming. They spent most of their time going to black clubs and soaking up and learning from the great Memphis soul of such local artists as Booker T. and the MGs.

Then they decided to try Florida. Neither of them knew anyone there; however, as Kirby says, "He and I both are very outgoing, able to make friends anywhere you go and talk to anyone…We'd just go meet people and have adventures and have fun…When we were young and strong, it was just an adventure, and it was something I'll treasure forever."

> We got off a bus in Orlando [Penick says]…One of my favorite memories is we played a gay, black, after-hours joint…Now[adays] you've seen people like RuPaul and others like that, but that was an *eye-opener* for us. I was trying to play the bass a little bit; he was playing, you know, drums—but we just had yucks over that. I mean that was more for fun. And then we did some other stuff, had a little day labor…
>
> While we were down there, some groups came through, like I remember Bobby [Goldsboro]…Lee knew him, and we went and hung out with them…Another guy…wanted Levon to come work for him that…had a bunch of good hit records too. Lee didn't like his music too well, though, so he wasn't up for it.

After that, they headed down to Miami and stayed at the Miami Beach YMCA, but they couldn't find a music scene they liked, so they didn't stop long. They answered an ad in the newspaper offering pay to drive a new Lincoln to New Orleans. The Big Easy was a ball. They got a room at the St. Louis Hotel in the French Quarter and stayed out all night listening to great music. "I had heard the New Orleans music [before], of course," Levon said, looking back in 1998. "Huey Piano Smith and the Clowns, those records were real big all through the Delta, and all the New Orleans music was on the radio and available, and was my cup of tea right from the very front. Earl Palmer has got to be the greatest rock and roll drummer that's still around, as far as I'm concerned."

In the French Quarter, the duo played in a couple of amateur-night contests for the prize money, and they earned a few dollars as street musicians, for a time backing a little tap dancer—Levon on guitar and Kirby blowing harmonica. "Then we ran into a couple of girls from New York and fell in love…" Kirby says. "They wanted to stay with us, so we had that little romance going."

> We lived in this St. Louis Hotel [Kirby continues], which was full of strippers, hookers and some of the strangest people you have ever met, and Levon took to it. You know, he fit right in there. He loves eccentric, odd people, and…the strippers were great, the hookers were great. I mean, if you're not a john, they were really fun.
>
> Anyway, I think the best one we found down there was a guy that lived in this hotel…We called him Commander Jack…Levon did it—he encouraged him and encouraged him until this guy finally just [went] over the edge. He now becomes a double-naught spy. He's wearing a trenchcoat, and now he says he's working for Israeli intelligence, and he's there to buy a ship to take it back to Israel…We'd be walking down the street. Here comes Jack. He'd look and he says, "Pretend like you don't know me," as he went by…It was amazing. He would call us down to his room. He had maps…and he was plotting all of this shit, and we were

going to be on the crew…then he wanted the girls to come and be on the crew too. It was all just fantasy, of course.

So that was about as fine a time as I've had. That was so crazy. And these girls were working in the Court of Two Sisters, one of them in the back bar. We'd go over there in happy hour, and they'd feed you red beans and rice as a complimentary dish. We'd go in there about five o'clock in the afternoon, nobody there. Hell, we could eat a bucketful of that and drink beer on the house.

Kirby had been working in the oil industry in a pipeline-casing crew, while Helm tried his hand in the restaurant business, at the Court of Two Sisters. It lasted only about a day and a half—he was fired for eating the entrées.

As money was running low, he and Penick were hired as deckhands on a pipeline barge that was laying pipe to connect the wells with big storage tanks that were built on pilings out in the Gulf. "It's tough," Penick declares, "and…it's like most of the oilfield stuff. You don't go in there and work nine to five; you do the job until it's done…Those were characters too. We loved that because they were, if anything, even weirder and wilder than the people who were living in the St. Louis Hotel 'cause most of them were wanted somewhere. They would get offshore where nobody could mess with them."

In their downtime, the workers played cards, Levon and Kirby entertained their crewmates—with Helm blowing harmonica and Penick on guitar—or they listened to the radio, where Dylan's current hit, "Rainy Day Women #12 & 35," had Levon wondering how the Hawks were doing without him.

The aspect of the work Levon and Kirby enjoyed most was bringing the barge back to New Orleans for shelter when storms were coming.

Couldn't get out on the Gulf, [Kirby says,] so we rode this barge they sent back up to New Orleans through the intercoastal…and it's a long way from there to New Orleans. You get to go and see all of the wildlife, you know, alligators and all of that stuff and then come back, and that takes several days…We made a lot of money because you're out there two weeks on and two weeks off. You go back to town, party and all of that, and then come back.

But eventually they'd had enough. Anna Lee chuckles as she reminisces:

Mary and me had an apartment in Memphis, and one Friday night, I think, or Friday afternoon—we'd come in from work—and there was a knock at the door, and it was Levon and Kirby. And they'd been working offshore in Louisiana on the oil rigs. And he said, "Well, you know, we decided we'd come and spend the weekend with y'all before we go on to Springdale."

So we had a great time. We laughed, joked and talked for the whole weekend, fed them and cooked. They would stay up at night, and because we only had a one-bedroom apartment they would stay in the living room on the couch and the chair, and they'd be playing the guitar and harmonica and Jew's harp—just making music. Come Sunday they didn't leave; Monday we got up and went to work. We'd come in; they were still there. "Well, we're going to stick around for a few more days," and they'd go down Beale Street or people would call from Beale Street: "Come on down and jam with us," and everything. And it was like over and over and over, every night.

When we'd get up and go to work in the morning, they'd jump in our bed. They'd sleep all day—they're ready to go when we'd come in...So we kept saying, "You know, if you're going to stay here, you need to get a job. You need to do something." And we'd come in in the afternoon...Levon would say, "You know, girls, didn't nobody knock on the door and offer us a job today."

Finally, after about three months, I had to move. I had to have some sleep. So I moved, and they stayed another two or three months with Mary. That's the way it was. We never knew when he showed up if he was going to be here for a day or if he was going to be here for a month. It was just his way. I mean, we loved him, and we loved him being there, and he kept us laughing, but we're trying to work, and they're trying to party.

THE CALL CAME in October 1967. Rick Danko told Levon that the Hawks had cut some demos the previous month and that Capitol Records was negotiating a recording contract with their manager, Albert Grossman. Danko said they'd be getting two hundred thousand dollars when the deal was struck. Would Helm be interested in returning to the band in their new home base near Woodstock, New York? Garth Hudson sweetened the deal by describing the forested Catskills and their rural lifestyle there.

Levon wasted no time starting his next adventure.

7

In the Pink with the Band

For nearly two years, Levon had led an aimless, itinerant existence without the Hawks. In the meantime, the band had completed Bob Dylan's North American, Australian, and European tours with a succession of replacements on the drum stool: Bobby Gregg, then ex-Hawk Sandy Konikoff, then Mickey Jones. In July 1966, during a two-month break before the beginning of an arduous sixty-four-date North American tour, Dylan was abruptly sidelined by a motorcycle accident. Still on retainer but unable to tour, the Hawks, minus Levon, moved near Bob in the Woodstock, New York, area to help him edit his documentary of their British performances, *Eat the Document*, and to find a quiet retreat in which to work on their own album.

The Hawks called their headquarters Big Pink. It was a three-bedroom house, with salmon-colored clapboard—what Levon later called "Saturday-night pink"—above unpainted concrete blocks at 2188 Stoll Road, halfway between the hamlet of West Saugerties and Woodstock. Set amid a hundred acres, with a large pond and a view of nearby Overlook Mountain, it offered the musicians complete privacy for the regeneration of the band.

Rick, Garth, and Richard were living at Big Pink. Robbie was sharing a cabin with his girlfriend a few miles away in Bearsville, on Albert Grossman's property. Dylan and his family had settled in Byrd-cliffe, a colony only a couple of miles outside Woodstock. All the elements were in place for an extraordinary collaboration.

Everyone, except the absent Levon at this time, converged at Big Pink. Robertson drove over every day to join the three other Hawks, and Dylan often appeared. Sometimes they'd just listen to music, smoke dope, play checkers, or throw around a football. There was no pressure, simply a sense of relaxation and playfulness. There were a couple of typewriters in the living room, and whenever a catchy phrase or lyric came to mind, it was hammered out on the keys. Then someone else might come along and finish it.

The music was mostly created in the basement, where Garth set up a Revox two-track tape machine, along with an inexpensive Nagra mixer and some first-rate Neumann microphones they'd liberated from their tours. With concrete walls and floor, and a large metal furnace—all hard surfaces that created reverberation and echo—it was a space antithetical to the usual baffling and soundproofing standard in recording studios. The only modifications were to seal the garage door, turn off the furnace, and throw a rug on the floor.

It was never meant to be a professional recording studio; it was a rehearsal space and a place to brainstorm. As ideas emerged, they were often taped as a way to remember them; the quality of the recordings was not an issue.

"It amazed us," Hudson recalls, "to watch Bob go upstairs and type out a tune without any erasures or backspaces, then he'd come downstairs and we recorded it." Dylan could write several songs a day. During his time at Big Pink, he churned out at least sixty original numbers—mostly meant for other artists to record. Between May and November 1967, Bob and the band produced an estimated 150 tracks. Until Helm rejoined the Hawks, most cuts had no drums, although occasionally Richard Manuel laid down the beat.

Jamming with Dylan was liberating and exhilarating, and an introduction to musical styles that were unfamiliar to the Hawks. But the band knew their collaboration with him was temporary. They'd recorded without Bob in fall 1966 when they cut "Beautiful Thing" in New York and taped more demos there in February 1967. By October, Dylan had left for Nashville to work on his album *John Wesley Harding*, with no input from the Hawks.

Danko badgered Albert Grossman, who was now managing the band, to get the Hawks their own record contract. In September 1967, Grossman arranged for them to cut more demos in New York—still without a drummer. Although the Hawks were unsatisfied with the results, Grossman shopped their songs to Columbia and Warner Brothers; both turned him down. Capitol Records, however, was interested. And with that, Helm was back in the picture.

LEVON IMMEDIATELY FELT an affinity for the rural Woodstock lifestyle. "The people here are like the people down in the Ozark Mountains," he said, referring to Fayetteville. "They're just as country in that good, kind, solid-citizen way as they are back home…Anyone who lives here is blessed." A rustic environment suited Helm. He and his roommates inherited a bearlike black dog—Hamlet—from Bob, there was good food and lots of beer, and Levon grew his own stash of pot in the forest. He invited Kirby Penick to join him, and Penick became the road manager of a band that played no gigs.

"At Big Pink there were lots of late-night parties," rock journalist Al Aronowitz remarked. "They'd pass the guitar around, and Levon was always the star of the evening. He'd play the mandolin and sing great old songs like 'Caledonia.'" Helm appreciated how the community welcomed and accepted the band. As one local commented, "You'd see them at the hardware store or drinking beer with firemen. They lit up the town." And all the girls loved them.

A group of Baul musicians from India, led by Purna Das and his brother Luxman, were recording in Woodstock at the time. "We got to be real tight with them," Penick says. "They'd come out to Big Pink. The main ingredient for them was, I mean, killer hash. They would come out and put down these Indian rugs on the floor, and everybody'd get mellow, and they would start playing these weird-ass instruments, and then the guys would start playing with them…[Jazz saxophone and flute player Charles Lloyd] would come up there, and they'd be making some wild-ass music."

Levon—always an auto enthusiast—and Richard tested the limits of their daredevil driving skills with rental cars on the clearing next to Big Pink. One night—feeling no pain and racing home from town to tear up the field—Manuel took a curve too fast and slammed into the ditch. Helm had a late start but was determined to catch up. In the meantime, however, the police had arrived at the scene of Richard's wreck. When Levon sped around the corner and saw the flashing lights, it was too late to stop. He clipped the police cruiser as a cop leapt into the ditch. A brawl ensued—Levon and Richard in a hopeless tangle with the officer and the chief of police. Helm was arrested but avoided jail; in fact, the judge became his friend and mentor.

Relationships within the band remained close, although Helm had detected a change in Robertson even before he left the Dylan tour. Then during Levon's absence, roles had shifted as Robbie assumed more of a leadership position. Additionally, Robertson had formed a deep bond with Dylan, so much so that the Hawks called him Barnacle Man. "He was stuck to Bob," Mickey Jones said. "It was like Robbie was there if Bob went to take a leak." Then Robertson became close with Grossman, increasingly aligning himself with management, whereas Levon harbored a degree of suspicion toward Albert and those he called "the greedy suits who ran the industry meat grinder."

"Robbie obviously had more of a head for business and taking care of things," says Happy Traum, the esteemed folk guitarist, singer, and educator. "The other guys were a little more free and easy and loose." As the exposure to Dylan stimulated Robertson's songwriting creativity, the former dropout was also expanding his intellectual horizons through film and literature, cultivating new interests the others did not share—another potential crack in the unity of the group.

AT FIRST, LEVON had some musical rust to shake off when Dylan and the Hawks congregated in the basement at Big Pink. It had been almost two years since he'd played at this caliber—but any lack of confidence was soon abated. There was no agenda here; these were relaxed, laid-back gatherings full of gaiety and good humor. As Levon put it, "No fun, no work was our policy." They would mine their musical memories, stretching their usual boundaries with a mix of covers and creativity. Fragments of lyrics torn from the upstairs typewriters could be shaped into songs or launch new avenues of exploration, captured on Garth's tape recorder. These tracks were never meant for public release. They were experiments, demos that other artists might want to cover.

"We would get together two, three, four times a week [with Dylan],"

Helm recalled, "sometimes every day—and go down and play, and the songs would pour out of Bob. The rest of us would sit around in amazement at this. We caught ourselves helping him, trying to put some music underneath it. It was a hell of an experience." For Levon it marked the beginning of a revitalized approach to music. "I'm sure that we profited more than Bob," he admitted. "But I know that we had a good time, and I would like to think that we rubbed a few good things onto him."

MOST OF WHAT became *The Basement Tapes* was recorded before Levon came to Woodstock. Dylan—grounded in Harry Smith's *Anthology of American Folk Music* while writing lyrics that spoke to the contemporary experience—led the way, yet the Hawks brought their musical influences to the gatherings as well: rockabilly, R&B, gospel, country, blues. "So we were learning more about folk music," Levon said. "I was playing certain things for Bob that I didn't think he'd come across: maybe some obscure tracks by the Impressions, particular blues tracks, or mountain music."

Word got out about this extraordinary collaboration, and bootleg tapes of their sessions became prized possessions. Then much later, in 1975, Dylan gave his permission to issue a selection of the recordings, and in June that year, Columbia Records released *The Basement Tapes*, a compilation of music recorded at Bob's house, Big Pink, and at the Cabot house where Levon and Rick later lived, plus some subsequent studio outtakes by the band without Dylan. The double LP was lauded by *The New York Times* as "the greatest album in the history of American popular music." Paul Nelson of *Rolling Stone* wrote, "The songs on *The Basement Tapes* are the hardest, toughest, sweetest, saddest, funniest, wisest songs I know, yet I don't know what they're about. Friendship, sex, death, heroism, learning from others. I guess history and inevitability are in there too. And sorrow and longing."

Dylan's influence on the Hawks was profound. Levon acknowledged that the band's exposure to Bob did "a lot for us in everything from trying to construct a song to being able to catch the attention of a recording concern…It was certainly one of the highlights of my musical career." As Hudson explains, "When we moved to [that] house…we stopped playing twelve-bar blues, stopped jamming, and concentrated on songs."

In addition to collaborating with Dylan, the Hawks used what they'd learned from him to develop their own style. Their creative process was largely trial and error; they lacked the knowledge to have a proven systematic method. Through experimentation, their music radically diverged from the Hawks' previous repertoire. Sequestered in the backwoods—isolated from current trends—they tapped into a vein of astonishing originality and discovered a renewed sense of Americana. Their music was evolving in terms of songwriting, theme, instrumentation, vocals, and delivery.

As Levon and the Hawks, the band had mostly performed covers. "We had never tried to put original songs together," said Levon. "We'd spent our whole time playing for dances, repeating popular songs. For the first time, we were trying to come up with musical ideas and stitch them together. It was a whole lot of fun. A brand new experience." He compared it with songwriting school—Dylan, in front of them, crafting music, igniting their creative spark. "Bob helped us more than anybody ever did," Helm stated. "Bob had set the band on fire, and everybody was starting to write, Richard and Robbie especially."

According to Levon, part of this education was learning to blend acoustic and electric sounds, another change for the Hawks. They cut their tempo and created space for what the song required, not simply filling it with sound. "There's only a certain amount of room in a song," Helm believed. "Some things just won't fit. But we're not there to do what we want to do. We're there to do what we're *supposed* to do. You either get the song to breathe or you don't, and that's the only way to get the song to play *you*." Danko concurred: "Levon would leave a backbeat open for me because he thought as much like a bass player as like a drummer."

"I would call Levon's drumming very crafty. *Very* crafty," says Garth.

> Somebody used this word: They said he was the "foxiest" drummer. He accompanied songs, just as I did. That's what we did a great percentage of the time, isn't it? It wasn't a jam band. There weren't many long solos—somewhat in the tradition of basic country music and jump music, rhythm and blues. We paid great attention

to the language of blues and jazz. We would hear twelve bars and we knew it as a work, a piece of art.

Levon had a great touch. His special thing: the pickup grace notes that precede the beat. He did it subtly, and he did it so you almost didn't hear it. It was a treatment—tapping to find out how close you are to being on the money. When I say on the money I don't mean precise like a machine, but having the same feel as the other people you're playing with.

Helm primarily credited Hudson with the unique sound they were generating, with no overplaying or gratuitous solos. "Garth knew instinctively the richest voicing for any chord and how it projected mood, color and movement," he said. "Garth also knew by schooling all the chord inversions and their suspensions...Best of all, Garth Hudson taught the band the patience to grow our tunes into songs we could cultivate and craft until there were no weak places." Their music was egalitarian, without a guitar focus so common among their contemporaries. Levon described their songs as "musical architecture," yet they had a loose feel without sacrificing the rhythm.

Increasingly, the themes the Hawks explored hearkened back to the rural or small-town America of the past, an era when fundamental values of community, family, tradition, and hard work were valued. Stemming from the folk and country music of Helm's childhood, their songs awakened a nostalgia for basic American values, a yearning for a mythical past distinct from psychedelia and the upheavals of the Vietnam and Middle East wars, the Cold War, race riots, and mass protests. And with Levon back in the group, a seal of Southern authenticity was stamped on the otherwise Canadian band. "With Levon's playing there was something in that that was so grown right out of the Mississippi Delta in its approach to the music," Robbie maintains. "There was no question from the very beginning when Levon would sit down to play that this is the real deal here. It just had that kind of authority to it...and [there was] something magical about the feel."

The Hawks also began to experiment with instrumentation. A song was rehearsed with different combinations to see what served the music best. Helm admired the drumming technique Manuel had developed during his absence—characterizing it as swinging, slightly behind the beat, loosey-goosey—but with Levon's return, the drums were no longer an afterthought; the Hawks had their funky, driving beat back. Helm's drums were on equal footing with the vocals and the other instruments. Yet when he could hear that Richard's drum style sounded better on a song than his own, Levon cheerfully picked up a guitar or mandolin. For him it was stimulating. He believed that playing a second instrument gave a drummer a deeper understanding of the interplay within the music.

Singing became a large part of their rebirth, deeply influenced by the vocal stackings of such gospel and soul groups as the Impressions and especially the Staple Singers. "One of the things that we were trying to do was learn how to sound good together," Levon said. "We had never learned how to blend our voices…We would take standard songs—'In the Pines,' right?—and we would sing those kind of songs, and take turns singing the lead, and the others would practice the harmonies." Levon's aim was to sing the middle part while Richard's voice could climb to falsetto, and Rick vocalized in many different spots—yet each voice retained its individual character.

The delivery of their music was determined by the dimensions and limitations of the basement at Big Pink. "It was a larger than average room space," Helm stated. "It gave us room to get in a circle and set our equipment up. Garth usually had one, maybe two microphones that would be placed closer to the singer than the rest of us, and that was pretty much our recording technique." Songs were worked on, recorded, modified, then rerecorded. In contrast with much contemporary music, the Hawks turned *down* their amplifiers. Danko acknowledged that "back when people were stacking up Marshall amps and blowing out their eardrums, we were down in the basement of Big Pink trying to get a balance." Lowering the volume showcased their intricately crafted songs but was also a necessity. When it was louder, sound rebounded off the hard, reflective surfaces in the basement, and the singers had to be able to hear the blending of their voices.

IN JANUARY 1968, before a final contract with Capitol was even signed, Grossman sent the band to A&R Recording's Seventh Avenue studio in New York City to lay down a reel of tracks they'd been working on at Big Pink as demos, not finished tracks, although they were used in the eventual album. Dylan offered his assistance with background vocals. The band declined; they wanted to remain egalitarian, one unit without a star.

These sessions marked the beginning of an important relationship with producer John Simon. Born in Norwalk, Connecticut, in 1941, he grew up surrounded by classical music—his father, a doctor, was schooled as a violinist at Juilliard. John studied piano from an early age and began composing before he was a teenager. He later played in jazz bands and graduated from Princeton University with a degree in music. He worked as a producer for Columbia Records, and he came to be introduced to Dylan and the Hawks as co-producer for the countercultural documentary *You Are What You Eat* and its soundtrack.

Simon found Levon to be the real deal, someone who never put on airs, a genuinely friendly person—most of the time. "For all his southern charm," he says, "Levon could really hold a grudge. Sometimes I joked with him that he was mostly still pissed about the outcome of the Civil War."

Simon credits Robbie for creating the sound of the songs, although, as he puts it, "All the music gets filtered through my musical tastes." And John acted as conductor for the group. "Because only Garth read music, sometimes I'd become a living page of music paper for the others—signaling the guys when a new section was coming up," John notes. "That was really the case with Levon. On 'Chest Fever' and countless times when we were recording, I'd lean on the baffles in front of the drums and point to different drums or cymbals to help him remember what was coming up next."

Studio A had been arranged to utilize the large space, with barriers separating each musician, but that didn't work for this band. Levon placed his kit behind baffles in the middle of the room, with the other musicians gathered closely around so they could see each other and get the pitch from the keyboards and guitar. Their goal was for this setup to be as similar to their basement configuration as possible.

First came the song, then Levon and Rick would explore ways of making the rhythm section interesting and distinct. One variation

Helm brought to the band was to cut the backbeat in half, what he called half time.* His interpretation of the music was brilliant; he was a lyrical and melodic drummer, always aware of dynamics, never predictable. Levon helped achieve the band's signature sound by the way he tuned his drums. By keeping the top heads loose, then tightening two of the lugs opposite each other, he created a band of tension that produced a descending pitch.

After the others built their parts around the rhythmic groove, Helm said, "We would start swapping it around, and different ones of us would sing the lead, and then we would back up and start it again, and somebody else would sing the lead. And that's how we'd determine really who would sing the lead and who would sing the harmonies on our songs." Through his vocals, Levon's unhurried drawl injected a soulful resonance into a song, a fusion of bluegrass, blues, and rock. If the lyrics had a Southern bent, Helm sang the lead. His was a voice alternatively jaded and hopeful, desperate and defiant.

Remarkably, Levon's vocals were completely independent of his drumming, although he admitted that

> sometimes there are spots in certain songs where it's a bit tougher going from a chorus to a verse while you're singing and drumming. The Band always tried to put sing-along choruses in a lot of our songs, and the gear-shifting between those different sections, combined with having a mouthful to sing, can get a little challenging at times. But if you can just ride it, "let it go" and don't count it out too strictly, singing while drumming becomes second-nature.

Regarding the tone of his drums, Levon said, "I like more of a padded sort of sound for my set. I'll usually throw a wallet on the snare drum or a cloth, a towel or tape. Sometimes a cymbal won't sound good to me until I put a piece of tape somewhere on it...The night,

---

* Levon considered what he was playing to be a quarter-note groove (where the bass drum is on beats 1 and 3, and the snare on beats 2 and 4) in half time (now the bass drum is only on beat 1 and the snare on beat 3). Today, some would call this an eighth-note groove.

my ear, or the weather—it all changes." Next to him, Garth was experimenting with new sounds on his Lowrey organ. Helm remarked that "it always helped having Garth playing beside you. He kind of bounced the ball back and forth with you."

"Tears of Rage," "The Weight," "We Can Talk," "Chest Fever," and "This Wheel's on Fire" were all recorded in two sessions on four tracks at A&R. Because they were aiming for a live sound, the group tried to capture a song on the first take. That way, as Helm believed, "It was more like making music and less like making tracks."

"[It was] at the zenith of the psychedelic music era, with its flaming guitars and endless solos and elongated jams, [and] we weren't about to make that kind of album," Levon said of the style and theme of their recordings. "We were hard-headed enough to not want to be a part of that whole thing. I was pretty much tired of the whole folk scene at the time, and the only American music that was having any impact was Motown." He conceded, "We wanted success, naturally, and we wanted to please our families and friends. But we wanted to do it on our own terms, and *that* was a conscious effort…Some things we would do, and some things we wouldn't." And that meant instead of using the electronic effects currently in vogue, the group delivered down-home Americana evoking the ethos of a century before. It was a music apart from trends, an amalgam of American genres yet an imitation of none.

To underscore their independence from mainstream rock, the funereal ballad "Tears of Rage," with Richard's anguished vocals, would be chosen as the LP's opening track. It has an antiquated sound, with Levon playing behind the beat, his snare tuned so deep it sounds like a tom—a tone he achieved by tuning his drums to the fluorescent lights. John Simon described the sustain on Levon's dampened drum notes as "bayou folk."

"The Weight"—perhaps Levon's signature song—was recorded only as an afterthought, yet in 2004 it was named number 41 in *Rolling Stone*'s 500 Greatest Songs of All Time. After Robbie's acoustic-guitar intro, the commanding thump of Helm's floor-tom triplet signifies the intensity of the song that follows. Helm plays in a simple but soulful, swampy, slightly behind-the-beat style with rhythm pushes and triplet fills that echo the introduction. In what *Rolling Stone* called "one of the greatest recorded pop vocal performances of all time," Levon's luminous voice, with his unmistakable southern twang, leads the first three verses, lending authority to lyrics peopled with characters from his Arkansas roots, including Anna Lee. Danko sings the fourth verse, then the two join forces for a powerful close.

In "We Can Talk," the vocals of Manuel, Danko, and Helm are interwoven in a comical parody of their everyday conversations. Levon's eighth-note groove, enhanced with captivating fills, shifts to a shuffle in the bridge. After Garth's masterful organ introduction in "Chest Fever"—taken from Bach's *Toccata and Fugue in D Minor*—the crash of Levon's drums sets the song in motion. His eighth-note groove transitions to quarter-note backbeats in the chorus, and when the tempo changes for an anomalous horn interlude, his drum suggests a heartbeat. Manuel takes the vocal lead here, with Helm and Danko providing backup. Then in the upbeat "This Wheel's on Fire," Levon sings harmony to Rick's lead vocals. Producer John Simon didn't realize until later that Helm's snare was too low in the mix, so reluctantly Levon had to overdub this track.

BOB DYLAN, WHO was heavily influenced by folk legend Woody Guthrie, was invited to play at a Tribute to Woody Guthrie on January 20, 1968, two concerts held to memorialize the folk-music icon who had died the previous October. The other performers were Tom Paxton, Judy Collins, Odetta, Richie Havens, Ramblin' Jack Elliott, Pete Seeger, and Arlo Guthrie. It was Dylan's first performance since his motorcycle accident eighteen months before, and he brought along Levon and the band, who were billed as the Crackers, a spur-of-the-moment name Helm came up with. He thought it hilarious that the band be called a disparaging term for poor Southern whites, and it seemed appropriate for the genre of music they were putting out.

"I don't think Pete Seeger was too thrilled to see us at first," said Levon, "but the audience was warm, and our evening show brought down the house. Bob tore it up!" They backed Dylan on three Woody Guthrie songs: "Ain't Got No Home," "Grand Coulee Dam," and "Mrs. Roosevelt."

With Robertson playing an acoustic guitar with a pickup and Danko on a fretless bass, they complemented the folk material, in stark contrast to the ear-splitting rock the Hawks put out behind Dylan in their 1965/1966 tours. "They kind of toned it down quite a bit," Happy Traum says. "It was a very energetic set, and they changed the songs around quite a bit from the way Woody did them, as I remember. But I think it was very well received. They were not terribly loud and rock 'n' rolly...They were more in the spirit of the folk side of things."

Larry Campbell, who would figure so prominently in Levon's last band, explains his reaction: "Then Bob comes on at the end with this band behind him and it just killed me because for the first time I'm seeing guys with a great rock 'n' roll attitude playing folk music!...Right then I was starting to explore the old-time acoustic thing—the Carter Family, Jimmie Rodgers, country, and bluegrass. And here are these guys doing basically rock 'n' roll with all that stuff present. It was a feast for the ears."

IN THE MEANTIME, Grossman had sent the A&R tapes to Capitol Records. The label was so impressed with the five songs that they asked the band to finish recording the album—which would be called *Music from Big Pink*—at Capitol and Gold Star Studios in Los Angeles. For a month, the musicians lived at the Chateau Marmont in West Hollywood, purposely drawing out their recording time to escape the winter in Woodstock. Levon discovered a lifelong passion for sushi at the restaurant next door, and everyone was kept happy with a steady supply of marijuana.

The most stirring track on these sessions is a prisoner's lament, "I Shall Be Released," with Manuel's heart-rending falsetto backed by Danko and Helm, whose voice was described by John Simon as "beautiful dirt." What sounds like military drum rolls from afar is Levon with his snare upended, strumming the wires on the bottom as he plays the bass drum.

"To Kingdom Come" is a complex arrangement with driving backbeats in 4/4 time, transitioning into 5/4. Helm's funky kick drum is complemented with rhythmic pushes and fills. "In a Station," with elements reminiscent of the Beatles, swings with Levon's iconic rim-shot backbeats.

Time signatures shift in "Long Black Veil" as Levon plays an almost syncopated groove behind the beat. In "Lonesome Suzie," backing Richard's haunting vocals, he also lags behind, doubling up on the snare in parts, with an almost inaudible hi-hat. Helm switches to acoustic guitar on "Caledonia Mission"—Manuel is on drums—with lyrics recalling the band's Toronto drug bust of 1965.

Their contract with Capitol was finally signed on February 1, 1968—a massive ten-album commitment, longer than they wished but a deal they couldn't turn down. On the document, the band was identified as the Crackers, the name they used the previous month at the Woody Guthrie memorial. When the group tried to come up with an alternative, Levon suggested the Honkies, and Richard proposed the Marshmallow Overcoat or the Chocolate Subway. But the Crackers won out. The Hawks were no more.

BY THE SPRING, Levon and Rick had moved out of Big Pink. Four men in a three-bedroom house was too crowded. They relocated to Bearsville, in a rental home owned by designer Petra Cabot at the end of a long, winding driveway off Wittenberg Road (now accessed from West Ohayo Mountain Road), and this house became the new meeting and rehearsal space for the Crackers.

When it was time for their album to be designed, Dylan contributed a colorful, primitive-style painting of the five musicians and a roadie for the front cover. And Grossman chose a young, relatively obscure New York photographer, Elliott Landy, to provide shots for the inner gatefold and back cover of the LP.

Landy was immediately struck by how different these musicians were from the other bands he'd photographed. Although they were only in their mid-twenties, these were seasoned professionals who seemed much older than their years. "You couldn't fool them," Elliott observed. "They were wise—and they were also very kind and very nice. I think that's what impressed me: how sociable they were. Up in Woodstock, where they lived, when they passed someone in the street who they knew, they were just really sincerely glad to see them, glad to say hello to them. It wasn't some phony stuff, and they were just very gracious human beings. And they were very gracious to me also." Landy remarked that Rick and Levon "genuinely liked people, regardless of how strange they were or how redneck, how liberal, how bright, how dumb." As for the relationships within the Band, he says, "They were so close to each other, and at that time, so trusting of each other, they were really five brothers...To me they were all equivalent. There was no leader; there was no boss."

Posing for photos didn't sit well with Helm. "Levon often felt uncomfortable [being photographed]," Landy says, "but yet personally I was very, very close to him—closer to him than some of the other guys." He regarded Levon as a "flawed human being," yet also, "as one of the most gracious people I ever met. He was very Southern in the best sense of the word." Landy's idea was to reflect the values of the band through his photos. He was influenced by a book on the Civil War, and this group—in beards, suits, ties, and hats, with old-school family values and a respect for tradition—looked and acted the part. Like the music, Landy's band shots were reminiscent of a venerable past.

Aside from one band photo and a picture of Big Pink, the other gatefold shot was entitled "Next of Kin." Taken in Simcoe, Ontario, on Rick's brother's farm, it featured the band members and their families, with an insert of Levon's parents as they couldn't make it up north. In an era when youth were disowning their elders, it was another way the group deviated from the mainstream. "They wanted to honor their parents," Landy says. "They wanted to say, 'We love our parents, they sacrificed, they made us who we are today.'" At the photo shoot, Levon persuaded Rick's uncle Lee—a poultry judge—to teach him how to hypnotize a chicken.

There was an air of mystery surrounding the band, and Grossman and the group preferred it that way. The musicians' photo was on the inside of the album instead of on the cover, and the band members were not individually identified in the shot. Capitol's rather juvenile promotional plans were scrapped: the band refused to be interviewed and they would not tour.

Despite that, *Music from Big Pink* triggered shockwaves in popular music months before it was released in July 1968. When Cream passed through L.A. that May, Eric Clapton obtained an acetate. He claims it not only altered his life but also the trajectory of American music. Clapton admits that "I became very, very discontent with my own lot… There's a group here who's finally amalgamated all of the influences— the black influences and the country influence—and they put them all into one thing with songwriting and musicianship, and this is what it's about, and I'm in the wrong place with the wrong people doing the wrong thing." He disbanded Cream that fall and made a pilgrimage to Woodstock.

Upon the release of the LP, Al Kooper wrote in *Rolling Stone*, "I have chosen *my* album for 1968. *Music from Big Pink* is an event and should be treated as one…Levon Helm is a solid rock for the band. He is an exciting drummer with many ideas to toss around." Of Helm's music, journalist Charles P. Pierce wrote, "He helped point the way home for all of us who thought we'd lost our country. He brought us back to what was really important: the fugitive grace of a young democracy, that America, for all its flaws and shortcomings, for all its loss of faith in itself and its stubborn self-delusions, was a country that was meant to rock."

The fallout from *Big Pink* buried psychedelia. Procol Harum and Traffic shifted direction; the Grateful Dead became more rootsy. Fairport Convention were inspired to probe their British roots as this LP had done with Americana. Jimi Hendrix commented that the album "has changed the musical landscape. It's like you turned the music world on its head." Roger Waters of Pink Floyd insisted, "That one record changed everything for me. After *Sgt. Pepper*, it's the most influential record in the history of rock 'n' roll. It affected Pink Floyd deeply, deeply, deeply." George Harrison had a similar reaction, and after his trip to visit the band, he started composing "All Things Must Pass," saying, "I wrote it after the *Music from Big Pink* album. When I heard that song in my head, I always heard Levon Helm singing it."

For such an influential album, the sales were not what one would expect, peaking at number 30 on the charts, although it charted for almost a year. It finally reached gold-album status in 2001, with a half-million copies sold.

But Levon was uneasy. The credo of the group since Ronnie Hawkins—that they were one unit, a democracy, no frontman—was undermined by Robertson's sole attribution as songwriter on several tracks, with no credit for Helm or Hudson, which in Levon's mind was the most glaring omission. Helm adamantly believed that their music was a group effort, an amalgamation of all their creativity. It wasn't about royalties; he was still quite new to the business side of recording and didn't yet recognize the financial security earned through songwriting and music publishing. Levon rationalized that he hadn't been back with the band for long, so he tried to let it go. Yet it remained—a discomforting feeling just on the edge of his consciousness. He hoped that on their next album, he—and especially Garth, their musical virtuoso—would be recognized.

"The actual process of writing *Big Pink* began there [on Yonge Street]," David Clayton-Thomas declares.

> I know that a great deal of that album was Levon Helm. Sure everybody contributed, but I just knew what a force he was in that band, and there's no way he didn't co-write some of those songs, and he maintained that right up until his death. And I believe him because I was privy to the process of that group and how they worked. Levon definitely was the driving force...It's more likely Robbie was smart and they were busy partying and drugging...I would have felt better about it had [Robbie] gotten the publishing but still credited the writers...because I knew how much they contributed.

As the record generated a seismic upheaval throughout the music world, it rattled the Crackers in another way. Capitol had disliked their name and without informing them, merely listed the musicians on the album under the heading "The Band," as if that were the name of the group. Helm was taken aback: "Calling it the Band seemed a little on the pretentious, even blowhard side—burdened by greatness—but we never intended it that way." Still, their Woodstock neighbors had always referred to them simply as "the band," so in that respect it was appropriate.

Nevertheless, barely nine months had passed since Levon—broke and lethargic, his future uncertain—had spent his time sprawled in front of Mary Cavette's TV. Now, as part of the Band, Helm was a key component in the shaping of musical history.

8

"The Only Drummer That Can Make You Cry"

Levon—naked—yelled at the state trooper, "Now's no fuckin' time to be asking for his goddamn license! Call an ambulance, for God's sake!" It was late at night in autumn 1968. Helm had been asleep when Bill Avis and his wife, Jeannine, sped up to the house with a bleeding, severely injured Rick Danko.

Danko had spent that evening with Bill, Jeannine, and Levon, sitting on the porch singing with them, before driving off at about eleven o'clock in a rare 1953 Bristol, borrowed from his girlfriend's brother.

> He was going too fast, [Bill says of Rick,] and he come around a bend. About maybe…thirty, forty-five minutes later, Jeannine and I decided to go home, and I come around a corner and I could see these lights pointing up into the sky…There was the car. It was virtually climbing up the tree. He had managed to get out of it… and crawl under it because it was raining…Now how he did that with a broken neck is beyond me…So anyway, I got him out of there, got him in the car. I'm driving. He's leaning up against Jeannine…His head flopped over onto Jeannine and bled onto her. [We] turned around and [went] back to Levon's. Levon was already in bed. We got him up…We phoned for the police and the ambulance.

Despite his protestations, Rick was rushed to the hospital, suffering from a broken back and neck. When the Avises saw him the next day, Danko had a contraption drilled into his skull with weights on it, and he could only move his eyes. Mirrors were positioned on the hospital table so he could see who was coming through the door. He was in traction for weeks, had to learn to walk again, and suffered recurring pain for the rest of his life.

In the aftermath of *Music from Big Pink*, this was only the most serious incident, as Levon, Richard, and Rick showed no restraint, leaving ruins of wrecked cars in their wake. Helm bought a new gold Corvette after *Big Pink*. He drove it from Woodstock to Fayetteville as fast as it could go, then finally turned it over when he got back to New York. Manuel, amping up his already-massive intake of alcohol, crashed a growing number of rental cars. All three were experimenting with prescription pills and other drugs. Meanwhile, Levon was working his way through every girl in town.

ONE OF DANKO'S crashes was unwittingly instigated by twenty-two-year-old Libby Titus, a dark-haired beauty with a larger-than-life personality, one of the most stunning women in Woodstock. A native of the town, she was born Elizabeth Jurist in 1947 to a mother who'd been a Broadway dancer and a Russian father who co-produced *Batman* comics for Stan Lee. By 1968, her two-year marriage to some-time novelist Barry Titus—grandson of the cosmetics tycoon Helena Rubinstein—was over, and she was raising her two-year-old son, Ezra, in upscale comfort in New York City's Gramercy Park. Libby had musical ambitions of her own; 1968 saw the release of her first album, *Libby Titus*, a compilation of pop and folk-rock covers.

Titus first glimpsed Levon in Woodstock as he and Andy Yarrow—younger brother of Peter, of the group Peter, Paul and Mary—were in the midst of an intense argument with two locals. As a ranting Helm smashed in the side of one of their trucks, Libby thought she'd never seen anyone as attractive, albeit dangerous. Mason Hoffenberg—co-writer of the erotic satire *Candy*, heroin addict, and confrere of the literary and rock worlds—introduced them. As the summer of 1968 progressed, she got to know Levon better and was captivated by his magnetism and wildness.

Titus was staying with Hoffenberg in Woodstock that fall when Danko and Helm decided to race to Mason's house, stoked by a bet that whoever got there first would sleep with her. Danko ended up in the ditch, and Helm—eventually—got the girl.

ERIC CLAPTON AND George Harrison each made a pilgrimage to Woodstock in late 1968. Clapton—who considered *Music from Big Pink* a seminal work in the history of rock 'n' roll—later admitted that he had embarked on the visit with the intention of asking to join the Band, but lost his nerve.

Harrison dubbed his hosts "the best band in the history of the universe." Helm was encouraged that the Beatles were inspired by the Band's music and credited George's enthusiasm for helping to establish them internationally. "George was certainly one of the easiest going, nicest people that I ever got to meet," Levon said. "I was always amazed at how outgoing and friendly he was."

Happy Traum vividly remembers the first time he met Levon, in the company of George and Pattie Harrison:

> My friendship with Levon Helm dates from our first meeting. It was Thanksgiving 1968 at Bob Dylan's home on the mountain above Woodstock, New York, in the heart of the historic Byrdcliffe artist colony. Sara [Dylan's wife] had mentioned that "the boys" would be coming over, and some time later there was a knock at the door and in walked five guys looking like they had just stepped out of a nineteenth-century daguerreotype. Broad-brimmed hats, string ties, beards, work boots—the iconic look that later distinguished the Band from all the tie-dyed, psychedelic, hippie rock 'n' roll fashions of the day. These guys looked like they were of the earth. They were new in town, but as Bob's backup band there was certainly a buzz about them, and their mysterious other-worldliness was intriguing and a little intimidating at first.

Nevertheless, Traum describes Helm as being "extremely friendly and warm." Happy's son Adam was about two years old, and when the Hawks walked in, he was playing in the entryway. "The first thing Levon did was scoop him up and start carrying him around and talking to him…He was very good with kids. He loved kids. My son to this day, he has very warm feelings about Levon; in fact, all my kids do." Another indelible memory from that night was when Richard sat down at the piano and Rick, recently out of traction, joined him for an impromptu rendition of "I Shall Be Released." The following Saturday, the same group, with several local artists and artisans, convened at Happy's house for a party.

Procol Harum came to Woodstock around that time specifically to visit the Band. "We had a good old drunken time," Levon recalled. "Best bunch of guys: they were as bad as we were for wanting to hang out and laugh and have a drink, and have some fun. We fitted well together, and we had one hell of a night in Woodstock…It used to be flattering to me, to be compared with Procol Harum, and we got that compliment a lot."

DESPITE THEIR GROWING fame, the Band was uninterested in overt trappings of success. They'd already declined to be interviewed and delayed until August a cover story in *Rolling Stone*. "We hoped they'd review the record and leave our personalities out of it," Helm said of the press. "They always turn things around and try to fuck you."

With Danko in recovery—and Richard suffering a severe burn on his foot from a barbecue mishap—they were unable to tour to support their new album, even if they wanted to. They kept their injuries to themselves, drawing an increasing curtain of mystery over the group. Plus, Levon felt the Band was on a roll. They'd developed what he called a formula for recording, and he thought that going on the road would break that momentum. "It's different playing in a studio than it is playing live, of course," he said. "So we had managed to develop some studio chops, and we didn't want to back away from it that quick." Meanwhile, Albert Grossman was getting offers of four thousand dollars a night, as bookers—wanting what they could not have—were clambering to get them to play at their venues.

FOLLOWING THE RELEASE of *Big Pink*, amid the turmoil and transformation it incited, the Band began to generate ideas for a new album. They rehired producer John Simon, though their intention was to do most of the production themselves. For a change of scene, a winter escape, and a retreat from their destructive lifestyle, the group decided to record in Los Angeles, but to retain the clubhouse atmosphere that had worked so well in Woodstock. Their new road manager, Jonathan Taplin, rented a house for them at 8850 Evanview Drive in the Hollywood Hills—owned by Sammy Davis Jr.—where the Band would live for two months while they cut their second album.

In February 1969, Helm moved into an upstairs suite in the pool house, and the rest of the structure was converted into a recording studio. Capitol Records soundproofed the building from the outside, and on the inside blankets were hung, carpet laid, and windows sealed to baffle the sound. While the Band waited weeks for Capitol's recording equipment to be installed and to have their gear shipped from Woodstock, they worked on their new music.

In early 1969, Helm was playing a Gretsch kit with two toms, and the snare drum tilted slightly away from him, the traditional jazz setup. While the L.A. studio was being assembled, he used the time to scour pawnshops for old instruments. In Santa Monica, he found an antique mandolin, and for $130 he bought what he called his hybrid kit, which he played on these sessions: vintage wooden drums that included two Gretsch toms and a twenty-six-inch Ludwig bass drum and snare, plus two Zildjian cymbals. "I like to hear the wood of the drum shell," he pointed out, explaining that his preference was for a wood sound over chrome. "That's why wooden rims are so much fun. That wooden rim gives you more of a knock when you play rim shots." Commenting on the tone of Levon's drums, Ringo Starr says, "The sound was so unique. He had that real dead sound which I'd always tried to create in the studio...He was going the same way—different countries."

JIM KELTNER WOULD become acclaimed as a session drummer for John Lennon, George Harrison, and Ringo Starr, as well as for such artists as Carly Simon, John Hiatt, Joe Cocker, Barbra Streisand, and Boz Scaggs. He first met Levon and the rest of the Band at the Davis house. Keltner had come from the jazz world, and his friend Carl Radle—the bass player with Delaney and Bonnie and Friends, and Eric Clapton—was schooling him in popular music and blues:

So Carl would tell me what I should be listening to because I started playing rock 'n' roll, and I figured I'd better know something about it, and one of the things that he told me about was the Band. He said, "You've gotta hear these guys." And it was the [*Music from Big*] *Pink* album. It blew me away, the album, and I became instantly a fan. Then at some point in time, Carl told me, "I'm gonna go up and see what's going on up at the studio. Robbie and the guys are up there." I went up with him, I think—I'm still not sure how that happened—but I ended up staying for a couple of days and just hanging out with Levon.

It was amazing…[It was] the first time I'd ever seen somebody making an actual record with what looked like student-type, very old instruments. I thought, "Wow, that's interesting." And then when they played, I could see what [Levon] was doing, why he was doing that, why he was playing those kind of drums because of the way he played…He had a completely unique, beautiful style. Just pure feel. And it helped that he sang, too…There has still not been a more soulful voice.

Levon's technique was a revelation for Jim:

He didn't play the drums exactly like a normal drummer would play. First of all, he didn't hit real hard, but he got plenty of volume out of the drum set, which is all you want really. You don't want to over-hit the thing, which is the way a lot of people do today—it crushes any kind of personality out of the playing. Levon, he played traditional grip with his sticks, and he played loose, but he had a tightness, so it's paradoxical—he's playing tight, but yet he's playing loose. How do you do that? Well, that's the mystery; that's the beauty of it. And, as I say, it helped that he was just an incredible singer with the most amazing phrasing, and so because of that the playing of the drums was enhanced even more. So it was a whole package that he had there.

Keltner noticed that Helm didn't hit the hi-hat when he played the backbeat on the snare, as is standard. "Because I saw him do that,"

Keltner says, "I started sort of naturally doing it, and then it became a thing with me, so that's the way I played for many years after that. I played exactly like that. And Charlie Watts told me years later that he saw me doing it on the [*The Concert for*] *Bangladesh* film, and so he started doing it. So then years went by, and Steve Jordan saw Charlie Watts doing it, and then he started doing it. So it all started with Levon."

Unlike many drummers, Helm seldom played the crash cymbal. Keltner explains, "A lot of the stuff he would do or not do was based on what was going to interfere or not interfere with his singing, with the phrasing of the song. And don't forget, his mic was open—his vocal mic was open—which gave the drum sound that really nice, cool sound, but crashing the cymbals would be something to try to be avoided, if possible."

"Levon…played very classically, but he did it with a real loose kind of technique," Jim says. "I used to love it when he would sound like he was going to play a fill, and he'd just hit one beat, or he'd play the fill and it would just be a portion of the fill. As a drummer, you're listening and you're thinking you know what's coming, but that was the beauty of his playing, that was the total beauty of his playing." After listening to Helm play at the Davis house, Keltner altered his own approach. "After that I completely changed as a drummer…I wasn't interested in playing a lot of stuff anymore like I was. I was always messing with my chops, trying to get fast and play a lot of different stuff. It just went away. I just kept wanting to hear Levon's feel when I played."

As for Helm's personality, Keltner declares, "He was one of my absolute all-time favorite people. I just loved him. I miss him because he's one of those type of people you just loved being around…If there's such a thing as a Southern gentleman, that's what he was. And he was no saint, but that's all I ever saw…Just go listen to 'The Night They Drove Old Dixie Down,' and listen to that guy singing, 'cause that's who he is, it seems to me—Virgil."

IT TOOK A month for the makeshift studio to be ready for recording. Originally scheduled for two months, their session time was now cut in half. At a group meeting, the musicians decided to push through with the help of what Richard called "them high-school fat-girl diet pills." John Simon scored a prescription from a neurosurgeon friend, thus fueling the Band's next album with copious amounts of amphetamines. They tried to stop Richard drinking before the sessions, but when shaky, he'd need a beer or two; as for the rest, they generally abstained until a song was in the bag.

Although Robertson considered himself the director of the sessions, according to Manuel, "Levon acted as the musical leader for the most part, although we traded." Robbie did concede that "if there was something about the feeling in a song, an angle I couldn't get, Levon would always find ways to get the feel I hadn't been able to express."

Helm positioned his drums in a corner of the pool house, behind a gobo, a panel that prevents the drums bleeding into other tracks. As they'd done at Big Pink, the rest of the musicians gathered around so they could play off each other. Helm enjoyed the recording process. It was an exacting system, experimenting with each person's part many different ways, trying a selection of microphones on every instrument. "Sometimes we would have to record a song for a while," Levon recalled, "until the song would come on and we could cultivate it voice-wise, arrangement-wise, and get all the choruses straight...I think all musicians want that advantage of being able to listen to themselves. That's when you have a chance to get a track that you like...You can go back, take a little tape off the snare drum or fix things around to get your kit sounding right."

Drawing on the experience they'd gained from recording *Big Pink*, Levon said, "We had actually figured out some methods of how to really turn the heat up and get the music to cook: how to blend our voices three different ways, how to get the track together and not make it so complicated."

While they aimed for as much live material as possible, this album had more overdubs than *Big Pink*. Helm admitted that he sometimes had to redo his parts: "I'll swear to myself that I didn't lose concentration, but something will just kind of waver there just for a brief instant. When it does, it's kind of like somebody's fingernails on a blackboard—my nail and my board...So I stumble back in there and re-sing it sometimes, but I don't like to...Playing live is more fun."

This album, like its predecessor, intentionally stood apart from those of the Band's contemporaries. Their music was not dated, yet their lyrical themes, instrumentation, and vocals evoked early Americana. West Coast psychedelia and surf music did not penetrate this pool house.

The vocal harmonies that Helm, Danko, and Manuel had worked on in Woodstock were still an integral part of their music. And when Levon sang lead, the old South came alive. Robertson said, "If I wanted this tremendous character in the vocal, that drummed up all kinds of timeless pictures, I'd want Levon."

John Simon notes that a lot of attention was paid to the drum parts in each song. "Levon was always open to suggestions," he says, "and to learning something new, always humble, never haughty." Then as Helm's kick drum and Danko's bass locked together, they were always mindful to leave space in the music for everyone else.

THE FIRST TRACK they recorded, and the one that took the longest, was a song of Southern pride and anguish, "The Night They Drove Old Dixie Down." In it, Levon delivers some of his most impassioned vocals. Helm owns this song. His Arkansas drawl resounds with grief and stoic dignity as he portrays a downtrodden Confederate lamenting the overthrow of the South in the Civil War. Helm's drumming is extraordinary. He plays with the rhythm through numerous time changes, and his half-time groove is swung and deftly embellished with triplet fills. And the crescendo of closed drum rolls—evocative of a military salute—opens each chorus with dynamic intensity. As journalist David Hepworth expressed it, without Levon's contribution, this song would be like an empty shell. "When the Band played it with Levon Helm singing," he writes, "suddenly the house is not merely built, the carpets are laid, the curtains are hung, every light is on and there's a deuce of a party taking place inside."

For Jim Keltner the standouts in the song are, "That beautiful feel, those stately fills, and the snare drum roll that makes you hold your breath. And the most amazingly soulful singing." He continues: "To this day when I hear that song, even just the intro, I start welling up. It's very powerful, a very powerful song and, of course, delivered with genius delivery. Levon was just so amazing. He was such a great actor. He made you believe the character in that song. It was just awesome." The late Richie Hayward, drummer for Little Feat, commented that "the drums are exactly what they should be. That's one of the hardest things to do: play it simple but keep it interesting and keep it working."

After this track was complete, the remaining songs took about two days each—one day of practice then recording on the second day. Helm utilizes his signature dampened beat enhanced with compelling breaks and fills on "Across the Great Divide," a song that for Levon elucidated Richard's gracious personality. Then Helm turns the kit over to Manuel and plays mandolin—accompanied by country-style fiddle and ragtime piano—while supplying bawdy, booty-shaking vocals in "Rag Mama Rag." Helm considered this tune a true Band collaboration, with input from everyone, especially Hudson.

Levon is also on mandolin for "Rockin' Chair," while supplying exquisite vocal harmonies with Rick behind Richard's lead. John Simon remembers working out the mandolin sections with Helm:

> We imagined a mandolin part for "Rockin' Chair" but there were more chords required than 99 percent of mandolin players would ever be asked to play. So he and I sat down in facing chairs to figure it out. It remains one of my favorite memories of working with Levon. We each knew something the other didn't know. I heard some chords that he didn't know. He could play the mandolin better than I could. So together we figured out unconventional mandolin hand positions for chords that would fit the song.

Levon's intricate, delicate embellishments introduce "When You Awake," as he plays on the rim of his snare, accompanied by swinging toms and kick-drum parts. "Look Out Cleveland" is propelled by rousing drumming that switches between sixteenth- and eighth-note grooves, and Helm plays a quarter-note shuffle with hi-hat triplets on "The Unfaithful Servant."

"Jawbone" is a combination of different time signatures and tempos. Levon laughed when he recounted Richard creating it: "I could always depend on a good workout when Richard was helping to write the songs. He might want to go from a shuffle to a march, and vice versa. It was stuff that kept you on your toes all the time." Because Levon could not read music, Simon—as he'd done with *Music from Big Pink*—became what he called "a living music chart for Levon, leaning on one of the gobos in front of the drums and pointing at a particular drum or cymbal as we entered each new section of the song and it would be time to change the rhythm pattern." The percussion in the choruses of "Jawbone" is striking as Manuel's piano and Helm's drums lock in rhythmic unison.

The hardscrabble life of the rural laborer is poignantly portrayed in "King Harvest (Has Surely Come)," one of Helm's favorite songs. Lyrically, it reflected much of Levon's outlook and rural experiences. Describing his drum work, Levon said, "I really like the bass drum pattern, and then we left a corresponding hole for the backbeat. That was one track where I got my drums sounding the way I wanted them to. There's enough wood in the sound. You could hear the stick, the bell of the cymbal and so on." It has a driving, swinging funk beat with a time change and push into each verse. The synchronicity between Danko's bass and Helm's kick drum contrasts with the shimmering and tapping of the cymbals when Helm's singing supports Manuel's lead. "I think that as an overall thing—sonically solid, groove-wise, the feel—it's a masterful thing," says Steve Jordan, the highly respected drummer, composer and producer, "and that's why I listened to it over and over and over again. It had me mesmerized. It's perfect—the groove, the whole thing."

BILL GRAHAM, ROCK impresario extraordinaire, finally convinced the Band—for twenty thousand dollars—to make its live debut at one of music's premier venues, San Francisco's Winterland Ballroom, on April 17, 18, and 19, 1969. They had not been onstage for more than a year, and that was as Dylan's backup band; moreover, it had been an interminable four years since they'd performed on their own as Levon and the Hawks. An entire generation was on tenterhooks. While recording in the Hollywood Hills, the group started rehearsals, and Levon admitted they were nervous about presenting their new music to an audience again.

That Thursday as their first show approached, Robbie grew increasingly ill, a combination of severe flu and nervous exhaustion. Cancelation was not an option; the schedule was set and their fans had intense expectations. As a last-ditch fix, Robertson was hypnotized, causing some improvement, but it was midnight when Graham finally introduced the Band to a progressively belligerent, impatient crowd. As Robbie summoned all his strength to go onstage, Levon encouraged him to just do his best. Queasy and weak, Robertson leaned against Manuel's piano as he tried to play guitar. He was spent after thirty-five minutes. As his bandmates followed him offstage, the crowd erupted in hostile jeers, evoking memories of the contentious Dylan tour. Yet, as Levon remarked, "I'll bet they didn't feel as bad as we did."

Negative word of mouth spread through the Bay Area, causing lower turnouts for the following nights. But on their next outing on Friday, the Band triumphed, playing songs from *Big Pink* as well as "Little Birds," a bluegrass waltz that Diamond Helm had taught his young son, "Ain't No More Cane" and "Don't Ya Tell Henry," culminating with Little Richard's "Slippin' and Slidin'." A reviewer noted that "Helm seemed to lose his mind without losing the beat, playing a small kit but making every beat count, with no extraneous cymbals." In an exuberant commentary in *Rolling Stone*, Ralph J. Gleason wrote, "The first thing that flashed into my mind was, 'This is Levon's band!' I had never thought of that. But there he was, bushy beard, swinging shoulders and his Mephistophelian visage pushed up to the mike on one side of him as he drummed. 'He's got a great voice!' I thought next."

Even with this flush of success, the Band still felt vulnerable before an audience, especially with no frontman to provide a focus. Helm recalled, "We were scared to death. You knew you were going to make a mistake, you just didn't know when. And none of us was the kind of performer who could stand up and tell jokes and entertain a crowd that way." But for Levon, when they carried it off, the elation was transcendent. He credited audience feedback as an equal component in making that happen.

Checking out an early Band show, Roger McGuinn of the Byrds thought it noteworthy that Levon's kit was set on a riser, stage right.

Robbie was next to him, Garth in the center, and Rick between Garth and Richard, who was on the far left—a configuration that signified equality among the musicians and their instruments. In the Band, drums never had a subordinate role. And without the kit in its traditional position behind a frontman, the group's essential sight lines were preserved.

Moving on to Bill Graham's Fillmore East on New York's Lower East Side, the Band played four sold-out shows on May 9 and 10. Dressed like country gentlemen, they attained what one enthusiastic columnist called "a genuine apogee of rock...with music that was utterly timeless, spiritually moving and surpassingly beautiful...The Band's music, putting it in basic terms, is an amalgam of rock 'n' roll and country sounds, which is like saying Duke Ellington's music is jazz. It is also something more, and that 'more' is forever indefinable, intriguing, the very essence of their music."

Again, during their appearances, the group played songs primarily from *Big Pink*, supplemented with selections from their upcoming album, plus "Don't Ya Tell Henry," "Slippin' and Slidin'," "Get Up Jake," "Loving You Is Sweeter Than Ever," and "Little Birds." During his lead vocals in "Don't Ya Tell Henry," Helm's lip touched an ungrounded microphone. A sudden flash momentarily blinded him, and the electric shock burned his face as he struggled to complete the song through welling tears of pain. "The Weight" was meant to close that weekend's final show, but the cheering, stamping crowd brought the Band back for two encores.

WITH THE END of this triumphant interlude, the Band still had an album to finish; only nine tunes were in the can. They reconvened in June at New York's Hit Factory on West Forty-Eighth Street to record "Jemima Surrender," "Whispering Pines," "Up on Cripple Creek," and "Get Up Jake," which was cut from the final LP.

In "Jemima Surrender," Levon rocks out on rhythm guitar while his lead vocals brim with twang and cocky confidence. His voice mirrors Richard's sublime lead in "Whispering Pines," as Helm's delicate touch on the hi-hat and ride cymbals create an ethereal underlay to a stunning performance.

"Up on Cripple Creek"—soon to be a Band classic—did not come easily. They'd tried it in Los Angeles, but no one was satisfied, then one night at the Hit Factory, they nailed it. Levon sings lead with carefree exuberance, enhanced with yodeling and a mischievous laugh. His inspiration for the drum intro came from Charles Connolly in Little Richard's "Keep a-Knockin'." Then with Helm's kick drum and Danko's bass playing off each other, Helm delivers a funky, implied half-time shuffle through snare and syncopated bass-drum combinations that vary as the song progresses.

The buoyant effervescence of the tune is heightened with closed drags spilling into the next bar, kick-drum fills, and the playful addition of Garth on clavinet. "It's probably a combination of everything that I grew up liking," Helm said. "It's got kind of a march feel in spots, and at the same time it's like a fatback shuffle. It's mainly as much fun as I can muster with the cowbells and the wooden rims."

Steve Jordan was amazed at Helm's artistry in "Up on Cripple Creek." "Very few drummers can play and sing with such fluidity and independence," he maintains. "There are people who do it but you can sense the mechanics. Levon has quintessential independence. And he's so natural. It makes it even freakier." For Jordan, this song "really is the personification of his half-time playing, and the vocal on it is so incredible, the fills, everything, the sound, everything about it. And I would say because it's so musical and there's so many twists and turns on it that it's my favorite." It would become the Band's most popular single, reaching number 25 on the *Billboard* chart.

The resultant album—eponymously named *The Band*—was a pastiche of rock 'n' roll and downhome country, replete with captivating characters—hardworking stiffs struggling to make a good life amid adversity who could also step out for a raucous good time. Much more than *Music from Big Pink*, *The Band* was easier for the average listener to appreciate. With this record, the Band solidified its identity apart from Dylan and showcased its own formidable talent—in originality, songwriting, and musicianship.

UNABLE TO GET him off her mind—even though she was dating anarchist leader, actor, writer, and heroin addict Emmett Grogan—Libby

Titus dropped in on Helm while he was recording at the Hit Factory. Sparks flew, but he didn't show up for the date they'd arranged until five o'clock the next morning. Undeterred, she fell in love, as Levon continued to keep his distance. Reluctant to be seen focusing on one woman, he'd only be with her in the middle of the night. Not until Jonathan Taplin made a move on her did Helm stake his claim and fly Titus to Arkansas to meet his parents.

BY 1969, HUDSON, Manuel, and Bill and Jeannine Avis were living in a house on Spencer Road, near the top of Woodstock's Ohayo Mountain, with a spectacular view of the Ashokan Reservoir, a dammed lake that provides water for New York City. Their large living room became the Band's new rehearsal space for their concerts in the months ahead.

They began that season's shows on June 21 in familiar territory, at the Toronto Pop Festival, a weekend event with an extensive lineup that included Johnny Winter; Chuck Berry; Steppenwolf; Blood, Sweat & Tears; the Velvet Underground; and Ronnie Hawkins and his current Hawks. Helm had looked forward to being back in Toronto, but he considered the outing a fiasco after their performance was marred by a rainstorm, a burned-out amp, and a poor PA.

On July 14, the Band headlined the first Mississippi River Festival, held in a huge tent sheltering three thousand fans at Southern Illinois University in Edwardsville. When they were called back for an encore, the group brought on an unannounced guest, and Bob Dylan—unrecognized by many in the audience—closed out the set with the Band.

SINCE THE LATE 1800s, Woodstock had been a vibrant arts, theater, and music center, and its allure as a hip address only increased as its fame spread. That summer Van Morrison, Tim Hardin, and Paul Butterfield joined legions of other musicians drawn to the town as they succumbed to the lure of the Woodstock vibe.

Attracted to the area by the mystique of Dylan and the Band, fledgling concert promoter Michael Lang and his associates decided to set up a recording studio there. To raise the funds, Lang proposed a music festival. When it was unfeasible to situate it in Woodstock,

Saugerties, or Wallkill, he moved the venue to Max Yasgur's farm in Bethel, retaining the Woodstock name to capitalize on its cachet.

Lang always intended the Band as a highlight of the Woodstock Music and Art Fair. They would be paid fifteen thousand dollars for their appearance on Sunday, August 17, although Grossman refused to allow his artists—Janis Joplin; Blood, Sweat & Tears; and the Band—to appear in the subsequent film or on the album soundtrack, regarding the payment offered for the movie rights to be too low.*

That Sunday, the Band was flown in by helicopter, arriving just before a hard summer downpour transformed Yasgur's field into a sloppy quagmire. Levon instructed Libby to stay home, that it was no place for a woman; she accompanied Janis Joplin instead. That evening, after an explosive performance by Ten Years After—defying the threat of electrocution in the rain—and after Alvin Lee had left the stage with a watermelon hoisted on his shoulder, emcee Chip Monck announced, "Please welcome with us...the Band!"

At 10:30, as the Band appeared on the thirty-foot-high stage, Helm heard an "inhuman roar from the dark hillside. We looked at one another in disbelief. Garth was shaking his head. He started playing, and so did I. I played my cymbal, and he hit the bend pedal on the Lowrey organ, and we had a little duet until he slid into 'Chest Fever.' We were off." Once again, the sound from the venue's PA was not up to their rigorous standards. With Levon on mandolin and drums, plus vocals—they played mostly *Big Pink* numbers, ending with "The Weight." When called back for an encore, Danko sang "Loving You Is Sweeter Than Ever," while a sodden audience of more than 400,000 waved lit matches and lighters in the air.

"I remember hanging out backstage with Levon," David Clayton-Thomas says. "They had just done their set, and we had a chance to schmooze a little bit...He said, 'Who would ever believe it from the Le Coq d'Or, and right now we're the two biggest bands in the world'... We had a laugh about that. We talked about some of the characters we knew on Yonge Street, but then they hustled us out of there." As Helm

---

* The Woodstock Festival performances by the Band and Janis Joplin were not seen on film until the twenty-fifth-anniversary director's cut of the movie was released in 1994.

recollected, "We took off from backstage in a rented station wagon, pulled through the mud by a bulldozer with a short chain. It took off with us, got us through a field, over a couple of ditches, and then finally onto some hard road. It took us a couple of hours to get the fifty miles back to Woodstock."

TWO WEEKS LATER, the Band was slated to appear with Bob Dylan at Britain's second Isle of Wight Festival, from August 29 to 31. This, Dylan's first full-fledged performance since his motorcycle accident, generated unrealistic expectations. Levon, with Libby and the rest of the group, arrived a few days early to run over the setlist with Bob, who had rented a building on the island where they could rehearse, although Rick admitted the focus was more on socializing. George Harrison dropped in to see his favorite musicians, and John Lennon and Ringo Starr followed, bringing the soon-to-be-released *Abbey Road* for Dylan and the Band to hear. The next night, Bob and the group performed an impromptu acoustic set at a local inn.

Dylan and the Band were the headliners for Sunday evening, the closing day. After festival management caused a long delay, the Band went on at about 10:30 before a tired, frustrated audience and played a forty-five-minute set. After a short break, a slightly unnerved Dylan fronted the Band and performed for a further hour. Although Lennon called Bob's performance flat, Eric Clapton thought the two sets were magnificent.

A FEW WEEKS later, on September 22, 1969, the group's second album, *The Band*—also known as the Brown Album—was released to widespread acclaim. "Masterful" and "essential music," wrote Susan Lydon of *The New York Times*: "The stuff of their songs is the stuff of life: birth, death, families, earth, crops, love, weather, people, feelings… Like a perfectly cut gem, every time you turn it, it shows you something else." Lydon credited Helm's drumming as the glue that "holds the Band together through its weird syncopations and timing changes." The great lyricist Bernie Taupin described Levon's vocals as "birthed from the land from which he sprang. Rich as Arkansas soil and raw as a plug of tobacco, gnarly as knotted pine and so expressive it seemed like he was chewing on the words before they left his mouth." Overwhelmed, Jim Carroll in *Rolling Stone* proclaimed, "Levon Helm is the only drummer that can make you cry."

"*Abbey Road* captivates me as might be expected," stated the reviewer for the *Village Voice*, "but *The Band* is even better, an A-plus record if I've ever rated one." The LP wasn't able to nudge *Abbey Road* from its number-one spot on the *Billboard* album chart, yet it did peak at number 11 on the week of December 13. Although it was an iconic recording, *The Band* was not the group's best seller.

NEVERTHELESS, THE SONGWRITING credits that Helm believed he, Manuel, Danko, and Hudson were finally entitled to were largely absent. Levon was listed as co-writer on one number, "Jemima Surrender"—even there, Robertson alleged that Helm's input was minimal—Richard was named as co-writer on three, and no songs were ascribed to Garth or Rick. In stark contrast, Robertson was attributed as songwriter on all twelve numbers.

"A lot of those songs were Levon's stories, without a doubt," Danko revealed. "And as far as the music, yeah, it was very much a collaborative effort on those first two albums. So there was a little greed there on Robbie's part—a lot of greed, actually." Helm was of the same mind: "In spite of the fact that Garth, Rick, Richard, and I had contributed to the writing of the songs on those first two records, the credits on most of them simply read J.R. Robertson." For Levon, the question was "How do you ever figure out who wrote what when you got five guys spending every day with each other, all playing, all contributing ideas?"

Bill Avis lived at the Ashoka Reservoir house in 1969 with Richard and Garth, and saw everyone involved all aspects of songwriting, including the lyrics. C.W. Gatlin, who knew Levon since he was a teenager, says, "I've seen him write 'em, so I know. He's a writer." David Clayton-Thomas hung out with the group in Toronto and Woodstock, and claims, "Knowing the Band as I did, I know they were a collaborative bunch. Most of the early songs were written by the whole group as a unit...The Band that I knew—both in Woodstock and

Toronto—total collaborators. Everybody got in a room, and they hashed out the songs." Jeff Carter says his father, Fred Carter Jr., who'd played with the Hawks in 1959,

> was definitely in Levon's camp on that one. He felt like Robertson kind of appropriated the Southern heritage and Levon's experience and Levon's sayings and Levon's wisdom…[Levon] was real funny about the way he said things, the way he talked, and some of that stuff made it into these songs apparently, according to Dad…and [the other members of the Band] just kind of felt like, you know, that Robbie was the guy who wasn't partying with the rest of them, who was hanging real close with Grossman…And Dad—please understand, he wasn't one to go about badmouthing anybody—he didn't say a whole lot bad about Robbie, but it was very clear that he didn't like any part of that whole situation and thought Robbie had done Levon wrong for sure.

Robertson himself acknowledged, "Everybody contributed something, it wasn't like there were two guys doing everything and the other guys were along for the ride." Yet Jonathan Taplin, who was with the group while *The Band* was recorded, says, "Robbie wrote the songs. He got up every morning and worked on writing. I *saw* it. And it wasn't because he wanted to hog it; it was because nobody else was doing it…There was no need for this myth that they all got screwed by Robbie."

Happy Traum believes there's truth on both sides, but agrees that Robertson was the main composer and wordsmith:

> Levon once said to me…"Do you think that Richard or Rick or I never had any ideas or ever contributed in any way?" He said, "That's totally crazy. We were all doing it together"…I can't make a value judgment. It is hard to believe that on those songs, like "The Night They Drove Old Dixie Down," that Levon didn't have some direct hand in the way that came out…but then Robbie would say, "Well, they didn't take care of business. They were off playing when I was working."

Part of the controversy could be founded on a misunderstanding of what constitutes songwriting. In the legal sense, a songwriter provides lyrics and the basic melody. The arrangement of that song—which may include a distinctive instrumental lead or hook—does not constitute songwriting. Collaborating on a song does not necessarily mean songwriting, although it could. It depends on what the collaborator brings to the song. If it's lyrics or melody, that's songwriting. If it's part of the arrangement, then it's not.

Robertson points to the fact that he wrote songs even before he joined the Hawks. "I'm sorry," he says, "I just worked harder than anybody else…The guys were responsible for the arrangements, but that's what being a band is, that's your fucking job." While Robbie admits that "Levon and Rick and Richard contributed tremendously to the arrangements, and to the sound of those records, and there's no way to explain how important Garth was in terms of taking us to new places musically," he refused to budge regarding songwriting accreditation.

Robbie alleges that whenever he got together with Levon to work on composing, "Levon would groove along on drums or mandolin, but he was much more comfortable accompanying. Making up a tune made him restless and uneasy, so I didn't want to push it." Referring to those few songs that Helm was credited for co-writing, Robertson says, "He was there when I was writing them, and just because he was being supportive, I gave him credit on a couple of songs. He didn't write one note, one word, nothing."

Robertson maintains that he "begged the guys to get involved in the writing, because I was the one who was up all night banging my head against the wall trying to write this stuff. And just because someone's in the room when a song is being written that doesn't mean they helped write it."

"It's a collaborative effort," Levon insisted. "Now you could say that Robertson was sixty percent responsible for the lyric, that Richard was twenty percent and maybe Rick got another twenty, and I got five or ten, then you talk about the music. You could give Garth chord credits, but the people who handle that stuff don't work for Garth or Richard or me. They work for Robbie and Albert."

However, when Levon spoke of collaboration in the songwriting process, he was never explicit as to what that contribution was—actual songwriting or arranging. His contention appears to be that Robertson did do a lot of the songwriting, but that it was fragmentary. He would bring part of a song to the group, then as a unit, they finished it together. Levon said, "Richard did some good work, and I always thought that Garth and Rick and myself was there all the way, no matter whose idea the song was or if it was halfway there… Most of our stuff then got finished under that workshop kind of circumstance."

A songwriter automatically owns all the publishing rights to his or her song. Those rights can be split with a music-publishing company—which is responsible for collecting licensing income from radio play, performances, recordings of that song by other artists, etc.—but that is up to the discretion of the creator. According to Robertson, he elected to share his music-publishing income with the rest of the Band, although he had no legal obligation to do so.

Because publishing income is divided between the songwriter and those who own the publishing rights, if Robertson did share his publishing income with the rest of the group, he would have received his full portion as the songwriter plus his cut of the publishing. The rest of the Band would get only what Robertson decided to give them out of his part of the publishing, nothing from the songwriting. There is no indication how long Robertson's benevolence lasted, although in 1998, Levon complained that Robbie and Grossman took all the publishing income.

As the rest of the Band slowly came to realize that so much of their future earnings rested on songwriting credits, Levon said, "There was always a way to cover up or divert our attention from any unfairness or shortcoming." They were placated with the promise of a partnership with Grossman in his new Bearsville Studios, but it never materialized. In addition, Robertson and Grossman were making crucial business decisions without consulting the rest of the group. A sizeable portion of their publishing income was invested—and lost—in a fraudulent apartment-building deal in Aspen. "It was a display of smoke and mirrors that would have made Houdini jealous," Helm declared. "Call us naive if you want. Maybe we were just too damn trusting. We were a family, and if you can't trust your family, well, who can you trust?"

Levon blamed it on the suits—management and lawyers—who he insisted wanted to set one person up as the star and leave the others in the financial dust; it was simpler that way. To several observers, the leadership of the group had transitioned from Levon to Robbie. "I never thought I was the boss," Robertson contends. "I was just trying to organize things so we could do things like make records and go out and play a show somewhere. It was not a big controlling thing on my part."

Levon tried to caution Robbie about this divide-and-conquer strategy and appealed for more fairness in the division of the lucrative songwriting income, reminding Robertson that "the Band was supposed to be *partners*. Since we were teenagers we'd banded against everything and anyone that got in our way. Nothing else—pride, friends, even money—mattered...as much as the band did."

"He'll say he did it all, if you give him the opportunity," Rick said of Robbie. "It was a Band project. All of a sudden what team we had started heading down the wrong trail." Looking back, Levon lamented, "From the time that he joined the Hawks at fifteen, Robbie and I were as close as brothers. All that changed overnight. By the time our second album came out, I started to realize that something was terribly wrong."

NEVERTHELESS, THAT FALL of 1969, the Band set off on tour to support their new album, which earned them a gold record for sales of a half-million. They were now pulling in an average of twenty thousand dollars per show. But the exacting musical standards of the group were taking their toll. Regardless of his confident demeanor, Helm felt the pressure, and sometimes his temper exploded. He'd soothe the edge with downers, which fortunately seemed not to hinder his onstage performance.

The crowds were enthusiastic and the reviewers in awe. After their show at Washington, D.C.'s Constitution Hall, an elated Carl Bernstein wrote that in the Band's music the various American genres coalesced to "become a beautiful whole, a wondrously stunning, mature sound...Like the work of rural craftsmen, the Band's music is hewn from the rough, then honed and smoothed and polished until it glistens." He described Levon as "almost gentle on his drums, seeming to coax them with an antithesis of attack which has never been heard before in rock. It makes him the only drummer in the same league as jazz-man Max Roach."

The Band declined the opportunity to lip-synch on *The Glen Campbell Goodtime Hour*, but were excited to be booked on the venerable *Ed Sullivan Show*—a Sunday-evening TV staple for North America. Intimidated at the national exposure—and the lineup of stars that included Rodney Dangerfield, Buck Owens, and Pearl Bailey—Helm admitted to nervous insomnia. On November 3, Ed presented the Band as "the new recording sensation for youngsters," then Levon sang "Up on Cripple Creek" to rousing applause, although without voice monitors the musicians were unable hear themselves. Still, Sullivan gave them his stamp of approval by calling the group to the side of the stage, introducing them individually and expressing his delight in having them on his show. "Levon thought they were just going to filmed from the waist up," C.W. Gatlin says, "so he wore blue jeans. And Ed made him come out there and line up, and he kinda started a trend with that."

The Band ended the year with four sell-out concerts in two days at New York's Felt Forum at Madison Square Garden, and then in Hollywood, Florida, on December 29. For New Year's Eve, Levon relaxed with Libby in an upscale New Orleans hotel, then rented a Cadillac and drove to the area around Helena, where he showed her his childhood haunts and introduced her to his grandparents.

UNDER A HEADLINE that defined them as "The New Sound of Country Rock," the Band kicked off 1970 on the cover of *Time* magazine, the first North American band to receive that honor. In the feature article entitled "Down to Old Dixie and Back," Jay Cocks observed, "Significantly, the Band's music is quiet. They once played hard-driving, ear numbing rock. Now they deal in intricate, syncopated modal sound that, unlike most rock but like fine jazz, demands close attention and rewards it with a special exhilarating delight. When the Band plays it is not for a trip but a musical treat." Regarding Helm,

Cocks said, "[He] approaches his drums with what is, in rock music, unparalleled subtlety and restraint."

On the subject of songwriting, Robertson told Cocks, "There are five guys involved, and everybody has a little different thing. Like one guy in the group would remember very impressive horn lines by Cannonball Adderley. Somebody else would remember a singing harmony that J.E. Mainer and His Mountaineers did years ago."

The Band continued their tour, including five sold-out concerts in Toronto and the surrounding area that January. The *Toronto Daily Star* described their performance as being "perfect," with "breathtaking artistry" and an "astounding level of musicianship…You feel you could peel layer after layer from their music and still not touch the essence of its density. It is truly profound music." Despite the demands of the road, Robbie remarked—somewhat surprisingly as future events would reveal—"I don't think we'll ever want to give up concerts and do strictly records…It's important to play for *people*."

BY THE BEGINNING of 1970, Libby Titus and her four-year-old son, Ezra, were settling into Levon's Wittenberg house in Bearsville, on the edge of Woodstock. The boy came to think of Levon as his father and a playmate, saying, "It sounds silly, but when I was four, Levon and I liked the same things. He was, in many ways, as much a kid as I was, so we were best friends." Helm had an ATV that he'd drive into the woods, where he and Ezra would shoot off fireworks—bottle rockets and powerful M80s—agreeing to keep it a secret from Libby. When she was away, Levon would let their two dogs into the house, which for Ezra was like a celebration.

Helm's relationship with Libby could be strained. She had been living in a world of privilege in New York City, among the avant-garde intelligentsia and social elite; Levon was an unsophisticated, down-home Southern boy who'd barely scraped through high school. Titus found herself in a backwoods house that could have been transplanted from Arkansas—two dogs on the porch, a couple of broken-down cars on the lawn.

"They were oil and water," Jonathan Taplin says of the couple. "But there was obviously a sexual attraction there, and they were very funny together. Libby and Maria Muldaur both had the same sarcastic sense of humor and could drop the bon mot that would just devastate you." Anarchist actor and writer Peter Coyote comments that "Libby was like a cross between Joan Didion and Fran Drescher. She was gorgeous; she was louche; she was languorous. I don't know how she got Levon, because there could not have been two more disparate souls on the planet."

Yet, as Titus concedes, "I was obsessed with him, and I became very isolated. He felt very competitive around other men, so he wouldn't take his beautiful girlfriend to parties. All the signs were there in front of me, but I ignored them."

BY THE TIME the tour for *The Band* ended in March, the excesses that can come with immense fame were taking their toll. When their behavior, as well as their cars, veered out of control, Levon, Richard, and Rick were enabled by Woodstock police and judges, who looked the other way at their transgressions. "I always thought people treated us almost *too* nice," Helm later admitted.

The Band was under more scrutiny than any of them felt comfortable with. Harold Kudlets, their former booker, confirms that "the more famous they got, the more they shied away from publicity." The Band had no aspirations to be music idols. "I never wanted to be recognized on the street and mobbed," Levon maintained. "I like going to places without all that star stuff. I like applause when I'm out on the stage, but I like to leave after the show and go in a bar and enjoy the rest of my life."

They wanted to keep it simple, just about the music. "We ain't never played no fruit rock, no punk rock; we never wore dresses onstage," Helm said. "We didn't wear tight pants and big rings, we didn't puke onstage or throw TVs out the windows." At times they were criticized for playing more for themselves than their audiences. "There weren't any jokes in our show or introductions or long-winded conversations," Levon acknowledged. "It might have hurt the personality of the group a little bit, but it left a lot of room for more songs."

With their success, came more money than any of them had dreamed of. That prosperity brought hangers-on, trying to ingratiate themselves with the Band through drugs. Jonathan Taplin already considered Helm's use of downers a problem, but now Levon, Richard, and Rick were snorting heroin. With perverse seductiveness and degenerate glamour, smack was running rampant through the arts world. Among the sophisticates in their circle, Libby recalls that there were junkies who were so compelling—with stories of shooting heroin with William Burroughs—that it was tempting to follow their lifestyle. Peter Coyote confesses, "I'm afraid Emmett Grogan and I might have been the people that introduced Levon to heroin."

As opioids sucked him into a deep morass, Helm became apathetic. Robertson, who stayed relatively clean, found it difficult to get through to him: "It was almost as if it had become this experiment to see how close to the edge of the cliff you could drive without falling off." Ronnie Hawkins saw Levon's personality alter. "He laughed all the time; everything was funny," he said of Helm before narcotics took their toll. "He was like that until all the Band got on too many drugs and changed all their personalities…Drugs is what messed them up in the end."

9

"The Shape I'm In"

"When you've had two records and you still can't pay your bills… you get to figure something ain't quite right," Levon declared. Yet, despite feeling short-changed over songwriting income, he was never one to hold onto what money he did have. These were young men living the dream; they had few thoughts of socking away cash for lean times.

"They did get money, and they pissed a lot of money away," Bill Avis says. "Rick Danko—bless his sweet heart, rest in peace, brother… Rick decides to rent a house in Malibu…for probably two, three grand [a month]. It wasn't gonna last, so down the tube. Garth bought a big, beautiful spot up there…fire, no insurance, and he lost everything." Ronnie Hawkins agrees: "Levon started wasting so much money when they didn't work, when they were off. *Two* suites at a time. You know, just showing off, pickin' up the tab for everybody." Harold Kudlets said, "Levon Helm would tip five people before he even got to his hotel room."

It's been said that Helm could have a hundred thousand dollars first thing in the morning and be broke by nightfall. In a restaurant, he'd pick up the bill for people he hardly knew. Jeff Carter cites the recollections of his father, Fred Carter Jr.: "Apparently whenever they would book into a hotel, Levon liked to just order everything on the whole menu, and then when it got there, he might eat a bite off of each tray. Just order like five hundred dollars worth of food and maybe take six bites of it and then say, 'Eh, let 'em have it.'" Steve Thomson, Ronnie Hawkins's former manager, remembers one of Helm's credos:

"You gotta spend the money. It's called *current*-cy. You gotta keep it flowing."

Helm liked to spread his money around. "He was the type of guy who'd give you the shirt off his back," Kudlets said. "He was very good-hearted in a lot of ways. He was a typical Southerner." Bill Avis concurs: "If you asked Levon for a fiver, and he had it in his pocket, he'd give you ten…Levon was very generous."

Morse Gist once asked Helm if he still had the Martin guitar he'd bought from him as a youth:

> And he said, no, he wished he did, but he didn't. And what happened to it? Well, he was in New York, and there was a fellow musician, a girl, who hadn't had a gig in a long time and came to him, to his room one time, and said she's got a gig for a night… but she had pawned her guitar or something. Didn't have an instrument. Could she borrow Levon's guitar? And he said yeah. He loaned her that Martin—and never saw either of them again… He was a generous person, completely generous.

"If Levon had money, he would give you his last dime," Anna Lee says. "If he didn't have money…[and] he asked you, 'Can I borrow it?' he's going to pay you back. If he said, 'Let me have it,' you could kiss it goodbye. But money didn't mean anything to him. He couldn't care less if he did have it or he didn't have it. He was just happy. As long as he felt good and could make music he was happy. He didn't care if he had a dime or if he had a million."

NEVERTHELESS, LEVON—DESPITE his largesse—felt a sense of unfairness, that he'd been ripped off, and it was with this mindset that the Band's next album, *Stage Fright*, was recorded. It didn't come easily. A sense of unease had seeped in where before there was only a tight-knit bond of brotherhood. Helm said, "Our success brought us a lot of money and a lot of greed. By *Stage Fright*, the writing was on the wall. That was no collaboration. It was Robbie and his manager Albert Grossman and their accountants and lawyers versus the rest of the band." Danko agreed, noting, "Ego is a funny thing, and after the first two or three albums, the Band pretty much became a Robbie thing, so there was conflict there."

Richard was downing quarts of Grand Marnier a day, and Rick and Levon were taking too many drugs. Helm's heroin use caused him to fall asleep in the studio and at the wheel of his Corvette, wrecking it. Robbie said of the others' drug and alcohol abuse, "It started very early on—way before the *Stage Fright* sessions—and it never went away again. As a result, making records became very painful. These were, and are, very talented guys, and it was a joy to hear them when they were on their mark. But then, when you go into the studio and everyone's not really there for it, it bruises you in your soul." According to Levon, "We could have had the Last Waltz between *Stage Fright* and *Cahoots*. That's when all the bad stuff started to happen. We never had fist fights, but…we hardly ever sat down and wrote songs with each other again, after *The Band* album and about half of *Stage Fright*."

Robertson confronted Helm about using heroin, and when he denied it, Robbie felt betrayed. From his perspective, a darkness was inching into Levon's personality:

> We were like brothers. I thought Levon was amazing. I thought he was such a great guy. He was such an amazing musician. He had music just running through his veins. And he was…the closest thing I ever had to a real brother. Over time, drugs started to come between him and I, and I felt something come over him and I wasn't sure if it was the drugs—maybe it was a coincidence, I didn't know. But anyway, something happened and he grew quite bitter, and he grew bitter about all kinds of people around us…Because him and I were so close, I tried to set him free from this; I tried to relieve him from carrying this burden and this bitterness and this anger around with him, but it grew deeper.

Ronnie Hawkins put it succinctly: "They could have been the biggest band in the world…if it hadn't been for drugs…It ruined the best band in the world."

Stage Fright was intended to be a live-audience recording in the Woodstock Playhouse, then the town refused permission, afraid they'd be swamped by fans, so the Band recorded there alone. For this outing, they were their own producers and hired engineer Todd Rundgren, who brightened the Band sound. But he got off on the wrong foot with Levon, especially when he called Garth "old man," and Helm, always a redneck and a staunch defender of Honey Hudson, knew how to nurse a grudge.

These tracks are looser, more experimental and less worked-out than those of the previous two Band albums—possibly because they produced the recordings themselves without John Simon's guidance, or maybe due to their loss of unity. From Levon's point of view, Robbie was steering the band in a direction that only he wanted to go. Without another member taking up that role, however, all that remained was resentment.

Robertson insists he tried to cajole the other musicians into participating in songwriting to little avail. Richard had almost stopped composing, and on this LP he would get only two co-writing credits. As a result of the collaborative process breaking down, Robbie was listed as either sole writer or co-writer for every song on the album.

"Strawberry Wine" was only the second Band co-writing credit that Levon shared with Robbie. It was a song he'd started during a recent trip to Arkansas. "I loved the idea that he was willing to try and do some writing," Robertson says. "On the other songs, he was there when I was writing these songs, and I really wanted to be encouraging for him to try and to participate in the songwriting. I just loved the feeling of him participating in that, and I was being a little naive in the idea that some people write and some people don't." Sounding like a rural rascal, Levon sings lead and plays rhythm guitar with Richard on drums in this Cajun-laced track.

Helm reclaims the drum stool for "Sleeping," a delicate, languorous waltz that shifts from minimum drumming in the verses to amping up the dynamics in the chorus through a driving, energetic beat with Levon's trademark rolls. He plays rhythm guitar again for "Time to Kill," weaving his swinging guitar parts underneath and through Robbie's solo, while Richard moves back behind the drum kit. "Just Another Whistle Stop" showcases Helm's drags through time signature changes. He transitions from a basic to a funky shuffle on the ride, then moves into a quarter-note shuffle. Levon's lead vocals on the ballad "All La Glory" portray a sense of vulnerable intimacy as he plays an eighth-note groove—likely using blast sticks—with a deadened snare drum while providing some interesting syncopation with the bass drum.

"The Shape I'm In" features three distinct drum parts. Levon plays a quarter-note groove with the ride cymbal, he switches to half-time where he orchestrates the toms, and he doubles up and goes into an eighth-note groove with quarter-note backbeats. It was this track that led a *Rolling Stone* reviewer to anoint Helm as "the best drummer in rock and roll."

Although it's solely credited to Robertson, "The W.S. Walcott Medicine Show"* is Helm's childhood memory. He sings lead, his Southern drawl giving the track added credibility. His drumming seems random here as he playfully intersperses parts on the ride and hi-hat with drags, all in an eighth-note groove. *Rolling Stone* raved, "*God,* what a great singer, what down-home locution…Levon is *cooking*—though he makes it sound as easy as shuffling a deck of cards."

"Daniel and the Sacred Harp" is like a beckoning to a country-church social with interplaying vocal harmonies that are largely missing from the rest of this album. Levon plays twelve-string acoustic guitar as he shares lead vocals with Richard, who's on drums. Helm kicks off "Stage Fright" with syncopation on the cymbal and kick drum, but he's not at the top of his game. The LP—a brief thirty-six minutes long—ends with "The Rumor," featuring vocal interplay between Levon and Rick. Helm is feeling free now as he breaks away from his usual groove and drags to swing out and play jazzy figures on the ride.

Stage Fright was released in August 1970, and was the most successful Band album in terms of sales, reaching number 5 on the *Billboard* album chart and achieving gold status, even though the reviews were lukewarm. The Band toured the South and Midwest to support the album through the fall of the year. Diamond sometimes joined his son on the road, at one point asking to be their tour manager.

---

* The correct name of the tent show was F. S. Walcott, but it was changed for the song in order to better fit with the lyrics.

THE BAND'S FOURTH album, *Cahoots*, was recorded at Albert Grossman's new Bearsville Studio in Woodstock beginning early the following year. The strains within the Band remained—substance abuse and rancor had not abated—plus there were technical challenges with the brand-new facility. Robertson felt the pressure of constantly trying to cajole the group into performing at their best. Whereas the lyrics of *The Band* album carried the listener back in time, Robbie's theme for *Cahoots* was looking back with despair at a vanishing past. Perhaps the same could be said of the Band itself.

In Rick's view, Richard and Levon seemed inattentive, only willing to contribute by rote. Members showed up sporadically as their parts were recorded, no longer creating as a cohesive unit. Robbie knew it wasn't their best work.

Nevertheless, "Life Is a Carnival," the first song on *Cahoots*, is rock solid, a staple of future setlists. It was credited to Danko, Helm, and Robertson, and Levon explained the creative process: "That was one of the tunes that we put together from a pattern that Rick and I came up with, between the bass and the drums down on the bottom. And we stacked the other stuff in on top." He adds an interesting dimension to the drum parts, implying the beat is backwards. He plays the back-beat with the tom on beat one and the snare on beat three; the downbeat is played with the kick drum on beats two and four.

"I wanted to get a different rhythmic feel in the choruses," Robbie remarks, "and Rick jumped right in and started to play along. Levon got behind the drums and worked on an unusual pattern to go along with my guitar and vocal. There was no getting around the fact that when we made music, sparks flew." Jimmy Karstein maintains, "That beat that Levon came up with on 'Life Is a Carnival'…that's one of his major contributions." Later, however, Robertson discounted Helm's input by saying, "He was just there when I was writing that."

For "Life Is a Carnival," the venerable New Orleans musician, songwriter, producer, and arranger Allen Toussaint was called in to compose the horn charts. With Big Easy flair, the horns veer off in separate directions, Dixieland style, which suits the theme of a free-wheeling carny, while Levon and Rick belt out the lyrics with a joyful swagger.

Bob Dylan's "When I Paint My Masterpiece" begins as a fade-in, with Garth on accordion and Levon playing mandolin, to set the continental mood of an artist in Rome. Helm's lead vocals sound unabashedly American with the naive bravado of a visitor in unfamiliar territory. In "The Last of the Blacksmiths," he varies his quarter-note groove with the hi-hat, ride, and cowbell on top of kick-drum syncopation. The polyrhythm of "Where Do We Go from Here?" is different for the Band, and Helm has fun playing odd-numbered groups of three, similar to progressive rock.

In "4% Pantomime," fellow Woodstock resident Van Morrison trades vocals with Richard while Levon plays a shuffle with triplet variations on the ride. He plays a quarter-note groove on "Shootout in Chinatown" and "The Moon Struck One," the latter at a challengingly slow pace. While Danko sings lead on "Thinkin' Out Loud," Helm switches to bass guitar. Levon sings lead again on "Smoke Signal" and plays a syncopated kick drum with quarter-note backbeats.

Helm has fun with "Volcano," swinging quarter-, eighth-, and sixteenth-note grooves. His wistful, crystalline vocals in "The River Hymn"—accompanied by Richard, Rick, and Libby—evoke images of a choir at the County Line Church in Turkey Scratch. His freewheeling eighth-note drum groove has the feel of a waltz.

With *Cahoots* in the can, the Band began a European tour that May, with several concerts in Germany, then Vienna, Paris, Copenhagen, Stockholm, London, and Amsterdam. The album was released in September 1971, with a dark, cheerless cover portraying the group behind a sarcophagus. *Rolling Stone* recognized that this wasn't the masterpiece of *The Band*, although it noted, "The Band is one of the few functioning units in rock worthy of the name *auteurs*. As such, their mistakes and failures are more interesting to me than the successes of dozens of lesser artists. And their triumphs, including the ones on the latest album, are among the most interesting things in rock altogether." It peaked at number 21 on *Billboard*'s album chart.

LEVON HAD BEEN led to believe that the Band would be in partnership with Grossman in his Bearsville Studios. "That's how dumb I was, right?" he said. "I could see myself with my own key and never having to break those drums down…'Course it didn't work out that a-way." Helm wasn't satisfied with the sound in that concrete-and-steel studio anyway. He had something else in mind.

"Levon and I used to drive around the Woodstock area here, looking for property," says Garth, recalling when they first started making money from *Music from Big Pink*. "We would be talking about the design, with the home studio in mind. It was pretty well set in his mind what his building would be, even back then." Levon bought eighteen wooded acres with a creek at 160 Plochmann Lane for about twelve hundred dollars. Consulting with his good friend Woodstock stonemason Ralph Shultis, they determined that a post-and-beam barn would have the best acoustics. Helm, who was highly knowledge-able about construction and architecture, described how the combination studio/home came about:

> We did a regular barn shape, pretty much standard procedure. 'Course, there ain't no more chestnut, and oak is a little expensive, so we went with hemlock timbers, used those big ten-by-ten hemlocks…About the only thing different that we done was put a big double porch across the back. Then we hooked another smaller barn on one end to make a little apartment…and on the other end we hung a truck shed, and upstairs there's a control room space. Got heat in '73.

But it was a slow process; the construction proceeded in fits and starts as album money and performance fees came in. "For years it was one of those white-elephant places," Levon said. "My dad once came up and saw the place, and I told him it was going to be a great studio one day. He said, 'Lee, you're tryin' to cut too big a hog with too l'il a knife.'"

IN THE SUMMER of 1971, the Band performed some dates in the northeast U.S. and into Canada. They went out again in November to support *Cahoots* and also as a warm-up for a live album they had planned for the next month. After their concert at the Civic Auditorium in San Francisco, in which Levon sang "When I Paint My

Masterpiece," the review in the *Los Angeles Times* read, "Helm's lead vocal, which brings out every ounce of feeling (and then some) that Bob Dylan put into the song, is not only one of his best vocals, but one of the finest I've ever heard in rock." Also that month, Elton John and Bernie Taupin's song "Levon" was released. Although it's not about Levon Helm, they acknowledged that he was their inspiration.

WITH CAPITOL EXPECTING another record, the Band decided to try again for a live-concert LP, this time in New York City's Academy of Music on the last four days of the year. Named *Rock of Ages*, the double album became Levon's favorite Band record. To add a different twist to the second half of each show, a horn section was added, and they called on Allen Toussaint once more to write the horn parts.

Howard Johnson, who'd focused mainly on jazz, played baritone sax, tuba, and euphonium in these concerts. He'd never met the Band: "I didn't know what to expect, you know. I talked to some of the guys in the Band, and when [Levon] came over and introduced himself, I heard that deep South accent, it gave me pause." As a black man from Alabama, he wondered if Helm had any racial hang ups. "It took very little time of actually talking to him to realize this guy was as much of a brother as you could want."

Johnson came to respect Helm's expertise as a drummer. He says, "Well, you know, I didn't really notice it at first and then pretty soon—after I heard a couple of other bands—it was like, 'Whoa, this guy's really heavy.' It's hard for anybody to even describe what about it is so compelling, but it is. Everybody recognizes that he's got a *big beat*, as they used to say." Howard points out that on technical issues, Robertson seemed to take control; for everything else, all members had an equal voice.

"Without horns, [Levon] told me, there was something missing, you know," Johnson reveals. "He wasn't so gung-ho about it at first, but when he heard it actually in a live situation, he got a conversion." Remembering those nights taping *Rock of Ages*, Helm stressed how much he enjoyed it: "That was a lot of fun. I love horns, and the bigger the band, the better it sounds to my ear."

Over eight shows in four days, December 28 to December 31, the

Band laid down some stellar tracks. Variations were made from their original recordings to accommodate the horns, and Helm played his crash cymbal, which he hadn't done in the studio. The enthusiasm and electricity of the audiences affected the musicians. "You can hear that excitement," Levon said, contrasting the live experience to one in a relatively insular recording studio. "It comes out in the music—the excitement that the crowd brings to the equation."

Rock of Ages wouldn't be released until August 1972. It was a definite improvement over *Cahoots* sales and reached number 6 on *Billboard*'s album chart.

NINETEEN SEVENTY-TWO HAS been called a lost year for the Band. They performed no concerts; each member had his own focus apart from the group. Robbie and his wife moved to Montreal, Rick was dealing with divorce, Garth was building a house, and Richard's drinking and drugging were frightening amid marital difficulties and more crashed cars. For Levon, it was an opportunity to get his life back in order.

Libby had given birth to Helm's daughter, Amy, two years before, and for Levon, she was miraculous. When he was on the road, he'd call Libby and have her hold the baby up to the phone just so he could hear her breathe. He had Amy to think of now.

Bill Avis was frank with his friend, saying, "'You know the path you're leading is not good.' [Levon said,] 'I know that, Bizz. I'm going to get straight.' And he did. I think he did it just cold turkey. He started drinking a hell of a lot of Coca-Cola." Levon went to Springdale to stay with his parents while he detoxed.

Helm wasn't satisfied with his drumming. Being exposed to the prodigious talent of Allen Toussaint at the *Rock of Ages* shows inspired him to want to know more about drumming technique and the rudiments of music. "[I] wanted to be able to do something about what I heard in my mind," he said. "To play what I was thinking. Timing is what it's all about. Split-second timing. You get that down, you're set."

And to achieve that, he went back to school. He moved to Boston with Libby, Ezra, and Amy, and spent one semester at the Berklee School of Music, registering as Mark Helm in an attempt to be incognito. It was a rewarding time for Helm. He enjoyed the city and its architecture, and he lived close to the eminent economist John Kenneth Galbraith and master chef Julia Child. "That winter was great," Libby says. "Levon was the greatest father, couldn't wait for Amy to wake up in the morning. He even read some books."

Back in Woodstock, Helm set out to instill his love of driving in six-year-old Ezra, sitting the boy in his lap so he could steer. One time, however, when Levon was concentrating on rolling a joint, Ezra smashed into a rock on the side of the road. "I listened as my stepfather told my mother over the phone that he'd wrecked the Corvette," Ezra wrote. "My mother wasn't surprised until Levon added, '…and Ezra was driving.' Then, I could hear every word she screamed into the phone from all the way across the room." Two years later, Levon taught Ezra to drive a standard.

WITH COLLABORATION A distant memory, Levon said of their next album, *Moondog Matinee*, "That was the best that we could come up with…We couldn't get along—we all knew that fairness was a bunch of shit. We all knew we were getting screwed, so we couldn't sit down and create no more music." He continued: "We knew what the score was by then. Everybody had come to realize that ugly word *publishing*, and we didn't have any of it…And the Band, for the music part of it, had pretty much busted up already. We did live things, and we did old ones and good ones, but we never collaborated with each other and wrote songs like we did for the first three records."

Tipping their hats to the R&B and blues that they loved, the Band cut only covers for this LP, recorded at Bearsville and in Los Angeles in 1973. Helm's rowdy vocals kick off the album with the boisterous rocker "Ain't Got No Home"—at one point singing through a hose— as he plays rhythm guitar while Billy Mundi, former member of the Mothers of Invention, mans the drums. Levon's voice stokes the engine of "Mystery Train," as Mundi and Manuel team up on drums, and Helm plays bass. His vocals smoke as he rocks out on Chuck Berry's "Promised Land" and "I'm Ready" by Fats Domino. "Saved"—with all the vibe of a revival meeting—is bolstered by Levon's supersonic train beat with cymbal shots, and on bass he backs Richard's plaintive showstopper "A Change Is Gonna Come." That October, *Moondog Matinee* was released to disappointing sales.

IT TOOK A hundred-thousand-dollar payday to lure the Band back to performing live after a hiatus of nineteen months. The Summer Jam at Watkins Glen was held on July 28, 1973, at a racetrack near the southern tip of Seneca Lake in Upstate New York. It was a day-long event with only three acts—the Band was slotted between the Grateful Dead and the Allman Brothers. It was expected that 150,000 fans would come, but 600,000 showed up, a new concert attendance record.

"That was a good show—that was a good time!" Levon exclaimed. Contrasting it with the Woodstock Festival, he said, "It was just mellow and easy and healthy—it was over in a day; that might have had something to do with it." But like Woodstock, the rains came. The Band's set was interrupted by a downpour, then—fueled by a swig of Glenfiddich—Garth retook the stage, launching into "The Genetic Method," and as if on cue, the skies cleared. On July 31 and August 1, the Band opened for the Grateful Dead at Jersey City's Roosevelt Stadium.

ROBERTSON FOLLOWED DYLAN out to Malibu in September 1973, and soon the others also relocated there. Helm recognized that the focus of the music industry had shifted to Los Angeles, so he rented a house near Malibu—owned by Robert Wagner and Natalie Wood—for Libby and the kids, and for himself, a suite at the Miramar Hotel in Santa Monica. Levon moved between the two residences in L.A. and his barn construction in Woodstock.

Libby and Amy flew out west, while Levon drove with Ezra, entertaining the boy with funny stories and with his fantasies about building the barn. "Levon loved to dream," Ezra remembered, "and I loved dreaming with him. Today, it seems magical to me that he actually did build that tremendous barn-house with a large lake, the home of the Midnight Rambles."

AFTER PAYING A huge penalty, the Band were now free from their management deal with Albert Grossman, and David Geffen at Asylum

Records suggested that Dylan—who'd been off the road for eight years—reunite with the Band for another tour. After the positive experience of Watkins Glen, the group was open to performing again, and they had *Moondog Matinee* to promote. While they rehearsed for these upcoming shows, Bob and the Band took time out to record *Planet Waves*.

Planet Waves was a Bob Dylan album with the Band in a backup role. It was recorded quickly at the beginning of November at Village Recorder Studio A in West Los Angeles. Because Levon was still in transit from a trip out East, he missed the first session that produced "Never Say Goodbye." Two versions of the classic "Forever Young" were recorded, the second with Helm on mandolin. Levon later commented that it was one of his favorite songs.

The Dylan/Band extravaganza—dubbed Tour '74—began in Chicago on January 3 and covered twenty-one cities across North America with forty concerts, ending in Los Angeles on February 14. *Time* magazine proclaimed, "Never in the history of American rock has a tour aroused so much public interest." The tickets were sold by mail order, with twelve million requests for 658,000 seats.

Here was a chance to stick it to the traditionalists who'd booed Dylan and the Hawks in their previous tour. This time they were received as champions. The world had come around, and the accolades felt good. "Between 1965 and 1974, times had changed," Danko said. "People were totally behind us…That was one of the most incredible tours. It was first class all the way. I've never done anything so extravagant in my life." Helm kept his feet on the ground, confessing, "I had to give Rick a lecture…I had to go back and talk to Rick about there's big stars and there's little stars, and we're little stars."

Earning about five million dollars, it was the highest grossing rock tour up to that point with all the attendant decadence. A lot of the profits were squandered on unsuccessful investments and excessive indulgences. Dylan and the Band traveled in a private forty-seat jet called *Starship One*, which had been refitted with private compartments. Cocaine was in vogue and readily available, as were willing women. Richard had the crew take Polaroids of aspiring groupies so none but the finest were permitted backstage. Only occasionally were wives and girlfriends allowed to attend. From Libby's perspective, "It was all so sad and pathetic."

Greil Marcus reported that Helm "played like a star…It was the authority of Levon's beat that let Dylan, Robbie, and Garth Hudson sing and play with a freedom that with any less of a foundation would have seemed merely personal; with Levon there it was still personal, and also shared, sympathetic, dependent—onstage and out in front of it." Paul Berry saw the last three shows in L.A. "It was different every time," he says. "It was one of the most thrilling musical experiences I've ever had…It was startling." Backstage, he had to walk through a series of rooms until he finally reached the inner sanctum where Ringo was declaring to Levon, "You're the most laid-back son of a bitch I've ever heard." The live album of the tour—*Before the Flood*—was recorded mainly from the final concerts in Los Angeles.

Helm was ambivalent, claiming on one occasion that the tour left him feeling less than excited. Conversely, he also said, "That was real satisfying for me—that was the first time we had ever been able to play with Bob and get a round of applause…All of a sudden it was a new dawn—a new light…It was fun to travel along with everybody and put that show on every night. All I had to do was play drums and do my part, so I was really enjoying it."

After the last concert, Bill Graham threw a party at the Beverly Wilshire Hotel: "Bill had set aside a room for the offspring of all these lunatics," Libby remembers with disgust. "The wives who'd been cheated on, the kids who were destined to be scarred."

THE BAND RETURNED to Malibu, but the veneer of super-stardom was wearing thin. After such exorbitance, real life could only be anticlimactic. Tour excesses had strained relationships. Richard was suicidal. Money was squandered without thought for the future. Levon and Libby were arguing and taking too many drugs. By that spring, they were spending more and more time apart. Finally they split, leaving Helm a part-time dad to Amy and Ezra.

According to Bill Avis, Libby and Levon had disagreements over how much time Levon could spend with their child. As Amy got older,

Helm asked to take her to Arkansas to visit his parents, but it was difficult for him to get permission.

Levon wanted Amy to be exposed to music, without forcing it, and took her to the studio with him whenever he could. "He wanted to make sure I knew who Muddy Waters was and Ray Charles and to hear the stuff you have to hear to round out your musical education," Amy says. "Levon was just salt-of-the-earth, right from the soil of Arkansas," Maria Muldaur observed. "While people like Libby were floating around putting on airs, he'd bring Ezra and Amy over to play with [my daughter] Jenni." Ezra remarked that when he was older, "[Levon] often said that Amy and I saved his life, as being responsible for us forced him to take better care of himself and remain relatively sober."

Helm enjoyed his time with the kids, taking them out for sushi—where he'd twirl his chopsticks like drumsticks—and having as much fun at Disneyland, Magic Mountain, or Knott's Berry Farm as the children, loving roller coasters and cotton candy. Levon had a special affinity for the aerial tram ride at Disneyland, which seemed monotonous to the children. It wasn't until they were older that they realized it was the only safe place in the park where their father could smoke a joint.

LEVON PLAYED DRUMS on "See the Sky About to Rain" and—joined by Neil Young, David Crosby, and Rick Danko—on "Revolution Blues" for Neil Young's *On the Beach* album, recorded in spring 1974. These sessions were notable for more than music and the debilitating, ever-present "honey slides," a pot-laced treat cooked up by guitarist Rusty Kershaw and his wife.

It was during this time that Helm was introduced to his future wife, twenty-six-year-old Sandra Dodd. Raised in Virginia, Sandy attended college in Florida, then was living in Lake Tahoe when she went to Los Angeles with some friends who were acquainted with Kershaw. Levon first saw the beautiful brunette in the swimming pool at West Hollywood's Sunset Marquis hotel and took her out for sushi. They kept in touch, even after she moved back to Virginia.

THE BAND HIT the road again that spring for a few dates, but the tour was cut short when Richard collapsed, incapacitated from substance abuse. Meanwhile, aiming to regain the camaraderie that they had at Big Pink, as well as a place to compose and record, the Band rented Shangri-La, a defunct bordello—complete with a bungalow that was the former stable of TV's talking horse, Mr. Ed—near Zuma Beach, California. They began converting the master bedroom into a twenty-four-track recording studio, while in the bungalow, Richard was drinking and drugging to an alarming extent. There was a bedroom in the house for Helm when he wanted to stay, and the rest of the group had homes nearby.

Beginning in July, the Band played in Orchard Park, New York, and in Pittsburgh with Eric Clapton, then set off throughout the U.S. and up to Vancouver and Toronto to support their *Moondog Matinee* album. Most dates were with the reunion tour of Crosby, Stills, Nash and Young, which also included Jesse Colin Young and at times, Santana, the Beach Boys, and the Elvin Bishop Band. It was another rock extravaganza fueled by copious amounts of money, drugs, and sex— what David Crosby called the Doom Tour. It came to a close on September 14 at London's Wembley Stadium with Joni Mitchell sharing the bill.

Bill Graham, the producer of the tour, had hired Dayton Stratton, from Fayetteville, as head of security. Stratton, who had been Ronnie Hawkins's good friend and partner in various clubs, had by this time become very close with Helm and assisted him in financial matters as significant money started rolling in. His son Randy recalls, "Levon was very confident in trusting my dad's business savvy and helping him get more out of what he had earned with the Band. Dad really stepped in and helped Levon with his financial advice because he really cared…My dad just felt strongly about keeping an eye on making sure nobody took advantage of him."

Helm had had some trouble with the IRS, so Dayton suggested they set up a corporation as a tax shelter. Stratton had his pilot's license and a Cessna airplane, and together with Levon, they formed a company called Daylee, a combination of both their names. Just before the summer 1974 tour began, they bought a twin-engine, eight-passenger

Beechcraft Bonanza. Dayton ran it primarily as part of his entertainment business—a way to get him and his production people to shows he was promoting—while Helm remained purely an investor. Because Stratton wanted to upgrade his license to an instrument rating, he flew the Beechcraft whenever he could.

After the CSNY tour played Tampa, Dayton returned to Fayetteville to deal with various business affairs. On August 27, he flew the Beechcraft to Fort Smith, Arkansas, to get some blueprints for his construction firm, taking three passengers with him—Gregg Jeko, Richard Belke, and Gene Hopkins. On the way back, Stratton tried to navigate around a thundercloud, but lightning slammed into the plane, blasting it apart. All onboard were killed. Dayton was forty-two.

"Life changed instantly," says Randy, who was preparing to go back to college for his sophomore year. He had to quit school, learn his father's music-entertainment business, and try to keep it afloat. For Levon, it was a devastating blow, the loss of a valued friend and advisor. He went to Fayetteville for the funeral and tried to support Randy:

> Levon flew me out to California right after my dad's accident for a birthday present…It was kind of before we knew all the hard feelings that were setting in. Robbie was nice, and he was kind of quiet, you know…Danko was a hoot; he was always a good guy. We went to see Garth at his place up in the canyon. Garth was always kind of a deep thinker. We visited him, and of course Richard too. They were all super-nice guys. They felt bad about my dad dying—having his accident—and helped me keep my spirits up, that kind of thing. It was nice of Levon to do that, for sure. He knew I had challenges ahead of me…Levon helped me a lot [to learn the music business], took me under his wing to show me the ropes…
>
> Those kind of experiences with him, I'll always appreciate. The guy really went out of his way to try to help me work through the tragedy. If that's what I wanted to do in life, to stay in music, he'd try to help me out as much as he could…He was one of a kind.
>
> We just had a lot of good times together. He did teach me

never to get star-struck…Levon was so down-to-earth, you know. It was easy to just feel like one of the guys.

A HIGHLIGHT OF Helm's career took place in early 1975 with the recording of *The Muddy Waters Woodstock Album*. Levon had kept in touch with Henry Glover, who'd produced some of the early Roulette records for Ronnie Hawkins and the Hawks, and now that Glover was in semi-retirement, he and Helm formed a company called RCO, for Our Company. Their first project was to record Levon's blues hero, Muddy Waters.

"I would give Henry Glover the credit for most of it," said Levon, who produced the album with Henry, "and…the next thing you know, a dream had certainly come true. You know, I'm down at the airport picking up Muddy and Bob Margolin and Pinetop [Perkins], man, and we're goin' to Woodstock in a hurry! It was fantastic."

Levon joined Muddy, Bob, and Pinetop on drums and bass, while other musicians included Garth, Howard Johnson, Fred Carter, and Paul Butterfield. The album was cut in the chestnut-timbered barn at Turtle Creek, part of the Bearsville Studio complex on February 6 and 7, 1975. It was recorded live in the studio to try to recreate the fabled Chess sound of the 1950s. "After we made sure [Muddy] had a big Neumann microphone to sing in, so we had his voice covered," Helm recollected, "then everybody just got right in his lap nearly. I got up real close with the drums so that I could really hear his guitar and everything and hear his voice and try my best to play with him. And it just made it a whole lotta fun to get up that close and, you know, tie right in to what he was pulling off."

Muddy decided to stray slightly from his deep-blues repertoire, although he did choose numbers that he often performed live.

> It kind of came off as a show unto itself, you know, [Levon said,] and we played it that way. We ended up playing some of those good show tunes by Louis Jordan and just things you would want to hear the Muddy Waters Woodstock Band play, just some of those songs, blues standards. At the same time, I wasn't disappointed because when you listen to "Fox Squirrel" and some of the

*Twelfth Grade
Mr. Personality*

LAVON HELM

Miss Personality

KAY COOKE

Twelfth-grade Mr. and
Miss Personality, Levon with
Kay Cooke, 1958

BEST DANCERS
Jimmie Lee Harpole and
Lavon Helm

Best Dancers in twelfth grade, Levon and
Jimmie Lee Harpole, who danced onstage
with the Jungle Bush Beaters, 1958

MOST TALENTED
Anne Holland and
Lavon Helm

LAVON HELM
"Wisdom, power, and "Goodness
Meet."
FFA 1, 2, 4; Band 1, 3, 4; Football 1;
Basketball 1, 2, 4; Class Officer 1, 2,
3, 4; Junior Play 3; Mr. Mustang
Candidate 1; Boys' State 3;
Commercial Club 3; Mr. Personal-
ity 2, 4; 4-H Club 1, 2, 3, 4, Pres-
ident 2, 3, 4; Who's Who 4.

Levon and Anne Holland, elected as
Most Talented, twelfth grade, 1958

Levon's graduation photo, 1958

All images on this page Marvell High School yearbook, courtesy of Ben Story

Levon's parents, Nell and
Diamond Helm

Playing in Ronnie Hawkins's band,
late 1950s

Ad for the Hawks at
Dayton Stratton's
Shamrock Club,
Fayetteville,
November 1959

A FULL WEEKEND OF ENTERTAINMENT
at the SHAMROCK

Friday Night
Ronnie Hawkins Band

f e a t u r i n g

LeVon Helm

from 8 til 12

Saturday Night
E M C E E S

8 til 12

Springdale High School prom: the Hawks with fan Shirley Overton (from left: Rebel Paine, Ronnie Hawkins, Shirley, Robbie Robertson, Stan Szelest, Levon), 1961

The Hawks perform at the Brass Rail, London, Ontario
(from left: Rick Danko, Richard Manuel at the piano, Ronnie Hawkins,
Levon, Robbie Robertson, Garth Hudson), early 1960s

Levon and the Hawks at Tony Mart's in Somers Point, New Jersey
(from left: Rick, Richard, Levon, Bill Avis, Garth, Robbie), 1965

Tony Mart's club

The Band at Big Pink, West Saugerties, New York (from left: Garth, Levon, Richard, Robbie, Rick), Easter Sunday 1968

Recording *The Band* album at Sammy Davis Jr.'s house, Los Angeles (from left: Rick, Richard, Garth, Robbie, Levon), 1969

Photo by Michael Friedman

First performance as the Band, Capitol Records executive meeting, Miami
(from left: Rick, Robbie, Levon), 1969

Photo by John Scheele

Levon and Rick performing at the Woodstock Festival, August 17, 1969

Courtesy of the Pryor Center for Arkansas Oral and Visual History, University of Arkansas

Levon with his mother, Nell, and his maternal
grandfather, Wheeler Wilson

Photo by Jack Clark

Levon and his mother, Nell

The Band playing at Felt Forum, Madison Square Garden, New York (from left: Richard, Garth, Rick, Robbie, Levon), December 1969

Photo by Michael Friedman

Robbie, Levon, and Richard during the recording sessions for *Stage Fright*, 1970

Levon and Bob Dylan performing at the Academy of Music, New York, for the *Rock of Ages* album, December 1971

In front of Levon's barn construction during the recording of *The Muddy Waters Woodstock Album* (from left: Henry Glover; Marvin Schlacter, president of Chess Records; Scott Cameron, Muddy Waters's manager; Muddy Waters; Levon), February 1975

The Cate Brothers Band with Levon (from left: Albert Singleton, Terry Cagle, Levon, agent and promoter Randy Stratton, Earl Cate, Ernie Cate), War Memorial Stadium, Little Rock, Arkansas, July 31, 1976

Bob Dylan joins the Band at the Last Waltz (from left: Richard, Rick, Bob Dylan, Robbie, Garth, Levon), November 25, 1976

Gary Fong / San Francisco Chronicle / Polaris

The finale of the Last Waltz (from left: Neil Diamond, Dr. John, Garth, Joni Mitchell, Neil Young, Rick, Van Morrison, Ringo Starr, Bob Dylan, Ronnie Hawkins, Robbie, Levon), November 25, 1976

Photo courtesy of Randy Stratton

Levon (left) with Ronnie Hawkins and Dr. John gathering at Shangri-La to record the album *Levon Helm and the RCO All-Stars*, 1977

Levon and Henry Glover rehearsing songs for the upcoming
RCO All-Stars album and tour, 1977

The reunited Band (from left: Levon, Richard, Rick, Garth), 1983

AF Archive / Alamy Stock Photo

Levon in his role as Ted Webb, father of Sissy Spacek's character, Loretta Lynn, in *Coal Miner's Daughter*, 1980

Levon as Jack Ridley, U.S. Air Force test pilot and aeronautical engineer, in *The Right Stuff*, filmed in 1982

Entertainment Pictures / Alamy Stock Photo

Levon (left) on the set of the 1987 movie *End of the Line* with Levon's nephew and stand-in double, Terry Cagle

Courtesy of the Pryor Center for Arkansas Oral and Visual History, University of Arkansas

On Ringo Starr's All-Starr Tour (front row: Jim Keltner, Levon, Nils Lofgren; middle row: Dr. John, Ringo Starr, Joe Walsh; back row: Clarence Clemons, Billy Preston, Rick Danko), 1989

Levon with wife, Sandy, and road manager Butch Dener at the Woodstock '94 festival

Keith Richards recording "Deuce and a Quarter" with Levon at Levon's barn/studio for the album *All the King's Men*, July 9, 1996

The Barn Burners
(from left: Pat O'Shea, Levon,
Amy Helm, Chris O'Leary,
Frank Ingrao), 2000

Bill Avis, Levon, and
Jerome Avis getting
together after a
Midnight Ramble, 2005

The Midnight Ramble Band
(from left: Amy Helm, Teresa
Williams, Larry Campbell,
Levon), December 16, 2006

other deeper things and heavier things that Muddy pulled on the album, I get real satisfied with it.

And the way that the melody line—the horn spaces—the way that Butterfield and Garth with the accordion played the harmonica and the accordion as a section almost. And it really did sound good, a real country kind of a horn section sound to it…

Muddy Waters certainly called the shots as to what we wanted to do, and at the same time, gave us a whole lotta freedom on how we wanted to do it, and just let everybody have a good time. It really did happen like you would want a dream come true to happen. It was just that much fun.

Although he had grown up revering Muddy's music and had seen him perform over the years, Helm hadn't met the great bluesman until they were brought together for these sessions. He had high expectations, but Muddy was "better than I had hoped, more of a gentleman. It made you tighten up a little to be around Muddy!" he said with a chuckle. "We'd sit down and eat and have a hell of a good time, laugh and talk and go on, you know." Levon was delighted by Muddy's sense of humor:

That's what made it so much fun. We got to eat supper with him for about two nights down at a restaurant down in Woodstock there, and boy that was fun. You know between him and Butterfield and Henry Glover and everybody else, there was a lot of laughs going on…We spent most of our free time eating and laughing and talking. We never would get very serious, unless we were playing…I hung out with him every minute that I could, without just bringing him down and making a nuisance of myself. I hope I didn't do that, but I sure did enjoy.

Levon arranged a parting tribute to the blues icon. That Valentine's Day, two hundred residents came out as the mayor declared it Muddy Waters Day in Woodstock and presented him with the key to the town. It brought a tear to Muddy's eye, and it was an immensely proud moment for Helm. For the rest of his life, he kept a photo on his kitchen wall of himself, Muddy, and Butterfield on that very special day.

The following year, *The Muddy Waters Woodstock Album* won the Grammy Award for Best Ethnic or Traditional Recording.

10

Out of Step with the Last Waltz

"If it hadn't been for Levon," Earl Cate says, "we probably never woulda went in the directions we did go or get…some of the breaks." When the Band was still with Albert Grossman, Helm arranged for him to call the Cates to discuss a possible management deal. Later, Levon took their demo out to Los Angeles and got it to the right people. Consequently, in 1975, Earl and Ernie signed with Asylum Records. The result was their first album, *The Cate Brothers*, which included their hit "Union Man."

Levon, always a big supporter of the Cates, hoped to produce it, but due to scheduling issues, he passed that task over to Steve Cropper and contributed on one song. When the Cate Brothers performed at a major show at Little Rock's Memorial Stadium, Helm and Danko came down to cheer them on. "Levon was that kind of guy," Randy Stratton states. "He wanted other people to do well. He was loyal to people."

Throughout his life, through ups and downs, Levon stayed in close touch with his friends and relatives. "Levon's top priority were his parents, of course," Stratton continues. "He was real fond of all his siblings, and then his nieces, nephews, the whole family. When he'd come home, they'd have a gathering of family members, and he really enjoyed that. Modena was kind of the one that would get everything organized with family for him. They'd have their get-together and always invite me like I was one of the family."

Growing up, Jerome Avis knew that when the phone rang after midnight, it was Levon calling his father, Bill. Helm would phone his nephew Terry Cagle, "and you never knew what time of the night it might be," he adds with a smile. Helm cherished his friendship with Mary Vaiden, as well as Sister. "He adored [Sister], and she adored him," Mary says. "He was very kind and sweet to her. She was handicapped, but he always made sure that Sister…got to go to everything, and when he was home, he went to see her. He would take her for a ride in the car." He'd sometimes phone Anna Lee two or three times a week just to reminisce with what she describes as "a memory like an elephant."

John Donabie, who worked at radio station CKFH when he first met Levon in 1969 at the Toronto Pop Festival, says,

> If you had a relationship [with Levon] going way back, then it just never stopped…He was quite a character. I love him; I just love him. And it's his kindness, I think, and the way he treated my children…[He was] unbelievably thoughtful…If you couldn't do anything for him anymore, it didn't matter. He just treated you as such a good friend…I could be a ditch-digger, and if I was at those clubs in the early days and we struck up a friendship, I'd be on a list to get invited somewhere. He didn't care what you did. Just the fact that you were loyal and that you were a friend…He loved seeing people from bygone days. He would always look at me and say, "John, stay on the good foot." That was his saying, meaning "good health."

NEVERTHELESS, HELM'S RELATIONSHIP with Band management was increasingly frustrating. Substantial money was rolling in, and he believed the financial schemes proposed to the group were too risky. His influential business friends in Arkansas knew of more reliable investments, yet Levon's suggestions were ignored. To separate himself from a difficult situation, he kept his barn in Woodstock and commuted to Shangri-La when necessary.

In March 1975, Levon, Garth, and Rick played at the largest rock benefit concert to date, organized by Bill Graham to support SNACK—Students Need Athletics, Culture, and Kicks—to raise money for extracurricular activities in San Francisco schools. Sixty thousand fans at Kezar Stadium enjoyed the Grateful Dead, Tower of Power, Santana, the Doobie Brothers, Jefferson Starship, Joan Baez, and the highlight of the day—surprise guest Bob Dylan joined by the three Band members plus bassist Tim Drummond, Ben Keith on pedal steel, and Neil Young playing guitar and piano.

Helm spent as much time in Arkansas as he could, taking Amy and Ezra to Springdale to visit Nell and Diamond. Anna Lee recalls Levon coming to Marvell for a school reunion. He was a day late, but most people remained in town to catch up. He invited Anna Lee's daughter and niece to stay at the hotel with him, Amy, and Ezra, and pampered the kids for a couple of days with room service and breakfasts in bed.

In Woodstock, Ezra said, "Sometimes I'd tell Levon I wasn't in a good enough mood to attend school. He'd usually agree and say; 'I don't see why they need to have you down there every goddam single day!'…Once the school bus had passed by our house, my mood would improve considerably. I'd hear Levon say to my mom, 'Honey, Ezra's had a miraculous recovery and now we got some important business to attend to in town'…Then we'd cruise around in Levon's Jeep and see what there was to see."

THE BAND OWED Capitol another album, but as with Helm, the rest of the Band had turned their focus elsewhere, and it took most of 1975 to record it. The tracks were cut at Shangri-La, and for the first time on a Band LP, all songwriting was credited to Robertson, and most of the vocals were overdubbed. The production quality of this album is improved, and one can clearly appreciate Helm's masterful ghost-note technique on the snare.

A tasty drum lick kicks off the album with "Forbidden Fruit," the lyrics encapsulating Robbie's frustration with the Band's substance abuse issues. Ironically, it's Levon's evangelizing vocals that preach the message. Richard, Rick, and Levon trade verses in the sumptuous "Acadian Driftwood" as Helm lays down the feel through ghost notes and syncopation. He plays his drums at the top of the beat with a funky kick-drum in "Ring Your Bell," then switches mood entirely with a laid-back, behind-the-beat lope for "It Makes No Difference" as he harmonizes behind Rick's tearful voice. In "Jupiter Hollow," Helm delivers some feisty vocals while, surprisingly, both he and Manuel play drums along with a drum machine.

A standout on this album is "Ophelia," a song that would be part of Levon's repertoire for most of his remaining years. His yearning cry of loss is supported by a bouncing beat with cool shots. While he sings, he scales back his sixteenth-note, bass-drum syncopation, but ramps up the patterns elsewhere to underlie the guitar and horn instrumentals. For David Clayton-Thomas, this song epitomizes Levon's strengths. "Go back and listen to 'Ophelia,' the way Levon recorded it," he says. "It's so real, so genuine. There's no artifice about his singing or his drumming. It's just right in the pocket. Every musician understands that. I think it reflects the man's personality."

Northern Lights–Southern Cross was released in November 1975, and although it garnered generally positive reviews—hailing it as the Band's comeback record—it climbed to only number 26 on *Billboard*'s album chart. "Twilight" was appended as a bonus track in the 2001 reissue of the album. "I hate to say this," Danko revealed, "but it's as much of a Rick Danko song as it is a Robbie Robertson song. I just forgot to seek [credit]. Robbie was very tight with sharing those responsibilities. That's why he's where he is, and that's why we are where we are."

THE FOLLOWING YEAR the tension had still not abated. Eric Clapton noticed it among the group when he recorded his album *No Reason to Cry* at Shangri-La in March 1976, which included all Band members. "It took us coming in there to get them all in the studio with one another," Clapton comments, "because there was a lot of bitching."

It was not until June 26 that the Band start touring to support *Northern Lights–Southern Cross*, soon followed by the release of *The Best of the Band*. Starting in Stanford, California, and extending across the U.S. with one date in Toronto, their shows were hit and miss, largely depending on Richard's condition. His alcohol and drug use, paired with a split from his wife, left him unable to sing some nights, and against the others' wishes, he insisted that former Band girlfriend Cathy Smith join the tour to take care of him. Partway during the run, the Band added a horn section.

Critics were mixed in their evaluation of the Band's performances, some writing unrestrained raves and others concerned that the group was relying too heavily on their earlier hits. Charlie McCollum called the Band's July 16 concert in Washington, D.C., "backward-looking," noting that

> it is disturbing that this set has remained the same for over five full years. No matter how brilliantly The Band does "The Weight" or "W.S. Walcott's Medicine Show," one has to wonder why it has chosen to remain so solidly in the past, to the point of including only two songs—"Ophelia," "It Makes No Difference"—from its latest album. It smacks of a group hanging onto past artistic achievements and past glories, as if to let go and stretch out would somehow destabilize its musical existence.

During their stop at Lake Austin, Texas, in early September, Richard, who had previously hurt his neck in a drunk-driving accident in Woodstock, reinjured it in a speedboat mishap when a wave threw him backwards. Manuel, in extreme pain, was told it was fractured. Doctors advised he go into traction for six weeks, effectively canceling the rest of the tour. A group of Tibetan monks was called in as a last-ditch effort, and Richard's condition miraculously improved enough that he was able to resume performing with a few days' rest.

After their Nashville show on September 25—one of the best rock concerts one reviewer had ever seen—the audience responded with almost no applause, and the Band left the stage without an encore. Robertson was despondent. "As the Band's ace guitarist Robbie Robertson walks past me on his way down the stage steps," Jon Marlowe wrote, "he stops for a few seconds and says to me: 'Ya know, it's nights like this that sometimes make me wonder what the hell I'm doing out on the damn road in a rock 'n' roll band."

INCREASINGLY, BAND MEMBERS were drawn to individual projects outside the group. They turned down Warner Bros.' six-million-dollar offer to record an album a year. Danko had signed with Arista Records to do a solo album and concerts, and Helm was collaborating with Henry Glover to come up with new ventures for RCO. Robertson produced Neil Diamond's successful comeback album, *Beautiful Noise*, which was released that summer, and he was working on two screenplays.

Suddenly, Robbie called a halt to touring. He claimed that the road had started to frighten him. "I was no angel during that period," he admits, "but, to put it really bluntly, I was just more scared than they were—I didn't have the balls to try everything that they were willing to try. It was almost as if it had become this experiment to see how close to the edge of the cliff you could drive without falling off."

At first, Levon passed it off as a joke, then protested to Robbie, saying, "I'm not in it for my health. I'm a musician, and I wanna live the way I do…It's a crying shame to take this band from productivity to retirement because you're superstitious, or for the sake of a final payday." But the decision was irrevocable. And it had been made without him.

Even though it was a unilateral choice, Robertson spun it to the press as if it were unanimous: "When we first thought about not touring anymore," he told *The Toronto Star*, "we decided to make sure we were making the right decision. We consulted every source we could think of—business sources, the supernatural, just about everything. And they all pointed to the same thing…It all pointed to our need to stop…We all feel pretty good about our decision to stop touring."

However, without going on the road, the Band no longer had the cohesion to stay together. Robertson had effectively signaled its termination. There was no incentive to even record. "Playing is part of my life—it's therapy," Danko said. "It wasn't me who said I was going to stop playing." Helm, who'd started with the Hawks nineteen years before, had a similar view: "I wanted to keep what we already had—a good rock 'n' roll band. One that could cut the mustard and be in the running for the best band award, or hell, something great. I still dreamed of recording a record that would almost equal the great ones I had worshipped all my lifetime. I wanted to try and satisfy that musical hunger that haunts you when you love it so much."

Howard Johnson, who was part of the horn section in that summer tour, recalls Levon's reaction when the decision came down: "He wasn't happy about it. He let it show that he wasn't happy about it. He'd be asking why it was happening." From Levon's point of view, Robbie and management had railroaded the rest of the group into a decision they weren't ready to make. "The Band never really had a chance," Helm said. "The Band was so surrounded by mismanagement and unethical behavior on different parts, that the Band only lasted as long as it did, about three records' worth of time, and it sort of got killed off."

Robertson's plan was that the Band's final concert—which he called the Last Waltz—be held on Thanksgiving evening, November 25, at San Francisco's Winterland Ballroom, where the Band had made its premiere in 1969. An album of the show was planned, and Robbie—with an eye to future Hollywood projects for himself—got Martin Scorsese onboard to film the event. Robertson immersed himself in the preparations without much input from the rest of the Band.

Their tour continued throughout September and ended in Oakland on October 3. Soon after, a single of Richard singing "Georgia on My Mind"—the Band's way of showing support for Jimmy Carter's presidential bid—with "The Night They Drove Old Dixie Down" on the flip was released but failed to chart.

The Band's penultimate appearance was in New York on *Saturday Night Live* on October 30, with Henry Gibson as the host and Chevy Chase ending his run as a cast member. Backstage the Band felt jittery, an excuse for Richard to snort heroin. A doctor administered a shot to counteract the effects, yet Manuel was not in good shape. They performed "Life Is a Carnival," "The Night They Drove Old Dixie Down," "Stage Fright," and "Georgia on My Mind."

LEVON CALLED IT "the last lie" and "the last rip-off." For Paul Berry, "The Last Waltz was the public execution of the Band."

"By the time the Last Waltz came up," Helm said, "it was no secret our collaboration and—I felt—that the quality of our music had suffered. I didn't hear us getting better. I heard us, you know, doing albums with old songs that we liked, as opposed to getting in and really trying to grow a fresh crop of songs. And so I certainly didn't want to end the Band. The Last Waltz, you know, didn't set right with me."

Jonathan Taplin saw it differently: "Levon was very cooperative…
I think anybody who pretends that there was a lot of anger at that time
is wrong. That all came later." Yet Happy Traum remembers that Helm
"did not want the Band to break up. He thought the Last Waltz was
not a good idea…I know Levon was not happy about that." Helm
invited Randy Stratton to join him in L.A. for the rehearsals. "The
other guys didn't want to break up," Stratton says. "It was kind of
dropped in their lap with not much notice." John Donabie, whom
Levon asked to the rehearsals and the concert, remarks, "He was not
happy at all…He said, 'John, I'm just really not ready for this to come
to an end, but Robbie wants to go off and do his own thing, and he's
ready to pull out'…He said, 'I guess I don't have any choice'…He was
disappointed because he loved the Band. He loved the music they
made."

The musical guests for the Last Waltz included Ronnie Hawkins,
Muddy Waters, Dr. John (Mac Rebennack), Bobby Charles, Eric
Clapton, Paul Butterfield, Neil Young, Joni Mitchell, Van Morrison,
Bob Dylan, and Neil Diamond. The latter inclusion completely mys-
tified Helm, but it was due to Robertson's producing Diamond's latest
album. The horn section, led by Howard Johnson, comprised James
Gordon, Tom Malone, Rich Cooper, Jerry Hey, and Charlie Keagle.
Larry Packer played violin, and John Simon was the musical director.

The inclusion of Muddy Waters was crucial to Levon. "That started
off to be the main thing to, you know, present as many of the heroes
as we could," he said. "Muddy knew early on that we certainly wanted
him to be in the show with us." When it appeared that the guest list
was too long, and it was suggested that Muddy be cut, that was a bridge
too far for Helm. If Muddy was leaving, Levon announced, he was
too. Ronnie Hawkins admits, "I don't think I'd have been in the Last
Waltz if it hadn't been for Levon. He was the one responsible for getting me and Muddy Waters." The Hawk went out early for rehearsals
in L.A. so he could watch the big stars review their numbers while he
roomed with Helm at a Santa Monica hotel to save on expenses.

It was an onerous job for the Band to learn more than twenty new
songs during two weeks of rehearsals at Shangri-La in order to back
their guests. When the run-throughs were finished, the Band laid

down the final tracks for their last album for Capitol, entitled *Islands*, then Levon drove up to San Francisco in a motorhome with Amy and Ezra for the big event. The Band stayed at San Francisco's Miyako Hotel, not far from Winterland. When Helm had to be out, Bill Avis took care of the kids.

The dress rehearsal at Winterland was twelve hours long. The night before the Last Waltz, Bill Graham threw a party for all the musicians involved. They got onstage, but played different instruments, with Dr. John on guitar and Eric Clapton on drums. "He wasn't that strong on drums," the Hawk says of Clapton, "but he wanted to play 'em."

A phenomenal two hundred thousand dollars was spent to decorate the auditorium and provide Thanksgiving dinner for five thousand attendees, each paying a then-astronomical admission fee of twenty-five dollars. Adorned with chandeliers and red velvet draperies from the opera sets for *La Traviata*, Winterland was transformed, bestowing on it an ambience of faded splendor. Diners feasted on 220 turkeys, 300 pounds of Nova Scotia salmon (contributed by Bob Dylan), vegetables, rolls, apple juice, and pies at long tables covered in white linen, embellished with candles and flowers. A thirty-eight-piece orchestra played Viennese waltzes during the meal, while dancers swirled around the floor.

Backstage, the guests were provided with another kind of bounty. Bill Graham had set up a cocaine room, painted white, with a white rug on the floor, a glass table and all the paraphernalia a serious partygoer would need.

The main event began in the darkened hall, with Levon's greeting— "Good evenin'"—as the Band launched into "Up on Cripple Creek." Helm sang with exuberance, his drumming masterful. Of his drum work that night, *Classic Drummer* reported, "It represents one of the finest individual performances ever captured on film, a virtual lesson on how to play with other musicians in any context."

Levon wondered at Robbie's odd onstage behavior. He wasn't concentrating on his guitar parts, leaning instead into the microphone, pretending to sing through a mic that was usually turned off. "After the show," Helm said, "it became obvious what had happened: As we tried to play the best concert of our lives, it was picture-taking time for Scorsese and Robertson…Now our group was being portrayed as Robbie Robertson and his back-up musicians. Years of history and hard work were corrupted in one fell swoop."

Without a break following their set, the Band brought out their guests. A star-struck Ronnie Hawkins paid tribute to the Band's genesis as the Hawks, followed by Dr. John, Bobby Charles, then Paul Butterfield performing "Mystery Train" in a duet with Levon. But for Helm, the highlight was Muddy Waters. His inclusion was a way to pay tribute to an icon, to acknowledge Muddy as a wellspring for contemporary music.

After a tentative start with "Caledonia," Muddy separated the man from the boys. If there'd ever been a doubt about his right to be there, he dispelled that with his rendition of "Mannish Boy." Accompanied by the Band, Paul Butterfield, Bob Margolin, and Pinetop Perkins, Muddy proclaimed his manhood before a crowd of believers. Robertson stated the obvious: "Wasn't that a *man*—Muddy Waters!"

Helm would have liked to have seen more of Muddy both in the concert and in the final movie. "I'm kinda disappointed because of the shortness of time that the camera is on Muddy," he confessed. "I could have personally took another song or two myself; a couple or three songs wouldn't have been too much for me." Nevertheless, he felt privileged to share the stage with Muddy. "He was just a master musician," Levon said. "When you did get to play with Muddy, it was a short ride, right. You know, you were so into it…that it was over way too quick."

Eric Clapton followed, then Neil Young—showing powdery traces of his backstage indulgence—and Joni Mitchell. Next came what *The New York Times* described as "the very Las Vegasy Neil Diamond…so jarring and unwelcome that the movie takes minutes to recover." Van Morrison soothed the audience with a lullaby then resurrected it with a rousing version of "Caravan." The Band performed "Acadian Driftwood" with Joni Mitchell and Neil Young singing backup, then finally left the stage for a break. Levon's hands were bleeding; they were all exhausted.

After an interlude of poetry readings, the Band retook the stage for "Chest Fever," "The Last Waltz," and "The Weight." Then Bob Dylan joined them for "Baby, Let Me Follow You Down," "Hazel," "I Don't Believe You," and then for the movie cameras, "Forever Young" and another version of "Baby, Let Me Follow You Down." Ronnie Wood and Ringo Starr joined the reassembled guests for "I Shall Be Released." As the musicians left the stage and the audience stood for what they thought was a final ovation, Levon and Ringo remained, breaking into a funky rhythmic jam. As other players, plus Stephen Stills and bassist Carl Radle, drifted back, they performed two long improvised instrumentals. It was after 2:00 a.m. when the Band, coaxed onstage again by the stamping, cheering crowd, played "Don't Do It." Then after almost five hours, the Last Waltz—and the Band—was over.

OTHER THAN THE two thousand dollars an overwhelmed Bill Graham gave each Band member, they didn't get paid. Bill Avis recollects that when Muddy Waters went to get his fee, he was told, "Sorry, we'll send it to you."

> Well, [Muddy] didn't have any money, so [he went] up to Levon's suite…He says, "Levon, I need to talk to you. They won't pay me."
> Levon says, "Bullshit!" That's where the redneck came out. He said, "Bizz, I'll be back. Look after the kids. Come on, Muddy." Took him down to the pay room and said, "You'll pay that son of a bitch right now or the shit's going to hit the fan." And they paid him…But a lot of them didn't get paid because the money was ate up.

Then there weren't enough cars to take Muddy and his band to the airport. Helm arranged for them to be driven in Don Tyson's limo, "so those fuckers that worked for us wouldn't try anything stupid," he declared, "like telling Muddy Waters he had to wait."

Looking back on the event as a summation of the Band, Levon said, "I'd like to think we never put out any real dogs, and that our children will see that we never joined up, that we got in some good licks and played some music that'll be remembered."

The next morning, he took Amy and Ezra to FAO Schwarz and

told them they could pick out any toy they wanted. As Helm put it, "That's how we celebrated the end of the Last Waltz."

BACK IN SHANGRI-LA months later, Scorsese interviewed the Band for the film. To many the musicians came across as apathetic and unemotional—at that point perhaps their fans cared more about their demise than they did. Helm was reluctant to participate. Robertson, looking dissipated, spoke of the hardships of the road, to which Levon said, "That's a bunch of crap. That was Robbie being theatrical and being directed." When they were told to report to the studio to overdub their parts for the album and movie soundtrack, Helm was so disgusted he refused. His drums and vocals are the only original recordings from the show.

Afterwards, to acknowledge the Band's country and gospel influences, which were missing from the movie footage, the Staple Singers joined the Band at MGM Studios in Culver City to cut another version of "The Weight." Levon invited his mother, Terry Cagle, and Terry's wife to the filming. The Staples had been a major influence on the Band's harmonies, and now Levon and Rick shared vocals with the gospel soul of Mavis and Pops. "He was such a beautiful, beautiful spirit. Singing 'The Weight' now, my mind goes straight to Levon," Mavis remarks. "He was always like a brother to us. Levon is the only person in the world that I heard call Pops by his real name—Roebuck! I am reminded of *The Last Waltz* often, as people always mention it to me how I whispered 'Beautiful' at the end [of 'The Weight']. His mother, Nell, was at the taping, and so it always felt like family, same as us."

Emmylou Harris and the Band sang "Evangeline," with Levon on mandolin, Rick playing fiddle, Hudson on accordion, and Richard at the drums. Then the Band closed with "The Last Waltz Suite." Levon said, "That day, it really was over. We done led the horse to the barn and took off the saddle."

Yet even at that filming, Terry recalls his uncle being upset about the songwriting credits. By this time, though, Helm was concentrating on other things: his new music projects and his growing relationship with Sandy Dodd, who had moved in with him at the Miramar Hotel.

When Libby found out, Levon was served with child-support papers, and a custody battle ensued.

"WE WERE JUST trying to get out of a contract," Robertson admitted. "We were not in an album mode." Not the best attitude for recording, but in order to comply with their Capitol contract and move on to Warner Brothers for the release of *The Last Waltz*, the Band had to come up with another album—and that was *Islands*. Perhaps their most unsubstantial LP, it was not released until March 1977, when the Band no longer toured, one factor in its being their poorest selling recording, reaching only number 64 on the *Billboard* chart.

Islands largely comprises previously unreleased material that didn't make it onto the Band's earlier albums—the song by the same name comes off as merely filler. Levon plays bass for the funky "Street Walker," but otherwise stays on drums. He romps through the shuffles "Knockin' Lost John" and "The Saga of Pepote Rouge," and his high-spirited vocals shine on the bluesy rocker "Ain't That a Lot of Love." He sings "Livin' in a Dream" with brash optimism, enhancing his vocals with zesty fills.

Although Robertson is listed as the dominant songwriter on *Islands*, it's notable that Danko—first out of the gate with a solo recording, *Rick Danko*, in 1977—provided proof that he was also a lyricist and composer, either writing or co-writing every song on his own album.

THE BAND'S FINAL farewell to the public came in spring 1978 with the release of *The Last Waltz* three-LP set—which reached number 16 on the *Billboard* chart—and the accompanying movie. "The film was more or less shoved down our throats, too, and we went along with it," Levon acknowledged. "Do it, puke, and get out." Robbie grabbed top billing in the film, perhaps because he worked with Scorsese to produce it—reportedly in a cocaine-induced binge. Helm said of Robertson, "He wanted to show that he was the leader of the Band, and that's what that movie's about…If I'd had all the lawyers and accountants working for me, then I'd have been the star of that movie. But I'll tell you what, I'd have had some shots of Richard

Manuel in it. Man, you should have seen what got pushed out of that movie to make room for Robbie taking credit for all the things he never done."

Although most reviews were enthusiastic, Levon wasn't the only one who noticed the unbalanced focus. A reviewer for *Film Quarterly* wrote,

> The movie's real subject is not The Band as a whole, but Robbie Robertson. The film represents a highly crafted and complex exercise in image-making. There is ample filmic evidence to suggest that Robertson influenced Scorsese's construction of the film in order to establish himself as a star within the Hollywood community and launch his post-Band career...The guitarist's dominance goes far beyond the amount of camera time allotted to him, however, because virtually every visual and thematic aspect of *The Last Waltz* is designed to showcase his talents at the expense of the other members of the group.

In *Film Comment,* the reaction was much the same:

> Robertson is shot lovingly by Scorsese, as the most devotional object in a film that's about devotional objects. Robertson has been described in several reviews as having the aura of stardom about him, but I have a feeling that this has a great deal more to do with the way he's shot, the way Scorsese makes the dissipation written all over Robertson's face seem symbolic of the ravages of the apocryphal time on the road, than with any innate quality. Robertson's everywhere, though: introducing the various celebrities as they come on-stage, dominating the interviews so severely that he rarely lets anyone (except Helm) finish a sentence. To me, this made him obnoxious—The Band has always pushed community as the most transcendent value in its music—but maybe I'm just old-fashioned.

"I saw exactly what I was afraid of," Helm concluded. "Scorsese and Robertson had fallen in love with each other and with all the money they were going to make." Even though Richard struggled through the performance, Levon said, "I really resent the way Richard Manuel was portrayed in *The Last Waltz* as a crazed, burned-out drunk. You'd never know from watching the movie that Richard, who has been compared to Ray Charles and Bobby 'Blue' Bland, was the lead singer of the Band, and was responsible for our most moving songs."

Despite the venom Helm directed toward Robertson and Scorsese, it wasn't mutual. Scorsese says that watching Levon sing "The Night They Drove Old Dixie Down" was one of the high points of the film. "Levon's touch was so delicate, so deft," he comments, "that he gave you more than just a beat—he gave the music a pulse…Levon was a gentleman, a consummate artist…and he loved music as deeply and truly as anyone I've ever met. I consider myself fortunate to have worked with Levon."

The entire Last Waltz project had been presented to Levon, Rick, Richard, and Garth as a vehicle to preserve their legacy and provide future financial security. "I've never gotten a check for it in my life," was Helm's response. "It was Robertson and Scorsese and that fucking crowd of thieves that got paid, and they still get paid, I guess." Comparing the Band to black blues artists who were cheated out of their royalties by unscrupulous record executives, Levon observed, "You thought us being white maybe we didn't get fucked as bad? Hey, let me tell you something, son. A nigger's a nigger to these motherfuckers. It got nothing to do with color." Decades after the film was released, nothing had changed. "I'm a patient man," Levon said, "but it's been almost thirty years and Garth and I are still waiting for our 'financial security' to materialize. The sad thing is there's no more waiting for Rick and Richard."

Robertson alleges that neither he nor Scorsese received any compensation either. Helm's assumption was that the cocaine budget for the duo ate up a good portion of the bottom line. Or as Bill Avis puts it: "Snort…That's where all the money went."

11

Restoring the Rhythm

Levon had a new band to showcase—the RCO All-Stars—when he appeared as a guest on *Saturday Night Live* on March 19, 1977. He wasted little time opening this new chapter of his life following the acrimony of the Last Waltz and had assembled an astonishing array of musical talent. By that spring, the recording studio in Helm's barn was completed, and he was ready for a new adventure.

The RCO All-Stars was a band of superstars within the music industry that, nevertheless, many in the public had never heard of. Immensely talented, but often relegated to a backing role, these musicians lacked the egos of many frontmen. It was an aggregation of friends who had all been raised along the Mississippi River, and their music reflected it. Booker T. Jones, Steve Cropper, and Donald "Duck" Dunn signed on from the MGs. Dr. John played keyboards along with Booker T., former Hawk Fred Carter Jr. joined Cropper on guitar, and Paul Butterfield sang and blew harmonica. Levon also enlisted members of the *Saturday Night Live* horn section—Lou Marini, Alan Rubin, Tom Malone, and Howard Johnson, the latter two who'd also played at the Last Waltz.

At first, the producers of *Saturday Night Live* told Fred Carter to take off his cowboy hat during the show. Helm stepped up and in typical fashion announced, "Well, if he doesn't go on with that hat, *I'm* not going on." Carter wore his hat. The RCO All-Stars performed two covers, Ben E. King's "Sing Sing Sing," and "Ain't That a Lot of Love," the Homer Banks song that appeared on *Islands*.

Cathy Smith had moved to Woodstock and claims that she'd

rekindled a relationship with Levon. In her opinion, Helm was smoking too much Thai weed, the result of the pressure he felt in starting a new band in the overwhelming shadow of the previous one. The band baby was never mentioned.

That summer and into the fall, the group recorded *Levon Helm and the RCO All-Stars* for ABC Records at Helm's barn studio and at Shangri-La under the supervision of Henry Glover. In the California sessions, Levon enlisted Garth and, surprisingly, Robbie to play on "Sing Sing Sing."

Levon was back to having fun with his music. "I had as good a time with that project as I've ever had," he said. "And of course, we had Henry Glover there, who was our main guidance system." As Howard Johnson and Levon were only a year apart in age, they grew closer as friends.

The album was a bluesy, countrified, R&B-infused celebration of all that the band members brought to it—many of the songs written by them. Helm and Glover wrote "Blues So Bad," which was later recorded by Maria Muldaur. "Milk Cow Boogie" is an example of how Levon played a shuffle against a straight eighth-note groove, an influence from Earl Palmer. "If you can equal them out," Levon said, "that's the sweet spot to be."

Levon was at the top of his game, both as a singer and drummer. Although not all reviews were positive, one critic in praising the album, exclaimed, "The music is nothing short of breathtaking. Helm handled all the lead vocals, and the overall feeling is one of listening to a bunch of old friends, who happen to each be the best at what he does, having one hell of a time together." The *Down Beat* review read,

> Without being stodgy or sermonic, it's an album about the possibilities of the blues, its derivations and variations, and it's an album about friendship…These men make a mature music, warm and subdued, and a bit overly meticulous…Even more delightful [than Levon's vocals] is Levon's drumming, as resilient and inflective as his best work with the Band. In his hands, "Havana Moon" and "Milk Cow Boogie" shuffle and skitter with a sway that can be described only as sexy.

That summer, Levon, Paul Butterfield, Dr. John, and David Sanborn on sax performed an incendiary version of "Slow Down" for the BBC show *The Old Grey Whistle Test*. Then on August 31, Helm held the First Annual RCO/ABC Picnic and Rodeo at his barn. The RCO musicians attended, along with the ABC Records people and a large press contingent from New York City. Opening the musical entertainment with "Wild Thing" was six-year-old Amy on vocals, accompanied by Ezra playing guitar. Steve Cropper, Duck Dunn, Fred Carter, and Dr. John took the stage at dusk, joined by Ronnie Hawkins. The evening concluded with fireworks. Levon had a dynamite album; the band was booked on a fifty-date tour—it seemed that a dream was coming true.

Unfortunately, it wasn't to be. In Howard Johnson's judgment, ABC Records didn't appreciate what they had, so Levon didn't get the support he needed. Although the LP sold almost a quarter-million copies, Helm had hoped for more. "I'd like for it to go faster and bigger, and for these guys to get the recognition they deserve," he said of the All-Stars musicians, many of whom worked mostly as session players. "They played on more gold records than all the rest of 'em put together."

Levon had a serious health scare while at Shangri-La, landing him in L.A.'s Cedar Sinai Hospital, causing major problems for the rollout of the album and the subsequent tour. "Kidney stones, bladder, prostatitis, all that stuff down there," he disclosed. "A case of runnin' at it too hard."

Almost all fifty tour dates had to be cancelled, resulting in serious financial losses for Helm and Glover. One show that was saved was New Year's Eve 1977 at New York's Palladium, formerly named the Academy of Music when the Band performed *Rock of Ages* there.

The New York Times reviewer was disappointed, and called the performance dispirited, finding the choice of songs too uniform, and their delivery lacking interest and excitement, which he blamed partly on the absence of Booker T. Jones and partly on Levon's recent illness. The concert was recorded yet not released until 2006 as *Levon Helm and the RCO All-Stars Live at the Palladium NYC New Year's Eve 1977*.

After the concert, Levon declared, "As far as I'm concerned, we're going to play forever." But John Belushi had other ideas. He loved Helm's lineup so much that a year later, he hired five of the All-Stars for his Blues Brothers Band.

The All-Stars played a concert in New Orleans during Mardi Gras and opened some shows for Neil Young's Canadian tour in spring 1978. Meanwhile, Rick Danko's self-titled album had been released, and Danko had a gig at L.A.'s Roxy on March 1. As his set neared the end, Levon, Garth, Richard, and Robbie joined him onstage to play "Stage Fright," "The Shape I'm In," and "The Weight"—the last time the original Band performed together.

NO MATTER HOW much Levon and Fred Carter wanted it, the RCO All-Stars couldn't coalesce into a permanent group. Each member had his separate career and commitments. It worked for a while, then as schedules began to conflict, it became impossible to keep the unit together.

When Levon returned from the RCO tour of Japan in July 1978, he embarked on his next project, a solo album for ABC Records called *Levon Helm*, recorded at Cherokee Studios in Los Angeles and at the famed Muscle Shoals Sound Studio in Alabama. His sidemen included the legendary rhythm section the Swampers, comprising Barry Beckett, David Hood, Jimmy Johnson, and Roger Hawkins, three of the horn players he'd used for the RCO All-Stars—Lou Marini, Alan Rubin, and Tom Malone—and Steve Cropper on guitar. It was produced by Duck Dunn. The Cate Brothers wrote "Standing on a Mountaintop," for which they sang backup. For Helm, a big part of the reason to do the album was the opportunity to work at Muscle Shoals with these musicians, and it seemed mutual. Jimmy Johnson said of Levon, "He was just like a guy from our hometown. He had the best attitude and was a pleasure to be around." Unfortunately, there was no tour to support the album, and it failed to even chart.

Starting back in 1976, Helm had played for political rallies supporting Bill Clinton's candidacy for Arkansas attorney general and then governor. Levon's good friend Paul Berry had been Clinton's college roommate, so when Clinton was first elected governor in 1978, Berry suggested Helm perform for his gubernatorial inaugural ball in January 1979. The young governor-elect agreed, and Levon played with Earl and Ernie Cate. Levon's 1990s road manager, Butch Dener, explains Levon's ties to political movers and shakers in his home state:

> Levon would play with the Cate Brothers fundraisers down there…All the way through the campaign, our friends were Arkansas lobbyists who became Washington, D.C., lobbyists, bankers—the kind of people when we were on the road and you got stuck, you would pick up the phone and call these people and say, "We need five thousand dollars." At the next hotel, there would be five thousand dollars. Those were the kind of people that we knew in politics in Arkansas who became Washington, D.C., politicians.

"TO TELL THE truth, sometimes I feel luckier than the town dog," Helm said. One of his Woodstock friends, the actor Brad Dourif, who'd won acclaim for his role four years earlier in *One Flew Over the Cuckoo's Nest*, introduced Levon to Tommy Lee Jones. Jones was signed to play the role of Doolittle Lynn, Loretta Lynn's husband, in the biopic of Lynn's life, *Coal Miner's Daughter,* opposite Sissy Spacek as Loretta. When director Michael Apted had difficulty casting Lynn's father, Ted Webb, Tommy suggested Levon. That he was an acting novice deterred no one. As Paul Berry tells it,

> Tommy Lee is the one that says, "Get Levon Helm in here. He can do this."…Tommy Lee was the real catalyst. Levon called me, and he said, "I've read for this part…and I told them to call you, that you are my agent."…I did get a call, and I did go over to Nashville where they'd gathered. I read his contract, and we signed it. I like to brag I was his agent—and I was in a way—but Tommy Lee Jones is the one that really did what agents do. He's the one that got the role for Levon. Tommy Lee was not only Levon's friend, but they stayed friends, and he cast him again in a couple of other productions that Tommy Lee had a major control of.

Helm hadn't previously considered working in film, yet he was certainly a movie fan. "I never thought about acting all that much," Levon admitted, "but you've got to play the hand you're dealt, right? I tried real hard to pull it off in *Coal Miner's Daughter*. Acting is like music, in a way." His primary concern in preparing for the role was to respect the ethic of hard work and deep love of family innate to Kentucky miners. He likened it to his own background: "My dad was like Loretta's dad, raising a family on not quite enough and enjoying it. He didn't whine about his lot. You learned to play the hand you were dealt." Helm felt a kinship with those struggling to provide for their families, decent people trapped in the cycle of poverty who nonetheless had a culture worth preserving. "That's a tradition where I came from," he noted. "I know exactly about coal-oil lamps and working for a living… I'm a little worried that the tradition is getting lost." In order to add authenticity to his role as Ted Webb, Levon spoke with Loretta's family, talked to the miners, and spent time in a coal mine.

With no acting experience, Levon drew on what he did know and approached it the way he would an album. "You try to do the same thing for a scene that you do for a song," he said. "You try to bring it to life and get it like the director wants it, the same as you do a record. [With a record], you're supposed to let your producer guide you. That's who's supposed to help you get it so that it's got the right ingredients in there: life and breath; heart and soul." For Helm, the goal for music and acting were much the same—each one was an intimate experience for the listener or viewer.

Levon's authenticity shines through the camera, a remarkable achievement for a first-time actor. Martin Scorsese called his performance "rich, understated, and very moving." He played the part to perfection—a poor, proud man tormented by the loss of his precious daughter. "He knew that character in his bones," Sissy Spacek says, "and his portrayal has such dignity and grace that it literally anchors the film."

Helm was apprehensive about lying in the open casket in the scene depicting Ted Webb's wake, so Michael Apted did it first in rehearsals. Then with cameras rolling, in full corpse makeup, Levon lay in the coffin, the mourners around him singing "Amazing Grace." Suddenly,

Helm sprang upright, insisting that the song be sung the traditional way, in call-and-response fashion. Thanks to Levon's input, the part of Loretta's mother was played by another musician and novice actor, the bluegrass performer Phyllis Boyens, and her father, former coal miner and revered Appalachian musician Nimrod Workman, was visiting the set. So in the final film, as in time-honored custom, Workman calls out the lyrics and the actors sing them back.

"*Coal Miner* was really fun to make," Helm said. But for Loretta, it was unsettling to see Levon in character, such a dead ringer for her beloved father that it brought her to tears when she first saw him. "While he was doing the movie," she reveals, "I couldn't be around him that much—I couldn't sit down beside him—[he] reminded me so much of my daddy. I just wanted to hang on to him."

The cast and crew were based at the Wise Inn in Wise, Virginia, a small town not far from the Kentucky border. Most nights, Levon commandeered the taproom in the basement of the hotel, and gathered around him banjo and guitar players to perform traditional mountain songs from the area.

When Helm was asked to sing "Blue Moon of Kentucky" for the movie soundtrack, he was taken aback. It had a stellar pedigree. "Now as you may recall," he said, "Bill Monroe first did that song, and Elvis Presley had a good shot at it too. I asked the producer how he'd like to follow Monroe and Presley! But I did it anyway." Fred Carter and the Cate Brothers played behind him on the track.

The film premiere was held on March 4, 1980, at Nashville's Belle Meade Theatre. Levon, Sissy, Fred Carter, and the Cates did a concert at the Roxy in Los Angeles, then Levon and Sissy co-hosted an episode of the *Midnight Special* TV program in April, where they performed several songs from the movie. Helm's idea was to tour with the musicians from the soundtrack, but again, conflicting careers intervened.

Levon used a portion of the money he made on *Coal Miner's Daughter* to buy a house in Springdale, coincidentally opposite the cemetery where Dayton Stratton—and later, his parents—was buried. He was living with Sandy, splitting their time between Arkansas and Woodstock, with visits from Amy and Ezra whenever possible.

Coal Miner's Daughter was a success, considered one of the top ten films of 1980 and earning a slew of prizes, including an Academy Award for Best Actress for Spacek. When the film was shown in Fayetteville, Anna Lee remembers Diamond standing outside the theater beside a movie poster, proclaiming to anyone who passed, "That's my son. That's my son."

THE SESSION WITH Fred Carter for "Blue Moon of Kentucky" went so well that Helm and Carter maintained the momentum and recorded twenty more tracks, ten of which appear on the 1980 MCA album *American Son*. Produced by Carter and backed by Nashville studio musicians in Bradley's Barn outside Nashville, it highlights some of Levon's finest vocals. In fact, until *Dirt Farmer* was released in 2007, it was considered his best solo effort. Helm played harmonica on two tracks, but left the drums to three session players, though he may have added some overdubs afterward.

Levon kicks off the album in an effervescent mood with "Watermelon Time in Georgia," and the rockin' toe-tapper "Dance Me Down Easy." Uncharacteristically, he delivers tender, sumptuous vocals in the love ballad, "Violet Eyes." He takes another unusual approach in "Stay with Me," written by Fred Carter, which has a distinctly Latin feel, with the kick drum on beats 2 and 4, and the electric piano sounding like a kettle drum. The patriotic rocker "America's Farm" speaks to many of Helm's own beliefs, and he sings about one of his favorite cities in a highlight of the album, "Hurricane." His vocals are audacious in "Nashville Wimmin," and he sings the cheeky, albeit politically incorrect, lyrics to "Sweet Peach Georgia Wine" with a southern swagger, accompanied by Carter's choice guitar work.

Jeff Carter remembers his father reminiscing about *American Son*:

> He loved Levon—don't get me wrong—but candidly there were some times that Levon frustrated Dad because he kind of felt like, you know, Levon just did exactly what he wanted to, and Dad was a much more regimented kind of a person...[Levon] kind of came and went as the wind blew, and that's what Dad loved about him. There was a story, I recall, about *American Son*...There were some issues going on, and the feeling was that he didn't maybe do all

that he could to promote that album, and it kind of slipped through the cracks…There definitely was some frustration [on Fred's part] with that just because really he thought that Levon was a huge star, and he thought he deserved a bigger slice than what he had after the Band. And so he felt like Lee kind of sabotaged himself here and there unnecessarily.

Also in 1980, Helm co-starred with John Heard in a Canadian film originally named *Misdeal*, then later called *Best Revenge*. Shot in Toronto and southern Spain, it was a drug-smuggling adventure in which Levon's character is captured by the drug kingpin who set up the operation. He sings "Straight Between the Eyes" on the soundtrack, accompanied by Garth on accordion.

That summer, Helm was touring with the Cate Brothers Band, comprising Earl and Ernie Cate, bass player Ron Eoff, and Helm's nephew Terry Cagle on drums. With Terry onboard, Levon had the flexibility to play other instruments or join him on drums.

"Somebody called him one of the last of the Southern gentlemen," Cagle says of his uncle. "He just was very kind and courteous and humble." Although Helm accused Robertson of going Hollywood, Levon also had many celebrities as friends. The difference, Ernie and Earl claim, is that their status wasn't important to him. In Helm's mind, everyone was the same.

> We played a lot of shows with big-name groups, but that wasn't as much fun or as, you know, as exciting as just workin' with Levon [Earl says] 'cause Levon had all these friends in the movie business or whatever, and you never knew who was gonna show up. Like one night in New York at the Lone Star, Rip Torn, Tommy Lee Jones, and Dennis Hopper, all three showed up at the same time [laughs] to the gig, right? So they're in the dressing room, you know, partyin'. Stuff like that, you know. And Bob Dylan, you know, comin' to a gig.

Helm was generally even-tempered; it took a lot to make him angry. Terry recalls one night, though, when Levon's patience was stretched to its limit: "Once we were playing at a place with a great big stage, a real deep stage, and he had been after the guys. 'Fellas, look, I need a new hi-hat stand.' Each time they didn't fix it. So finally the last time [at the end of a song] we're holding the note, and he takes the stand and throws it to the back as far as he can. We're all loving it. As it lands, we played the final note. They fixed his stand."

For the next couple of years, Helm and the Cates gigged mostly in New York State—at New York City's Lone Star Cafe or at the Joyous Lake in Woodstock—and in Canada, through Kingston, Montreal, Ottawa, Hamilton, and Toronto. Levon was a day late for one five-night run at the Nickelodeon in Toronto—he was filming in Spain—and the band had to go on without him. When he did appear, he was smoking a Cuban cigar and wearing a T-shirt that read, "Too Many Women and Too Little Time." Helm said, "Money and fame and fortune is fine, but the *work* is the whole thing." When asked about his advancing age, he answered, "Forty years old? It feels great. I'm lucky to be here."

After the losses associated with the RCO All-Stars and two failed albums, Helm was suffering financially. "It was tough coming back after the Last Waltz," Helm acknowledged. "There were some times it didn't seem like very many people were pulling for us at all, except when we would go and play, and the people that showed up to hear us play wanted to hear 'Cripple Creek' and 'King Harvest,' and all those old songs. That's what got us through." He made a conscious effort to use the contacts he'd made during the Band era, saying, "If I'd sat around and thought about it, it might have gotten to me, but I took advantage of who I knew and the musicians I was able to meet, and I got to play with quite a few of them. It's in my plans to play with the rest." His philosophy was "Just to stay with the music and don't give up and keep learning. Keep, keep becoming a better player."

It was during this time the Cate Brothers became aware of the extreme animosity Helm harbored toward Robbie Robertson. Earl says, "It just seemed like right from the get-go, after he did *Coal Miner's Daughter*, during that time when we really started playing a lot, he pretty much constantly griped about the situation with Robbie and [music] publishing and all that." He didn't want to perform Band songs anymore. He tried to satisfy the audience with "Up on Cripple Creek," "The Weight," and "Ophelia," but to him, those songs belonged to the past, and he wanted to put that behind him.

Levon got top billing in 1980 as a vocalist, drummer, and harmonica player on the country-music album *The Legend of Jesse James*, written by Paul Kennerley and recorded for A&M in Nashville. He sang the part of Jesse James on this album, presented like a movie soundtrack. It also included Johnny Cash as Jesse's brother Frank, Emmylou Harris, Charlie Daniels, and Albert Lee. The songs spanned a wide swath of country music, from early folk and mountain numbers up to the present. Grammy-winning country instrumentalist Mark O'Connor described Levon as "the best country singer alive." Helm, though, characterized his vocals differently: "I'm really not a singer— I don't think I have a voice. But I love music so much that if I can get close to the pulse, the *real thing*, I can't wait to try it."

ALTHOUGH LEVON HAD never wanted to get married—other than to escape the U.S. military draft—he and long-time partner Sandy succumbed to pressure from their parents and tied the knot in the recording studio in Helm's barn on September 7, 1981. It was a small affair, with no friends or family from Arkansas except Terry Cagle and the Cate Brothers. Harold Kudlets, whose relationship with Levon was like father and son, was Levon's best man.

That same year, Levon recorded an album of covers, again at Muscle Shoals—confusingly also called *Levon Helm*. Back from his previous session were Jimmy Johnson, Barry Beckett, David Hood, and Roger Hawkins. He had a new horn section, and the backing musicians included the Cate Brothers on guitar and keyboards, and Terry Cagle as one of the backup vocalists. In spring 1982, following the album's release, Helm toured with the Muscle Shoals All-Stars to support the album, yet it went nowhere.

FOLLOWING HIS SUCCESS in *Coal Miner's Daughter*, Levon got the call to act in the critically acclaimed epic *The Right Stuff*, filmed between March and October 1982. He narrated the film at the beginning and end, and had the role of Jack Ridley, a highly respected U.S.

Air Force test pilot and aeronautical engineer from Oklahoma, the brains behind supersonic flight. As a character, Ridley is a secondary figure who nonetheless ties the movie together, bringing the celebrity of the high-flyers back to earth. General Chuck Yeager, a technical advisor for the film, was on the set every day, and Levon enjoyed having lunch with him while hearing his stories.

When Helm was in Los Angeles with Sandy and Bill Avis to do the overdubs for *The Right Stuff*, various executives dropped by to say hello. In typical fashion, he wanted nothing to do with the suits, although he remained polite. Levon saved his ire for the person he knew used the same recording studio, as Bill relates:

> He looked at me, and he said, "You know, Bizz, that fucking Robertson is right upstairs. I know that son of a bitch is up there."…He says, "I feel like going up there and seeing that son of a bitch."…Levon would just get so friggin' mad, and I'd say, "It's okay, bro. We're out of here soon. We're out of here soon." And he'd calm down…
>
> Sandy was with us, and we had that Ford Econoline. Boy, it was a nice piece of equipment. Sandy and Levon could lay there in the back, and I'd be driving. If I got to the point where I couldn't drive any longer, I'd say, "Okay, Lee, your turn." "Ah, shit. All right."…We're coming from L.A. Destination: Woodstock, New York…
>
> So we head out. He said, "We got to make a detour…I want to go down to Helena to Shadden's to get some barbecue sauce"… So, sure as shit, I make the right turns and down into Shadden's for a couple of big buckets of Shadden's barbecue sauce. It was good sauce. It really was.

HELM BEGAN 1983 as a no-show on *Late Night with David Letterman*, due to a fire that destroyed his pickup truck. He did appear the following week on January 11, and as a peace offering to Dave, he presented him with a jar of the sauce he got on his detour going home to Woodstock. Levon claimed he still hadn't mastered the skill of singing while playing drums, despite evidence to the contrary. He sang

"Rag Mama Rag" while on mandolin, then sat in with the band for the remainder of the show, singing and playing harmonica on "Caledonia," "Hand Jive," and "Just Goes to Show You (the World Is Mad)."

Rick Danko had recently moved back to Woodstock, and early that year, the two of them did an acoustic tour of colleges and clubs through the United States and Canada. "Rick is like a musical sponge," Levon said. "You can drop just one bit of music out there and, boy, he can soak it up and squeeze out a cupful...If you got some musical balls to bounce around, he's the guy to play catch with." Their performances were intimate, with no drums—Rick on guitar and Levon on harmonica and mandolin. They played a mix of blues and country, sprinkled with a few Band favorites, such as "Caledonia" and "Evangeline." At a Lone Star gig in February, a very inebriated Bob Dylan sat in for the last part of their set, which dissolved into a musical mess.

When Helm and Danko performed in Toronto at B.B. Magoons that April, a reporter for the *Toronto Star* wrote, "It was one of the headiest musical experiences this reviewer has had in recent years. They shared a sense of genuine joy in being together again and Danko couldn't keep from smiling all through the set." Their fans demanded four encores.

About this time, the duo expanded to form the Woodstock All-Stars. Since she'd never met Levon, Woodstock resident and Dobro player Cindy Cashdollar was surprised to receive an invitation to his New Year's Eve party along with her husband, bass player Frank Campbell. The party became a jam, and a few days later, Levon asked if they'd join Rick and him for a gig at the Lone Star Cafe. That night, they played all Band songs—it was the Band unplugged—with Helm on mandolin and harmonica.

Larry Packer played fiddle with the group, Stan Szelest came in on piano, Randy Ciarlante was hired as a second drummer, and Artie Traum played guitar. After a while, Traum passed the torch to Jim Weider, a Telecaster player who'd first met Levon as a teenager working in a Woodstock stereo store in the early 1970s. The Woodstock All-Stars performed mostly country blues with one or two token Band songs. They were frequently booked at the Getaway in Woodstock and at the Lone Star Cafe, and Richard Manuel and Paul Butterfield occasionally sat in.

Of one of their performances in July 1984, *The New York Times* reported, "Mr. Helm demonstrated his offhanded virtuosity both as a singer and as a band leader...As a singer, he combines the sharp twang of classic honky-tonk with the rolling rhythmic inflections of blues singers like Sonny Boy Williamson and Jimmy Reed. Singing the blues, the quality Mr. Helm expresses is a mixture of patience, true grit and spiritual fire."

"It was a really fun time," Cashdollar says. "And what sweet, wonderful people everybody was. Just working with Levon was such an education."

12

And the Band Played On

Harold Kudlets had assumed all the Band members were multi-millionaires until Helm set him straight. Kudlets claimed it was his idea to reform the Band. "Levon and the Cate Brothers were doing very good," he said, "and I suggested maybe we should put the Band together, and we started…Garth Hudson and Richard—they were in California—I had to send them the airline tickets to come to Woodstock to rehearse."

Danko and Manuel signed on—Robertson was not asked. Levon said the whole experiment hinged on whether Garth would participate, that he always made the rest of the group sound great, and he decided to come onboard. Levon also included the Cate Brothers Band, with Earl taking on the onerous role of replacing Robbie on guitar. "All the Cate Brothers sing and they sing well," Helm noted, "so when we play together, even if we do one of our old tunes, the tune sounds better having three keyboards instead of two, and five voices instead of three. It sounds like more fun and it is." He added, "Miners get hooked on mining, particularly coal mining. They can't do without it. That's sort of the same with me and playing on the road. I guess that's *my* reason for always going out again with those boys after the [original] Band broke up."

The Band Is Back tour began in June 1983 at the Joyous Lake club in Woodstock, then they performed at the University of Chicago before traveling across Canada, down to California, and ending in Washington, D.C. They played blues, some of Helm's RCO All-Stars material, and a few Band numbers. It could be discouraging at times, though, when the audience seemed to be there only to hear classic Band songs, although that was what got the group booked.

Among themselves, they called these gigs the Doomsday Tours. The venues were smaller than when the original Band was in its heyday, but Levon didn't mind. As Kudlets said, "He was a 100-percent musician." Helm enjoyed being within handshake distance of the audience. According to Bill Avis, who was back onboard as road manager, the person it *did* bother was Richard.

At the end of August, the Band began a series of concerts in Japan, then toured the U.S. for the rest of 1983. They closed out the year as a last-minute addition to the Grateful Dead's Winterland concert on New Year's Eve, where Bill Graham, decked out as Father Time, descended over the audience on a cable. Once again, Richard was losing his battle against alcohol and drugs, occasionally causing tension with Levon, who only wanted the best for him.

A major setback occurred when Helm was preparing for the role of a U.S. marshal in Willie Nelson's film *Red Headed Stranger*. Practicing his quick-draw technique at home with live ammunition, he shot himself in his right leg—his bass-drum leg—and severed the tibial nerve, which extends the length of the limb into the foot. At first there was doubt that doctors could even save his leg. Then once the nerve was repaired, they were unsure he'd ever be able to play drums. But after some time off, Levon was back with the Woodstock All-Stars—playing guitar—as his finances continued to be problematic, with IRS problems, an onerous mortgage on the barn, and a child-custody suit.

The Band—with Levon back behind the drum kit—toured through North America in 1984, playing some shows with the Grateful Dead. They made a memorable stop in Fayetteville on August 31. They hadn't played there since 1964 because the original Band was too big for local venues, but now on the tenth anniversary of Dayton Stratton's tragic death, Helm decided to perform a concert in his memory. Although Dayton's former venue, the Rink, had only 1600 seats—and they could have sold it out many times over—Levon wanted to play there in Stratton's honor. It was an emotional night. Half of Fayetteville was out in the parking lot, and the doors were kept open so the overflow crowd could hear. Levon began the show with a dedication to Dayton and to another friend from Fayetteville, his recently deceased attorney Jim Gallman.

DESPITE HIS SEMESTER at the Berklee College of Music, Helm still confessed to some musical shortcomings: "I've worked on some of my fundamentals a little bit and I've taken it maybe a notch above an elementary level, but I'm really not schooled at all. I don't read well, I don't write well." He believed that he'd have been a more effective musician if he'd had more formal training.

Levon was using 7A sticks, which he said, "I try to play as hard as I can without breaking them. That seems to be acoustically correct too, when you're having fun." His snare heads were textured Remo plastic heads, which he chose because they traveled well in all types of weather. As for his kit, Helm explained,

> I've got a couple of different bass drums that I like and that travel well. I've got a couple of tom-toms that are louder. They don't have to match as long as I've got a 13-inch or 14-inch tenor tom, a 15-inch or 16-inch baritone tom and a good snare drum. I usually prefer just a regular wooden snare. I stay away from the all-chrome snares. I like that wood sound better...My hybrid set now is a Ludwig snare, some Gretsch tom-toms, a Ludwig bass and some Zildjian cymbals. I usually like a couple of those, a good set of sock cymbals and a couple of cowbells. That's about as far as I usually take it.

BILL AVIS HAD left the Band after Japan and was back in Canada, although he and his family continued to be close with Levon and Sandy. Helm was godfather to Bill and Jeannine's son, Jerome Levon Avis, and was like a second father to Jerome and his sister, Rebecca.

Levon and Sandy had an affinity for children. Jerome and his sister spent their summer vacation in 1983 at the Helm barn. Levon would be away on tour for a couple of weeks, then back home in Woodstock for three or four days at a time. He played catch with Jerome, or they'd watch football on TV. Levon and Sandy were such film buffs that their bedroom, which doubled as a mixing room, was lined floor to ceiling with VHS tapes, and Jerome and his sister would crawl into bed with them to watch movies. "He was the real salt of the earth," Jerome says of Levon, "and he'd do anything for you. Also, if you pissed him off, that was the end of it for you too…If you were straight with him, he'd be straight with you."

Helm encouraged Jerome with his interest in drumming and vocals:

> Whenever we got together, he would show me different things on his leg, his thigh, with hambones or just sticks on a pillow. Not just playing drums, but singing, building up your jaw—chew your steak for twenty or thirty times each side of your mouth before you swallow it. That would help to build up your jaw muscles. And to think about when you're singing how you're going to phrase the song, where you're going to take your breath, when you're going to exhale.

Bill had tapes of live Band shows, and Jerome played air drum or air mandolin along with them. Levon showed him how to get some extra sizzle from his kit by cutting his dog's choke chain in half and attaching it to the cymbal stand. When Jerome was thirteen and Helm and the Cates were playing at Toronto's Diamond Club, Levon invited him to sit in on drums while Levon blew harmonica and Little Freddie played the tambourine.

IN 1984, HELM co-starred with Jane Fonda in *The Dollmaker*, a made-for-television movie set during World War II. He was cast as Clovis Nevels, an Appalachian sharecropper fed up with his family's grueling life on the land, who moves them to Detroit and the lure of a steady factory job. Helm delivers a powerful, emotional performance as a loving, hardworking man who tries his best, but deaf to his wife's wishes is unable to hold his family together. His wife, Gertie, played by Jane Fonda, carves dolls as a means to get the family back on track. Fonda won an Emmy Award for her performance, and the director, Daniel Petrie, won a Directors Guild of America Award.

Fonda was impressed by Levon's acting ability. The interior scenes were shot in a converted factory in Chicago. Helm admitted to Bill Avis that there was an embarrassing moment during filming:

> She's in bed with a nightie...and the scene calls for him to get in bed with Jane Fonda!...They're supposed to lay there and talk a little bit, like a husband and wife would do in bed about the day...He said once he got in bed, he had to piss. "Oh, God," he said, "I jumped out of that bed." They were getting ready to cut it, but he's up and out of the bed. She's laying there, right? And it's in this factory, and there's no toilet. He said he ran down the set, and he saw a side door. He opened that side door and just stood there and [pissed.] He got back on the set and apologized to everyone—which he would do—got in bed, and [in] one take they got it.

While Levon was in Chicago, he took the opportunity to visit Muddy Waters:

> He invited me out and fed me a good home-cooked dinner. Muddy understood. Muddy was a musician himself and knew that when he could put one of them cornbread dinners on you, he had done you a good favor.
>
> I carried us two big bottles of [champagne], and we sat in the shade and just relaxed, and I hung with him as much as I could until I knew it was time to get back on the road. But I got to eat dinner with him that day, you know, and hang out with him for a couple of hours. I sure did enjoy it. I almost got to introduce him to Jane Fonda, too. We were in Chicago working on a show and that was going to be fun. They wanted to meet each other.

IN THE SUMMER of 1985, the Band toured as the opening act for Crosby, Stills and Nash. Harold Kudlets had left the group, and their new manager saw little financial reason to include the full Cate Brothers Band in one bloated unit. Levon was heartbroken. The new lineup for the Band was Levon, Rick, Richard, and Garth, with Jim Weider—from the Woodstock All-Stars—on guitar.

It was Helm who pushed for Weider to join the Band. A Woodstock native, Jim had moved to Nashville, learned some licks from Lenny Breau, and played with Johnny Paycheck and blues and country artist James Talley. In Atlanta, he performed with Harvey Brooks and Richard Bell. He came back to Woodstock in 1983 to tour with Robbie Dupree, and soon after he became part of the Woodstock All-Stars. His first gig as a member of the Band was with no rehearsal in front of 25,000 people in Dallas.

When asked if there was any pressure to play guitar like Robbie Robertson, Weider replies,

> [Levon] never talked to me about that. It was all about the music with Levon and Rick and Richard and Garth—they were just into playing music and doing the best they could at all times. They never told me how to play or to play this like Robbie. If there were intros that Robbie did on the songs, which he did a lot, I would do the classic, trademark intro, but then when it came to soloing, they'd let me solo the way I wanted. Levon just liked me to keep that rhythm thick and leave an open stop for the backbeat—and he had the best backbeat that I ever heard. And so they just let me be myself, and they gave me a lot of confidence, and really if it wasn't for Levon, I wouldn't have had the experiences in life musically I got to do. I really owe it to all those guys.

In response to some reviewers, Helm said, "Let's quit talking about who *was* in the Band. Let's talk about who is in *this* Band." Levon was Jim's mentor. "He's taught me just about everything in terms of being a professional musician," Weider states. "His approach to music comes from the roots of the Delta so there was a lot to learn just from the people who inspired him." As well as being a legendary drummer, Levon was admired by Jim for his ability on harmonica and guitar. Of course, on top of that, was Helm's sense of fun. There were always a lot of laughs on the tour bus.

> [Levon] was so open to making people around him feel like they're comfortable [Weider says]. He'd bring in people, and he'd make

them feel like you've known him forever. He was that kind of person…I owe my whole musical career, really, to him. What I learned from him is play 110 percent, and it's all about the music. And it's just not about you. You gotta listen and listen to other people, then you're playing music as a band.

"Very strong-willed," is how Jim describes Levon's personality:

When he wanted his way, you know, he had a very powerful personality, and he would get the point across to you. [laughs] Always cordial, but when he had to deal with problems, he would get the point across…[He was] very focused, and you learned a lot about being a band leader by working with Levon. He always considered everybody else—how they were feeling musically and overall—and he was a great band leader.

"Oh, yeah," Weider says. "Levon ran the show. He would discuss stuff [with the others], but he was pretty much the leader." Helm's relationship with the other Band members was

very, very close. They really looked out for each other. It was a nice vibe to be on the bus and on tour with them. When people needed their space, they took it…When I wasn't feeling right, Levon would check in with me; he was right there for me…All those guys were good guys…Funny bunch, too. [laughs] There was a tremendous amount of laughing. It was a cool thing.

That October when the Band played at Toronto's Diamond Club, a reviewer reported that they'd never sounded better. Ever the optimist, Levon said,

Some of our best songs are still ahead of us, and we love playing together again…Everything we've done—from the years we spent in Toronto saloons to splitting up—has conspired to bring us here. The feeling in this band is family love, and what motivates us is simply the desire to be better entertainers…I'm like a farmer. The more crops he grows, the more bad weather he endures, the better he gets. And as long as Garth Hudson wants to play, I'll play with the Band.

IN 1985, THE movie *Smooth Talk* was released. In it, Levon played the role of Laura Dern's father and husband to Mary Kay Place in a coming-of-age drama that won the Jury Prize at the 1986 Sundance Festival. That winter, Helm had a leading role in a low-budget thriller filmed in Fayetteville—*Man Outside*. Looking very slicked-back and conservative, Levon played Sheriff Leland Laughlin alongside Robert Logan, Kathleen Quinlan, and Bradford Dillman, with more minor roles going to Rick, Garth, Richard, and Levon's Fayetteville friend Dash Goff.

TRAGEDY STRUCK ON March 3, 1986, after the Band's performance at the Cheek to Cheek lounge.

Levon told the police in Winter Park, Florida, that Richard Manuel had been in an upbeat mood after their two good sets. The way Bill Avis heard it, Rick had gotten on Richard's case about his heavy drinking—even during the show. Members of the audience kept supplying him with alcohol. Afterwards, Manuel made a point of visiting every Band member's room in the nearby Quality Inn, finally stopping by to see Helm.

In Levon's statement, he said that Richard did not appear to be depressed, that they spoke about music and people, and then Manuel went back to his room. "Levon avoided anything that was depressing or negative," Mary Vaiden says. "He avoided those conversations, but he did tell me about it, and he said it was just horrible. He said Richard had been down in his room smoking pot and Richard said he had to go back to his room for something, and he never came back. Levon said, 'Oh, I just thought he went to bed.'" This was around 2:30 a.m.

But by the time Richard returned to his room and woke his wife, Arlie, he was upset, complaining about the piano he had to play at the venue. She convinced him to go to bed. He lay there with his clothes on until she went to sleep. Sometime before 3:30, he went into the bathroom, looped a belt around the shower-curtain rod and around his neck, then lifted his feet as he jerked down hard.

Arlie discovered his body the next morning. Screaming, she brought Levon, Rick, and Rick's girlfriend, Elizabeth Grafton, into their room. "It took us five minutes to get him down from there," Helm said. "It just drained me." The autopsy showed that Manuel was under the influence of alcohol when he died and that he had also taken cocaine. He didn't leave a note. "I don't know what got crosswise in his mind between leaving the foot of my bed and going into his own bathroom," Levon conceded. Richard was forty-two.

"Levon Helm wanted to play music, and so did Garth and Ricky," Paul Berry says. "Richard just was tortured, and it was too much for him. Maybe the most difficult subject I ever talked to Levon about was Richard's death...That haunted Lee. He had nightmares about that." As Helm put it, "Richard wasn't afraid to go early, or leave late. And that was one time he decided to go early. And it's a decision that's strictly between him and his higher power, and I've never tried to second-guess it, or have too strong an opinion of my own about it."

Levon told Mary that they didn't go through official channels to bring Richard's body back to Stratford, Ontario, for burial: "They wrapped him up in a quilt and put him in the back of a truck and took him to Canada...He said, 'We just wrapped him up and took him home.'"

THE BAND SURVIVED, but only coasted through the late 1980s, together for a time with guitarists Blondie Chaplin and Fred Carter. Helm could be resolute when it came to certain aspects of performing, as Fred told his son, Jeff: "Levon was real bad about not wanting to go on on time. I remember Dad laughing about that, saying, 'Lee, we'd better go and hit the stage. That crowd's getting pretty restless out there.' He said Levon just waved his hat and said, 'Oh, hell, Fred. Just let 'em take the night off.' Then a couple of hours later, they'd finally go out and play." But if the sound on stage wasn't right, Levon could get upset. "He would really get after the production guys or sound guys from the stage if his monitors weren't right," Jeff remarks. "I definitely saw him put his foot through a kick drum a time or two and just let the monitor guy have it." About this time, the Band had some gigs in

Europe, and at least once, Terry Cagle—who looked, acted, played, and sang remarkably like Levon—took Levon's spot on the drum stool. The audience didn't know the difference.

Levon also performed with the Woodstock All-Stars, which in its later configuration included Stan Szelest, Paul Branin, Frank Campbell, Cindy Cashdollar, Larry Packer, and Randy Ciarlante on a second drum kit. Helm played with the Cate Brothers Band, as well, and kept his hand in on various other projects. He and Sandy appeared on a CBC-TV special, Murray McLauchlan's *Floating over Canada*, and Levon narrated the 1987 documentary *Elvis '56—In the Beginning*. In 1989, Levon, Rick, and Garth appeared on a Pay-TV special *This Country's Rockin,'* with Ted Nugent, Gregg Allman, David Crosby, Stephen Stills, Carl Perkins, and Ronnie Hawkins. Helm sang a verse of the title song of the album *Will the Circle Be Unbroken, Volume 2* with Emmylou Harris, which was nominated for a Grammy Award.

In 1987, Levon performed in *End of the Line*, a movie with Kevin Bacon, Wilford Brimley, and Holly Hunter, filmed in Arkansas. He played the role of Leo Pickett, a railroad worker who, along with Brimley's character, steals a train to protest the closure of their local station. Terry Cagle was Helm's double, and whenever there's a shot of the train traveling past, it's Terry, not Levon, as the engineer. Fellow Arkansan Mary Steenburgen, who played Leo's wife and was also the executive producer, commented on Helm's performance: "Levon is really bizarre in his ability to be a character. I've never met an actor like that. He has a strange ability just to walk into a scene and be completely natural and tell the truth at any moment. I don't really believe he knows the camera's there." Director Jay Russell said, "He has an amazing chameleon personality so that you never know exactly which Levon you're going to meet off the set or the bandstand on any given day. All of them are fascinating. There are days when he suddenly looks ten years older, then the next time you see him he looks ten years younger."

ON FEBRUARY 9, 1989, Levon's beloved mother, Nell, died of lung cancer and was buried in Springdale. Diamond went to Woodstock to stay with Levon and Sandy. Then tragedy struck again with the death of Rick's seventeen-year-old son, Eli, the result of asphyxiation after a drinking binge.

Helm's animosity toward Robertson was unabated that March as he skipped the induction of the Band into the Canadian Music Hall of Fame, which honors Canadian musicians for their lifetime achievements in music, knowing Robbie would be there. Although the group included an American, the academy noted, "The roots-rock pioneers The Band have influenced generations of musicians and are widely regarded as one of the most important Canadian musical groups." Instead of attending the ceremony, Levon brought his band to Toronto the next month, where he had a musical reunion with Ronnie Hawkins. As a striking blonde brought Helm's award onstage for the presentation, the Hawk quipped, "Here comes your prize, boy."

"He never considered himself a big star," Anna Lee says. "He was so humble about it." Levon played an active role in supporting the heritage of the Helena area and trying to reinvigorate the town through his assistance with and participation in the King Biscuit Blues Festivals. He usually closed the show on Saturday night, but he thought local bands should have the opportunity to showcase their talent in that slot instead. He would ask Anna Lee, "Why can't I come on Thursday night?" She says, "He never felt that he should be on the pedestal that people put him on. He always thought there was someone better. All he wanted to do was to entertain people. He didn't want to be a big star; he didn't want to be an icon in the music world, which he was. So many people looked up to him and thought he was the greatest drummer ever, and he never felt that he deserved all that."

In May, his favorite time of year in Phillips County, Helm returned to Helena for the opening of the Delta Cultural Center. Back on June 28, 1988, Levon had endorsed the center in his presentation before the United States Senate:

> Mr. Chairmen, while economic progress must take place, there is no reason why this progress should so drastically change our way of life that we lose our culture, that sense of who we are. That is perhaps the most important reason that this commission should pursue projects like the Delta Cultural Center in Helena, Arkansas,

which would help to preserve and interpret the rich cultural heritage of the Arkansas and Mississippi Delta region. Through organized events, exhibits, and programs, this center would give the people of the Delta the sense of community that is so badly needed there as well as work to preserve the region's unique cultural aspects. I have seen the importance of doing this through my work at the Helena [King Biscuit] Blues Festival. This October will be the 3rd year that the event has taken place and I would like to take this time to invite each of you to come and join us. You could then understand what an event such as the Festival can do for the morale of the people in that area.

On this rainy day in 1989, underneath a leaky roof, he appeared with Governor Bill Clinton to open the restored Missouri-Pacific Railroad depot in Helena as a visitor's center for researchers and tourists. During the hiatus of *King Biscuit Time* in the early 1980s, Max Moore, president of the Interstate Grocery Company, the long-time sponsor of the radio show, gave the band's guitar and Peck Curtis's drum kit to C.W. Gatlin, who then passed the drums on to Levon. Helm took them to Muscle Shoals, where they remained for a time, until he brought them back to Helena and donated them to the Delta Cultural Center, where they remain on display today.

DAVID FISHOF HAD a proven background as a manager and for packaging music tours, including those of the Mamas and Papas, the Association, the Turtles, and the Monkees. For the twenty-fifth anniversary of the Pepsi Generation, Pepsi asked Fishof to organize another tour for the summer of 1989. His idea—Ringo Starr and the All-Starr Band. Ringo loved the concept, but said, "I have certain people I want to put in the band…I want Levon Helm and I want Rick Danko—I want my favorite musicians." As well as occasional appearances by Garth Hudson, Ringo's choice of musicians for this band also included Joe Walsh, Mac Rebennack, Billy Preston, Nils Lofgren, Clarence Clemons, and joining Ringo and Levon on drums, Jim Keltner.

Keltner recalls, "I remember thinking when [Ringo] said, 'Well, maybe we should have the three of us do it on the drums,' I remember thinking, 'Wow, what a trip,' you know. 'Let's do it!'…Ringo is very hands-on, so it wouldn't have been somebody just telling him that's what we're gonna do. He would have sanctioned it, big time. He loved Levon so much." Generally, Keltner avoided playing double or triple drums—if one of his favorite drummers were playing, he wanted to hear that person clearly—but with the caliber of the All-Starrs, this was an exception.

Helm, on the other hand, loved playing with other drummers, even though some people said it wouldn't work. "But three drummers are more fun than two, just like two are more fun than one," he said. "There's a way of playing with each other without stepping on each other's toes, and at the same time, when a song like 'Hand Jive' comes up, well, with three of you, you can just tear the place down, you know. Yeah, you can really rough 'em up." When Levon was singing "The Weight," he held back on drums and let Ringo go ahead with some of the fills and patterns:

> And that just made the song new and made it more fun for me to do it. And we had those kind of spots that would come up in the music—certain songs—and we knew that Jimmy Lee [Keltner] was going to fill it up, and me and Ring would just kinda lay back on the ropes and double up, you know, and we'd have a lot of fun, you know. And then when we'd get a chance, of course, we'd all three come blistering out of there with them three backbeats, and if you could get 'em to fit in that wide a band [indicates about a one-inch span]…where it's all *pow*, that's a fine ol' time.

Helm also played harmonica and mandolin on the tour, and performed such favorites as "The Weight," "Hand Jive," and "Up on Cripple Creek" to thundering applause. "Oh, it was mutual admiration, lots of mutual admiration," Keltner says of the relationship between Ringo and Levon. "Ringo just thought the world of Levon. That tour was so much fun."

Everyone told David Fishof that a production of this caliber could never happen. A one-day event, such as Live Aid, was one thing, but an entire tour with these egos would end in disaster. "Still, I took the shot," Fishof recounts. "I mortgaged my house to put together the deposit. That's how confident I was. I just knew it would be great." To keep David on his toes, however, Helm and the guys hatched a prank that shook the young entrepreneur to his core.

On the fourth date, Clarence Clemons told Fishof he was quitting, that the musicians were fighting over the setlist and weren't getting along—he couldn't take it any longer. Nils Lofgren told David the same thing. When Fishof walked into the dressing room—his heart in his mouth, hoping he could save the tour, his reputation, and his house—Jim Keltner had his camera rolling.

"I see Joe Walsh with a knife in his hand, and blood all over him," Fishof exclaims, "and Levon Helm's holding a bottle and [he's] all bloody, and Levon throws a glass over Joe's head and it smashes on the wall, and I'm freaking out…and then they stick their tongues out at me…Rubber knife, fake blood…They set me up."

In fact, the musicians got along well and had an enormous amount of fun, especially Helm.

> Levon was so quirky [Keltner says]. He would open his room—he always had a suite—so both doors to the room were open at all times in the evening after the shows. If you were walking down the hall, and you wanted to step in, you could just step in. He had a tray of beers and wine and all kinds of food. He just was having a ball. He just loved it, and he wanted to share it with people… he'd have sushi, he'd have sandwiches. It was amazing. He spent a fortune. I think he spent all the money that he made doing that. That's just the way he liked to do stuff.

"Ringo had just gotten sober," Keltner remarks, "so he was 100-percent sober for that tour. Levon and myself and everybody else were not quite sober yet. I mean, we weren't outrageous or anything." When David was dreading the long flight from JFK to Japan for their dates there, the guys showed him how easy it could be: "I said to Levon, 'It's a long flight.' He said, 'Nah, you take one of these, and [before you know it] you'll land in Tokyo,' and I went to Rick Danko, and I said, 'It's a long flight.' He said, 'You take one of these, and you'll get there.'" David laughs when he says, "I took 'em both and *eventually* I woke up." Although Ringo became Helm's clean-and-sober sponsor, Jim didn't see him having any substance-abuse issues during this tour.

Keltner and Helm had remained good friends since meeting during the recording of *The Band*, and like so many others, Jim was charmed by his personality:

> Levon was the same from the time I first met him to the time I last saw him. He was just one of the most gracious, humble and helpful [people]. He's the guy that would see somebody come in the room, and he'd go immediately and find a chair for them. He was just one of those kind of guys, one of those kind of people. I got to hang out with him on the Ringo tour—we did a lot of serious hanging out then—and he was just really, really even and sweet-natured and everything. Now, he had a side of him that you didn't want to cross. I kinda figured that, although I never saw it...He's what I would call a perfect Southern gentleman, the ones that you read about...That's the way I always perceived Levon, just one of the easiest, wonderful people to hang out with ever.

Even as a renowned drummer himself, Keltner loved the sound that Helm got from his kit and the way he played:

> He and I were talking one night late into the evening, and I was telling him how blown away I was by how he just played so easy, with such economy. It was such a beautiful sound and feel. And he said to me, "Oh, yeah, Jimmy, but if I could just play all those goddamn little rolls that you do." And I said, "Oh, man, Levon, I would trade you those rolls for one hit on the floor tom the way you do it"...He just had a way—he would reach down there and play that floor tom. Just one beat, that's all. He'd just hit it one time. But it's *when* you did it, *when* you do it. Levon was a tremendous influence on not only me but so many drummers. It's hard to imagine how many.

Through that tour, David Fishof came to appreciate Levon for much more than his musical skill. The Arkansas farm boy and the son of a rabbi became friends:

> Levon had a mind of his own…I learned from him to be authentic. He never sold himself out…We came from two different backgrounds but respected each other…And while he was difficult to a lot of people, he taught me a lot…Here I was a young guy, excited, and he showed me the truth, what the business was really like. He was authentic; he didn't suck up to anybody, confident in who he was. There was no changing once he made up his mind; you weren't changing his mind. Money didn't drive him. Many artists today, it drives them, and he was not driven by money…I feel honored to have gotten to know him…
>
> He was so good to me. He listened to me, and I listened to him. I enjoyed our relationship…It changed my way of life… [When we met,] I looked at this business as money, money, money—you know, it's a business—and he showed me a different way of authenticity. It's not always about money, and don't sell yourself out, and don't do things you don't believe in. He could have made a ton of money if he'd got together with Robbie Robertson, but he really didn't like the guy.

As a result of this tour, Fishof was approached with a record deal for the Band—the album that became *Jericho*—and signed on as their manager until about 1991. Also, because he'd had such a ball hanging out with rock stars and he realized others would too, David went on to establish the Rock and Roll Fantasy Camp.

Levon had a small part in the movie *Staying Together*, which was released that November, starring Sean Astin and Stockard Channing, and directed by Lee Grant. He played the role of Denny Stockton, the proprietor of a small-town general store and the leader of a local band, which included Jim Weider, Randy Ciarlante, Paul Branin, Frank Campbell, and Stan Szelest. Helm sang several songs on the soundtrack, and shared songwriting credit for "Big Love in a Small Town" with the rest of the band. He also earned praise for playing the part of an aging ex-con in the television series *Midnight Caller*, in which his character, C.W. Blanchard, misses his life behind bars and gets involved with gangsters, hoping to be sent back inside.

LEVON WAS PERFORMING with Ronnie Hawkins at the Deer Park Inn in Stouffville, Ontario, when the call came from Roger Waters, formerly of Pink Floyd, asking the Band to play at the historic concert to celebrate the collapse of the Berlin Wall. Ever mindful of assisting Hawkins when possible, Helm passed the phone over to the Hawk's manager, Steve Thomson, who responded, "If you want the Band, you gotta take Ronnie Hawkins." That's how the Hawk got to Berlin.

Close to nine months after the demolition of the wall, on July 21, 1990, a huge audience—estimated at between 300,000 to almost a half-million—gathered in Berlin, with a staggering television viewership of one billion, for the concert The Wall – Live in Berlin. It was a massive, elaborate production, which in addition to Roger Waters, the Band, and Ronnie Hawkins, included Van Morrison, Bryan Adams, Joni Mitchell, Cyndi Lauper, the German rock band Scorpions, the Hooters, and Sinéad O'Connor.

"They were so happy," Jim Weider says of Levon and Ronnie. "They were having such a blast. Those guys were really funny. Of course, they were always talking about the old days, and you'd hear some funny stories." The Band put on a late-afternoon show, then Levon, Rick, and Garth performed with Sinéad O'Connor on "Mother" and with Van Morrison for "Comfortably Numb."

Waters said of the Band, "I loved their music and they were all absolutely amazing. Levon came up to me after the show. He scratched his beard and went, 'Roger, I like your style, man. I want you to have my hat.' He took off his Arkansas Razorbacks baseball cap and handed it to me. It's been my fishing hat ever since, and it's one of my most treasured possessions."

13

From the Ashes

The 1990s began and ended with life-altering challenges for Levon Helm.

By this time, the Band had two drummers, with Randy Ciarlante—who'd played with Helm in the Woodstock All-Stars—manning the second kit and providing third vocals. Levon wanted the freedom to break away and play mandolin and harmonica, plus he loved double drums. He trusted Randy to, as he put it, guard his gun side. "One of us sort of holds down home plate," was how Helm described it, "and frees the other one up to throw more accents in, do whatever the music is asking for, and how also on some tunes—when we play a tune like 'Life Is a Carnival'—we can both just raise all kinds of sand on that one, you know. The rules don't always stay the same."

"I had to try to find parts that would complement the classic drum arrangement that Levon had created, without getting in the way," Ciarlante says. "There's a big difference between swinging and playing straight," he continues, "and what made Levon so special was that he combined the two. I used to love when he got off the hi-hat and laid into a march feel. When you played alongside Levon, you had to learn how to stay out of the way. You can practice double bass drum technique, paradiddles, funk beats, all that stuff, but none of that is going to work, because he doesn't come from that. He just plays. It's a musical, lyrical, and melodic thing." The way Randy saw it, Levon was the leader of the Band: "The other two [Rick and Garth] would always say, 'If Levon wants to do it, then we'll do it.' He has that charisma."

In addition to Randy, Rick, Garth, Stan Szelest, and Levon, Rick brought Sredni Vollmer in on harmonica for a short time, and they made some appearances in the western states. Soon after Ciarlante joined, Butch Dener came aboard at first to provide security, then as the road manager for the Band. "He was a gift from God, you know. He really was," says Dener recalling Helm. "It was amazing to be around him."

"Every room we were ever in, it was Levon's room," Butch says. "I don't care if Elizabeth Taylor was in the room; I don't care if Eric Clapton was in the room. Levon was as real as it got."

When they traveled, Helm liked to ride with Dener. "I had a Saab with heated seats—Levon loved the heated seats. He said, 'Drummers always got that drummer's curse—hemorrhoids. Heated seats are good for a drummer.'"

Butch never had a contract with Levon: "He knew I was a moral person, a person of faith. He was a big believer in faith. He may not have been a big believer in organized religion, but he always gave credit to a higher and stronger power…He knew that if I said something, it was my word. That's how he was."

ON JANUARY 20, 1991, forty-eight-year-old Stan Szelest died of a heart attack, a massive shock for his family and for the Band. Levon and Stan had been especially close. Known as "the great Stan Szelest," the dean of rock 'n' roll piano had toured with Neil Young, Jackson Browne, Maria Muldaur, and Graham Nash, as well as the Band, and recorded with Roy Buchanan, Lonnie Mack, Stevie Ray Vaughan, Jesse Ed Davis, and Delbert McClinton. That April, Helm was also shaken by the passing of his mentor, Henry Glover, who died of a heart attack at age sixty-nine.

At almost the same time, in the middle of the night, the Helm barn burned to the ground. Carolyn Szelest was staying with Levon and Sandy after the death of her husband, and Diamond was there as well. The barn had caught fire before—causing damage to the kitchen and part of the studio—but not like this. They were lucky to escape with their lives, although Diamond, running around outside in his pajamas, wanted to return to the burning building to retrieve his teeth.

"Levon had one of those small refrigerators, and he had that in the bedroom," Terry Cagle says. "And I think that got a hot wire...And he had a cat that woke him up. He used to kinda kid around with that cat a little bit, but after that cat saved his life, he started being really sweet and gentle to that cat."

Levon and Sandy checked into a Holiday Inn, and the next morning, Butch took them shopping at a Jamesway discount store. Nothing remained in the smoking rubble except a concrete vault that held artifacts such as recordings from the RCO All-Stars, Levon's guns, and a singed Ludwig drum kit Ringo gave him after their 1989 tour. "Levon [was dressed in] a bathrobe, his boxer shorts and his boots. That's all," notes Dener. Levon was so desperate for something to wear that he put on a Yankees T-shirt, something a red-neck Southern boy would never usually do. They moved into a rental house in Bearsville, and Diamond returned to Arkansas to live with his daughter Modena.

The insurance money was a hundred thousand dollars short of what was needed for reconstruction, and Helm borrowed the balance to rebuild the barn from wood and stone, making it better than before. He had an amazing knowledge of architecture and construction. "This is how I know the genius of this man who barely got through high school," Butch says. "He and the architect and his other business manager, Joe Forno, designed the house that Levon had in his head. Everything that you see there came out of Levon's design, his dream vision." From the prototype of a small cardboard model, the new barn was rebuilt by Paul Shultis and Paul Shultis Jr.—the son and grandson of the original contractor.

"One of the most incredible buildings you'll ever see anywhere," Dener declares. "Not a nail in the wood in the studio anywhere. It's all post and beam; it's all hand done...Levon said, 'I want a cupola... and I want to make the music and have it go up in there and boil around and dance, and then when it comes back down then that's when the people will hear it.'" No metal nails or supports were used as they cause a false frequency when sound hits them, resulting in white noise on recordings. "They won't sound bad," Helm said, "but they will never have the depth and purity that only wood, stone, and natural materials can deliver."

In addition to his interest in architecture, Levon had a curious mind in general. "Levon was a smart person," Anna Lee recounts.

> You wouldn't think it from school 'cause he had been dumber than dirt, but he absorbed a lot of stuff. History—he could tell you things that happened years ago that who would ever thought that he'd picked up on...He knew a lot about American history and Arkansas history. He knew an awful lot about different musicians, different animals. He just absorbed everything.

AS THE REBUILDING of the barn proceeded, the Band had commitments, and Billy Preston was brought in on keyboards and vocals. That soon went awry, however, when Preston pleaded no contest to cocaine and sexual-assault charges and was sentenced to drug rehabilitation followed by a term of house arrest. Richard Bell, a Toronto native who'd played piano with Ronnie Hawkins and Janis Joplin, then joined the group.

Sony pulled out of the Band's record deal, citing bad sales for Robertson's recent album. Then Geffen Records proposed that the Band reunite with Robbie for an album and tour. Danko said it was out of the question: "After the first two Band albums it really wasn't a band anymore. We were on somebody's ego trip. Success can be a very strange thing. It can rear its head like an ugly beast." There's no record of Levon's response.

IN THE SUMMER of 1992, Rick was in rehab during several gigs, so the Band hired Frank Campbell on bass and Toronto songwriter and musician Colin Linden on second guitar and vocals. Colin had workshopped ideas for *Jericho* with Levon and Rick two years before, and now that they had a new deal with Pyramid Records, they resumed their work in earnest.

Linden had first been introduced to Helm in the early 1980s when the Band played the Nickelodeon Tavern in Toronto, then again when he opened for them at that city's Diamond club.

> [Levon] was about as charming as any human being could be [Colin says]. He would look you in the eye, and he shook your

hand. He made you feel like you were really welcome in his presence. And he was as down to earth as anyone could be… When I was a little kid and I dreamt of being a musician, and I dreamt of working with people whose music I love…he was the kind of person who in my most idealized sense, that was what you were supposed to be like. That was the graciousness and that was the warmth that made a real true musician. He was that.

Colin did some recording and gigs with Rick, then met Levon again in 1988 at a Band gig in Barrie, Ontario.

He came up to me, [says Linden,] and he remembered me immediately. He said, "Rick says great things about your record. You gotta come down and visit us." I was thrilled, and it was really amazing…I think he had a bit of—in the most literal sense—a supernatural thing. I found this a lot from the great old blues players that I knew as well. But he had very, very strong instincts. He was a very, very astute observer and listener.

The sushi-laden sessions for *Jericho* were mostly recorded at Helm's barn with some tracks cut at Bearsville and BearTracks. Recording in his own studio gave Levon more control and some separation from the suits at the record company. The control room, located on the second story of the barn, was open to the studio below, but it was not equipped with recording gear. "My plan was always to call in a truck: Back 'em in, plug 'em up, record 'em, and get 'em the fuck out of here," Helm stated. "I never did want to spend no damn half-million dollars on the electronics of it."

John Simon was brought back onboard as a musician and co-producer, along with the Band and Aaron "Professor Louie" Hurwitz. Simon must have had second thoughts, though, when he spent a night at the barn in between sessions and woke up to find Helm aiming a gun at him, mistaking him for an intruder.

Colin Linden struck a deal with Simon and Helm that in exchange for helping with the recording of *Jericho*, he could use the barn in the mornings to work on his own album, *South at Eight North at Nine*. He describes Levon's approach to music:

> He thought of music in such a holistic fashion that for him, I think, he could be playing the drums, he could be playing the mandolin, playing guitar, playing bass, it all was sort of the same for him. Interestingly enough, his feel, his actual time…permeated every instrument that he played. So when he played guitar, he sounded like Levon playing guitar. When he played mandolin, it sounded obviously like Levon.
>
> [His music is] influenced by a lot of different things, but to me there are a few identifiable things. He sounds like somebody who learned how to play in the '50s…in the earliest days of rock 'n' roll. I think a lot of what influenced him was music that existed before rock 'n' roll, so he was never what you would call a basher drummer. He was a very astute player and a very nuanced player. He really had his own style, and his playing and his singing were so integrated. That really, I think, had a big influence on his playing. Yes, it was behind the beat, but it also drove the song in the right direction.
>
> He was adamantly against using click tracks, and for that I thank him so much because when I'm in the studio producing something and somebody wants to use a click track—you know, once in a blue moon there's a reason for playing to a loop or something like that—but nine times out of ten at least I don't. And when I don't, I often cite Levon saying that music should not be played to a grid like that—and I'm paraphrasing him a little bit—but…he said music should speed up and slow down a little bit and breathe right.
>
> And he was always very conscious of taking the song in the right direction. It was never a mindless thing for him, and his way of interpreting it was really oriented to the song and his way of feeling it. Like in some ways it was almost like the top of the beat would land a certain way and the backbeat would be a little behind—and this is a great generalization, by the way—and that same kind of feel, when…he'd show you a song on the mandolin

or showed you a guitar part that he wanted you to play, he had the same purposefulness, and his actual sense of time was so unique to him, and so purposeful, that it felt the same...[In the Band, Levon] mapped out the rhythmic feel of everything.

Co-producer Louie Hurwitz first met Levon when he and Garth recorded the Bauls in the early 1980s, then he worked with the Band in 1987 on a PBS special in New Orleans at Tipitina's with Allen Toussaint, Jo-El Sonnier, Fred Carter Jr., and Thumbs Carllile. Hurwitz formed a group he called the Crows—he wanted the bird connection with the Hawks—to cut demos he thought the Band may want to record, as well as to back Levon, Rick, and Garth in some of their solo projects. Later, to differentiate themselves from several other bands who'd adopted *Crows* as part of their name, the Crows became the Crowmatix.

Louie acknowledges the tight relationship among Levon, Rick, and Garth: "Like any marriage, at times it was great—you couldn't get anything better—and at times it got pretty dysfunctional." Colin saw occasional tension between Levon and Rick. "There was never any lack of love," he points out, "but sometimes there was a week when Rick would be pissed off at Levon or Levon would be pissed off at Rick, and then sometimes Rick was just not around." But when they were together in the studio, Hurwitz says, "It was always a very positive experience because we were working on recording, and these fellows were true recording artists...The guys really enjoyed being in the studio once they got going." Regarding Helm, he recalls,

He was one of the greatest guys I've ever worked with in the recording studio...Levon talked a lot, so he was the leader. Garth doesn't say much, and Rick was just busy doing his things. If Levon said we were going to do something, we would do it. If Rick said we were going to do something, it was always, "Well, we gotta talk to Levon."...It always looked to me that Levon kept getting his band taken away from him [by Dylan then Robertson]...so I think he was always protective of that.

"The one thing I can say about Levon and Rick and Garth is they're great contributors to songs," Hurwitz continues.

> Somebody would have an idea, and Levon would jump in with another idea. They were great co-writers....Joe Flood brought in ["Move to Japan,"] and Jimmy Weider, and then Levon started adding things to that...He really had good ideas when somebody brought something in, and once in a while, he'd come in and say, "I've got an idea for a song"...and everybody would get to work, you know, like Richard Bell's "The Caves of Jericho."

Although Helm is credited as co-writer on only two songs—"The Caves of Jericho" and "Move to Japan"—Jim Weider maintains that Levon pulled his weight as a songwriter: "We wrote stuff together on that record. [Levon] would come in with a really good line...come up with some words. So we were working together on that record a lot."

The buoyant "Remedy" was written by Weider and Linden specifically for Helm and Danko to sing. Levon plays drums with hot rods; Randy uses sticks. They're likely both on drums in "Blind Willie McTell," with Levon's drums higher in the mix, the rhythm orchestrated on the toms. Danko's voice soars, and Helm brings the song earthbound with his sonorous vocals. Blues artist Champion Jack Dupree, who passed through Woodstock on his way back home to Germany just prior to his death in 1992, sits in on piano. "That's one where I had to fight the record company to record that song," Hurwitz reveals. "They didn't want to use 'Atlantic City' either." Ironically, the rousing "Atlantic City," with Levon on mandolin, became a staple of their live performances.

"Country Boy" is a melancholy reminder of the Band's missing comrade, showcasing Richard Manuel's lavish vocals from a 1985 performance. The Band rocks out on Muddy Waters's swinging shuffle "Stuff You Gotta Watch" behind Helm's declaratory voice. Staying in the blues vein, Levon gets down and lascivious in "Same Thing," with one drummer using blast sticks on the snare and tom, and the other on the ride.

Steve Jordan plays drums on the 12/8 shuffle "Blues Stay Away from Me." An esteemed drummer in his own right, Jordan came late as a fan of the Band. On his way back from Japan in 1977, he spent some time alone at a beach in Hawaii with two cassettes. One of them was *The Band*:

> I remember...really being overwhelmed by the recording "King Harvest," and I would listen to it over and over, and then of course "Rag Mama Rag"—those two in particular. It was the combination of the song, the feel and [Levon's] drumming...
>
> When we finally got to sit down together at length it was during the making of *Jericho*. And it was a thrill. Of course, I was elated about it...Obviously, before that watching [Levon's] performances, you know, in *The Last Waltz* and stuff, I just became a huge fan...Little do you know you're going to become someone's friend. I was always intrigued by how he could sing and play and sound like two separate people.
>
> When you're singing and playing the drums, sometimes the tendency is to phrase everything the way you're playing the instrument. So some drummers, they'll phrase to go along with the drumming. He actually phrased things like two completely different people, which was extraordinary. And he did the same thing when he played mandolin. Great mandolin player, 'cause his feel was just like his drumming, so the feel on the mandolin was just remarkable. I loved it.
>
> Obviously, I was intrigued by his gift, and then, of course, I became friends with him. You couldn't get a more genuine person. I mean, he is that guy, you know. And you felt that while he was singing on all of the records. You believed the story because you felt like it was his. To me, the key of the Band was his honesty and believability in delivering these songs. That's really the key.

Jordan describes Helm's drumming this way: "Levon plays the song. He was born with this beautiful rhythm. When you have a brilliant musician like Levon who has an inherent take on music—he's a great singer, he's a composer—with that combination you can't lose. His drumming is gorgeous, and his interpretation of the song is magnificent. He has that feel and he knows how to get that sound. I just love what emanates from the drums when he plays."

Two things Jordan learned from Helm were "his taste and also his sound. He knew sound, and that's always the quest, you know, to get the sound, and the appropriate sound for the appropriate song…The more muffled sound that, I guess, he might be known for was a very musical sound. There was a reason for it. It wasn't just to deaden the sound. It was appropriate for the music."

Levon rarely used the crash cymbal, yet Steve notes,

> Neither did Al Jackson, neither did Benny Benjamin…Some drummers do it because they're bored, so they feel like they have to crash all the time. It's not very musical to crash all the time, that's for sure. Some people have been taught to do that—they've been given the wrong message…because people want to hear something big going into a chorus or big going into a verse or something like that. But it's more of a musical decision. But of course, music and sonics are all kind of combined when you want to make a great-sounding record, so there are a lot of reasons.

THE BAND WAS invited to perform at Bob Dylan's Thirtieth Anniversary Concert Celebration, paying tribute to his years of recording for CBS, which was held at Madison Square Garden on October 16, 1992, only six days after the passing of Levon's dear father, Diamond. Robertson wasn't there.

The house band was Booker T. and the MGs, and the other guest artists included Tom Petty and the Heartbreakers, George Harrison, Willie Nelson, Johnny Cash, Stevie Wonder, Ritchie Havens, Neil Young, Roger McGuinn, and Eric Clapton, who introduced the Band. The Band had held a rare rehearsal for this event, going over "When I Paint My Masterpiece" at the barn, and Levon was happy with the result, especially gratified to honor a musician who had contributed so much to the Band's success.

Also in 1992, Helm hosted an instructional video called *Levon Helm Teaches Classic Rock, Country and Blues Drumming* for Homespun Tapes, founded by Woodstock neighbors and friends Happy Traum and his wife, Jane. On it, Levon played with Promark 7A drumsticks, which provided him with medium weight and power. He preferred wooden to nylon tips, saying that wood, "makes the cymbals sing in a truer voice for my ears." In order to prevent blisters from the sweat that ran down his arms when he played, Levon sometimes wore a black Zildjian glove on his left hand. He used Zildjian cymbals, and his kit was Yamaha, including a piccolo snare drum that he was given in Osaka on the Ringo tour. "It's about three inches of dynamite there," he said of the drum. "It sounds like a regular six-inch or seven-inch snare drum. It's amazing. It's so explosive, so loud." In his lesson, Helm encouraged drummers to experiment with their drums, trying different tunings until they find their sound.

AS PART OF Bill Clinton's presidential inaugural celebrations, the Absolutely Unofficial Blue Jeans Bash was held on January 17, 1993, at the National Building Museum in Washington, D.C. The house band was the Band, joined by the Cate Brothers, Clarence Clemons, Ronnie Hawkins, Kim Wilson, Dr. John, Dickie Betts, Stephen Stills, and Bob Dylan in blue jeans and a cowboy hat. The venue was so crammed with party-goers that Clinton himself couldn't come due to security concerns.

Although Levon had supported Bill Clinton, Anna Lee says, "I tried not to discuss politics with him because he'd get so frustrated. And you can tell by some of his songs…he had strong opinions about it. I guess he was more Democrat than anything…I think at the end he just kind of thought all politicians were crooked…He could get into some deep conversations about politics." In Butch Dener's opinion, "That boy loved America. He didn't love politics or politicians—I don't think he ever registered to vote a day in his life…He just didn't trust those suit people, whether it was from the record company on to the very top." Honesty was essential for Helm, and to a large extent he assessed it by intuition. "I've seen Levon walk away from big-time record people because he'd look at them and [say], 'I don't like his shoes,'" Dener declares. "He'd go on instinct. Levon didn't survive everything he survived without having real good gut instincts."

MONEY WAS STILL short for Levon in the early 1990s, as Butch soon realized:

> You always think that when you meet a rock star—and these guys were rock stars—you just think, oh, wow, they're rich. They have all these records, they're rich. But then I would be the guy in charge of handing out the daily per diems or the meal money, and it dawned on me very quickly that these guys needed and wanted that twenty-five dollars as much as I did…Those guys were hurting. Whenever they would get a royalty check, it really meant something.

Levon did some voice-overs and TV ads. "We had a friend in Chicago who did jingles," Butch says, "and Levon got a Coca-Cola commercial, and Rick got a Levi's commercial, and those checks, as they used to call them, were 'checks from God.'" Helm also sang for a Bud Light TV commercial and for Wrigley's gum. With the Band, he did some ads for jeans and a telephone company. "We did a lot of commercials…" Louie Hurwitz recalls. "Levon…was really quite respected as a great talk-over artist, easily identifiable. So we would get called from ad agencies for Levon to put his voice over the ads, and we did quite a few of them." In 1994, Helm and Mary Chapin Carpenter did narration and introductions for the Nashville-based weekly syndicated TV series *The Road*, which showcased new and established country-music performers.

As much as he needed to keep earning a paycheck, Levon was always generous in giving back to the community he loved. "We did so many benefits for the police department and the fire department up here in Woodstock," Jim Weider remembers. "He would always do a benefit, you know. That was just the way he was." George Lembesis, who would soon come onboard as the Band photographer, explains, "Those guys [Levon and Rick] were pillars of the community…and when each of them passed away, it was a big blow, and it affected the community pretty personally."

WHEN DAVID FISHOF brought up the idea of an autobiography to Levon, he was reluctant at first. Upon meeting Helm, co-author

Stephen Davis forewarned him that his experience was mostly with English rock bands. Levon responded, "Son, I need the money so bad, I'd work with Stalin."

This Wheel's on Fire was published in 1993 to excellent reviews. Paul Berry hired a trooper on leave from the Arkansas State Police to be Levon's driver and provide security as the book tour took him across the U.S. As was usually the case, they became good friends. "Levon loved the guy, and the guy loved Levon," Berry says. "There wasn't much they didn't talk about. Helm still smoked his joints, but he was discerning enough not to do it in the trooper's face. When Levon looked up from signing books at West Hollywood's Book Soup, he was delighted to see Ringo standing in line to surprise his friend.

Jericho was released in November to several negative comments. Some said the Band was looking backward; some professed that they'd lost their spirit. *Rolling Stone* claimed that the slick production subsumed their individual mastery.

WHEN THE BAND was inducted into the Rock and Roll Hall of Fame in January 1994, there was hope in some quarters that the living members of the original lineup would reunite for the ceremony. Butch Dener knew it would never happen:

> That supposed reunion was total bullshit, because Levon hated Robertson. He hated everything about him. He resented him. It was a betrayal, and it was a betrayal of brotherhood, and if you know anything about Levon and his feeling about loyalty, once you betray that red-neck son of a gun, you're done. Robertson was done…Robertson ripped them off, and when there was a time he could have helped, he was nowhere to be found. I know because I was out looking.

Rick, Garth, and Robbie were there for the honor, which was presented by Eric Clapton. As they were about to leave the stage, Clapton advised the audience—surely with tongue in cheek—to be patient, that Levon was on his way in a limo with Jerry Garcia, another no-show that year. The remaining Band with Clapton performed "The Weight," a sorry substitute for Helm's version.

Aside from his feelings for Robertson, Levon was ambivalent about awards in general. On one hand, he liked to be appreciated, but he also saw behind the facade. "How could I be part of that hypocrisy?" he asked. "Most awards are just bought and sold to the highest bidder, anyway, and they don't always acknowledge true excellence and artistry." Also, the induction was for the original Band, and for Helm, the Band was definitely not over. He gave his Hall of Fame jacket to someone he believed deserved it more—the great blues guitarist Hubert Sumlin.

THAT YEAR WAS a busy one, with a tour across North America and Japan to support *Jericho*, including *The Tonight Show with Jay Leno*, the New Orleans Jazz and Heritage Festival, the Canada Day celebration on Parliament Hill in Ottawa, and at Woodstock '94 with Bob Weir, Hot Tuna, Roger McGuinn, Bruce Hornsby, and Rob Wasserman. For Levon, performing with Garth and Rick still held rewards: "I can't call it a surprise, but every time I hear Garth play, I hear something that shakes me. Same with Rick. I've heard him sing a lot of nights, but every show he hits one note that really hits me, really makes me feel."

THE BAND BEGAN 1995 with an appearance on *The Late Show with David Letterman* then *Late Night with Conan O'Brien*, and in between, they performed in Toronto to help celebrate Ronnie Hawkins's sixtieth birthday.

Joining Ronnie and the Band for a rocking good time at Massey Hall were Jerry Lee Lewis, Carl Perkins, Jeff Healey, and Lawrence Gowan. Helm was a long-time fan of Carl Perkins and realized his dream that night when they played together. "That's the kind of drumming I like," Perkins said of Levon's style. "That's rockabilly...He just hit right at the bottom of the beat with that drum. That's where that boy was and still is."

Another memorable occasion that year was opening for the two final Grateful Dead concerts with Jerry Garcia, held on July 8 and 9 at Chicago's Soldier Field. The running joke was that the Band liked playing with the Dead because they had female fans, whereas the Band's audiences were mostly male. Also, during that appearance, Helm met with manager Ron Rainey about the possibility of the Band becoming his clients, and he signed on as their manager that August. "I had a lot of fun," he recounts. "Levon Helm was one of the most interesting people that I've probably ever met in my life...He was the leader while denying being the leader. It was kind of one of those things where if Levon didn't want to do it, it didn't get done. And if he did want to do it, pretty much everybody went along."

Rainey says of Helm, "He was spontaneous and he was infectious. If he set his mind to doing something, then he would become engaged, and it was hard not to follow his direction. He was a powerful personality." A case in point was Levon suddenly insisting at 11:30 one night that Butch Dener drive him to Arkansas. "We drove all night and the next day," Butch remarks, "and he hated to stop. When the sun came up and my eyes were closing, we'd pull into the rest area, and he'd open his eye and go, 'Are you stoppin'?' and I said, 'Well, just for a minute.' 'Well, all right. That's all we've got is a minute.' He goes, 'I know there's catfish waiting for me.' And we would just get back on the road. He just loved being on the road."

Whether it was for Levon and Butch or for the entire band and guests, whenever Helm was down home, Anna Lee prepared a feast:

> He would always call ahead of time and ask me what I was cooking, and I'd say, "What do you want?" He'd say, "I want red beans and rice, stewed potatoes, buttermilk cornbread and wilted lettuce salad." And he would come...sometimes it'd be eleven or twelve o'clock at night. We'd all go to my house, and we would eat. Paul [Berry] would come. Paul would bring some of his friends... and the whole band would come. And we would eat and laugh and joke until two or three o'clock in the morning...When he would eat, he would eat well. He had so much energy, he'd work it off. We was always trying to fatten him up. But he was the same way when he was a kid.

And when Levon was in the Memphis area, Mary Vaiden made him his favorite mandarin-orange cake, which he'd wash down with copious amounts of Coca-Cola.

LEVON'S VOICE IS more weathered with a slight nasal quality on the Band's next album, *High on the Hog*, mostly recorded in 1995 and released in February 1996. Louie Hurwitz, the engineer and co-producer along with the Band, says that although the Band only wrote one song for this album, the others were contributed largely by friends who were around at the time. "The Kentucky Headhunters were playing some gigs with us, and they gave us 'Back to Memphis,'" Hurwitz says. "Bruce Channel was on the bus all the time. He gave us 'Stand Up.' And 'Crazy Mama.'…[J.J. Cale] was hanging out with us a lot at that time." Regarding the song selection, Danko commented, "We choose everything very carefully, it's a great democratic system in the Band, it's a way of life."

En Vogue's "Free Your Mind" is an unexpected inclusion. With a streetwise snarl, Levon pleads for tolerance in this funky, horn-driven arrangement. "It's a patriotic song—and besides, it really lends itself to two sets of drums…" Helm explained. "We changed the lyrics a little to come from a less pretty place than En Vogue comes from. We had to rough it up a little to fit our style," he added with a chuckle.

Levon sings with swagger on "Stand Up," and Levon, Rick, and Randy trade vocals on Dylan's "Forever Young," resurrected from 1974's *Planet Waves*. Dylan also wrote the high-octane rocker "I Must Love You Too Much" for the Band, sung here by Danko and Ciarlante. The stomping R&B track "The High Price of Love," co-written by the late Stan Szelest, features Helm on harmonica and in a duet with Danko.

Again, this album includes a bittersweet performance by Richard Manuel—"She Knows"—recorded live at New York City's Lone Star Cafe a few weeks before his death. Champion Jack Dupree sings on "Ramble Jungle," a number he co-wrote with the Band when he recorded with them in the early 1990s.

Levon was busy as a sideman on other musicians' albums. "It's like we do each other favors," Helm said.

I got to sing on John Anderson's record, and got to play some shows with John, and it's because we like each other and get along and like to play with each other...We should take everything we can get and really enjoy it, and expect it to mean something. I've made myself that way, open to anything, and people know that I love to try anything new. Because of it, I've gotten to sing with Emmylou Harris, and Sheryl Crow, and Martina McBride, and some great people.

The Band appeared on *The Late Show with David Letterman* on March 26 to support *High on the Hog*, then Ron Rainey got them started on their tour in style. "I revered the Band," he says, "and what they'd accomplished musically—everybody knew what they meant to the music business. I was proud to sort of lift them up a bit when I came in." And Rainey did that lifting by renting Carnegie Hall. With one ad in *The New York Times*, the show on March 29, 1996— with J.J. Cale opening—sold out. Ron did the same thing the following March.

In John Simon's opinion, the Band had been doing really well, but after *High on the Hog* everything started to decline. That June, the Band played shows in Europe to some negative reviews, noting that Danko seemed distracted and his performances lackluster, and Helm had to carry a lot of the load. Yet in Dublin, Levon was seen smashing his mandolin into a wall and falling into the drums, then announcing how pleased he was to be in London.

ABOUT THIS TIME, George Lembesis started helping the Band at their gigs and became their official photographer, observing the relationship among Levon, Rick, and Garth:

> They were almost like brothers, right. You could tell they had been friends forever. There was a lot of non-verbal communication... Especially onstage, they'd kind of look at each other and communicate without really speaking...
>
> Garth is a unique individual. It's not true, but people would think he was aloof or anti-social, but nothing could be further

from the truth. You just had to know how to speak to Garth and what subjects to speak to him about, because late at night on the tour bus if I brought up, let's say, accordions or polka players or sea shanties or something, Garth could speak for three hours nonstop. The general public would not see that.

Levon and Rick were different. They were both down-to-earth, friendly guys. You know, when you first met them, they each had their own kind of charisma. You knew they were rock stars, but they didn't act like rock stars; they didn't carry themselves like rock stars. They were very open to their fans. If you approached them and asked for an autograph or a photo, they were always very accommodating...

Rick and Levon would be at the forefront of dealing with management decisions, then Garth would be brought in...For the most part, they came up with a consensus...It was a kind of democracy, and you could tell that they had mutual admiration and respect for each other. And, you know, just like every other group of people, everybody has their own little quirks and eccentricities, and you know, when you're on a tour bus with ten guys or whatever, you all have to get along. You all have to figure out the path of least resistance.

By this stage in their careers, the original Band members were not so eager to embark on long tours, as Lembesis recalls:

You have to understand that they were in their late fifties at the time, but they had led a pretty rough life on the road, and so I believe they had aged more than the average person and so as long as they could do shows locally and still have some kind of an income coming in, I don't know that they were relishing the thought of pulling together a twenty- or thirty-day tour and leave home for six weeks. They really were kind of homebodies, and they liked to hang out at home and being around Wood-stock. And from Woodstock, within a five-, six-hour drive, you could be in Toronto, Washington, D.C., and be in New York, Boston, Pittsburgh.

IN WHAT *ROLLING STONE* dubbed "one of the coolest gatherings in rock 'n' roll history," rock royalty gathered in Levon's barn on July 9, 1996, to record "Deuce and a Quarter" for *All the King's Men*, a tribute album to Elvis on the twentieth anniversary of his death. Elvis's guitarist, the immensely influential Scotty Moore, and his drummer, D.J. Fontana—one of Levon's major influences—were joined by Keith Richards (and his father, Bert), rockabilly guitarist Paul Burlison, Helm, Danko, Hudson, Weider, Bell, Ciarlante, and Stan Lynch, former drummer for Tom Petty and the Heartbreakers who produced this cut. In "Deuce and a Quarter," a foot-tappin' rockabilly gem, Levon swaps vocals with Keith—two of rock's most distinctive voices.

Levon laid down his vocal track before Keith arrived. As George Lembesis recollects,

> What they needed on that day was for Keith to do vocals and for Keith to do a guitar solo…It was hysterical because Keith was having trouble with the lyrics. He had a lyric sheet in front of him, but he was kind of stuttering and stumbling over the words. At one point he made a joke about how this stuff is as difficult to recite as Shakespeare, which everybody thought was hilarious. And then Levon started becoming his vocal coach, basically helping him get through the lyrics. And then at one point, Keith said to him, "That's what I needed, Levon, a real hillbilly cat like yourself to help me out."
>
> So when they recorded the vocals, Keith was doing the vocals live, and they were playing back the other vocals on the backing track, and Levon was basically standing next to him coaching him on and lending moral support. Then they stopped recording, then everybody would start laughing and slapping each other on the back, drinking and smoking and having a good time. And then they'd all go back up into the control room where they would listen to the playback…At the end of the tape, Keith would say [to his dad], "It sounds pretty good. What do you think, Pop?"

For Levon, having Scotty and D.J. in his studio was an honor and made for one hell of a good time. "Those guys were just talking constantly off in a corner, sharing a laugh," Lembesis says of Fontana and Helm, "and then, of course, the most natural thing for those guys, they just wanted to sit behind the drum kit and talk and compare notes, compare equipment or whatever."

With such an assemblage, the musicians couldn't leave after one song. "The jam session was still going strong at 4 a.m.," Scotty Moore reported. "They tore through cover after cover, including a hair-raising version of 'Willie and the Hand Jive' that found Richards playing a floor tom while Fontana and Helm dueled on their kits."

Levon was the host of a documentary for the PBS series *Great Drives*. His segment was close to his heart—the stretch of Highway 61 from Memphis to New Orleans. The Band recorded the theme music for the series, and on this episode, Helm performs with two of his best musical buddies, James Cotton and C.W. Gatlin.

He also had the small role of an earnest Bible salesman in Las Vegas in *Feeling Minnesota*, a sometimes-farcical drama of bumbling brothers and the woman they both desire, starring Keanu Reeves, Vincent D'Onofrio, and Cameron Diaz. "He's a good guy," Levon said of Reeves, "and he plays bass, so we talked about being in a band." Helm had no scenes with Diaz, but concluded, "She is a sweetheart too, and being around her just the little bit that I was, I know right away why everyone's so excited about her. She is really, really good and super-down-to-earth. Beautiful all the way through."

BAND MEMBERS HAD their own projects, and one of these was Danko's five-concert tour in Japan starting on April 30, 1997, with musical collaborators Jonas Fjeld and Eric Andersen. As the tour was finishing on May 6, a package was delivered to Rick from his wife, Elizabeth, that contained a magazine with .04 ounces of heroin tucked inside. He was arrested, charged with smuggling heroin, and held in jail until the ruling on July 25. Danko pleaded not guilty, claiming it was a misunderstanding, that he'd asked his wife to send him codeine, for which he had a prescription. With Levon's permission, Louie Hurwitz put together a CD of live performances by Danko, Hurwitz, and Ciarlante, called *Rick Danko: In Concert* to help raise funds for Rick's legal expenses and for Elizabeth, who had no money. Although the prosecution asked for a two-and-a-half-year prison term, the three-judge panel gave Danko a suspended five-year sentence, and he was permitted to return to the States.

While Danko was incarcerated in Japan, the Band had bookings that had to be canceled, meaning no pay for the rest of the musicians, although on a few occasions, they hired Mike Dunn to fill in on bass. "[Levon] was, from that point on, eternally pissed off at Rick for that because that cost him a lot of money," future bandmate Pat O'Shea says. As Louie Hurwitz puts it,

> [Levon] got a little ticked off at it, obviously...After the *High on the Hog* record, the Band had built a stable relationship with a lot of promoters and a lot of show people, and their manager at that time, Ron Rainey...set up a whole tour...across the country...and when Rick ran into his trouble, unfortunately he didn't want to change the configuration of the Band, so therefore the tours got canceled. So nobody was too happy about that...They just finished working hard for eight or nine years, and now they're going to finally reap some rewards and [they] don't. So it did cause problems.

"Levon loved Japan," Lembesis says. "He loved playing there, he loved everything about it," and even though Danko was permitted to return to Japan after a year, Helm was concerned that Rick may have negatively affected any future touring opportunities there. "I do remember one show that we did in Beverly Hills—it was a charity benefit show—where Rick was back..." George recalls, "and it was kind of tense up there. You could tell that Levon was just not happy about the whole situation."

HELM PLAYED THE Reverend Bob Goodall in the action movie *Fire Down Below*, starring his friend Steven Seagal, who spent a lot of time with Levon in Woodstock. Helm's character is a Kentucky preacher helping an Environmental Protection agent investigate toxic-waste dumping. Levon sings "Mr. Spider" in the film while playing acoustic guitar.

It was a musical cast, which also included Kris Kristofferson, Harry Dean Stanton, Randy Travis, and Marty Stuart. "Steven likes to get together at night and play music," Levon said. "And between shots we pull out our guitars and jam." In fact, Seagal enjoyed Helm's company so much that he kept him on salary after his character died off just to have him around. After the movie had wrapped, Seagal sat in with the Band in Trenton, New Jersey.

Levon held what he called a Midnight Ramble on a Mississippi riverboat during the King Biscuit Blues Festival in Helena in October, with the Cate Brothers Band and James Cotton. One song from that gig, "Going Back to Memphis," appeared on the album *River of Song: A Musical Journey Down the Mississippi.*

Two days later—October 12, 1997—was proclaimed Levon Helm Day in Marvell. "People in Marvell and Phillips County always thought Levon was special, from the very beginning," Mary Vaiden maintains. It wasn't only after he became famous. "The people of Marvell are very proud of Levon, and if there's anything negative ever said, you'd get your head bit off in a minute." Anna Lee says Helm seemed mystified: "He thought with his friend C.W. Gatlin, the Cates and other Arkansas musicians being so good, why did they want him?" A new sign was posted on Highway 49, on each side of town, reading, "Welcome to Marvell—Home of Levon Helm." At the event, he was presented with a large cake bearing his picture and scenes from the area, declaring him in icing as Marvell's son.

But those who knew Levon well were shocked. As George Lembesis relates, "Paul Berry pulled me aside, and he said, 'Listen, I think we have a problem with Levon...I think he was coughing up blood.'" Mary was dismayed. "He was so thin," she says. "Modena said to me, 'What is wrong with Levon?...He is sick. He really looks like he doesn't feel well.'" When Modena confronted her brother, he said, "'Naw, there ain't nothing wrong with me. I'm fine. I just need some rest." Despite his bravado, Helm knew it was serious, but he couldn't acknowledge it even to himself.

Bubba Sullivan saw Levon during this trip. "We had the Headhunters here, we had Johnnie Johnson, we had Cotton, and Levon could not talk. He came by the shop on Monday, heading back to New

York. I said, 'Levon, you better go see a doctor.' He said, 'No, if I go see a doctor, he's gonna tell me to quit smoking.' I said, 'Shit, man, if you don't quit smoking, you ain't gonna be here.'" Levon—a three-pack-a-day cigarette smoker—had disregarded good-intentioned pleas from friends such as Harold Kudlets and Paul Berry to stop smoking. Looking back, Levon confessed, "I think that there's that secret little spot back there in your mind where you know something's wrong, but you don't want to admit it."

LEVON'S VOICE IS cracked and rough in a small role he performed in the quirky film *The Adventures of Sebastian Cole*, the story of a mixed-up teen with a good reason for being so, starring Margaret Colin, Clark Gregg, and Adrian Grenier. Levon played the role of Juvie Bob, who chats up Sebastian's father, a man midway through his transition to becoming female. The movie was selected for the following year's Sundance Festival.

Louie Hurwitz first noticed Levon's gravelly vocals and declining health when they recorded *Levon Helm and the Crowmatix: Souvenir*. Then by fall 1997 when the Band began cutting *Jubilation*, it was obvious.

JUBILATION, THE BAND'S tenth studio album—and their last—was recorded at Helm's barn from fall 1997 to the following spring. It was meant as a tribute to *Music from Big Pink* on the thirtieth anniversary of its release. To tie into that theme, engineer and producer Louie Hurwitz says, "One thing I tried on that CD was to make it little bit more acoustic like the *Big Pink* record, which is fairly acoustic, and more original material with the guys co-writing." Levon agreed: "That acoustical sound and style and attitude with the emphasis more on voices and blends, that was akin to *Big Pink* a lot, and *The Basement Tape[s]* ensemble way of doing stuff." They used a similar approach. "We went back to the way we cut *Big Pink*," Helm said, "which was to get in the building together in the studio, and record the song, then tear it up and rewrite it and do it again, and do that until it was right... We all kind of co-wrote the things with each other."

The songwriting process was largely a group effort. "I'd make a suggestion," Louie remarks, "Levon would make a suggestion, and before you know it you've got a real good song, like 'Last Train to Memphis'...Or 'Don't Wait' by Kevin Doherty—Levon started adding things to that. So Levon was a very good co-writer." Helm, who co-wrote six of the tracks, said, "If I can make it irresistible for you, if I can just make the song so good you couldn't stand to not hear it, then that's what I'm supposed to do." On top of that, he aimed to prove that the Band still had its chops thirty years later.

In addition to Levon, Rick, and Garth—who, as usual, is impressive on keyboards, accordion, and saxophone—the lineup included guitarist Jim Weider, Richard Bell on keyboards, and Randy Ciarlante on second drums, plus special guests. As well as drums, Helm plays harmonica, mandolin, and acoustic guitar. The instrumentation on the album is mostly acoustic, with stand-up bass on several tunes. "I really enjoyed making *Jubilation*," Levon commented, "because I'd grown tired of the electric bass over and over and over. It hums and gets into everybody else's space, and I needed a little bit of rest from it."

It had been a long struggle for the Band to reclaim some of the recognition they were due, but by this time, Helm's voice was ravaged. Hurwitz says, "The sad part of that after working for ten years to get to that point was that Levon got sick...That wreaked a lot of havoc on a lot of levels. I felt terrible for him; he felt terrible...First, he thought he had the flu or a virus. It took a little while to diagnose. But he kept soldiering through it. I had actually asked him if he wanted to pull the record at one point...He said, 'No, we have to make this record.'"

Beginning with a drum roll, *Jubilation* kicks off with the warm, down-home sound reminiscent of *Big Pink* with "Book Faded Brown," a song that was part of Danko's solo repertoire even before *High on the Hog*. Helm sings lead and plays acoustic guitar on "Don't Wait." He added verses to Bobby Charles's "Last Train to Memphis," and plays a variation of a train beat, somewhere between straight and swung, behind his sweeping vocals. The tape was sent to Eric Clapton, who recorded two guitar tracks, and the Band chose the one they preferred.

Levon's hoarseness is evident on "Kentucky Downpour," a swinging, Motown-tinged song he started writing with Marty Grebb on the set of *Fire Down Below*. He plays mandolin on "Bound By Love," then John Hiatt, a longtime friend of the Band, overdubbed his voice in a hymn-like duet with Rick.

Ronnie Hawkins came to the studio to hear "White Cadillac," the Band's tribute to the Hawks, and gave his stamp of approval to this rockabilly foot-stomper. Following in the pathway of "Life Is a Carnival," with its inventive drumming, "Spirit of the Dance" is rhythmically infectious through funky, displaced backbeats. Levon accompanies his raw-throated vocals on Allen Toussaint's "You See Me" with loose, swinging drum work, likely with blast sticks. *Jubilation* was released in September 1998 to generally good reviews.

LEVON'S VOICE ISSUES and ill health did not improve. That winter he tried healing oils to no avail. "Finally, we went to this local doctor [in Newburgh] who did a horrible test," states Butch Dener. "They put a tube down his nose to his throat. They numbed it, but he grabbed my hand and squeezed it, but he didn't say nothing. He took it like a man, but it was horrendous…[The doctor] had no idea who Levon was. He said, 'Mr. Helm, I'm very sorry but you have throat cancer.'" Helm's first reaction? "Get me the fuck outta here!"

That doctor recommended a laryngectomy, the removal of the vocal chords, then equipping Levon with what Helm called "those Donald Duck voice boxes." Butch contacted his aunt Ruby in New York City, a retired psychiatrist and a cancer survivor. She arranged for Levon to see the top oncologist at Memorial Sloan Kettering Cancer Center, Dr. Dennis Kraus. Kraus not only believed he could save Helm's life, but also his voice. He couldn't be sure, however, that Levon would ever sing again.

Without Levon, the Band had difficulty booking shows. Dener remembers, "There was nobody around. Nobody. People had turned their back on him…He was cantankerous…He was angry and pissed off about stuff not being fair…At that time, Levon and Amy were not as close as they later were. There was a little bit of an estrangement going on at the time. I called Amy, and I said, 'Amy, your father's sick. He's got cancer. He needs you. All the other bullshit is bullshit. Get over here.' And she came."

Amy had grown up in Woodstock and Los Angeles, then attended the prestigious Trinity High School in New York City, where she studied jazz. Although she earned a degree in psychology at the University of Wisconsin, she realized that music was her first love. "I guess I had the same hopes for Amy that my parents had for me," Levon conceded. "I wanted Amy to be a scholar…And I'm so proud of her. But the same bug bit Amy that bit me and she fell back in with the rhythm section as soon as she got out of school."

After Helm had surgery to remove the tumor in his throat, he called Bill Avis and in a barely audible rasp said, "When are you coming down, Bizz? When are you coming down?" Avis left the next day.

C.W. Gatlin was another friend Helm leaned on. "He and C.W. just were very close," Mary Vaiden says, "and when Levon got sick, he would call C.W. to come stay with him, and C.W. would go up there and stay weeks at a time. He was very supportive of him in the dark days."

The surgery was followed by twenty-eight radiation treatments. Helm was fitted with a mask that had three holes at his throat and bolt holes at the back. For every radiation session, he'd wear the mask and be bolted to the table. Each time the radiation was shot through the center hole, and alternate weeks it was aimed through one of the side holes. It left his skin burned and raw, and ravaged Levon's vocal chords. "It didn't really bother me that much not being able to sing," he claimed, "but I couldn't really talk either. I couldn't explain myself. I'd have to whisper or write a note."

At first Butch took Levon to his radiation treatments every morning, then afterwards,

> we'd hang out by the pond, and [musician] Jimmy Vivino would come over…and we'd sit out by the pond. Levon would make a little fire—the country boy that he is—he would make a little fire to keep the bugs away, with pine needles to make a little smoke—he knew what to do. And we hung out there. He couldn't smoke weed, but I made pot brownies…Jimmy Vivino played guitar, and Levon would pat, and we would just hang out…He was always strong. He never doubted for a minute that he could get through

this. He had faith. I don't know how strong Sandy was or she wasn't, but she was always there. She never came to the hospital or to the medical stuff, but she always kept the home, and Levon would always come home to Mama. Mama would cook for him whatever he felt like eating—mostly Coca-Cola—but he was as strong a spirit as you ever wanted to see. He had faith. He believed in the doctors. We got him the best, and they saved his life.

After that, Amy took over and drove her father to his treatments. "He completely inspired me and kept me cool because of how blindly courageous and strong he was," she says. "It really transformed our relationship, turned it into what I would call a huge gift…There's something about linking arms with someone and going deep into that fear and hell that makes you just laugh and celebrate and feel a different joy, which I'm entirely grateful for." Levon admitted that when he got the cancer diagnosis, "It scared the hell out of me. But thank God for my baby," he said of Amy. "I didn't want her to see me scared, so I acted like I wasn't."

Until then, Levon had been a more distant presence in Amy's life, a giant figure of whom she was slightly in awe. Now, she declared, "I could see a man I had never seen before, a hero."

14

"Blues Before Sunrise"

Levon had to earn a living yet could no longer sing. Without the voice that delivered some of rock's most-loved music, Band bookings were scarce amid a stack of medical bills and a mortgage to pay. In October 1998, he and Sandy filed for bankruptcy.

Helm tried to make the best of it. "That's fine," he declared. "I never wanted to be a singer anyway. All I ever wanted is to be a drummer." Happy Traum says, "I'm sure there were periods of darkness, but I saw a positive guy all the time…He was just always striving to see the positive side of things. When his barn burned down, he said, 'Well, we'll just build a better one.' When he got sick in '98, he said, 'Whatever life I got left I'll just build a better Levon.'"

Helm pinned a lot of his hopes on a venture in New Orleans. Carmen Marotta, who had grown up at Tony Mart's club in New Jersey and revered Levon and the Band, decided to open a supper club in New Orleans. He and his investors raised a million dollars, acquired an old rice warehouse—a four-story structure in the French Quarter on the corner of Bienville and Decatur—and set about building Levon Helm's Classic American Café. Helm was not an investor; in exchange for the use of his name, he would receive a percentage of the profits. The announcement was made in spring 1998, and construction to turn the structure into a first-class music club with living quarters above continued for the rest of that year.

The club, which could hold about six or seven hundred patrons, offered two bars with seating on the main floor and on an upstairs mezzanine that looked down on the stage. The menu included such

Band-inspired dishes as "Up on Cripple Creek" seafood, "King Harvest" salads, and Last Waltz desserts. Levon was excited. His goal was to use this venue as a southern base and to play with the rich talent that lived in the city, particularly two local musicians he especially admired, Allen Toussaint and Earl Palmer.

The grand opening was on December 26. With no voice, Helm stuck to drums and mandolin with the Cate Brothers Band. James Cotton and New Orleans musicians Banu Gibson, Barbara Shorts, Brint Anderson, and Luther Kent also played. On New Year's Eve, 1998, the Band appeared with Levon's daughter, Amy, the Crowmatix, and a horn section. It was a momentous occasion—the final performance of the Band.

THE DEMISE OF the Band was not caused by Danko's passing. Its death knell sounded well before that. Levon could no longer sing the iconic songs he was renowned for, and it seemed pointless for others to do it while he sat at the kit. He lost his desire to even be in the Band—their repertoire of Robertson-credited material only rankled him. The last time he performed with Rick was in a trio with Louie Hurwitz at a private party in 1999 for Woodstock businessman Norman Clancy.

Helm went back to his first love. "At that point," Hurwitz remarks, "he said he only wanted to play blues; he wouldn't play any Band songs. And the Crowmatix, even though we play blues and stuff, we're not a blues band." So Levon was on the hunt for a new group.

PAT O'SHEA AND Chris O'Leary were part of the Eldorado Kings, a busy regional blues band out of Poughkeepsie, New York, with Frank Ingrao on stand-up bass and Mike Severino on drums. They were about to record their first album when George Lembesis, a friend of Pat, offered to ask Levon if he would play drums on a couple of tracks. Helm was struggling financially and scrambling for work. "He was interested," O'Shea says,

> so he came down…to that studio, and we recorded two songs with
> him, hung out all day and night…It was the first time that…any

of us had ever met him…and we just had a great time. A lot of laughs, a lot of storytelling. We were at that point just lifetime fans of the Band and of Levon, so it was really quite an experience, you know, meeting somebody like this and getting to play and getting to record with him for a bunch of blues hounds that were in their mid- to late-twenties. This was really kind of a big moment for us, personally and musically, and little did we know what it would lead to.

Levon could speak, but his voice was a raspy whisper with little projection. "He had broken one of his front teeth," Pat comments. "One of his favorite things to eat was frozen marshmallows. The night before, he had broken his tooth on it, so he came in looking like he was straight out of the woods, man. He looked like a backwoods hill-billy…It was hysterically funny."

About a week later, they got word that Helm wanted to see them.

He had a fire going in the fireplace [O'Shea says], and he was literally sitting in a rocking chair next to the fire with a blanket across his lap. We hung out all day, all night—I was there for probably eight to ten hours. He…could captivate a room like nobody's business, you know, with his charm and his wit and his colorful stories. It was easy to fall in love with him, and it happened instantly. Just about anybody who met him, I think, would agree that Lee was probably one of the most charming and welcoming people that they've ever met…He was just holding court, smoking weed, hanging out. We had a great time…At one point, he looked at me, and he said, "I want to join your band."

Pat was stunned. Levon's idea was for this group to be the house band at his club in New Orleans. Helm told O'Shea,

"We're going to work five nights a week, we're going to back everyone who comes through the club, and I'm going to use my influence to have friends of mine come in and play shows"…

For a twenty-nine-year-old blues upstart—someone who was

just in the trenches trying to make it happen for himself and for his band—this was like hand-of-God kind of stuff. I just couldn't believe that this is where my life was headed. This was my dream since I was four years old.

Levon and this new band, which he named the Barn Burners, went down to the club in April. Chris O'Leary, their harmonica player and vocalist, admits, "I would have done it for free...I owe that man everything." When he met Helm, O'Leary had tunnel vision as far as music was concerned, focused only on the blues greats. New Orleans blew his mind. "Levon was it," he says. "He was the catalyst for me being an eclectic artist, for sure...What you heard on the records is exactly who he is. There was no rock-star crap about him...I know his voice was rough those last three records, but you can hear all the miles, you can hear the cancer, you can hear everything."

O'Shea revered Helm's musicianship:

> He was a phenomenal shuffle drummer. He had a shuffle that nobody could duplicate. He was one of those great musicians that had a sound that was instantly recognizable...You hear Levon play a drum fill, and there's only one person that can play that fill that way, and it's Helm. His American roots, his Arkansas southern American roots were so audible in his playing it was unlike any other musician on any other instrument that I have ever heard. He played drums, and he was saying something. It told a story.
>
> So many musicians out there are just playing notes; they're not saying anything. And when Helm played drums, the sounds you heard were him. It was his life; it was his story...It didn't matter if he was playing Band songs or if he was playing a Muddy Waters song or if he was playing...a Johnny Cash song—it didn't matter. Every song he played became his.

Despite performances at Levon Helm's Classic American Café by such artists as James Cotton, Allen Toussaint, Marcia Ball, Kenny Neal, Irma Thomas, and Anson Funderburgh and the Rockets, by the spring of 1999, the club was in trouble. "The lowest night the take was four thousand dollars; the best night it was twenty-one thousand," C.W. Gatlin says. "But Levon was sick. That was the trouble."

Levon's relationship with Carmen became strained. There was the constant expense for Helm and the Barn Burners to live in hotels because their accommodation above the club wasn't ready. Levon complained that he could get his friends to perform for a nominal fee, yet management was going through official channels and paying the going rate. Café bookers, on the other hand, argued that a lot of the headline acts Helm promised did not materialize. Then there were claims that the development company was over-charging the club. As he saw the club's future in jeopardy, Carmen Marotta was heartbroken. He and his wife, Nancy, had worked tirelessly to keep it afloat.

> It never got the momentum it needed to succeed [Marotta says]... It was successful in the sense that it was a great club...We had a successful Jazz Fest...We were beginning to have bookings, and we were in the convention market...but we did not have enough cash to sustain, to get through the long hot [summer]...We had bookings for the fall, and we wanted to go forward, but we were just simply out of money in terms of subsidizing the operation. The attorneys and accountants said, "You have to close the club down."

Despite Helm's allegation that the club was a real-estate scam, Marotta emphasizes,

> This was a very big, complicated project. Attempts to over-simplify and point fingers are really a disservice to all the great people that worked so hard to make it happen...[Nancy and I] and all the investors in Levon Helm's Classic American Café certainly did not deserve to be besmirched...What a great club it was and how unfortunate it was that it just didn't make it...That's the story of Levon Helm's Classic American Café, not some kind of intrigue nonsense about somebody ripped off somebody and somebody got away with the money.

On May 13, 1999, Levon's New Orleans club closed its doors for the final time.

STILL, THE BARN Burners persevered. With Levon's precarious finances, it was a necessity. He rehearsed the young musicians, schooling them in the blues he adored. Based back in Woodstock, the band played a regular gig at the local Joyous Lake and at other clubs in the area. Without Helm's distinctive voice as part of the package, however, bookers weren't interested in hiring them for the kind of money a Levon Helm band would normally earn. And it was disheartening when audiences yelled out requests for classic Band songs, a constant irritant the group faced night after night.

> That was something that we fought for probably [for]…half of our existence [as] the Barn Burners [O'Shea says]. People expected and wanted and called out for "The Weight," "Cripple Creek," and "Ophelia" and whatever else, and all that did was just piss the Old Man off out of frustration. I'm going to guess that he felt a little diminished, and I'm sure he wanted to deliver what he was known for.
>
> And then the other part to that whole scenario is, "Hey, screw you guys. I've been at this for…forty-odd years, and I'm a drummer first, so let me drum. Let me do what I do." It took a while for us to kind of break the ticket-buyers out of that mindset.

"Levon had a lot of guts," George Lembesis observed, "because he went out…[as] the drummer in the band. He couldn't sing…Levon refused to put a Band song in the setlist. [He said,] 'We're not doing Band stuff. We're not a nostalgia act. We're in a blues band, and we're playing blues songs…If you like it great, if you don't, go see somebody else. This is what I've got. This is who I am—take it or leave it.'"

Helm put the best face he could on the situation. He was happy to just be out there in any capacity, stating, "After being as ill as I was, and faced with the possibility of not being able to perform, makes me appreciate the opportunity a whole lot more. I kind of took it for granted." Butch Dener remembers a night in Nashville when the club was almost empty: "Bonnie Bramlett, from Delaney and Bonnie, comes in to say hello to Levon; Bobby Keys, the saxophone player from Elvis Presley to the Rolling Stones, comes in. They joined the band...and there's thirteen people in the room, and they didn't give a damn. They just rocked. That was all about Levon. They came to see Levon. They came to play with Levon, and they didn't care if he could talk or not."

"Playing these little clubs—people screaming and yelling and dancing—that's all he ever wanted," Dener says. "He just wanted to make the music for the people." It wasn't about the size of the venue or about accolades. "I never wanted that damn mess," Helm claimed, referring to fame. "I'm doing the best work I've ever done. Maybe I can get back to singing again. That's a joyful thing, singing. We'll have to wait and see. But whatever happens, I might not ever fill Madison Square Garden again. That's all right with me."

Levon delighted in meeting aspiring drummers. If a parent came up to him at a show and said his child was learning drums, "That's all he needed to hear," Lembesis notes. "[Helm would say,] 'Come here, son. How long have you been playing? What do you like? Who do you like? Let me show you a couple of things. Here's a pair of drumsticks.' He *loved* that stuff."

Sometimes, however, his friendliness was a detriment. "We'd be playing a show in New York," George mentions as an example, "and people would say, 'We're coming up to Woodstock next week,' and he'd generally say, 'Oh, look me up and come visit. Stop by.' And then these people *would* show up!"

"People like to focus on gossip and drama, you know," George acknowledges, "and all the b.s. that goes with show business. What it really came down to was the music. [For] the musicians in the band, the people who were in the inner circle around [Levon], it was just about the music. That's all it was. We didn't care about anything else... Music dripped out of his pores...Even the way he walked was kind of musical and to the beat."

Those who knew Levon best saw his musicianship rise to new heights. Amy said, "There are these amazing nuances and subtleties to his drumming now. I watch him play and my jaw just drops to the floor...It's like he's beating out all the stuff he couldn't talk about. I think his drumming has become his voice and he is playing the hell out of it. It just makes me smile ear to ear."

> When we were doing the Barn Burners during his cancer, he wasn't singing [Butch says]. We were playing hardcore blues. And, man, I never saw him play those drums like he did because he couldn't sing. Everything was channeled into the drum kit. And we traveled around—a four-piece band—and people were expecting him to sing, you know, "Dixie" or "The Weight," and we were doing Muddy Waters and, you know, Howlin' Wolf and Little Walter, James Cotton's stuff. And after a while, the word got out that we weren't doing the Band, and the people stopped yelling for "Cripple Creek"…
>
> Every show Lee gave 200 percent. He didn't know how to give 100 percent. If there was ten people in the room, he played like it was Madison Square Garden. And the band always felt Levon's flow, man. He had that flow of music that was unbelievable to watch, and I was blessed so many nights to be there just watching it. He thought he had the best seat in the house—you know, the drummer's chair's the best seat in the house—well, let me tell you something, being Levon's road manager on the side of those stages all those nights, I had the best seat in the house…It was just a beautiful thing to be part of, and I'm honored and blessed that I could see it.

Rick didn't sit in with the Barn Burners, although when they had a local gig, Garth was often there. "Old Honey Boy would come and play with us, as Helm used to call him," O'Shea recounts. "They loved each other, no doubt, but like any other long-term relationship, they also annoyed the hell out of each other." Everyone recognized Hudson's brilliance. "His music might not have fit with a traditional blues band," Pat adds, "but I always loved having him there."

Levon's friend James Cotton was another favorite sidekick. "He would play with James any chance he got," Lembesis says of Helm.

> There were a couple of times where the band played in New York, and James happened to be in that neck of the woods, and he would

sit in with them. And then they would play together again in Helena and at the grand opening of the Alltel Arena in Little Rock. Then when the blues band started touring, James would show up, and he would especially do it in New Orleans at the club...You know, those two guys, they were like two little kids together. They were always having a good time and laughing and snickering and getting into trouble. It was like two little kids in the back of a classroom. It was pretty funny to watch.

Sax virtuoso Bobby Keys—a fixture with the Rolling Stones—was a Barn Burner whenever his schedule allowed. "It was absolutely just a dream come true—the greatest sax player ever," O'Shea asserts. "He had that tone; he had that honk...The two of them together was hysterical—they were two old, crazy pals. You could instantly see what it was like when they lived together...He was a good man, and I miss him."

Second drummer Mike Severino didn't last long with the Barn Burners. "[Levon] kind of methodically pushed Mikey out over time," O'Shea observed. "He took more and more of his freedom away until it became a point where Mikey says, 'What am I even doing here? I'm not on the drum riser, so I'm not seen. I'm not allowed to play certain drums, so it's not fulfilling.' We all understood it." He was not replaced.

RICK DANKO HAD been immersed in projects outside the Band, and in September 1999, he released his album *Live at Breeze Hill*, featuring Garth Hudson, Jim Weider, Randy Ciarlante, and Louie Hurwitz as part of a nine-piece ensemble. That fall, despite declining health, Danko, like Helm, had to keep performing in the face of extreme financial difficulties. Ciarlante recalls playing with Danko: "He was having a really difficult time, he had to sit in a chair to play, he was running out of breath, he was in rough shape." Evicted from their home, Rick and Elizabeth were living in a motel near Kingston, New York. According to Bill Avis, "She tried to get hold of Robertson more than once, trying to get some money out of him...to help, but it was not forthcoming."

Once again drugs were an issue with Danko. Jim Weider says, "It's a shame he got back into it, and it took him down. I tried to get him to go to the doctor, the local doctor. I was setting it up to go see him, but Rick, he just didn't want to go to the doctor. I don't think he wanted to hear any truths and deal with what he'd have to deal with. He wanted to live his life the way he wanted, and boy, he did." The sweet man with the celestial voice died in his sleep on December 10, 1999, less than three weeks before his fifty-sixth birthday.

Filled with equal parts grief and rage, Levon attended Rick's funeral, and although he tried, he couldn't force himself to go to the memorial, knowing Robbie Robertson was there. "I don't want to sit there with a bunch of guilty-ass people who had their hands in Rick's pockets," Levon pronounced. "You want to know what killed Rick Danko? He worked himself to death. That's what happens when people steal your money." Helm couldn't stomach what he called Robertson's crocodile tears and his efforts to put himself in the best possible light. As he addressed the spirit of his former bandmate from the podium, Robbie drove home his innocence in the face of Rick's passing, declaring, "I wrote the words you sang."

Levon and the Barn Burners played their usual gig at the Joyous Lake club that night as Helm tapped into his raw feelings for inspiration for the blues. Years later, Levon still said of Rick, "I miss him every goddamn day."

AS THE BAND got tighter, they toured more and more. Pat O'Shea describes the experience of going down to Arkansas with Levon:

> We traveled in a van, my van, a typical fifteen-passenger Ford. Helm always wanted to travel alone [often in his own convertible], which was good. You know, we needed separation from him because he was as crazy as hell. So he and Amy would always travel by themselves…So we were driving through the night…We came through Memphis just before daybreak, and I always led the way… Helm would always follow the van, which got kind of daunting because frequently you weren't going fast enough for him. I would look in my side-view mirror, and he would be right on my ass,

about a half-car width to the left so I could see his angry face and read his lips as he was mouthing words like "Let's go, mother-fucker!" and stuff like that. And he'd swing back out behind me and swing out again.

Once we got off the highway outside of Memphis and started to hit local roads, Helm passed me...We're driving on local roads into Helena, into West Helena, and there's mist everywhere, a little bit of fog. It's daybreak now; it's probably quarter to six or six a.m....and Helm drops the hammer, and he's doing, I don't know, eighty down these two-lane country roads and taking the turns out. He's cutting across the center line and just straightening the road out.

Harold Wieties booked Levon at Chester's Place in Fayetteville. Even though audiences there would have loved to hear Helm sing the iconic Band songs, Wieties says, "What they came for beyond that was to be in the same room as Levon Helm...As long as he was there playing drums, as long as they could see him and see his expressions on his face and feel him, who he was, they were happy with that...You could tell that it made the people sparkle just to be in the same room as Levon."

Wieties saw Helm as "very down to earth and very humble, but at the same time, he had some pretty...defined views of the world." Two examples were his propensity to smoke dope in public and his ongoing bone of contention with Robbie Robertson.

Not only did Levon believe there was nothing wrong with smoking marijuana, he felt there would be no consequences. "He didn't mind walking down the street [smoking dope]," Harold comments, "I remember one time we...decided to walk somewhere to get something to eat or something. He had a joint, and he was smoking it. I said, 'Levon, you can't do that out here,' and he said, 'Why?' And I said, 'You're going to get arrested. You can't do that. Put it away.' And he said, 'No, Harold, it's okay. It's like I'm invisible. Nobody's going to care.'"

The other issue Helm returned to time and again was Robbie Robertson. In addition to laying blame on Robertson for the end of the original Band and for cheating the remaining bandmates out of songwriting royalties, he accused Robbie of causing the demise of Richard and Rick. "He blamed both of those deaths on Robbie," Wieties says. "That's kind of the way he would talk to me. It was easy to get him talking about it, so I learned to try to back off when it would go into that, because as open and as wonderful as he was, that was the thing he was carrying, and that door would open at any time that you mentioned [Robertson] or anybody came up with something with Robbie's face on it or whatever."

Levon was a genial host at his shows, spending time speaking to fans and signing autographs. But his animosity regarding past wrongs was so extreme that when fans lined up afterward for Helm's signature, Harold was told to screen what they brought for him to sign. If it had an image on it of Robertson or of the Last Waltz, Wieites asked the person to put it out of Levon's sight, that he would be happy to auto-graph something else. "Boy, he was carrying a lot of anger or disappointment or resentment or whatever you'd say on that," Harold says. "He considered the ending of the Band to be all on Robbie. Otherwise, he was a very happy-go-lucky guy."

Helm's ongoing antagonism toward Robertson was in the spotlight again in the summer of 2000 with the release of re-mastered, expanded versions of the Band's first four albums:

> It don't mean anything to me 'cept another screwin'! Capitol Records haven't even sent me copies of the new records! They hate me, and I hate them, and I guess it's even. You would think that I'd be a wealthy man. I've made a lot of records, I worked for them for 12 or 15 years, I fulfilled my contract with the bastards, but as far as payin' me...even The Beatles had to sue 'em...so you can imagine what chance a poor bastard like me has got! People think that every year The Band sells, and I get my million or two, what-ever it is, and that I'm out in Hollywood livin' it up off the fat of the land, and that's not it at all. The Band is one of those same old stories: the record company and one or two guys—the man-agers and the turncoats—are fat, and everybody else is on the poor farm.

A year later, Garth Hudson declared bankruptcy for the third time, and his house was in foreclosure. Helm's turn came in January 2002, when he filed for bankruptcy in order to avoid the foreclosure of his property. Although he was offered twenty-five thousand dollars to play for the 2002 reissue of *The Last Waltz* four-CD box set, he turned down the financial lifeline knowing Robertson would be part of it. Instead, the Barn Burners drove to Fayetteville for a gig they lost money on. Looking back and laughing derisively at Robbie's role in the 1980 movie *Carny*, Levon sneered, "Robertson is still acting…He's playing the part of a genius musician who doesn't have time to play music."

"I think that some people, when things don't work out the way they want it to work out, they get bitter," Robertson said about Helm that year. "I don't have any hard feelings, I don't have any venom. For me, I don't have a problem. I'm doing what I want, and I'm having a great time doing it. I wish Levon all the best. Somewhere in there, he's a great guy, a very talented guy. I wish things went better for him so that he didn't have to feel whiny and sorry for himself."

THE BARN BURNERS toured North America throughout 2001, playing at such places as B.B. King's club in Memphis, the King Biscuit Festival—where Helm received an appreciation plaque for his ground-floor support of the event—and for Hubert Sumlin's seventieth birthday gig in New York City. The next year was spent performing mainly around the northeast.

Miraculously, in 2002, Levon's singing voice began to come back. "After a couple of years [following radiation], I would try and double Amy's vocal…and sing some background part," he said. "And I sang in my head all the time. Someone told me that even though you're not physically singing, just to do it inside your head affects those parts of you that do the singing. I just kept doing that."

The Barn Burners made a surprise appearance at the retirement party for Joe Ford, the CEO of Alltel, in Little Rock that July. Ford was an alumnus of the University of Arkansas and had been a fan of Levon and the Hawks. "It was the first time, the absolute first time, that Helm sang in public since his radiation," O'Shea reports, "and it wasn't bad. Joe was a big fan of ours and loved us—a big supporter. [He] got us a lot of high-paid gigs through Alltel, stuff he didn't have to do for us. He did it for Levon. He loved Levon."

A Tribute to Ronnie Hawkins was held at Toronto's Massey Hall in October, and Levon and Garth came to support their former bandleader. Two young musicians who were then part of Ronnie's Hawks were bass player Ryan Weber and his brother, guitarist Sam Weber, who only discovered at the last minute that they were slated to play a set with Helm and Hudson. "Levon was one of our biggest heroes and still is," Ryan says. "We were scared as fuck, you know, shaking, but I'd turn around and look at Levon, and he'd be smiling. That was like, 'Okay, I'm not sucking that bad!'" he adds, laughing. "You talk about why he gets the love. It's probably about how much he loves playing, and it always comes across."

Sam, who was eighteen at the time, remarks on "the kindness that he showed, 'cause he knew damn well that we were shaking in our boots and that he was our hero—he knew it—but he just went out of his way to make sure that we had fun...And then we felt respected by him, which meant so much." Later that year when the brothers were home in Maryland, they went to see Levon perform at a Baltimore blues festival. Characteristically, he recognized them right away and took time to chat.

PAT O'SHEA ADMITS that being a member of Levon's band wasn't always smooth sailing: "That relationship that I had with him—and many of us had with him—was not an easy one...More frequently than anyone would want, he was difficult to deal with and difficult to be around...Despite all that, I always loved him, and he used to tell me that he loved me like a son that he never had."

Throughout his time with the Barn Burners, Helm received many offers to play with other artists on their recordings or for performances, even though he couldn't sing.

> It was frustrating for us [O'Shea says] because it diluted our
> product and frustrated our booking agent for the same reason;
> however, despite that, I, at least, understood it. He didn't have a

steady stream of income, and if you're struggling financially and someone says, "Hey, man, come down to Long Island and play with us in a bar for a thousand bucks," I'd take the gig too...To the Old Man's credit, there were plenty of times that he stood by us and passed on gigs too. I always made sure to tell him thank you and thank him for being loyal and standing by us. I don't think he enjoyed playing with a lot of these people...Despite some of the hairy situations and despite some of the cantankerous moments—which were frequent—he still loved playing with us, he loved playing the music we were playing. So I think a lot of those gigs that he took and situations that he took were solely for the money.

Levon appeared on albums by such artists as Ronnie Earl, Ronnie Hawkins, Hubert Sumlin, Carl Carlton and the Songdogs, Emory Joseph, Kate Taylor, Rufus Wainwright, Guy Davis, Louisiana Red, and Little Feat, and on tribute albums for Nick Lowe and Charley Patton. He and Garth recorded with the gospel quartet the Dixie Hummingbirds for their album *Diamond Jubilation*. The Long Island–based rock roots band the Last Hombres hired Helm to play on their 2003 album, *Redemption*, then Levon stayed on, gigging with the band whenever he had a chance.

Levon remained staunchly thankful to those who hired him when he had no voice, specifically musicians Jimmy Vivino and Steve Jordan. But from Jordan's perspective, he was the one who was lucky:

His illness didn't ever, in my opinion, make him any less musical [Jordan says]. He was always brilliant, no matter how much of him you could get, and I just loved him so much. First of all, there was never a thing where he wasn't going to beat this thing—that's number one. Number two, he was always an incredible musician no matter what capacity he was in...And number three, you were happy that he accepted wanting to play when you asked him. You know, he could have easily said, "No, I'm not feeling well" or something, but he was always there and would always say, "Yeah, okay, I can do it." That was always a blessing for us.

Jordan hired Helm for recording sessions and concerts, such as the Rainforest Alliance show and later for the movie *Lightning in a Bottle*, a concert film of prominent blues artists such as Buddy Guy, B.B. King, Solomon Burke, and Dr. John. "I was the musical director and producer of the music," Steve remarks, "so I put together a house band to play behind all these brilliant musicians, and I hired Levon to play drums, along with myself."

DURING THE YEARS since the Ringo Starr All-Starr Tour and his subsequent management of the Band, David Fishof had kept in touch with Levon. He'd go to Woodstock to visit Helm, and they'd sit in the woods and talk. "There was something magical about him," David maintains.

In 1997, Fishof had established the Rock and Roll Fantasy Camp, but at first it stalled. He tried again in 2002 and went to England to try to get the Who's Roger Daltrey to participate the following year. As an inducement to lure him to the camp, he asked Daltrey whom he most wanted to meet and jam with. He told Fishof, "You get me with Levon Helm, and I'll do your Rock and Roll Fantasy Camp." When David explained that Levon had fallen on some hard times financially, Roger's response was, "Whatever you [were going to] give me, give it to him. I want to meet him, and I'll do your camp." Helm came down to New York City and hung out with Daltrey at the Bottom Line. "I was so happy to get Roger and Levon together," Fishof says. "It was great for both of them."

HELM HAD A genuine affinity for the regular, blue-collar residents of Woodstock. "He actually loved the local working people—the stonemasons, the carpenters, the plumbers, the local cops and firemen—much more than the other guys," Happy Traum says.

> In fact...a guy named [Ralph] Shultis...he was one of the old, local stone guys, and Levon had him over to the house a lot, they used to hang out together. [Levon] was definitely a man of the people. He had no airs about him at all; he had no illusions to stardom...He just had an affinity for the local[s]...You didn't

necessarily socialize with the guy who owned the garage or the hardware store or the guy who built the stone walls for you or something like that, but Levon did. He liked those guys.

And till the end, you could go into his living room even on the night of one of his shows at the barn, and there might be a local sheriff sitting there or some guy from the fire department. He was very much a down-to-earth person when it came to that kind of thing. And he had no patience for people who had pretensions, which was what I like most about him. That was a very strong part of his personality.

One of his close companions was Joe Lore, a heavy-equipment operator in the area. He had backstage access, they socialized together, and Levon was the best man at Joe's wedding.

I used to go on the tour bus with him, just riding along [Lore says]. He had a wealth of knowledge about architecture, geography. And we'd be driving through the Deep South, and he would just tell you *all* about the area, all about the churches, the steeples, the architecture. He was just so interesting to listen to, you know…

He knew his way around this country too. I'm talking about the roads. He never wanted to travel a road where the heavy tractor trailers were. He always liked taking those cartways, a little less truck traffic and *move*—he liked to move. He was pretty heavy with the pedal.

When Helm was on tour, "He'd have a brown paper sack," Dener comments, "and he called, 'Son, come over here. Mama made biscuits and sandwiches for us.' Sandy made homemade biscuits with porkchop sandwiches for the road. They never lasted more than two or three hours." As Lembesis recollects, "Sandy did not travel with the band. Sandy would come to our special occasions. I believe she came to New York City when we played Carnegie Hall, occasionally local shows. But Sandy was holding down the home fort…Anytime we were on the road, [Helm would say,] 'Come on, we gotta hit the road 'cause we gotta get home to Mama 'cause she's frying up pork chops or whatever, and we gotta be home for breakfast,' so we'd drive all night so we could be home."

Even though he was referred to as the Old Man by the Barn Burners, Levon hadn't lost his sense of fun. Chris O'Leary points out that Barn Burners' audiences were predominantly male, with a scarcity of attractive women. Chris laughs when he recalls one night in Alabama when the female situation looked promising:

> So this particular night, there was a slew of [women], and they're all at the front of the stage. And we start playing, the place is packed. And there's this one—auburn hair, green eyes, tanned, sun dress—she's looking up at me…Everything is going great. Amy comes up, and she's doing "Shake a Hand"—it's her showcase number—and she kills it; she's killing it. And there's these guys right in the crowd that are talking. There's things you can do around Levon—and he was an easy-going guy—but the one thing you couldn't do was in any way disrespect Amy, you know.
>
> I can hear him: "George, George," as he's playing, so George [Lembesis] comes over. [Levon says,] "Tell those motherfuckers to shut up." So [George] goes over. You can see George saying something to them, and they laugh, they laugh it off. George comes back, and they're still talking. I'm playing guitar, and I'm singing harmonies with Amy, and all of a sudden there's no drums…Over my left side I see [Levon] go to the edge of the stage…And he gets down like this, with a smile, and he's like, "Fellas, fellas, come on over." And they're like, "Oh, my God, it's Levon Helm. Holy shit!" So they come over, and he's like, "Listen, either shut the fuck up or get the fuck out!"…Not only did they leave; they took *all* the girls with them! All of them. They all just filed right out…If somebody had a trumpet with like a mute, it'd be *wah wah wah wah*. And he's like, "Chris, I'm sorry. It just had to be said."

Pat O'Shea still remembers when the group played at a festival in New York State, and at the end, all the bands joined them for an encore. It was the first time the Barn Burners had played a number from the Band repertoire.

> I just turned around and watched Helm—all of a sudden he was a completely different drummer when he was playing a Band song, and he played all those parts just like falling off a log for him. And I watched him do a matched-grip press roll…Holy shit, Helm really is a master drummer. Because before that, I only heard him play shuffles and slow blues and ballads and strolls and that kind of stuff, right, maybe a rumba beat.

Levon was switching back and forth between the traditional grip he'd started with and matched grip. With matched grip, Levon aimed to keep it simple with his left hand overhand on the snare, concentrating on the backbeat. "When you play traditional," drummer Jerome Avis explains, "your left hand has a tendency to bounce around a bit more, so he'd be putting more notes on the snare. [He wanted] to get away from that."

Jerome says, "He had very soft, smooth hands, and even after playing all those years, even though he had calluses, some of them would still bleed," so Levon sometimes wore a black glove on his left hand. "He'd wear it when he got sweaty," O'Shea remarks. "He'd yell, 'Where's my glove?' and then, of course, we'd all start laughing and start yelling stuff like, 'No glove, no love!'"

BY 2004, CHRIS O'Leary and Frank Ingrao had left the Barn Burners, and it comprised Levon, Pat, Jeff Sarli on bass, seventy-five-year-old Little Sammy Davis as lead singer and harmonica player, and Sammy's guitarist, Fred Scribner. Because Sammy fronted the group, they began playing only Davis's repertoire of old blues classics. "It was no longer anything special," Pat says about the Barn Burners. "It wasn't good…It had turned into an okay pickup band, basically, which is a shame given the members. There's no reason why that band couldn't have smoked at that point." Sammy wasn't at his best, and Pat and Jeff could no longer get behind it. Levon was becoming more irritable and was difficult to work with. O'Shea was booking the band, and it became harder and harder to sell.

The second-to-last show the Barn Burners played was in Washington, D.C., a private party for a group of senators and their staffers. Helm brought a new keyboard player onboard whom the band didn't know and had no background in blues. It was not a good night musically. Then Levon took a dislike to the audience, particularly one well-known senator:

> So all these senators are there, and everyone's wasted and we're on a stage and we're playing [O'Shea reports]. They're the type of people Helm hated. They were like rich college frat boys, as he used to call them. And they are drunk and they're rude and they're not listening and not paying attention. And somehow this senator winds up with a washboard strapped to his shoulders. And he thinks he is the funniest thing in the world, and he is standing right in front of the stage with his senator–frat boy pals playing the washboard with spoons, and it's loud as hell. And Helm is getting so pissed off, and he's yelling—now Helm still doesn't really have a voice at this point, but *we* can hear him—and he's screaming, "Motherfucker, hey, stop that! Hey, asshole!" He's yelling from the drum riser. This guy is just ignoring [him]…I know what's going to happen, so I'm just kinda hanging back…
>
> Helm ends up getting from up behind the drum set in the middle of the song, and he makes a beeline for this guy…and he takes a swing at the guy with his drumstick. At that moment, this senator just happens to turn and walk away, and Helm missed hitting him in the back of the head by, like, eight inches. And Helm was about to go after him in the crowd, and myself and our sound guy—A.P. [Al Pierce], rest in peace—grabbed Levon by the shoulder, and I kind of put my arm like a bar in front of him… and Helm turned around and let the guy go.
>
> The guy never knew it…He literally almost got his ass kicked by Levon Helm. There's not a doubt in my mind that if Helm had got closer to the guy, he would have clocked him in the head, and he would have knocked him out. One of the nicknames we used

to have for Helm, totally behind his back, was Captain I-Don't-Give-a-Fuck…The keyboard player was shaking in his shoes. He couldn't believe what was unfolding before his eyes. Same with Fred Scribner and Little Sammy, whereas Sarli and I and A.P., we were just laughing because it was the kind of shit that we had seen many times before.

They played one more show at the end of the summer, at a festival in New Jersey, but no one was into it, and Levon wasn't himself. "It also felt like there was some sneaking around and some sketchy shit going down from everybody," O'Shea reveals. "They…had pushed Butchy [Dener] out. Helm wasn't returning any of our calls. He was very guarded anytime he would speak to us." When Pat came to the barn at Levon's request, Helm wouldn't let him in, dismissed him rudely, and said, "See you around"—the last words he ever spoke to Pat. It was the typical way Levon approached a situation he didn't want to deal with—he wouldn't address it directly. Without knowing why, that was the end of the Barn Burners. Pat attended one of Levon's early Midnight Rambles but was ignored.

"Writers and historians act like the Barn Burners never existed," Lembesis says.

> The Barn Burners were a crucial part of his career. Not a major one, but a crucial one. Because the Barn Burners bridged the gap between the Band and before cancer to the Rambles…And unfortunately, the Barn Burners never released an album, although they did record a lot…It's a real shame that the Barn Burners don't get their proper due and don't have their appropriate place in his legacy because I would argue they saved his life and helped him when he needed help the most, and nourished his soul with the blues.

"WE DIDN'T MAKE that song to be a fucking jingle," stated Levon, referring to the use of "The Weight" in a television commercial for Cingular Wireless in 2004. Helm filed a lawsuit against the ad agency, BBDO Worldwide, claiming it had used the song without his permission. Even though he did receive a royalty payment, Levon believed that he wasn't adequately compensated, saying, "It was just a complete, damn sellout of the Band—its reputation, its music: just as much disrespect as you could pour on Richard and Rick's tombstones." The suit was ultimately adjudicated in BBDO's favor, the court ruling that Capitol Records had the right to license the song and its performance based on the contract Helm signed in 1968.

"YOU CAN'T AFFORD to pay your bills and buy your medicine— you've got to give up one or the other," Helm confessed. "I got behind on my mortgage. The only way I could hang onto the place was to declare bankruptcy." Ironically, 2004 was the same year *Rolling Stone* placed the Band on its list of the hundred greatest musical artists of all time.

Levon had a far-fetched idea that he wasn't sure he could pull off: "I didn't know if I was going to be able to hang onto the place. But I thought, well, I'm going to go out with a bang." That's how Helm's Midnight Rambles began. The Rambles harkened back to the tradition of old-time rent parties—where blues artists, strapped for cash, charged admission to their homes for a night of musical fun. So Levon did the same: opened his barn to the public, invited some musicians, and sold tickets.

It had always been Helm's intention to stage his own performances based on the tent shows of his boyhood. The Rambles were Levon's personal medicine show, a sure-fire cure for whatever's ailing. It was his aim to create an intimate interaction between musicians and the audience, a place where everyone felt like friends and neighbors sitting in his living room. In that, he equated the Rambles to the camaraderie of all-day singing and dinner on the ground at the County Line Baptist Church when he was growing up. And with that hospitality and warmth came an overpowering musical experience. Some likened it to church.

"He always wanted to do things in an easier way," O'Shea maintains, "and I know that he had dreams of having shows at his house where he basically could just roll out of bed at four o'clock in the afternoon, fire up a joint or two in the kitchen, hold court, walk into his studio next door, play a short set and get paid."

Norman Clancy, who was president of Levon Helm Studios, was

instrumental in assisting Levon financially and for launching the Rambles. "At the time we started, I had more bills than I had just about anything except friends," Helm announced. "Thank God for that." The events were entirely staffed with volunteers. Levon said, "It's a labor of love for everybody. I've never been able to do anything for any of them—just return their friendship."

"I did the first Ramble with him, the very first one," Steve Jordan says.

> It was an incredible experience. It was just like an idea that he had. It wasn't fully realized, but he explained to me how he always loved the carnivals—he wanted to be a carny in a way—and the road-show kind of things always intrigued him…Johnnie Johnson was there—the late great Johnnie Johnson—and Jon Smith was there, the saxophone player who played with Edgar Winter's White Trash. A kid named Sean Costello, who later passed away at too young an age, played guitar…It was quite something.

Despite his own uncertain situation, Levon continued his generous musical contribution to community fundraisers for local schools, the Little League, veterans, and farmers. Barbara O'Brien, the administrative assistant for the Ulster County Sheriff's office, would see Helm at these events, and they became friends. With his home in foreclosure and scrambling for a lifeline, Levon offered Barbara a job. Under her management, beginning in 2004, Helm was able to consolidate his debts and the Rambles started earning a profit.

But with administrative changes came an abrupt break with parts of Levon's past. Suddenly old friends had difficulty reaching him. "Sometimes it's good to have a flak," George Lembesis says, referring to the protective barriers installed around Levon. "Sometimes it's good to have a bad cop to tell people things you don't necessarily want to tell them…According to [new management], the Barn Burners never existed…It was like they were persona non grata." Pat O'Shea agrees: "The Ramble regime flexed their muscles and shut certain people out by design: myself, George, Butch…They didn't even acknowledge the existence of the Barn Burners."

LARRY CAMPBELL, WHO had played in Bob Dylan's band for eight years, and his wife, singer-guitarist Teresa Williams, joined Helm in 2005. A singer and superb musician who's at home on almost any stringed instrument, Campbell became the musical director for the Midnight Rambles and producer of Levon's later albums. "I've played with a lot of people in my career, but it's the most fulfilling musical experience I've had," Larry asserts. "Levon can do any vein of American music, any genre, with complete authority. There's no pretense in any of it." Of Helm's concept for the Rambles, he says, "All he wanted to do was make good music and have a good time doing it, with no other agenda involved. If we made some money, great—and certainly starting these Rambles was an attempt to get himself out of debt—but the means to that end was only about playing music you enjoyed playing."

Teresa Williams, a native of rural Tennessee who is well grounded in folk, country, and bluegrass, observed that Helm always brought out the best from the musicians he played with. "Just being around Levon elicits your truest self, musically and otherwise," she says. "For decades he was my artistic touchstone, as an actor and as a singer and musician, and I never believed I'd meet him much less work with him."

The Rambles house band comprised Levon, Amy, Larry Campbell, Teresa Williams, Little Sammy Davis, guitarist Jimmy Vivino, Byron Isaacs on bass, and Brian Mitchell on keyboards. Helm played drums and mandolin. For him, it was a safe haven, a place where he could still play and work on getting his voice back in a comfortable environment without pressure. The band included plenty of strong vocalists to carry the shows until Levon was able to sing himself.

> You know it really was one of the more pleasurable things that I've ever had the opportunity to do [Levon said]. I counted on Amy, Larry Campbell, Teresa Williams…everybody, especially the singers to keep me from singing myself into a hole. Even though I had my voice back enough to attempt the songs, I would have days where I'd start too early and I couldn't find my voice. It was a concern for me, but having Amy especially helped guide me through those spots and I was actually able to perform better than I thought I could.

Three CD volumes of *The Midnight Ramble Sessions* were released in 2005, 2006, and 2014. Musical guests through the years included Garth Hudson, Elvis Costello, Diana Krall, Phil Lesh, Donald Fagen, Emmylou Harris, Dr. John, Mavis Staples, Chris Robinson, Allen Toussaint, John Sebastian, Pinetop Perkins, Hubert Sumlin, Kris Kristofferson, Phoebe Snow, Boz Scaggs, Luther "Guitar Jr." Johnson, John Hiatt, Steve Earle, the Holmes Brothers, Shemekia Copeland, Billy Bob Thornton, the Muddy Waters Tribute Band, Norah Jones, Hot Tuna, David Bromberg, and Amy's own band, Ollabelle. In coming years, the Rambles opened with local musicians to provide them a showcase, and for a while, there were children's Rambles on Saturday afternoons to encourage their interest in music. As Helm put it, "My job is to make people feel good, show them a good time, and, my God, what a blessing."

Levon loved the fact that when the show was over, he could walk off the stage into his home. Jacob Hatley, who spent about three years with Levon while filming his documentary on Helm, *Ain't in It for My Health*, recollected his favorite moments: "After the crowd had gone home, Levon would go back to his kitchen table [and] pour everybody a Coke. You'd light up and he would hold court from about midnight to 2:30 in the morning and let us listen to stories—everybody just staring at him, wide-eyed." Hatley says, "Levon's place was the place to be. There was always such a giddiness and an excitement to him. He loved to laugh. He loved to party."

"There's some history in that kitchen," Amy pointed out. "After every Ramble, they hold court. Dad likes to call it the Cannabis Cup, and it's like Cheech and Chong back there. You have to get out quick if you don't want a contact high."

IT'S BEEN SAID that while Levon always tried to pay his musicians and his local bills, a trail of other debtors was left in the dust. Levon and Sandy filed for bankruptcy again in the summer of 2005. Then a dispute with a company Helm hired to collect unpaid royalties led to another lawsuit, which was judged in his favor. John Simon recalls joining Levon at the barn to view football on TV: "There, watching the Super Bowl with him was the VP of the bank...Levon was courting him in order to get the favor of the bank, to have his finances a little more in order."

Through it all, Helm kept working on strengthening his voice. "I can sing my share of the songs for the first time in a long time and not be quite as scared as I was," he admitted in 2005. "I didn't have any plans on even being here, much less being able to try and sing some harmonies with everybody, so it's a wonderful life." Larry noted that Levon's voice after cancer was different. "You hear the damage that's been done," he says, "but it's got all the honesty and fire that's always been there. None of that is missing. It might even be enhanced by the grittiness in his voice now. The guy is amazing, just amazing."

"The things that matter to him have changed," Amy remarked. "He knows what counts and what doesn't. And there's a power in that, and a confidence and a self-reliance that all musicians—or anyone who loves music—can hear and respond to. He did have to get his confidence back. Part of what makes his singing now so strong is that he wasn't afraid to acknowledge that he was very scared. He was scared to lose his voice and to get back up on stage and know that people had high expectations."

Levon's recovery was a triumph. "It's certainly a miracle for me and a dream come true," he said. "I never thought I would sing and play like I used to be able to do. I thank God. Every song is a celebration for me."

15

"God Wasn't Through with You"

For those lucky enough to attend one of Levon's Midnight Rambles in Woodstock, it was a musical and communal occasion they wouldn't forget. Driving down the long, winding driveway off Plochmann Lane, they'd arrive at Helm's green-roofed, wood-and-bluestone barn located in a bucolic, forested setting not far from another of Levon's creations, a deep three-acre pond.

Rambles were held two Saturdays a month for around two hundred people, with an admission of a hundred dollars a ticket, rising through the years to two hundred dollars. To increase the down-home spirit, attendees were encouraged to bring a potluck dish or snacks to share before the show. Downstairs, various items were available for sale: CDs, posters, books, T-shirts, and popcorn. Everything was simple and efficient—no pretention, no excess baggage. The focus was on community, joy, and a collective appreciation of good music.

On the main floor in the performance space, draped with flags, there were folding chairs; alternatively, attendees could bring a pillow and sit on the floor in front of the musicians or stand in the balcony above. From whatever vantage, it was an intimate musical experience. The stage wasn't raised; the musicians performed on a rug on one part of the floor.

The tone was casual, with nothing too structured. "Go out there and just kind of let it happen," Levon said. "Because it's a ramble, if we make a mistake, we can stop and start over again, which happens frequently. And people are free to come and go and sit in and participate." The audience, Helm observed, "don't feel like strangers. They feel like friends and relatives and we're all here for the same thing, to have a good time and celebrate music." Happy Traum says, "Levon had deep southern roots, a graciousness and infectious quality that played out in his life and music. And he loved the fact that in his hometown, local stonemasons and carpenters and policemen became part of this. I think these were the happiest days of his life, that he could invite all these people into his living room and treat them like house guests for the evening."

Helm said of the Rambles, "That's the most peaceful time in my day, when I'm playing. There's nothing to worry about, I don't owe anybody anything, just play the songs and try to make them good… After the show's over the other things can come back." It was as entertaining for him as it was for the audience. "Just playing here in the studio for a couple of hundred people is just as much fun as playing Madison Square Garden," Levon insisted. "It's actually more fun. It sounds better, and it's a lot easier, and when the show's over, I just walk next door and take my boots off."

At first Helm avoided Band songs, but gradually he incorporated them into the show. The repertoire was typically a mélange of all things Americana, as Larry Campbell said: "What's rare about Levon is that he can shift seamlessly between genres in American roots music, which is what the Band did. They took all those genres, threw them in a pot and came out with a unique sound in which you can hear those elements in everything they do…At a Ramble, you're not going to hear a blues concert, or a country concert or a rock show—you're going to hear all those things and nothing will seem out of place."

"I always say it was like the revivals I grew up in as far as the vibe," comments Teresa Williams. "The windows were thrown open, the doors were thrown open…The place would be packed to the gills. Outside, there were a lot of people roaming around, and the music [was] just full on with only the best spirit about it, not about industry, not about career. It was just music for the sake of music…Not a lot of egos flying around."

When Levon incorporated horns into his band, he called on Howard Johnson. Howard saw the Rambles as a blessing for Levon and was pleased he was playing at the top of his game. Johnson says,

"Some people like Barbara O'Brien were always telling him, 'You don't need to have these horns to play the gig,' and he said, 'Yes, I do because it's the sound I want to hear coming at me...But she and some other people were saying [to the horn players], 'You're taking money out of Levon's pocket.' I said, 'As soon as Levon wants me to go, I'll go.' He just never did."

During these years, the friendship between Johnson and Helm grew deep. "He knew that I was a cancer survivor and he feels very close and protective of other cancer survivors," Howard points out. "He often spoke about how we're still going on against all odds...So, between that and our musical history, we were a lock." Helm joked about Johnson's musical diversity, saying, "Howard can go in a hardware store and play anything in there."

HELM HAD A cameo role—along with Kris Kristofferson, Merle Haggard, and Ronnie Hawkins—in the quirky mockumentary about the mysterious life of a Canadian country superstar, *The Life and Hard Times of Guy Terrifico*. In February 2006, *The Three Burials of Melquiades Estrada* was released in the U.S. It starred Tommy Lee Jones as the best friend of murdered Estrada, and as he sets out to fulfill his friend's final wish, he runs into a blind desert hermit with a death wish, an unforgettable character played by Helm. When asked if he prepared for his role, Levon answered, "I don't know enough about it to prepare myself. You know, I try and sleep as good as I can and just enjoy it. I enjoyed being with people who do know how to do that stuff, and I've never had anything but a good time around any of those shows that I've had the opportunity to be part of."

LEVON'S MIDNIGHT RAMBLES had a positive economic impact on the entire Woodstock area, as attendees often spent the weekend in the region, visiting restaurants, shopping, and staying in local accommodation. Even beyond that, Helm was recognized for his generous support of many charitable causes, such as performing at benefits for the victims of September 11 and to help pay Hubert Sumlin's medical bills. He could always be counted on to support the local firemen, police, the Little League, or the military. "Levon was big on...

American troops and firefighters and cops," Butch Dener says. "[It's] pretty funny that an outlaw like him loved the cops so much, but he did." Each year on May 30, starting in 2001, he presented a beautiful floral bouquet to Mrs. Shulte, the only gold-star mother in New Paltz—a town just south of Woodstock. Then he would either ride with her in the local Memorial Day Parade or drive with veterans who could no longer walk.

In 2008, Levon sang an Arthur Alexander number, "You Better Move On," on *The Imus Ranch Record*, an album compiled by his friend and fan Don Imus, with all proceeds donated to the Imus Cattle Ranch for Kids with Cancer. Helm performed Dylan's "It Takes a Lot to Laugh, It Takes a Train to Cry" for the second volume of the record, released two years later.

Levon offered his studio at no charge for the Congo Square Project, a volunteer organization that produced several CDs to help New Orleans musicians in the wake of Hurricane Katrina. He performed on tracks with Steve Jordan, Hubert Sumlin, Danny Kortchmar, Larry Campbell, and Teresa Williams. To assist in disaster relief for victims of Hurricane Irene in the Catskills, he played a concert at the Ulster Performing Arts Center in 2011 and donated the following night's proceeds at his Ramble to the cause.

Helm felt strongly that music in schools should be supported, and he performed at several school benefits over the years. "Socially, it means a lot," he said of music education. "It gives even the quiet kids that chance to enjoy and maybe learn to express themselves musically, something we all should have. Right now, in the prime of their school years, there's a real value to helping them to build friendships and gain confidence in their own playing abilities. It can be so important to their lives, and it only takes a little bit of effort on our part to make it happen."

Levon was a musical mentor to two ten-year-olds, one of whom joined him onstage at a benefit concert at Onteora High School in nearby Boiceville, which was having difficulty funding its music-education program. "Man, it sure was fun," Helm declared. "If only the audience enjoyed it half as much as we did." He invited the drum-line from the school's marching band to his studio for free lessons and practice. Levon continued to support schools throughout the rest of his life, saying, "If we receive any wealth, we're willing to share it. We've got to give more support to our great teachers."

Levon Helm Day was proclaimed by the Town of Woodstock on May 20, 2006, and Helm was presented with a scroll and a key to the city. There was a town-wide party, featuring music from students in the jazz ensemble from Onteora High School paying tribute to their benefactor. Watching them with pride, Levon exclaimed, "It's the most fun you can have, watching those kids."

One of Levon's most rewarding experiences was with Amy, singing and playing guitar and mandolin for children at Memorial Sloan Kettering Cancer Center. "Sometimes you have to put on the medical gowns and the hats and sing with a mask over your face," he said. "But it's okay. The amazing thing about some of these children that can't really move a lot, you can start to play music with them and all of a sudden they can clap their hands and make movements that they couldn't do before. And it's so satisfying and so rewarding to get those smiles from those little kids. It warms my heart. I've never done anything that's meant more to me or made me feel any better."

AFTER HE HEARD Alexis P. Suter's powerhouse vocals at a benefit for a musician with cancer, Levon invited her to a Ramble, and beginning in 2005, he brought Suter and her band onboard as his regular opening act. From there, he became not only her mentor but a dear friend. At the end of a Ramble, Alexis would head back to the kitchen before anyone else arrived, "and just tell Levon how much I love him," she recounts. "He always treated me with respect…He saw something in me…and he gave us a chance."

Suter says, "He was a shy gentleman, too—a lot of people don't know that—but all that Levon wanted anyone to do was treat him like a normal human being…He was the furthest thing from Tinseltown. He was a country boy, a country dude. He loved nature; he loved animals; he loved his wife, Sandy; he *loooooooved* his daughter, Amy… I'm just blessed and very humble that my path crossed his path."

"I learned a lot from Levon, especially in business," Alexis continues. "He showed me how to deal with people: the good ones, the bad ones, everybody. He always dropped wisdom." If someone did something Levon didn't like, "He wasn't violent," Suter says, "he didn't throw threats, he didn't do none of that. He'd just cut you off. 'Okay, I'm not going to deal with that. I'm too old to deal with that. I've been through too much in this industry to deal with that'...The bottom line is Levon knew how to deal with people, you know. He was a great guy. I wish the entire music industry was like him."

Suter knew Helm had health challenges, although she maintains,

> He didn't want no sympathy from anyone. And anything he ever asked for, he worked for...One thing about Levon—and I'm just seeing it now—throughout this whole thing he never showed depression, he never showed desperation, he never showed sadness, he never showed anger, he never showed disappointment, he never showed despair. He was always on a positive note, smiling and "How ya' doin'?" and "Yeah, darlin', everything is fine." He never complained.

And of course, there were a lot of laughs. There had been a close call with a black bear that had squeezed through the pet flap for Helm's black Staffordshire, Muddy—named in honor of Muddy Waters—and had roamed around inside the barn until the dog chased it out. Alexis remembers a similar experience one time when she and her keyboard player, Debbie Hawkins, and another fellow were visiting Levon:

> At the time, Muddy, his dog...was barking, and we wondered why's this dog barking like this. Come to find out he's barking at a bear. So [the dog] runs out of the house behind this bear...Levon runs after Muddy who's running after the bear. Then we had this gentleman who was with us in the house, he grabs a cap gun, runs after Levon who's running after the dog who's running after the bear. Big Mama and Debbie stayed in the house because if something happens, somebody had to be able to call the police...If you could have seen Levon running after Muddy, it was the funniest thing in this world, you know...It was like a circus.

Helm kept Suter's band as his opening act until 2008; perhaps for the sake of providing the audience with some variety, he gave them a longer run than he should have. But, "He loved us," Alexis says, "and he let it be known that he loved us, and I know for a fact, he was our biggest fan."

LEVON TOOK HIS Rambles on the road in March 2007. At first, he was hesitant, not sure how the format would work in a less intimate venue. The tickets for his two shows at New York City's Beacon Theatre sold out in fifteen minutes.

"He gave it everything he had and then did it again the next night," Campbell declares. "The crowd was with us from beginning to end." As emcee Lou Ruffino tells it, "It was the most unbelievable musical experience I've ever been in." After the last song, the audience refused to leave. "They were screaming, 'Levon,' for about ten minutes to get him back out…I can't even describe how incredible it was…People were not sitting; they were standing the whole show." It proved to Helm that he was indeed back. He donated a portion of the proceeds from the concert to Memorial Sloan Kettering Cancer Center and thanked his doctor from the stage, saying, "He's part of the band."

The Alexis P. Suter Band opened the concerts. "That was great, let me tell you," Alexis says. "My mother was in her eighties then…and she got to meet Levon, and Levon loved my mother. He said, 'I can feel that motherly love. This is a *real* mother right here. This reminds me of home.'" After that, Helm kept in touch:

> He used to call my mother from time to time and check on how's she doing. I remember one year on his birthday, there was this big birthday cake…He told them to pack it up, give it to me to give to my mother so that she could give it to the church, and that's just what my mother did. And another time, Levon called me in the back, and he pulled out a wad of money—it had to be about six or seven hundred dollars—and he gave it to me in my hand, and he said, 'Give this to your mother, and tell her to pray for us.'…He loved my mother.

THE POLITICAL THRILLER *Shooter* was released in March, starring Mark Wahlberg. In one of the film's most engaging scenes, filmed in Vancouver, Levon played a myopic, wily old codger living in the Tennessee backwoods, whom Wahlberg's character pronounced as the greatest gunsmith east of the Mississippi.

That June, the Levon Helm Band was back in New York City, in Central Park for SummerStage, performing for another enthusiastic crowd, despite the rain. Then in Woodstock, Levon held a Ramble for young children and their families, sharing vocals with a ten-year-old. His goal was to pass on to the next generation the music that was important to him. He gave the audience—some in diapers, shaking maracas and strumming inflatable guitars—a show that ranged from Robert Johnson to Chuck Berry to the Velvet Underground. He said, "Kids need to see real people playing real songs on real instruments. There's too much phoniness in the world."

In July, the band took their show to Nashville for a fundraiser for the Americana Music Association, which had awarded Helm its Lifetime Achievement Award as a performance artist in 2003. Dubbed Ramble at the Ryman, it included special guests Emmylou Harris, Sam Bush, Buddy Miller, Sheryl Crow, John Hiatt, Ricky Skaggs, and Lee Roy Parnell. Levon brought his down-home atmosphere with him—at several points, his dog was seen wandering onstage. He described the show as being "as good as having Muddy Waters come to Woodstock… Gosh, everybody showed up! The Ryman was just a wonderful, special night. There's so much history there. It was a thrill of a lifetime to work with some of the nicest people in the world." That night, Emmylou exclaimed to Levon, "You are an American treasure."

"NATURALLY, AS SOON as I could sing, I wanted to record again," Helm said. "Thank God for music." So twenty-six years after the release of his previous solo recording—the second *Levon Helm* LP—Helm left no doubt that he was back with his new CD, *Dirt Farmer*, on the Vanguard label. It had been a heroic struggle, but he was finally ready to regain the spotlight as a lead singer. "Every now and then I feel like my voice is as good as it's ever been," he revealed, although at times it could be unreliable.

The concept for *Dirt Farmer* came about after Levon played for Amy some of the old songs from his childhood, such as "Little Birds," "Dirt Farmer," "The Girl I Left Behind," and "Blind Child":

> And we started doing those tunes together [Levon said] just to celebrate getting my voice back a little bit, and I would sing harmonies behind her and behind [Little] Sammy [Davis]. Amy's idea was to go back and do those very first songs that I had heard. They're still good songs. That's the thing about music. Music don't wear out like you and me...Music just stays young forever. These are the songs that...my mom and dad and their friends sang and played and partied with each other when they were coming up.

Once he was on a roll, Helm recalled more music from his childhood, and through those songs, felt a connection with his parents and old friends:

> I sure feel Rick, Richard, and Stan [Szelest's] presence. They're my three brothers if you will...When we were working on "Blind Child" and "Little Birds" I couldn't quite remember a couple of spots...I would either dream them or they'd come to me in other ways. It was wonderful. Vocally, for the first time it was like all of us who were singing were as comfortable with each other and reached that level that Rick, Richard, and I used to aim at. For sure, I copied Rick and Richard...we sang together so many times and I tried to sing like they would sing and phrase like they would phrase. I love 'em that much.

Amy, who co-produced the album with Larry, says, "I knew how important it was to have these songs recorded that he had learned from his parents—from my grandparents. In that regard, I think I was very conscious of wanting to preserve those songs and record them so that they could be passed along and shared." Levon dedicated *Dirt Farmer* to Nell and Diamond.

Of his many challenges, Helm said, "Tough times can make you more reflective, and make you long for better and simpler times. So I guess that's what led me back to those songs, which were already old when I heard them as a boy. I wanted to get back to the community feeling the music used to have." He continued, "Songs don't wear out. Good songs are good now. If they were a comfort during those hard times in the past, they'll be a comfort in today's age."

"[Levon] said it was a music utopian sandbox," Teresa says of the recording process. "It [was] safe and...he just pulled the very best out of everybody." Amy recalls, "It was very exciting to be in the studio with him because he would come up with an idea and we'd try a take and hit the record button, and he would just execute these songs and be kicking so much ass! As a musician, sometimes I would have moments in the studio with him where...Larry and Byron [Isaacs] and Teresa and I would be there with our jaws dropped because we just couldn't believe what this man was doing."

Like the title suggests, *Dirt Farmer* was stripped of all artifice. "If you want something to sound real, just have Levon sing it or play it, and all the fat gets trimmed away," Campbell maintains. "You get to the basic beauty of the music." In Larry's opinion, the essence of Levon's music "comes out of the woods, the dirt, the mountains... There's nothing manufactured about it."

The tracks were recorded as live as possible with only necessary overdubs. The instrumentation was acoustic, and to keep it rocking, Levon and Amy alternated on drums, with percussion by George Receli and Byron Isaacs on bass. On this album, Levon rarely played the hi-hat, which gives the music a more rootsy feel. "We taped the toms down a bit and had a pillow in the kick with a port on the front head," says production manager and engineer Justin Gulp. "The snare had a zero ring on it as well as some additional taping. Just when I thought they were dead, Levon would deaden them a little more. Part of the sound is the way he hits them with the sticks."

Levon also played acoustic guitar and mandolin; Campbell was on guitar, fiddle, mandolin, dulcimer, and percussion. Regarding the superb vocal support, Helm said, "One of the great gifts from *Dirt Farmer* for me is the sound of Amy and Teresa's harmonies."

From the first track, "False Hearted Lover Blues," Helm sounds every bit his sixty-seven years with a voice that lays bare an earthy honesty and hard-won gravitas. Following two dry cracks of his drum, his vocals explode through the gate as he plays the hi-hat part on his snare, creating a martial quality. His artistry shines on "Poor Old Dirt Farmer," with a meter in three, but Levon shifts the backbeat around in order to keep it engaging, a prime example of playing for the song. His voice here is weathered and poignant, eliciting all the pathos of a hardscrabble life on the land. He aches with empathy in "The Mountain" while playing an engaging variation of his hi-hat pattern.

Levon picks up the acoustic guitar for "Little Birds," and proclaims through pure, stark vocals a story of misguided love, enhanced with harmonies by Amy and Teresa. Their background singing intensifies "Calvary," where Levon, with his snare sounding like dead wood, alternates the beat between 3/4 and 4/4 time. His rustic vocals blaze through "Got Me a Woman," accompanied by his mandolin.

"A Train Robbery" evokes a special memory for Amy. "We were all sitting upstairs in the other part of the control room," she says, "and he did that song in one take. All of us, we just couldn't believe it, to hear his voice in the room sounding so strong. As a singer, he's just brilliant. It was like taking a master class. There's a part of that that's just very cool to be around. That was my favorite performance because I remember getting chills hearing him sing that."

Of "Wide River to Cross," Levon commented, "It may be the first time you've ever heard it, but that song's about you, your life, your sorrows and joys." He sings it with authenticity, a spiritual essence, the instrumentation reflecting its church-like quality.

"I don't have any big plans for it," Levon said modestly of *Dirt Farmer*. "If people like it, then I've gotten away with another one." Emmylou Harris affirmed, "Levon is one of my favorite singers and drummers. He has a groove unlike anybody else, and his voice is extraordinary...This album is a triumph of spirit and his miraculous recovery."

IN OCTOBER 2007, everything changed for Helm. Levon and Sandy emerged from Chapter 11 bankruptcy with their creditors paid in full. Then a couple of weeks later upon the release of *Dirt Farmer*, Levon received a deluge of praise. "This isn't an album; this is a miracle…" one San Francisco reviewer wrote, "nothing less than a return to form by one of the most soulful vocalists in rock history… Acoustic, timeless and rich with the kind of Southern pastorals that loomed over the Band's finest work, *Dirt Farmer* would be a major work by any consideration. Under Helm's circumstances, it's a triumph over adversity of immense proportions." Helm performed songs from the album in free concerts in the Woodstock area, on one occasion attracting so many fans that Highway 209 had to be closed.

LEVON'S FIRST GRANDCHILD, Lavon Henry Collins, was born in February 2008 to Amy and her husband, sax player Jay Collins. "He's quite a character," Levon remarked of his namesake. "He likes to play drums…He uses one stick to play with and one stick to chew on…It's been the best thing that's ever happened in my little life."

It was only one of many blessings. The day after his grandson's birth, Helm won a Grammy Award in the category of Best Traditional Folk Album for *Dirt Farmer*. The Recording Academy also bestowed its Lifetime Achievement Award on the Band. But with his disdain for the big-business of music and knowing Robertson would be there, Levon declined to attend the ceremony. He said it was less phony to have his own celebration at the barn. At that party—dubbed the Midnight Gramble—he sang "Tears of Rage" in memory of Richard and Rick.

That month also marked the release of *Toolin' Around Woodstock Featuring Levon Helm* by the guitar master Arlen Roth. As well as drumming on most of the tracks, Helm sang lead on "Sweet Little Sixteen" and "Cryin' Time." Roth describes Levon as "just so giving and open as to be disarming! He really made you instantly fall in love with him, and with his incredible legacy of music to back it up, you always knew you were in the presence of real American music royalty." Roth recounts the experience of recording with Helm:

> Once in his presence, you simply never forgot that magic that he commanded. He took the recording sessions so seriously, and many times was the last one who wasn't satisfied with a track when the rest of us were ready to move on to others. He and I cut 11 tracks

in merely 2 days, and his drumming was something you could set your watch to! No click tracks for him…every beat existed in its own space and time, and when he did that little "bob" with his head each time he hit that snare drum, you *knew* he was right on the money!

The Levon Helm Band scored another grand slam at their return performance at New York's Beacon Theater in March, delivering music from a wide swath of Americana roots, including folk, bluegrass, blues, gospel, R&B, and some enduring favorites from the Band. Portrayed by one reviewer as "an old bantamweight fighter," Levon led his group to one more knockout in Baltimore that April, followed by a performance at Merlefest in North Carolina.

By the summer, baby Lavon was on tour with his mother, his grandfather, and the rest of the band. "We put drumsticks in his hands and earphones on him," Levon said. "He seems to be real happy as long as he can be part of it. If you want to protect him and put him off to the side where he can take a nap, that don't work. He wants to be right in the middle of it. That is exactly like his granddad." Some highlights that summer were Warren Haynes's Mountain Jam Music Festival in Hunter, New York; the Bonnaroo Music and Arts Festival in Manchester, Tennessee; and the Newport Folk Festival.

In September, upon being named Artist of the Year by the Americana Music Association, Helm quipped, "Even a blind chicken gets a piece of corn once in a while." Then he and his band staged another triumph at Nashville's Ryman Auditorium. Levon invited Bill and Jerome Avis to the show and asked them to come to his room for a visit. "He reached in his small, little duffel bag that he always carried," Jerome says, "and he pulled out two thousand dollars…He put a thousand in his pocket, and he threw a thousand at Dad and said, 'Here, you guys have a good time. We'll just keep this to ourselves, right.'"

With musical guests Billy Bob Thornton, John Hiatt, Sheryl Crow, Buddy Miller, Little Sammy Davis, and Sam Bush, that concert left no doubt that Helm was an American icon. A recording of the show—*Ramble at the Ryman*—was released in 2011 to rave reviews. One critic wrote, "There was little question of Levon Helm's importance, within that group—but also within the broader landscape of American roots music—as inventive interpreter, as country proselytizer. His sermon, shouted before a jubilant crowd in Nashville that night: As long as these songs have been around, from his former group and from much further back, they will always provide us with a lasting communal joy." Helm donated a portion of the proceeds of the album to the Americana Music Association.

VINCE GILL LET out "the biggest cheer you can ever imagine" when told that Levon would be joining him onstage at the second annual All for the Hall New York Benefit to support the Country Music Hall of Fame and Museum in Nashville. "I think he possesses maybe the greatest voice in America's music," Gill said. "The music he made with The Band is arguably the best music America ever put out." In an event hosted by Arkansas native Billy Bob Thornton, Levon was joined onstage by Gill, country singer-songwriter Rodney Crowell, and Emmylou Harris.

The year was capped off by another honor when *Rolling Stone* named Helm one of the hundred greatest singers of all time, describing his vocals as encompassing a spirit of family and deep country: "[Levon's voice] is ageless, timeless and has no race. He can sing with such depth and emotion, but he can also convey a good-old fun-time growl...[It] is the equivalent of a sturdy old farmhouse that has stood for years in the fields, weathering all kinds of change yet remaining unmovable."

Helm played the acid-induced hallucination of Confederate General John Bell Hood who haunts the film noir detective movie *In the Electric Mist*, released in February 2009. It starred his friend Tommy Lee Jones, John Goodman, and Mary Steenburgen, and included a cameo appearance by blues artist Buddy Guy. Although it went direct to DVD, it was nonetheless praised for its supporting cast, "especially Levon Helm, former drummer with The Band, who brings an otherworldly seasoned dignity to the role of the dead General."

"THE MAN IS still vital, you know," Campbell said of Helm. "The guy's still got plenty to give, and I wanna be there to help him give it," he added with a laugh. For Levon's next album—*Electric Dirt*—his vision was to build on the success of *Dirt Farmer* by maintaining the acoustic feel while incorporating some electric instruments and horns to jack up the energy and create a fuller, more complex sound. Songs were selected from a wider range of genres than *Dirt Farmer*, and ran the gamut from bluegrass to country rock, blues, gospel, and Dixieland, with one original track and others from diverse artists such as Pops Staples, Randy Newman, Muddy Waters, Jerry Garcia, and Happy Traum. Even the more recent numbers have a well-worn feel.

The personnel included Levon, Amy, Larry, Teresa, Byron, Brian Mitchell on keyboards, and Jimmy Vivino. Levon played drums and mandolin, a Gibson F-9. Several tracks incorporated a horn section comprising Howard Johnson, Erik Lawrence, Jay Collins, Clark Gayton, and Steven Bernstein. The album was produced by Campbell and recorded at Helm's barn.

Levon's voice is more robust here than on *Dirt Farmer*, and his confidence had increased. "This go-round has been a lot more fun," he admitted. "Now I know I've got enough voice left to do it." He hits his stride in *Electric Dirt*. "I feel like it's the best I've been able to sound," he said. "And it's about time. For the most part the solo records I made before this were just opportunities to record in, say, Muscle Shoals or Nashville. But this is the first time ever really that—after being sick for a while and not being able to do it—I had a real *want* and a *need*."

Levon was gratified at how the band had coalesced and enjoyed performing with so many younger musicians, especially his daughter, who played mandolin and drums on this album. Amy's and Teresa's backing harmonies were especially effective. "They're the most different background singers you'll ever hear," Helm acknowledged, "but they really cover whatever flavor we're in, and really add that color or tone to it."

The horn charts for "Kingfish" and "I Wish I Knew How It Would Feel to Be Free" were compiled by Helm's old pal Allen Toussaint. "The beauty of this horn section, like with those Band records," says Larry, "is that what Levon does is not a jazz gig, it's not R&B, it's not swing. It's something in between…If it was just a standard blues or

R&B horn section it wouldn't be right. It has to have some of that Salvation Army in it, some of that New Orleans thing."

In the jubilant Jerry Garcia number, "Tennessee Jed," often on the band's setlist for live performances, Levon belts out the lyrics with exuberance as he plays a swampy drumbeat, moving seamlessly through time-signature changes. He countrifies two Muddy Waters shuffles, beating out a call and response in "Stuff You Gotta Watch" and barking out with gusto the slow blues "You Can't Lose What You Ain't Never Had."

Helm digs deep into his rural roots in "Growin' Trade," singing with gritty determination, backed with a half-time shuffle. A song of survival he wrote with Campbell, it portrays a destitute farmer who resorts to growing marijuana. "There's a lot of people that are just haunted by the idea that they will be the first one in the family to lose the family farm," Levon noted. "I've seen it a lot, and it's a horrible thing. The 'Growin' Trade' is about a guy trying to hang on to the family farm, and he has to go a little bit undercover to try and do it."

Levon plays drums and overdubs mandolin on Randy Newman's "Kingfish." With no change in tempo, the feel shifts from languorous to energetic as he alternates between drumming in the cracks and playing it straight with lots of hi-hat openings amid rollicking horns. Of the Happy Traum–penned ballad "Golden Bird," delivered with stark, unadorned vocals, Helm said,

> That song is one of my favorites on the album, it really is…We had it very stripped down, almost a cappella, and just built the verses as the song progressed…We've all had that experience where you've destroyed something you love. My mom stopped me from doing that one time. I had a BB gun and I was taking aim, you know, and all of a sudden she comes up behind me and says, "You're not gonna shoot that songbird, are you?" Yeah, we've all hurt things we should be loving.

Levon confronts death with elation in the gospel-infused "When I Go Away," a fast shuffle with high-hat openings that are likely over-dubbed. Written by Larry, it first appeared on the Dixie Hummingbirds

CD *Diamond Jubilation*. Helm plays a driving eighth-note groove with an in-the-cracks lilt as guest vocalist Cat Russell joins him for another church-inspired exaltation, "I Wish I Knew How It Would Feel to Be Free."

Electric Dirt was released in summer 2009 and spent six weeks at number 1 on the Americana Radio Chart. A reviewer for *The New York Times* wrote, "[Helm's] voice is vigorous and unbridled, with his Arkansas drawl intact as he bends notes toward the blues and the backwoods… The music struts and cackles through every earthly travail."

WITH THE DEPARTURE of Jimmy Vivino, Levon asked Jim Weider to rejoin his group. "It was so great to be back playing with him…" the guitarist says, "and see how happy he was with this band." The Levon Helm Band was performing in summer 2009 with John Prine at Red Rocks Ampitheatre in Colorado when Helm started to experience problems with his voice. Thinking the altitude might be a factor, he continued to Tulsa and Fayetteville, where it became apparent something was wrong. They played on *The Late Show with David Letterman* that July to promote *Electric Dirt*, but Levon's voice faltered as he sang "Tennessee Jed." By the time, he appeared at the Gathering of the Vibes festival in Connecticut at the end of the month, he was under doctor's orders to not sing. In August, a benign lesion was removed from his vocal chords. He continued to perform, playing drums with Allen Toussaint, Nick Lowe, and Richard Thompson on the Canadian–U.K. television series *Spectacle: Elvis Costello with…*, filmed at Harlem's Apollo Theatre, and did not resume singing again until December.

THE RECORDING ACADEMY introduced a new award in 2010— the Grammy Award for Best Americana Album—and Levon Helm was its first recipient, winning for *Electric Dirt*, beating out Willie Nelson and Bob Dylan.

On the heels of his Grammy win, Helm maintained a demanding performance schedule on the road and at his barn. He brought his Ramble to Nashville's Ryman Auditorium again in April, inspiring one reviewer to write,

If you need proof that getting old doesn't have to suck, Levon Helm is Exhibit A. The iconic Band drummer, who's just a month shy of his 70th birthday, brought his Ramble to the Ryman Wednesday night, and the sinewy septuagenarian rocked the Mother Church like a guy a third his age, unleashing three solid hours of roadhouse rock and soul that was a roots lover's wet dream…

And the best part of the evening was witnessing how much fun Helm was having. It's rare to see performers enjoy themselves so much, particularly in this day of calculated pop performances and studied hipster detachment. For three solid hours, Helm was the proverbial pig in shit—an image we're sure is familiar to the pride and joy of Turkey Scratch, Ark.

Later that month, Helm appeared at the New Orleans Jazz Festival with friends Dr. John and Allen Toussaint sitting in, then traveled on to Charlottesville, Virginia. On May 22, to celebrate his seventieth birthday, Levon did what he loved best—hosted a Midnight Ramble at his barn. Beginning with a barbecue and a performance by John McEuen, founder of the Nitty Gritty Dirt Band, the Levon Helm Band took over with special guest Donald Fagen. Then on June 6, the festivities continued in front of ten thousand fans at the Mountain Jam, about thirty miles from Woodstock. Closing the festival with the Levon Helm Band were special guests Mountain Jam co-presenter and Allman Brothers guitarist Warren Haynes, Sam Bush, Alison Krauss, Donald Fagen, Jerry Douglas, Steve Earle with Allison Moorer, Jackie Greene, Ray LaMontagne, and Patterson Hood and his father, David Hood. Levon was presented with a huge birthday cake in the shape of his barn. One of Helm's birthday messages was from Billy Bob Thornton: "There's a sound from the Arkansas delta that doesn't exist anywhere else. It's called Levon Helm."

His Ramble on the Road traveled to Massey Hall in Toronto later in June for a performance with John Hiatt, then on to the Winnipeg Folk Festival and the Ottawa Bluesfest. Helm looked frail, but he was happy. By this time, he was trying everything he could—inhalers, steam, oxygen—to loosen his throat so he wouldn't disappoint his fans. Bill and Jerome Avis joined him there.

When he came to the Ottawa Bluesfest [Jerome says], there was just him and I and Dad sitting on his bed in his back bedroom on the bus, and he was sucking a little bit of oxygen at that time to get through the first two or three songs, then that would be pretty much it for his singing. He said, "You know, boys, all I want to do…I just want to go and play shows and get paid well for doing it."

One of the sad things I noticed at that time…Levon would never say no to anybody. When they put out *Dirt Farmer* and then *Electric Dirt*, and he was doing all these Rambles, and then they took the Ramble on the road, and they had some pretty big shows, you know, but they'd take everybody and their brother with them. So then, instead of getting away with one bus, now he's got to take two buses. It would cost more for the buses, then you've got all those people and even if they weren't taking pay, they were still getting looked after for their rooms and their food. That added up to thousands and thousands of dollars. I know he would never say no, but I was always upset that those people couldn't see that. He had a second mortgage on that place.

Helm performed at the Gathering of the Vibes festival in Connecticut, then at Radio City Music Hall, prompting one reviewer to observe, "[Willie] Nelson really came off as a mellow fellow in contrast to show opener Levon Helm…[who] swung like a New Orleans sledgehammer…His voice all but gone, Helm still sang what he could with admirable fervor…routinely bringing the crowd of around 5000 to its feet so long…that we almost forgot about Willie." The next night, back at the barn, Levon hosted a Ramble with guest Phil Lesh, attended by Jane Fonda and Catherine Keener, who were in town filming their movie *Peace, Love and Understanding*.

August saw Levon perform at the Newport Jazz Festival, then in Edmonton, Vancouver, San Francisco, Los Angeles, and New York. Backstage at L.A.'s Greek Theatre, drummer Jim Keltner had dropped by to say hello to his old friend and icon. Helm asked him to back the band on drums while he played mandolin on "Deep Elem Blues."

"That was the last time I saw Levon," Keltner says. "He had already

had the operation and everything, and he'd lost quite a lot of weight…
and it was sad because he was still so sweet in the dressing room,
making sure everyone was comfortable. As I can recall it, I think he
still sang good. He wasn't as strong as he normally was…That was
tough to see him hurting like that."

LEVON TOOK HIS Rambles on the road again in spring 2011,
touring southern Ontario and the U.S. Midwest, Northeast, and South,
with various special guests that included Donald Fagen, Warren
Haynes, Los Lobos, and Paul Barrere and Fred Tackett of Little Feat.
On March 4 and 5, he played at Toronto's Massey Hall with Lucinda
Williams, and Colin Linden sat in for a couple of tunes and the encore.
Helm's final appearance in Toronto was at the BlackCreek Summer
Music Festival on July 16, opening for John Fogerty.

Other notable stops were at the New Orleans Jazz Fest in May and
then at New York's Central Park in July. At the Gathering of the Vibes,
a few days later, Levon's voice was clearly shot, but not his spirit, especially evident as he played mandolin in a rousing rendition of "Deep
Elem Blues" with Bob Weir. And although his voice was no better in
September at the Fredericton, New Brunswick, Harvest Jazz and Blues
Festival, in every other way he was still a magnificent musician. "You
could have watched him the whole show and had a master class in
roots music. That, and his smile were enough," said one critic. "The
vocal shape he's in didn't matter at all. He was happy to be there, they
were happy to have him."

"MY HEALTH RIGHT now seems to be pretty good," Helm
remarked. "I'm not the poster boy for good health, but I'm not doing
too bad. I've still got the energy to make music so as long as I can do
that I'm great." Levon felt blessed. "He was just the happiest guy the
last years of his life," Happy Traum says, "because he was getting
accolades from fans, respect from his fellow musicians and [was creating a] very fulfilling musical output. Also, his very positive
association with his daughter Amy—that was such a strong and pal-
pably fulfilling thing for him. To see him onstage with her singing you
could just see the pride in his eyes."

Jim Weider concurs: "It was a joyful thing to see how happy Levon was towards the end of his life, and he loved the band that he was playing with. To see him get that much success made me so happy, and I know it made his daughter happy, and everyone around him. I was so glad to be there with him." Mary Vaiden had great respect for her old friend. "He pulled himself out of [drugs]," she says, "he pulled himself out of bankruptcy. By the end of his life, he had accomplished everything that he wanted to accomplish. I just admire him greatly for it."

Friends and family often wished he didn't drive himself so hard. "He wouldn't listen to anybody, you know," Howard Johnson says. "He wanted to do what he wanted to do when he wanted to do it. I didn't feel like denying him any of that, but I feel that it had consequences." One thing Helm did eventually do was cut down on his colossal Coke consumption and drink mostly water instead.

Steve Jordan experienced firsthand that you could never count Levon out:

> The last time I saw him, he had called me, and he said he might need some help on this Ramble because he wasn't feeling all that great, and he had never said that to me before. So I said sure. So I went there, and I believe it was December…and we started to do a rehearsal, to work out a couple of things in the basement before we hit the stage, and we were playing, and he sounded great and everything. And then we were playing this one song, and he had a lot of energy and everything. It's like, "Hey, you're supposed to be sick!"
>
> And then the craziest thing happened. I'm playing, and I heard this bell-tone type of vocal, and I'm looking around the stage to see who's singing, and I don't see anybody's mouth moving, and I'm going, "Well, who's singing this thing?" and I look over to my left, and it's him. I was completely confused—he sounded amazing! There was no rasp or anything.

When the CD *Ramble at the Ryman*, compiled from the band's 2008 performance in Nashville, was released in 2011, the reviewer for

Modern Drummer wrote, "Helm doesn't let anything slide, doesn't take one measure of rhythm for granted, never gives one beat less than his full attention. He works the hi-hat from all angles, pops the snare with holy conviction, and maintains a strong drive…On a stage full of excellent musicians—Buddy Miller, Sam Bush, Sheryl Crow, and Larry Campbell, to name a few—Helm inspires the lot."

At the 54th Annual Grammy Awards on February 12, 2012, *Ramble at the Ryman* won for Best Americana Album. As Anna Lee expressed to Levon, "God wasn't through with you."

Helm was ambivalent about recognition and awards. "He was just very humble and never thought that he deserved the rewards," Anna Lee says. Mary remembers receiving a couple of Levon's gold records in the mail. He told her he'd found them under the bed when they were cleaning house and just wanted her to keep them. Another time, Mary says, "I'm up there [in Woodstock], and I'm in the kitchen making some coffee, and I see this sitting in the window—it's his Grammy. It's sitting on the soap dish."

Helm's awards meant more to his loved ones than himself. "He was very successful, getting Grammys, and his daughter, Amy, was doing really good, and he was so happy that she was singing great, and he had a grandchild," Weider affirms. "And to see him come back, the most award-winning comeback you could ever see and to see how happy he was, it was kind of like a great ending. Sad that it ended, but he ended full blast. I was so happy to see him be so successful and to be part of it. I was very honored."

Chris O'Leary says, "I'm so happy with those last three records because he finally got the recognition as a singer and as a performer that he deserves with the Grammys and all that stuff, which didn't mean crap to him. But still, it meant something to me, that finally people were recognizing what a treasure he was."

Amy gave birth to another son in 2011, named Hugh Collins, in honor of the great blues guitarist Hubert Sumlin, who died that December.

THAT FALL, LEVON asked his former drummer Randy Ciarlante to come back to the second drum stool, which he was pleased to do:

It was and is a phenomenal band. He was visibly happy I was back in the fold, though, and I really felt that we recaptured some of that old magic. I know we laughed a lot. Whether he knew how sick he was or not, he never complained. He was the most intense warrior I've ever seen. He loved what he was doing so much and was an inspiration to the end…The feel, the voice, the undeniable presence took hold of you every time he played, sang, or told a story. Lee also had that distinct quality of making everyone around him better. He was the quintessential band component.

Helm rarely let health issues interrupt his performance schedule. Around Christmas 2011, a spot was found on his liver and his back began to ache, but he persevered. "It's the most fun that a musician can have," he said about performing with his band. "I've got the best players in the world that I get to play with, and they can play anything and do anything so I don't have to worry about nothing. It's just a free ride for me."

He did admit, however, that he was having some problems: "Last week my voice was pretty much there. Tonight it lasted about a song and a half, and started going funny on me. And that's when Larry and all the other musicians—Amy, Teresa—they all come to the rescue. Brian Mitchell's got a great solo voice so I just gotta back up a little and let the show roll on. I couldn't make it without [their support]. And I wouldn't have done nearly as well as we've done without it."

"I was able to cherish every moment," Teresa says, "'cause you know he had like twenty lives he had burned through. You kind of knew it was precarious, and how long could this last because how long could *he* last?" Following a medical procedure in late January, Helm postponed some road dates and missed three Rambles in February. "He did everything he could to keep that same ball rolling," Howard Johnson recollects, "until he just really couldn't anymore…He did what he wanted to do and he carried it as far as he could. Otherwise, it wouldn't have been meaningful at all to be given a few more years of life."

"He played music great," confirms Weider, "even though he was in pain…but he knew music heals, and that's about the only thing [that] kind of saved me through it all, too: music." Following performances in Milwaukee and Ann Arbor, the Levon Helm Band hit the Tarrytown Music Hall on March 23. Teresa recalls sitting in the dressing room with Levon. "He's got his head down; he's just sitting quietly," she says. "It's right before the show. And out of the blue, he looks up and raises his head and says, 'All I want, all I ask for, is just those two hours onstage.' It was heartbreaking 'cause his voice was so fragile." Yet onstage that night, though he wasn't singing, Helm looked rejuvenated, hitting that backbeat with vigor.

Larry was performing "When I Go Away" and just when he was opening his mouth to start the second verse, he says, "I hear this strong voice—sounds just like Levon—come busting into that second verse. And he was sitting there at the drums just giving it up like he had this new burst of energy…And he finished the song from there. It was like chills. For that few minutes, we felt like we had him back and like everything was going to be okay again." At the end of the song, not only the audience, but also the band erupted in applause. Then Helm joined Teresa, Larry, and Amy for an a capella version of "Gloryland"— sitting on a stool, he belted out the lyrics with inhuman strength. It was his last performance on the road.

On March 31, Levon played his final Ramble at the barn despite pain in his back and head. Los Lobos were his special guests that night, and as band member Steve Berlin discloses,

> We knew he wasn't well. But he said the Barn show was still on the next day. When we got there, someone said: "Hey, Levon wants to talk to you guys." He had like a little bedroom in the back of the barn, more or less, and we walked in there—and he looked about as close to dying as I've ever seen anybody. It was just terrifying. He looked small and frail; he was shivering. He could barely talk. We just sort of shot the shit with him for a while, and then we walked out of there going: "There's no way this guy is going to play a show tonight. There's no way." He looked like he was basically about to go. So we did our set, and here comes Levon. He's dressed to the hilt, and he sits down and plays his ass off. He

was unbelievable. He just killed it that night. An unbelievably powerful performance.

Helm, however, was dissatisfied, saying to the Rambles manager, Tony LoBue, "I wasn't on my game tonight. I just couldn't do it. It hurt." According to Jim, "He was upset and said that he didn't play as good, and everybody said, 'Aw, don't worry about it.' That was the last show we did. He asked me to play his favorite song, 'Deep Feeling,' an instrumental that he turned me on to—it was a Chuck Berry song— and we did that. I guess he just really wanted to play it one more time, you know."

THE FOLLOWING WEEK, an MRI showed that the cancer had spread to Helm's spine, and he was admitted to Memorial Sloan Kettering Cancer Center in New York City. One of the last things Levon said to Amy, Larry, and Barbara O'Brien was, "Keep it goin'," meaning the Midnight Rambles and the recording studio.

Anna Lee and Mary arrived as soon as they could, but Levon was already unresponsive. Robbie Robertson had offered love and prayers to Helm at the induction ceremony at the Rock and Roll Hall of Fame on April 14, then flew to New York to visit his former bandmate the next day. Anna Lee points out that Levon remained unconscious, so any reconciliation Robertson hoped for was impossible. On April 17, Sandy and Amy posted the following message on Levon's website:

Dear Friends,

Levon is in the final stages of his battle with cancer. Please send your prayers and love to him as he makes his way through this part of his journey.

Thank you fans and music lovers who have made his life so filled with joy and celebration…he has loved nothing more than to play, to fill the room up with music, lay down the back beat, and make the people dance! He did it every time he took the stage…

We appreciate all the love and support and concern.

From his daughter Amy, and wife Sandy

"They'd taken him off of life support," Anna Lee says, "but the night before he passed away, I sat with him all night long and talked to him. And he couldn't talk back. He didn't make any sign, but I just felt that he heard me. And I just went back over our childhood and things we'd done and the laughs we'd had."

Howard Johnson and several other friends and bandmates saw Levon a few minutes before he passed away on April 19, 2012. "All his friends were there," Campbell recounts, "and it seemed like Levon was waiting for them." Then with Amy, Teresa, and Larry still in the room, they sang to him as he faded away. "He did it with dignity," Campbell says. "It was even two days ago they thought it would happen within hours, but he held on. It seems like he was Levon up to the end, doing it the way he wanted to do it. He loved us, we loved him."

Garth Hudson wrote, "Levon Helm left us today at 1:30 p.m., Thursday, April 19, 2012. I am terribly sad. Thank you for 50 years of friendship and music. Memories that live on with us. No more sorrows, no more troubles, no more pain. He went peacefully to that beautiful marvelous wonderful place. He was Buddy Rich's favorite rock drummer...and my friend. Levon, I'm proud of you."

New York Congressman Maurice Hinchey paid tribute to Helm in the United States House of Representatives on April 25, stating in part,

> Without a doubt, Levon's contributions to American music cannot be overstated. But beyond the music, we cannot forget Levon the man. I knew him well. He was a beacon of our Hudson Valley community. He was always willing to open his doors to help raise money for important local causes. He was a tremendous supporter of local agriculture. He worked to bring music into our schools and communities. He was a great person, and a great friend... Watching Levon perform over the years, you get the sense that despite all the fame, awards and notoriety, at his core he was just a man who felt music deeply in his bones. It's what made him one of the world's great performing artists...
>
> Levon will forever be remembered in our community, throughout the world and in our hearts. He was our neighbor, and

my good friend. I will miss him dearly. Levon has gone home, but his music will live on forever.

A DAY OF visitation was held for the staff of the studio, then the next day about two thousand fans were transported by school buses from Woodstock to a public wake held at the barn on April 26. Family members met the visitors, who were directed down a hallway lined with Levon's memorabilia, photos, and Grammy awards. Upstairs, they filed past his closed coffin surrounded by bouquets of flowers and placed next to his red drum kit. A slide show of family photos flickered by on a screen above.

A plumber from Long Island had left home with his family at six in the morning to get on the first bus to Levon's wake. "He wanted everyone to know they were welcome, they were among friends," he said. "He was just the realest, most soulful person who ever made music, and it was euphoria to be a part of it."

"It was hard for everybody," Anna Lee declares. "Pat O'Shea came, and the night he passed away, he wrote a song in his memory and named it 'Crazy Old Man.' And he was sitting with me at the [wake], and when we got up…Pat said, 'I wanna say a prayer.' And he got down on his knees and said a prayer before we walked out. It was just that type of loss and closeness and well-wishers…You felt the love in the building."

The following day was cold and bright for Levon's private funeral. In Arkansas, Governor Mike Beebe ordered all flags in that state to be lowered to half-mast. The service, held in the barn studio, was a tearful celebration of his life and music. Musical guests, including Garth Hudson, Howard Johnson, Happy Traum, John Sebastian, Rosanne Cash, Alexis P. Suter, and the Levon Helm Band with daughter Amy performed gospel hymns, blues, and songs from the Grateful Dead, Bob Dylan, and the Band. Jerome Avis, who attended with his father, Bill, says,

> I'll never forget it, and I'll never forget Garth getting up—as slow as Garth is—and getting at the piano, and he had a notebook with him, his piano music…Everybody's quiet and he flipped the pages,

and you could hear his mumbles to himself, and after what seemed like forever, he just shut the book and sat down at the piano and just did his own thing and played. And then he stood up. Nobody said anything…[Garth] sticks both arms out in the air and points two fingers up. He faced Levon's casket, did that, and then walked right out of the room. Very powerful.

John Donabie, Levon's pal for more than forty years, recalls one musician who spoke at the ceremony: "[He] stood there and said, 'Good morning, I'm Levon Helm's best friend.' And he paused, and he said, 'Well, all of us in this room can say, "I was Levon Helm's best friend," because you know what? Levon made everyone he met feel like he was your best friend.'"

New York State Troopers closed the route from Helm's property to the Woodstock Cemetery—the same location where Rick Danko was buried more than twelve years earlier—for the extraordinary procession of a hundred cars. Admirers lined the road, playing music, holding signs, waving drumsticks, or standing silently in respect. John Donabie was in the cavalcade and remembers, "When we left Plochmann Lane and made our way up Tinker Street…it was like a head of state had passed away—the lineups [of townspeople] on both sides. And when the hearse went by, you could hear all the applause." Anna Lee says, "It was really a great thing…[Levon] would have got a kick out of it… He would have been honored at the crowd that turned out."

"There was a lot of cars in the procession," Anna Lee recalls, "and one of them in place of turning, went straight. Well, then the ones behind him just kept following, so finally the police came and caught up with the lead car and turned him around to go back to the cemetery. And [Levon] would have got the biggest laugh out of that. He just would have enjoyed the heck out of that."

"We were in the line going to the cemetery," Donabie says, "and we were still quite a ways from getting there, and all we could hear— because we had the windows down—all we could hear were drums. Levon wanted one of the best drum corps they could find." It was the Jaguar Memorial Band drumline from Jackson High School in New Jersey.

The gates of the cemetery were closed for the private interment, but lines of spectators and media gathered along the fence hoping to get a glimpse of the ceremony. The drumline marched past Danko's grave, then played a military tattoo at Helm's burial site. "All the drummers were in a big, giant semi-circle..." John continues, "drumming away, and other musicians were there playing—Happy Traum and all these different people. A lot of legends were there, playing. It was very fitting." As mourners sang the gospel hymn "Angel Band," Levon Helm was laid to rest.

Led by Larry Campbell, Jimmy Vivino, and Steve Jordan, the musicians played "Ophelia" as the mourners wended their way from the gravesite back to the cemetery entrance, while Levon's dog, Muddy, bounded around them. A few stray snowflakes drifted from the sky.

Behind the gravesite is a wooden wall, built by Helm's friend Paul Shultis. On it are fastened the musical notes from one of Levon's most memorable songs, "Life Is a Carnival"—a fitting metaphor for the joy he bestowed on the world.

He was my bosom buddy friend to the end, one of the last true great spirits of my or any other generation. This is just so sad to talk about. I still can remember the first day I met him and the last day I saw him. We go back pretty far and had been through some trials together. I'm going to miss him.

—BOB DYLAN

Acknowledgments

When I had the privilege of interviewing Levon Helm in 1996 for my biography of Muddy Waters, I was immediately struck by his friendliness and generosity. It felt like talking to an old friend. Little did I know at the time that Levon made most people feel that way—it was part of his immense charm. When it finally came time to write another book, my criterion was to make it about someone I respected as much as Levon. Like a bolt from the sky, I had my answer.

So many friends and colleagues of Levon's helped to make this book possible. They either assisted me with contacts or photos or delved into their memories and took time to help me understand what he was all about. I sincerely thank the following:

Barry Avis
Paul Berry
Sandra Cox Birchfield
Bill Boatman
Terry Cagle
Randy Cale
Jeff Carter
Earl Cate
Ernie Cate
David Clayton-Thomas
Larry Crowe
David Daniloff
John Donabie
David Fishof
Alec Fraser
Michael Friedman
C.W. Gatlin

Dash Goff
Joe Griffith
Ronnie Hawkins
Bruce Hay
Tim Heagerty
Aaron "Professor Louie" Hurwitz
Howard Johnson
Steve Jordan
Jimmy Karstein
Jim Keltner
the late Harold Kudlets
George Lembesis
Colin Linden
Carmen Marotta
Pat O'Shea
Kirby Penick
Shirley Overton Quick

Ron Rainey

John Scheele

Philip Slayton

Ben Story

Bubba Sullivan

Alexis P. Suter

A.B. Thompson Jr.

Steve Thomson

Happy Traum

Barbie Washburn

Ryan Weber

Sam Weber

Jim Weider

Harold Wieties

My literary agent, Beverley Slopen, exemplifies the qualities of experience, optimism, and extraordinary patience that everyone would wish for in an agent, and I am most grateful for her support and advice through this long process.

Diversion Books shared my enthusiasm for this project, and I heartily thank CEO and publisher Scott Waxman and editor-in-chief Keith Wallman for their faith in me. Editorial Assistant Marc Greenawalt and Marketing and Publicity Manager Shannon Donnelly were a pleasure to work with. In addition, I appreciate the expertise of cover designer Libby Kingsbury and copyeditor Elisabeth Evan.

Scott Lunsford, associate director of the David and Barbara Pryor Center for Arkansas Oral and Visual History at the University of Arkansas in Fayetteville, kindly allowed me access to their archives of interviews and photos, and I wholeheartedly thank him and the center for their invaluable addition to my research. I am also appreciative of Mark Stein on behalf of Max Weinberg, Minnie Yorke at the Ritchie Yorke Project, and Tracy Kearns at *Modern Drummer* for permission to quote extensively from the writings of Max Weinberg, Ritchie Yorke, and Robyn Flans.

Murray Creed—my drum teacher at Groove Studios and the author of five educational books on drumming—opened up a new world to me through his love of the instrument, his deep knowledge of the subject, and his extraordinary ability as an educator. Thanks, Murray.

It was such a pleasure to spend time with Bill Avis, his wife, Jeannine, and their son, Jerome Levon Avis, and I was very gratified that they welcomed me into their home and reminisced for hours about their beloved friend. Jerome remained very helpful throughout the writing of this book. For all the Avis family, Levon was clearly a treasured part of their lives.

Butch Dener was passionate about this project from the start and was a resource I could call on throughout. He not only shared his joyful as well as painful memories of a man he loved, but he paved the way for my remarkable interview trip to Arkansas. I thank him heartily for his assistance.

I am indebted to Randy Stratton for opening so many doors for me in Fayetteville and beyond. Levon holds a very special place in his heart, and it showed through his enthusiasm for this book and his ongoing willingness to help whenever he could.

What can I say about the generosity of Mary Vaiden and Anna Lee Amsden? It was an honor to get to know them and to hear their stories of growing up with Levon. With abundant goodwill, they entrusted their precious memories to me. And how lucky was I to get a guided tour of Marvell and Turkey Scratch with Anna Lee. This would have been a lesser book without them. You both have my sincere thanks.

Notes

Chapter 1: Best Seat in the House

1. became rock 'n' roll.": Jay Russell [producer/director], "Highway 61," *Great Drives* [PBS series], Four Point Entertainment, 1996. https://vimeo.com/128143366 (accessed January 6, 2019). **1. beat that show.":** Levon Helm, interview with Marco Werman, *Sound Tracks: Quick Hits* [series], the Talbot Players in association with PBS Arts, February 2012. www.youtube .com/watch?v=KVey5eGRZqk (accessed June 27, 2018). **1. at him all night.":** Austin Scaggs, "Profile: Up All Night with Levon Helm," *Rolling Stone*, August 6, 2009, p. 28. **2. was like, 'Goddamn!'":** Ibid., p. 28. **2. F.S. Walcott's stage.":** Mikal Gilmore, "Levon Helm 1940–2012," *Rolling Stone*, May 10, 2012, pp. 38–41. **3. took place down there.":** Morse U. Gist, interview with Scott Lunsford. "Helena, Arkansas, Project." October 25, 2012, courtesy of the Pryor Center for Arkansas Oral and Visual History, University of Arkansas. **3. sharecroppers of Arkansas.":** Harry S. Ashmore, *Arkansas: A History* (New York: W.W. Norton and Company, 1978), pp. 168–69. **4. it was all about.:** Jay Russell, *Great Drives*. **4. mom and daddy.":** Paul Berry, interview with author, April 22, 2018. **5. situated Turkey Scratch.:** A.B. Thompson Jr., "Turkey Scratch," self-published [n.d.]. **6. your hide right off,":** Butch Dener, interview with Scott Lunsford, "Helena, Arkansas, Project," October 9, 2015, courtesy of the Pryor Center for Arkansas Oral and Visual History, University of Arkansas. **7. always been friends.":** Anna Lee Amsden, interview with author, April 24, 2018. **7. and sister forever.":** Ibid. **7. wound up laughing.":** Ibid. **7. nobody else had one.:** Ibid. **8. was very outgoing.":** Mary Vaiden, interview with author, May 1, 2018. **8. it wasn't Diamond.":** Ibid. **8. a crease in them.":** Ibid. **8. not make him behave.":** Ibid. **9. in charge, she thought.":** Ibid. **9. loved him to death.":** Anna Lee Amsden, interview with author, April 24, 2018. **10. he could eat all day.":** Mary Vaiden, interview with author, May 1, 2018. **10. troubles and misfortunate times.":** Bonnie Langston, "At the Helm: The Rebirth of a Legend," *Daily Freeman* [Kingston, NY], February 17, 2008. www.dailyfreeman.com/news/at-the-helm-the-rebirth-of-a-legend/article_6e758fac-3ba9 -5ca1-ad35-6fa27bee1086.html (accessed February 10, 2019). **10. so many times.":** Anna Lee Amsden, interview with author, April 24, 2018. **10. play for each other.:** Ashley Kahn, "Not Far From 'Big Pink,' Levon Helm Is Back Performing," *The Wall Street Journal*, February 7, 2008, http://levonhelm.com/articles/Not%20Far%20From%20Big%20Pink.htm (accessed November 29, 2016). **11. to play percussion.":** Levon Helm, interview with David Bianculli, "Levon Helm: The 2007 *Fresh Air* Interview," *Fresh Air*, NPR Music, April 29, 2012. www .npr.org/2012/04/20/150886425/levon-helm-the-2007-fresh-air-interview (accessed July 20, 2018). **12. a big deal.:** Bubba Sullivan, interview with author, April 26, 2018. **12. their own musical styles.":** *Levon Helm Teaches Classic Rock, County and Blues Drumming* [DVD], Homespun Tapes Ltd., 1992, 2005. **12. from then on.":** Levon Helm, "The Music," *Razor* magazine, February 2004. http://theband.hiof.no/articles/the_music_razor_february_2004. html (accessed February 9, 2016).

Chapter 2: From Turkey Scratch to the Hawk

13. ate everybody's lunch!": Anna Lee Amsden, interview with author, April 24, 2018. **13. out every time.":** Ibid. **14. my bicycle again.":** Ibid. **14. going to the *big* school.":** Ibid. **15. loved to aggravate people.": Ibid. **15. we just waited.**: Mary Vaiden, interview with author, May 1, 2018. **15. wouldn't turn over.'"**: Anna Lee Amsden, interview with Scott Lunsford, "Helena, Arkansas, Project," October 9, 2015, courtesy of the Pryor Center for Arkansas Oral and Visual History, University of Arkansas. **16. plenty of it.":** Paul Berry, interview with author, April 22, 2018. **16. bought him a watermelon.:** Anna Lee Amsden, interview with author, April 24, 2018. **16. it was over with.:** Ibid. **17. gonna be so mad!'":** Mary Vaiden, interview with author, May 1, 2018. **17. I still favor.:** PJS Productions, "The Band Documentary of 1 Making of the Hawks," February 1, 2014. www.youtube.com/watch?v=KmHsLzcyvBE (accessed March 31, 2018). **18. piece of the pie.":** Berbon "Bubba" Sullivan, interview with Scott Lunsford, "Helena, Arkansas, Project," courtesy of the Pryor Center for Arkansas Oral and Visual History, University of Arkansas. **18. hear all year.":** Levon Helm, interview with author, July 3, 1996. **19. he could do.":** Anna Lee Amsden, interview with author, April 24, 2018. **19. show that evening.":** Craig Harris, *The Band: Pioneers of Americana Music* (Lanham, MD: Rowman and Littlefield, 2014), p. 47. **19. got him for that!":** Terry Cagle, interview with author, April 19, 2018. **19. Both of us did.":** Mary Vaiden, interview with author, May 1, 2018. **19. be around it.":** Anna Lee Amsden, interview with author, April 24, 2018. **19. get on that guitar.":** Jay Cocks, "Down to Old Dixie and Back," *Time*, January 12, 1970. http://theband.hiof.no /articles/time_1970.html (accessed November 7, 2016). **19. couldn't get otherwise,":** Berbon "Bubba" Sullivan, interview with Scott Lunsford, "Helena, Arkansas, Project," courtesy of the Pryor Center for Arkansas Oral and Visual History, University of Arkansas. **19. get out of work!":** Bob Girouard, "Levon Helm: The Classic Drummer Interview," *Classic Drummer*, August 2008. www.levonhelm.com/articles/CLASSIC_DRUMMER_8_08.pdf (accessed November 9, 2016). **19. got a dime!":** Anna Lee Amsden, interview with author, April 24, 2018. **20. We had a ball.":** Ibid. **20. gin that cotton.":** Paul Lieberman, "Levon Helm Is Still Ready for the Load," *Los Angeles Times*, February 10, 2008. http://articles.latimes.com/2008 /feb/10/entertainment/ca-helm10 (accessed January 2, 2017). **20. New York or somewhere.":** Vicki Mabry (interviewer), "Comeback Kid: After a Year When the Music Came Back," *Nightline* (ABC-TV program), December 30, 2005. http://theband.hiof.no/articles/lh_nightline _12-30-2005.html (accessed February 9, 2016). **21. tell Mama that I died saving Sister!":** Mary Vaiden, interview with author, May 1, 2018. **21. the storm cellar.":** Ibid. **21. stay in the house.":** Ibid. **22. Rotaries, 4-H Clubs.":** Max Weinberg, "Conversations with Rock's Great Drummers: Levon Helm," *The Big Beat: Conversations with Rock's Great Drummers"* (Chicago: Contemporary Books, 1984). http://theband.hiof.no/articles/the_big_beat_lh.html (accessed February 9, 2016). **22. in my neighborhood.:** Paul Berry, interview with author, April 22, 2018. **22. and he could.":** Paul Berry, interview with author, April 22, 2018. **23. with his father.":** Morse U. Gist, interview with Scott Lunsford. Helena, Arkansas, Project. October 25, 2012, courtesy of the Pryor Center for Arkansas Oral and Visual History, University of Arkansas. **23. up your dress.":** Mary Vaiden, interview with author, May 1, 2018. **24. do his gyratin',:** Steve Dougherty, "Down Home with Levon Helm: The Band Legend Returns to the Delta Where His Music Began," *People*, May 9, 1994, vol. 41, no. 17. **24. was truly electrifying.":** Helm, "The Music," *Razor*. **24. you ever heard.":** PJS Productions, "Making of the Hawks." **24. drummer—full throttle.:** Weinberg, *The Big Beat*. **25. up on their chairs.":** Ken Micallef, "Playing for the Song—and More: Steve Jordan Interviews the Great Levon Helm," *Modern Drummer*, 32.4 (April 2008). **25. watched him go.":** Anna Lee Amsden, interview with author, April 24, 2018. **25. was his teacher.":** Mary Vaiden, interview with author, May 1, 2018. **25. bologna and cheese.":** Paul Lieberman, "Levon Helm Is Still Ready for the Load," *Los Angeles Times*, February 10, 2008. http://articles.latimes.com/2008/feb/10/entertainment /ca-helm10 (accessed January 2, 2017). **26. refurnish their home.":** Mary Vaiden, interview with author, November 27, 2018. **26. shit in sports,":** Bubba Sullivan, interview with author, April 26, 2018. **26. we had the ball.":** Steve Dougherty, "Down Home with Levon Helm: The Band Legend Returns to the Delta Where His Music Began," *People*, May 9, 1994, vol. 41, no. 17. **26. look at you!'":** Brian Hollander, "Oh, Those Daze … Levon and Friends Talk about Onteora Show and High School Times," *Hudson Valley Times*, October 21, 2010. www.ulsterpublishing.com/view/full_story/9998087/article--Oh--those-daze-Levon-and

-friends-talk-about-Onteora-show-and-high-school-times-? (accessed September 26, 2016).
26. with a band.": Helm, "The Music," *Razor.* **27. wild damn sound.":** Scott Jordan, "Levon Helm," *Offbeat,* December 1, 1998. www.offbeat.com/articles/levon-helm (accessed July 6, 2018). **27. King Biscuit Boys.:** Harris, *The Band: Pioneers of Americana Music,* pp. 49–50. **28. dance one night.:** Weinberg, *The Big Beat.* **28. more of a social thing.":** Kay Cordtz, "Reading, Writing and Rhythm: Levon Helm, One Time Drummer for the Band, Now Devotes His Time to Bringing Music to the Classroom at Local Schools," *Hudson Valley Magazine,* August 22, 2006. www.hvmag.com/core/pagetools.php?pageid=6054&url=%2FHudson-Valley -Magazine%2FAugust-2006%2FReading-Writing-Rythym%2F&mode=print (accessed February 9, 2016). **28. day after day.":** Anna Lee Amsden, interview with author, April 24, 2018. **29. rock 'n' roll anymore.":** Terry Cagle, interview with author, April 19, 2018. **29. they all liked us.:** Anna Lee Amsden, interview with author, April 24, 2018. **29. five good ones.":** Hollander, "Oh, Those Daze," *Hudson Valley Times.* **30. spanked with that paddle.":** Anna Lee Amsden, interview with author, April 24, 2018. **30. movie in West Helena.:** Ibid. **30. always had the prettiest girlfriends, always the best ones.":** Mary Vaiden, interview with author, May 1, 2018. **31. died by ourselves,":** Anna Lee Amsden, interview with author, April 24, 2018. **31. pulling tricks on people.:** Mary Vaiden, interview with author, May 1, 2018. **31. would have never graduated.'":** Anna Lee Amsden, interview with author, April 24, 2018. **32. came to see them.":** Mary Vaiden, interview with author, May 1, 2018. **32. how great he was.:** Helm, "The Music," *Razor.* **32. all about to me.":** Levon Helm, interview with Marco Werman, *Sound Tracks: Quick Hits* [series], the Talbot Players in association with PBS Arts, February 2012. www.youtube.com/watch?v=KVey5eGRZqk (accessed June 27, 2018). **33. there and play.":** Berbon "Bubba" Sullivan, interview with Scott Lunsford, "Helena, Arkansas, Project," courtesy of the Pryor Center for Arkansas Oral and Visual History, University of Arkansas. **33. clean house, man,":** Ibid. **33. biggest hall in America.":** Bubba Sullivan, interview with author, April 26, 2018. **33. music a disservice.":** Micallef, "Playing for the Song" *Modern Drummer.* **33. anything, anyway, anyhow,":** Anna Lee Amsden, interview with author, April 24, 2018. **34. my personal taste.":** Robyn Flans, "Levon Helm," *Modern Drummer,* August 1984, vol. 8, no. 8, http://theband.hiof.no/articles/modern_drummer_08_1984_lh_interview.html (accessed February 9, 2016). **34. bottom of the music.:** Weinberg, *The Big Beat.*

Chapter 3: "The Wildest, Fiercest, Speed-Driven Bar Band in America"

35. pussy than Frank Sinatra.": David Hepworth, "Levon Helm 1940–2012: Master Musician, True Leader of the Band," *The Word* (June 2012): 46–47 (accessed online February 10, 2016). **36. style with a back beat.":** Ronnie Hawkins and Peter Goddard, *Ronnie Hawkins: Last of the Good Ol' Boys* (Toronto: Stoddart Publishing, 1989), p. 50. **36. they'd all play.":** Dash Goff, interview with author, April 20, 2018. **37. whiskey all over it.":** C.W. Gatlin, interview with author, April 26, 2018. **37. set of drums.":** Scott Jordan, "Backtalk with Levon Helm," *Offbeat,* December 1998, www.offbeat.com/articles/levon-helm (accessed November 10, 1016). **37. got them together.":** Edwin Leo Burks Jr., interview with Scott Lunsford. "Arkansas Memories Project." July 20, 2011, courtesy of the Pryor Center for Arkansas Oral and Visual History, University of Arkansas. **37. can play drums.'":** C.W. Gatlin, interview with author, April 26, 2018. **38. we started practicing.":** Ronnie Hawkins, interview with author, May 19, 2016. **38. great humanitarian.":** Robyn Flans, "Levon Helm," *Modern Drummer,* August 1984, vol. 8, no. 8, http://theband.hiof.no/articles/modern_drummer_08_1984_lh _interview.html (accessed February 9, 2016). **38. never mind a dime.":** Hawkins and Goddard, *Ronnie Hawkins,* p. 83. **39. steal my licks.":** Steve Thomson (director), *Let It Rock: At the Crossroads of Rock 'n' Roll* (DVD), Backstage Productions International and Eagle Rock Entertainment, 2005. **40. his own eventually.":** Ronnie Hawkins, interview with author, May 19, 2016. **40. make it sound right.":** Hawkins and Goddard, *Ronnie Hawkins,* p. 81. **40. crackin' and knockin'.":** Max Weinberg, "Conversations with Rock's Great Drummers: Levon Helm," *The Big Beat: Conversations with Rock's Great Drummers* (Chicago: Contemporary Books, 1984), http://theband.hiof.no/articles/the_big_beat_lh.html (accessed February 9, 2016).

40. could take that abuse.": Robert Cochran and Ronnie Hawkins, "Long on Nerve: An Interview with Ronnie Hawkins," *The Arkansas Historical Quarterly*, vol. 65, no. 2 (summer, 2006), p. 110. www.jstor.org/stable/40038292 (accessed November 6, 2016). **40. Robbie Robertson was early on.":** Hawkins and Goddard, *Ronnie Hawkins*, p. 81. **40. they'd let you in,":** Ibid. **40. We outdrew everyone.":** Robert Cochran and Ronnie Hawkins, "Long on Nerve: An Interview with Ronnie Hawkins," *The Arkansas Historical Quarterly*, vol. 65, no. 2 (Summer, 2006), p. 110. www.jstor.org/stable/40038292 (accessed November 6, 2016). **41. I was in heaven.":** Levon Helm with Stephen Davis, *This Wheel's on Fire: Levon Helm and the Story of the Band*, updated edition (Chicago: Chicago Review Press, 2013), p. 49. **41. note with me.":** Levon Helm, *Levon Helm Teaches Classic Rock, Country and Blues Drumming* (DVD), Homespun Tapes Ltd., 1992, 2005. **41. were mental giants.":** Ronnie Hawkins, interview with author, May 19, 2016. **42. loved their music.":** Ibid. **42. places we played.":** Ritchie Yorke, "Ronnie Hawkins," http://ritchieyorke.com/2015/04/17/ronnie-hawkins (accessed June 8, 2016). **42. you off the stage.":** John Poppy, "The Band: Music from Home," *Look*, August 25, 1970. http://theband.hiof.no/articles/music_from_home.html (accessed November 9, 2016). **42. a woman's tit.":** Ritchie Yorke, "Ronnie Hawkins," http://ritchieyorke.com/2015/04/17/ronnie -hawkins (accessed June 8, 2016). **42. now and again.":** Ian Wallis, *The Hawk: The Story of Ronnie Hawkins and the Hawks* (Kingston, ON: Quarry Press, 1996), p. 46. **42. ashamed to attend.":** Yorke, "Ronnie Hawkins." **43. girls in one day.":** Hepworth, "Levon Helm," *The Word*, pp. 46–47. **43. some crazy things.:** Anna Lee Amsden, interview with author, April 24, 2018. **43. cook up a storm.":** Yorke, "Ronnie Hawkins." **43. Mr. Marvell—I won!":** Terry Cagle, interview with author, April 19, 2018. **44. listen to Chuck Berry.":** Ibid. **44. the train laughing.":** Anna Lee Amsden, interview with author, April 24, 2018. **44. kind of big deal,":** C.W. Gatlin, interview with author, April 26, 2018. **44. I wanted to be in.":** Flans, "Levon Helm," *Modern Drummer*. **44. bitch of a band.":** Hawkins and Goddard, *Ronnie Hawkins*, p. 109. **44. he was a rocker.":** Ronnie Hawkins, interview with author, May 19, 2016. **45. recommended Ronnie Hawkins.":** Harold Kudlets, interview with author, June 3, 2016. **45. messin' up, takin' pills,":** Ronnie Hawkins, interview with author, May 19, 2016. **45. Really wild.":** Hawkins and Goddard, *Ronnie Hawkins*, p. 94. **45. hillbillies outta here.'":** Ronnie Hawkins, interview with author, May 19, 2016. **45. next ten years.":** Ibid. **45. young he looked.":** Wallis, *The Hawk*, p. 46. **46. distance from everybody.":** Harold Kudlets, interview with author, June 3, 2016. **46. he *was* twenty-one.":** Ronnie Hawkins, interview with author, May 19, 2016. **46. never miss a beat,":** Harold Kudlets, interview with author, June 3, 2016. **46. He was a typical Southerner.":** Ibid. **46. he'd laugh about everything.":** Hawkins and Goddard, *Ronnie Hawkins*, p. 82. **46. anyone's ever enjoyed.":** Adrian Chamberlain, "At the Helm of the Band," *Times-Colonist* [Victoria, BC], July 7, 1994, p. 1. **46. money on doctors.":** Wallis, *The Hawk*, p. 48. **47. kinda wore out.":** Ibid. **47. have any underwear.":** Hawkins and Goddard, *Ronnie Hawkins*, p. 117. **48. really play drums.":** Aaron Howard, "The Rock of Aged: Former Band Drummer Levon Helm Lends His Experience to the Youthful Barn Burners," Houston Press Online, January 25, 2001. http://theband.hiof.no/articles/barn_burners_mucky_duck_houston _press.html (accessed February 9, 2016). **48. world to rock 'n' roll.":** Paul Berry, interview with author, April 22, 2018. **48. "It was like dreamin',":** Ronnie Hawkins, interview with author, May 19, 2016. **48. something underground,":** Ibid. **48. sounded like chipmunks playing.":** Ibid. **49. they loved doing it.":** Kirby Penick, interview with Scott Lunsford, 2018, courtesy of the Pryor Center for Arkansas Oral and Visual History, University of Arkansas. **50. reality of the blues.":** Ibid. **50. out at that point.":** Ibid. **50. born to do it, I guess.":** Ibid. **50. "Always a fight.":** Earl Cate, interview with Scott Lunsford, Bob Cochran, and Eric Johnson, "Arkansas Memories Project," April 2010, courtesy of the Pryor Center for Arkansas Oral and Visual History, University of Arkansas. **50. never lost a fight.":** Hawkins and Goddard, *Ronnie Hawkins*, p. 38. **50. get the door shut.":** Hayden McIlroy, interview with Scott Lunsford and Barbara Pryor, "Arkansas Memories Project," April 25, 2011, courtesy of the Pryor Center for Arkansas Oral and Visual History, University of Arkansas. **50. places we played.":** Ronnie Hawkins, interview with author, May 19, 2016. **51. had a lot of bands.":** C.W. Gatlin, interview with author, April 26, 2018. **51. amount of energy.":** Cleve Warren, "What Do You

Know About Tulsa Time?" Facebook, Blues Society of Tulsa, July 3, 2012. www.facebook .com/bluessocietyoftulsa/posts/what-do-you-know-about-tulsa-timejimmy-karstein-chuck -blackwell-david-teegarden-/109535709190668 (accessed November 12, 2018). **51. kind of a character.**: Jimmy Karstein, interview with author, December 12, 2018. **51. who's gonna drive!"**: Ronnie Hawkins, interview with author, May 19, 2016. **52. have in your band.**: Hawkins and Goddard, *Ronnie Hawkins*, p. 185. **52. you might say."**: Weinberg, *The Big Beat.* **52. aimed for the laughs."**: Ibid. **52. motherlode for me."**: Bruce Blackadar, "Levon Helm at 40: Music Is Still the Key," *Toronto Star,* June 22, 1980, D9. **53. we were paying $2000."**: Wallis, *The Hawk,* p. 49. **53. Absolutely movie stars."**: Ronnie Hawkins, interview with author, May 19, 2016. **53. Bony wasn't sure."**: Ronnie Hawkins and Peter Goddard, *Ronnie Hawkins: Last of the Good Ol' Boys* (Toronto: Stoddart Publishing, 1989), p. 142. **54. every frigging night."**: Paul Rellinger, "Peterbio: Bill Avis," My Kawartha.com, November 6, 2013. http:// www.mykawartha.com/whatson-story/4193985-peterbio-bill-avis (accessed December 16, 2016). **54. that's all I needed."**: Howard, "Rock of Aged," Houston Press Online. **54. I love that man."**: "Ronnie Hawkins," *Toronto Daily Star,* March 27, 1976, p. 6. **55. bar band in America."**: Helm with Davis, *This Wheel's on Fire,* p. 9. **55. guts fell out."**: Kliph Nesteroff, "Mobsters, Scoundrels, Comedians and Rat Finks." http://blog.wfmu.org/freeform/2012/03 /mobsters-rat-finks.html (accessed July 22, 2016). **56. ...and worse.**: Ibid. **56. Simple as that."**: Ibid. **57. recording an album."**: Jason Schneider, *Whispering Pines: The Northern Roots of American Music from Hank Snow to the Band* (Toronto: ECW Press, 2009), pp. 53–54. **57. "Life with an option."**: Ronnie Hawkins, interview with author, May 19, 2016.

Chapter 4: Gambling on Roulette

59. looked like gangsters.": Ronnie Hawkins, interview with author, May 19, 2016. **59. Bad friggin' dudes,"**: Bill Avis, interview with author, March 18, 2017. **59. time with him, loved him."**: Ibid. **60. him up a little bit."**: Ian Wallis, *The Hawk: The Story of Ronnie Hawkins and the Hawks* (Kingston, ON: Quarry Press, 1996), p. 59. **60. called it 'Forty Days.'"**: Ronnie Hawkins, interview with author, May 19, 2016. **60. just keeps on going."**: C.W. Gatlin, interview with author, April 26, 2018. **61. was a disc jockey,"**: Ronnie Hawkins, interview with author, May 19, 2016. **61. were somebody then."**: PBS Productions, "The Band Documentary of 1 Making of the Hawks," February 1, 2014. www.youtube.com/watch?v=KmHsLzcyvBE (accessed March 31, 2018). **62. Levon and Jimmy Ray."**: Ronnie Hawkins, interview with author, May 19, 2016. **62. hear the record."**: Ibid. **62. out of their minds, dancing."**: Bill Avis, interview with author, March 18, 2017. **63. make us stars.**: Ronnie Hawkins, interview with author, May 19, 2016. **63. paid very little."**: Ian Wallis, *The Hawk,* p. 69. **63. out of themselves."**: Jeff Carter, interview with author, September 6, 2018. **64. him as his brother.**: Ibid. **64. on top of that."**: Ibid. **64. live up to this stage,"**: Robbie Robertson, interview with Shelagh Rogers, "Robbie Robertson on His Storytelling Roots," *The Next Chapter,* CBC Radio, January 23, 2017. http://www.cbc.ca/radio/thenextchapter/robbie-robertson-on-the-story-telling-roots-of-his-new-memoir-poet-sylvia-legris-on-the-pull-of-the-body-1.3944459 (accessed January 23, 2017). **64. great to hear."**: Joshua Baer, "The Band: The Robbie Robertson Interview," *Musician—Guitar Special,* no. 43, May 1982, p. 58–71. http://theband.hiof .no/articles/1982_interview_band_rr_musician.html (accessed November 9, 2016). **64. just lit up the room."**: Anthony Mason, "Robbie Robertson: For the Record," *Sunday Morning,* CBS-TV, December 18, 2016. **65. He was the real deal.**: Craig Harris, *The Band: Pioneers of Americana Music* (Lanham, MD: Rowman and Littlefield, 2014), p. 57. **65. it was addictive."**: Robbie Robertson, *Testimony* (Toronto: Alfred A. Knopf Canada, 2016), p. 5. **66. didn't write anything.**: Ronnie Hawkins, interview with author, May 19, 2016. **66. crazier than he was."**: Jeff Carter, interview with author, September 6, 2018. **67. anybody I *ever* heard."**: Bubba Sullivan, interview with author, April 26, 2018. **67. Robbie in! [laughs]"**: Carol Caffin, "Ronnie Hawkins Talks About 'The Boys'—Then and Now," *BandBites,* vol. I, no. 5, April 15, 2007. http://theband.hiof.no/articles/RonnieHawkinsBandBite5.html (accessed November 16, 2016). **67. He was the leader."**: Ibid. **68. wheels go around."**: Kirby Penick, interview with

Scott Lunsford. "Arkansas Memories Project." Courtesy of the Pryor Center for Arkansas Oral and Visual History, University of Arkansas. **68. had musical talent.":** Paul Berry, interview with author, April 22, 2018. **68. experimenting with life.":** Ronnie Hawkins and Peter Goddard, *Ronnie Hawkins: Last of the Good Ol' Boys* (Toronto: Stoddart Publishing, 1989), p. 109. **68. real great combination.":** Ronnie Hawkins, interview with author, May 19, 2016. **69. just vanish on me.":** Nicholas Jennings, *Before the Gold Rush: Flashbacks to the Dawn of the Canadian Sound* (Toronto: Viking Press, 1997), p. 30. **69. It broke my heart.":** Hawkins and Goddard, *Ronnie Hawkins*, p. 86. **70. back to him onstage.:** Jeff Carter, interview with author, September 6, 2018. **70. "Hey Bo Diddley.":** Ronnie Hawkins, interview with author, May 19, 2016. **71. hysterical in those days.":** Hawkins and Goddard, *Ronnie Hawkins*, p. 123. **71. play on the record.'":** Peter Viney, "Influences on The Band: Country Connections," Band website. http://theband.hiof.no/articles/band_and_country.html#sdfootnote12sym (accessed January 5, 2019). **72. singing in the church.:** Bill Avis, interview with author, March 18, 2017. **72. they'd listen to you.":** Tony Glover, "A Wonderful New Group," *Eye*, issue 7, November 1968. http://theband.hiof.no/articles/eyes_7_november_1968.html (accessed November 8, 2016). **72. had it then.":** Bill Avis, interview with author, March 18, 2017. **72. we sold the jukebox.":** Ibid. **73. and start crying.":** Ibid. **73. make musicians steak.":** Ibid. **74. cars or whatever.:** Kirby Penick, interview with Scott Lunsford. "Arkansas Memories Project." Courtesy of the Pryor Center for Arkansas Oral and Visual History, University of Arkansas. **74. gum and smoke cigarettes.":** Bill Avis, interview with author, March 18, 2017. **74. play football, still drunk.":** Ibid. **74. got mustard all over it.":** Ibid. **75. We're afraid. [laughter]:** Earl Cate, interview with Scott Lunsford, Bob Cochran, and Eric Johnson. "Arkansas Memories Project." April 2010, courtesy of the Pryor Center for Arkansas Oral and Visual History, University of Arkansas. **76. He was hurting.":** Ronnie Hawkins, "Rick Danko: December 29, 1943 – December 10, 1999," *Toronto Life*, February 2000. http://theband.hiof.no/articles/hawk_danko_feb_2000.html (accessed November 16, 2016). **76. loosey-goosey rhythm section.":** Levon Helm, "The Music," *Razor* magazine, February 2004. http://theband.hiof.no/articles/the_music_razor_february_2004.html (accessed February 9, 2016). **76. book with his accomplishments.:** Ibid. **77. good drummer in my estimation.":** Henry Glover, interview with Scott K. Fish, "Henry Glover: Remembering Levon Helm," posted April 7, 2018. https://scottkfish.com/2018/04/07/henry-glover-remembering-levon-helm (accessed August 5, 2018). **77. blues like they did.":** Ibid. **78. lot of blues stuff.:** Levon Helm, interview with author, July 3, 1996. **78. heard the playback,":** Lee Gabites, "A Conversation with Levon Helm, *Band fanzine*, October 1996. http://theband.hiof.no/articles/interview_levon_oct_96.html (accessed November 10, 2016). **78. what we had.":** *Classic Albums: The Band*, DVD, Bob Smeaton (director), Isis Productions in association with Daniel Television, 1997. **79. anybody you knew.":** Max Weinberg, "Conversations with Rock's Great Drummers: Levon Helm," *The Big Beat: Conversations with Rock's Great Drummers*" (Chicago: Contemporary Books, 1984). http://theband.hiof.no/articles/the_big_beat_lh.html (accessed February 9, 2016). **80. a lot more fun.:** Baer, "The Band," *Musician—Guitar Special*, pp. 58–71. **80. icing on the cake.":** Weinberg, *The Big Beat*. **80. hustle the women.":** Ronnie Hawkins, interview with Steve Dawson, "Episode 42: Ronnie Hawkins," The Henhouse Studio, July 12, 2017. www.stevedawson.ca/makersandshakers/episode-42-ronnie-hawkins (accessed July 9, 2017). **80. fun to be with.":** Paul Berry, interview with author, April 22, 2018. **80. rock 'n' roll band ever.":** David Clayton-Thomas, *Blood, Sweat and Tears* (Toronto: Viking Canada, 2010), p. 38. **81. hang on every note.:** David Clayton-Thomas, interview with author, April 5, 2017. **81. He's a showman.:** Ibid. **82. make a living at this.:** Ibid. **82. lot more, believe me.":** Bill Avis, interview with author, March 18, 2017. **82. I'd still be in jail!:** Ibid. **84. place to party.:** David Clayton-Thomas, interview with author, April 5, 2017. **84. learn a new song.:** Bill Avis, interview with author, March 18, 2017. **85. feathers would get up.:** Ibid. **85. as much as possible.":** Randy Stratton, interview with author, April 19, 2018. **86. "Me? Naw, it's him,":** Hawkins and Goddard, *Ronnie Hawkins*, p. 124. **86. regards to the draft.":** Bill Avis, interview with author, March 18, 2017. **86. You could trust her.":** Ibid. **86. already married here.":** Ibid.

Chapter 5: The Hawks Take Wing

89. Real dudes, man.": Ritchie Yorke, "Ronnie Hawkins." http://ritchieyorke.com/2015/04/17/ronnie-hawkins (accessed June 8, 2016). **89. smarter than me."':** Ian Wallis, *The Hawk: The Story of Ronnie Hawkins and the Hawks* (Kingston, ON: Quarry Press, 1996), p. 110. **89. got too good.":** Ronnie Hawkins, interview with Steve Dawson, "Episode 42: Ronnie Hawkins," The Henhouse Studio, July 12, 2017. http://www.stevedawson.ca/makersandshakers/episode-42-ronnie-hawkins (accessed July 9, 2017). **89. Muddy [Waters] and J.B. Lenoir.":** Levon Helm, "The Music," *Razor* magazine, February 2004. http://theband.hiof.no/articles/the_music_razor_february_2004.html (accessed February 9, 2016). **89. we were doing.":** Ronnie Hawkins and Peter Goddard, *Ronnie Hawkins: Last of the Good Ol' Boys* (Toronto: Stoddart Publishing, 1989), p. 128. **90. music or personalities.":** Wallis, *The Hawk*, p. 103. **90. back and book them,":** Harold Kudlets, interview with author, June 3, 2016. **90. them for that figure.":** Wallis, *The Hawk*, p. 244. **91. Bobby Bland band.":** Aaron Howard, "The Rock of Aged: Former Band Drummer Levon Helm Lends His Experience to the Youthful Barn Burners," *Houston Press Online*, January 25, 2001. http://theband.hiof.no/articles/barn_burners_mucky_duck_houston_press.html (accessed February 9, 2016). **91. blazing rock 'n' roll.":** Levon Helm, "The Music," *Razor*. **91. best singer—Richard Manuel.":** Paul Berry, interview with author, April 22, 2018. **92. it's worth it.:** Max Weinberg, "Conversations with Rock's Great Drummers: Levon Helm," *The Big Beat: Conversations with Rock's Great Drummers* (Chicago: Contemporary Books, 1984). http://theband.hiof.no/articles/the_big_beat_lh.html (accessed February 9, 2016). **92. music more danceable.":** Ken Micallef, "Playing for the Song—and More: Steve Jordan Interviews the Great Levon Helm," *Modern Drummer*, 32.4, April 2008, pp. 52–58, 60–64, 66, 68. **93. music should do.":** Levon Helm, *Levon Helm Teaches Classic Rock, County and Blues Drumming* (DVD), Homespun Tapes Ltd., 1992, 2005. **93. play other instruments.":** Ibid. **93. rhythm of the song,":** Robyn Flans, "Levon Helm," *Modern Drummer*, August 1984, vol. 8, no. 8. http://theband.hiof.no/articles/modern_drummer_08_1984_lh_interview.html (accessed February 9, 2016). **93. drink on the bandstand.":** Brian Hollander, "Oh, Those Daze...Levon and Friends Talk about Onteora Show and High School Times," *Hudson Valley Times*, October 21, 2010. www.ulsterpublishing.com/view/full_story/9998087/article—Oh—those-daze-Levon-and-friends-talk-about-Onteora-show-and-high-school-times-? (accessed September 26, 2016). **93. anybody you see.":** Cutler Durkee, "Levon Helm's Rock Led to a Role: Loretta's Coal Miner Daddy in the Movie," *People*, vol. 13, no. 20, May 19, 1980. https://people.com/archive/levon-helms-rock-led-to-a-role-lorettas-coal-miner-daddy-in-the-movie-vol-13-no-20 (accessed February 9, 2016). **93. gravel getting out of town.":** Helm, "The Music," *Razor*. **93. through the hard times.:** Ibid. **94. take the floor.":** Levon Helm, interview with David Bianculli, "Levon Helm: The 2007 *Fresh Air* Interview," *Fresh Air*, NPR Music, April 29, 2012. www.npr.org/2012/04/20/150886425/levon-heln-the-fresh-air-interview (accessed July 20, 2018). **94. Muddy Waters and Cannonball Adderley.":** Rick James with David Ritz, *Glow: The Autobiography of Rick James* (New York: Atria Books, 2014), p. 62. **94. Canadian rock and roll.":** John Goddard and Richard Crouse, *Rock and Roll Toronto: From Alanis to Zepplin* (Toronto: Doubleday Canada, 1997), p. 134. **94. really good friends.":** Sid Griffith, *Million Dollar Bash: Bob Dylan, the Band, and the Basement Tapes* (London: Jawbone Press, 2007), p. 95. **94. plans for the future.":** Ibid., p. 92. **95. play the twist.":** Craig Harris, *The Band: Pioneers of Americana Music* (Lanham, MD: Rowman & Littlefield, 2014), p. 28. **95. Junior Parker material.":** Griffith, *Million Dollar Bash*, p. 90. **95. sing his ass off.":** John Hammond, interview with Marc Maron, WTF [n.d.]. www.johnhammond.com (accessed June 15, 2018). **95. took you to dreamland.":** Goddard and Crouse, *Rock and Roll Toronto*, p. 133. **95. sharing of music.":** Mary Martin, interview with Jay Orr, "Louise Scruggs Memorial Forum: Mary Martin" Ford Theater, Country Music Hall of Fame and Museum, Nashville, November 17, 2009. https://countrymusichalloffame.org/louise-scruggs/mary-martin#.WyLb-KdKjIU (accessed June 14, 2018). **96. close to him in bed.":** Cathy Smith, *Chasing the Dragon* (Toronto: Key Porter Books, 1984), p. 21. **96. most of the time.":** Nicholas Jennings, *Before the Gold Rush: Flashbacks to the Dawn of the Canadian Sound* (Toronto: Viking,

1997), p. 57. **97. outcome of this tour.**: Sandra Cox, "Levon and the Hawks: 'A Real Treat in Store,'" *Echoes of the Ozarks*, posted August 8, 2013. https://echoesoftheozarks.wordpress.com/2013/08/08/levon-and-the-hawks-a-real-treat-in-store (accessed May 28, 2018). **98. didn't have Ronnie.**": Earl Cate, interview with author, April 19, 2018. **98. playin' music, good music.**": Earl Cate, interview with Scott Lunsford, Bob Cochran, and Eric Johnson. "Arkansas Memories Project." April 2010, courtesy of the Pryor Center for Arkansas Oral and Visual History, University of Arkansas. **98. them some pussy.**": Bill Avis, interview with author, March 18, 2017. **99. are going to jail!'"**: Ibid. **99. wearing his jacket.**: Ibid. **99. we might some day.**": "Drug Case: 6 to Face the Music But Later," *The Globe and Mail*, April 8, 1965, p. 2. **100. her to "look after"**: Bill Avis, interview with author, March 18, 2017. **100. being used until later.**": Smith, *Chasing the Dragon*, p. 22. **100. and he *farts*.**": Bill Avis, interview with author, March 18, 2017. **102. Southerners were against blacks.**: Anna Lee Amsden, interview with author, April 24, 2018. **102. we really dug him.**": Tony Glover, "A Wonderful New Group," *Eye*, issue 7, November 1968. http://theband.hiof.no/articles/eyes_7_november_1968.html (accessed November 8, 2016). **102. had some big plans.**": Scott Jordan, "Backtalk with Levon Helm," *Offbeat*, December 1998. www.offbeat.com/articles/levon-helm/ (accessed November 10, 2016). **103. for us as children.**": Carmen Marotta, interview with author, July 22, 2018. **103. rockin' the house with it.**": Ibid. **103. ying and yang there,**": Ibid. **104. Levon and the Hawks.**": Ibid. **104. them the greatest.**": Treble Clef, "Bob Dylan and the Band—Down in the Flood, Part 2," April 3, 2013. www.youtube.com/watch?v=27Le13exEP4 (accessed March 31, 2018). **104. but so was Levon.**": Griffith, *Million Dollar Bash*, p. 94. **105. pretty good too!'"**: Carmen Marotta, interview with author, July 22, 2018. **105. play with the sticks.**": Ibid. **105. intense it was.**: Ibid. **106. Ray Charles stuff.**": Earl Cate, interview with Scott Lunsford, Bob Cochran, and Eric Johnson. "Arkansas Memories Project." April 2010, courtesy of the Pryor Center for Arkansas Oral and Visual History, University of Arkansas. **106. talent of that caliber.**": John Goddard, "When Dylan Got Rocked," *Toronto Star*, November 18, 2000, J17. **106. "a rather persevering soul"**: Jann S. Wenner, "Bob Dylan: The *Rolling Stone* Interview," *Rolling Stone*, issue 47, November 29, 1969. www.rollingstone.com/music/features/the-rolling-stone-interview-bob-dylan-19691129 (accessed July 7, 2016). **107. stuff like that.**": Robert L. Doerschuk, "Rick Danko—The Last Interview," *All-Music Guide*, December 7, 1999. http://theband.hiof.no/articles/rd_120799.html (accessed November 10, 2016). **107. the band that was the Hawks.**": Carmen Marotta, interview with author, July 22, 2018. **108. Dad loved them.**: Ibid. **108. onwards and upwards.**": Bill Avis, interview with author, March 18, 2017.

Chapter 6: Dylan Plugs In and Helm Checks Out

109. music from dog shit,": Howard Sounes, *Down the Highway: The Life of Bob Dylan* (New York: Grove Press. 2001), p. 102. **109. work with him,**": Ibid, p. 103. **109. was diametrically opposite.**": John Goddard and Richard Crouse, *Rock and Roll Toronto: From Alanis to Zeppelin* (Toronto: Doubleday Canada, 1997), p. 137. **110. really related to it.**": Harvey Brooks, "Forest Hills and the Hollywood Bowl: The Days After Bob Dylan Went Electric," *The Times of Israel*, August 28, 2015. https://blogs.timesofisrael.com/forest-hills-and-the-hollywood-bowl-the-days-after-bob-dylan-went-electric (accessed October 5, 2018). **110. enormous iron metronome.**": Barney Hoskyns, *Across the Great Divide: The Band and America* (London: Viking Pimlico, 2003), p. 96. **110. both liked it.**": Brooks, "Forest Hills and the Hollywood Bowl," *Times of Israel*. **110. how weird it gets!**": Ibid. **110. little self-satisfaction.**": Hoskyns, *Across the Great Divide*, p. 98. **111. watching from below.**": Brooks, "Forest Hills and the Hollywood Bowl," *Times of Israel*. **111. Good for him.**": Mary Martin, interview with Jay Orr, "Louise Scruggs Memorial Forum: Mary Martin," Ford Theater, County Music Hall of Fame and Museum, Nashville, November 17, 2009. https://countrymusichalloffame.org/louise-scruggs/mary-martin#.WyLb-KdKjIU (accessed June 14, 2018). **112. heard it before.**": John Goddard, "When Dylan Got Rocked," *Toronto Star*, November 18, 2000, J17. **112. but really beaming.**": Clinton Heylin, *Bob Dylan: Behind the Shades, Take Two* (London: Viking, 2000), p. 235. **113. music or total bullshit.**": Ibid., p. 235. **113. fast lane all right.**": Robyn Flans, "Levon Helm,"

Modern Drummer, August 1984, vol. 8, no. 8. http://theband.hiof.no/articles/modern_drummer _08_1984_lh_interview.html (accessed February 9, 2016). **113. enjoy their fellowship.**": Max Weinberg, "Conversations with Rock's Great Drummers: Levon Helm," *The Big Beat: Conversations with Rock's Great Drummers* (Chicago: Contemporary Books, 1984. http://theband .hiof.no/articles/the_big_beat_lh.html (accessed February 9, 2016). **113. walking on the edge.**": Flans, "Levon Helm," *Modern Drummer.* **114. beatniks was tough!**": Barney Hoskyns, "Levon Helm," commissioned but never published by *Rolling Stone,* 1998. http://theband .hiof.no/articles/hoskyns_lh_interview_2000.html (accessed February 9, 2016). **114. like I usually do.**": Levon Helm, interview with David Bianculli, "Levon Helm: The 2007 *Fresh Air* Interview," *Fresh Air,* NPR Music, April 29, 2012. www.npr.org/2012/04/20/150886425 /levon-heln-the-fresh-air-interview (accessed July 20, 2018). **114. pain in the ass.**": Andy Gill, "Back to the Land," *Mojo,* November 2000. http://theband.hiof.no/articles/back_to_the _land.html (accessed November 8, 2016). **114. stuff like that.**": Andy Gill, "Dylan and the Band: Obviously Five Believers," *Q* Magazine's Maximum BOB! issue, October 2000. http:// theband.hiof.no/articles/Obviously_Five_Believers.html (accessed February 9, 2016). **114. so we kept doing it.**": Sounes, *Down the Highway,* p. 192. **114. do at a concert.**": Jason Schneider, *Whispering Pines: The Northern Roots of American Music from Hank Snow to the Band* (Toronto: ECW Press, 2009), p. 80. **115. rock 'n' roll band,**": Nicholas Jennings, *Before the Gold Rush: Flashbacks to the Dawn of the Canadian Sound* (Toronto: Viking, 1997), p. 97. **115. that stinging slur.**": Levon Helm, "The Music," *Razor* magazine, February 2004. http://theband.hiof.no /articles/the_music_razor_february_2004.html (accessed February 9, 2016). **115. then getting booed.**": Heylin, *Bob Dylan,* p. 235. **115. shitty day in paradise,**": Weinberg, *The Big Beat.* **115. I really couldn't.**": Sounes, *Down the Highway,* p. 192. **115. the way through.**": Russell Hall, "Levon Helm Exclusive Interview: *Gibson.com*'s Tribute to a Legend," Gibson Guitar, April 20, 2012. www.gibson.com/news-lifestyle/features/en-us/levon-helm-exclusive-interview -0420-2012.aspx (accessed July 5, 2018). **115. kind of music.**": Hoskyns, *Across the Great Divide,* p. 95. **115. making good music.**": Anna Lee Amsden, interview with author, April 24, 2018. **116. times to catch up,**": Max Weinberg, "Conversations with Rock's Great Drummers: Levon Helm," *The Big Beat: Conversations with Rock's Great Drummers* (Chicago: Contemporary Books, 1984). http://theband.hiof.no/articles/the_big_beat_lh.html (accessed February 9, 2016). **116. Texas–Arkansas football games.**": Eric Hisaw, "Feature Story: Bobby Keys," Lone Star Music (record label), [n.d.]. www.lonestarmusic.com/magazine/mag_html/may11 /bobbykeys.html (accessed June 21, 2018). **116. Thank you, Levon.**": Bobby Keys with Bill Ditenhafer, *Every Night's a Saturday Night: The Rock 'n' Roll Life of Legendary Sax Man Bobby Keys* (Berkley, CA: Counterpoint, 2012), p. 66. **116. [Levon] up there.**": Jimmy Karstein, interview with author, December 12, 2018. **116. trouble than we did.**": Lee Gabites, "A Conversation with Levon Helm, *Band fanzine,* October 1996. http://theband.hiof.no/articles /interview_levon_oct_96.html (accessed November 10, 2016). **117. 'Are you kidding me?'**": John A. Ware, interview with Scott Lunsford, "Arkansas Memories Project," February 18, 2011, courtesy of the Pryor Center for Arkansas Oral and Visual History, University of Arkansas. **117. 'No, we don't.'**": Ibid. **117. just a little bit.**: Adam Gold, "Bobby Keys: The Cream Interview," *Nashville Scene,* March 2, 2012. www.nashvillescene.com/music/article/13042122 /bobby-keys-the-cream-interview (accessed June 21, 2018). **118. damn day together.**": Keys with Ditenhafer, *Every Night's a Saturday Night,* p. 66. **118. calmed me down.**: Bill Boatman, interview with author, December 14, 2018. **119. show was over.**": Kay Cordtz, "Roger Tillison, Oklahoma Jukebox Poet: 1941–2013," *Roll Magazine,* [n.d.]. www.rollmagazine.com /roger-tillison-oklahoma-jukebox-poet-1941-2013-2 (accessed January 8, 2019). **119. special thing…charisma,**": Earl Cate, interview with author, April 19, 2018. **119. known them for years.**": Ernie Cate, interview with author, April 19, 2018. **119. loved the guys,**": Earl Cate, interview with author, April 19, 2018. **119. Bob's backup band.**": Harris, *The Band,* p. 75. **119. without a dime.**": Paul Berry, interview with author, April 22, 2018. **120. I'll treasure forever.**": Kirby Penick, interview with Scott Lunsford. "Arkansas Memories Project," courtesy of the Pryor Center for Arkansas Oral and Visual History, University of Arkansas. **120. he wasn't up for it.**: Ibid. **121. far as I'm concerned.**": Scott Jordan, "Backtalk with Levon Helm," *Off-*

beat, December 1998. www.offbeat.com/articles/levon-helm/ (accessed November 10, 2016). **122. beer on the house.**: Kirby Penick, interview with Scott Lunsford, "Arkansas Memories Project," courtesy of the Pryor Center for Arkansas Oral and Visual History, University of Arkansas. **122. mess with them.**: Ibid. **122. then come back.**: Ibid. **123. trying to party.**: Anna Lee Amsden, interview with author, April 24, 2018.

Chapter 7: In the Pink with the Band

125. "Saturday-night pink.": Levon Helm, interview backstage at the Queen Elizabeth Theatre, Vancouver, 1983. www.youtube.com/watch?v=zgVxszM42DI (accessed June 19, 2018). **126. downstairs and we recorded it.**: Jason Fine, "The Summer of Love: Woodstock," *Rolling Stone* (July 12, 2007–July 26, 2007), pp. 98, 140. **127. here is blessed.**: Barney Hoskyns, *Across the Great Divide: The Band and America* (London: Viking Pimlico, 2003), p. 144. **127. songs like 'Caledonia.'**: Barney Hoskyns, *Small Town Talk: Bob Dylan, the Band, Van Morrison, Janis Joplin, Jimi Hendrix and Friends in the Wild Years of Woodstock* (Philadelphia: Da Capo Press, 2013), p. 85. **127. lit up the town.**: Fine, "The Summer of Love," *Rolling Stone*, pp. 98, 140. **127. wild-ass music.**: Kirby Penick, interview with Scott Lunsford, "Arkansas Memories Project," 2018, courtesy of the Pryor Center for Arkansas Oral and Visual History, University of Arkansas. **128. Bob went to take a leak.**: Howard Sounes, *Down the Highway: The Life of Bob Dylan* (New York: Grove Press, 2001), p. 209. **128. industry meat grinder.**: Levon Helm, "The Music," *Razor*, February 2004. http://theband.hiof.no/articles/the_music_razor_february _2004.html (accessed February 9, 2016). **128. easy and loose.**: Happy Traum, interview with author, October 12, 2018. **128. work was our policy.**: John Harris, "Mixing up the Medicine: Robbie and Levon on *The Basement Tapes*," *Mojo*, December 2003. http://theband.hiof.no /articles/john_harris_rr_lh_mojo_2003.html (accessed February 9, 2016). **129. hell of an experience.**: Ibid. **129. things onto him.**: Robin Flans, "Levon Helm," *Modern Drummer*, August 1984, vol. 8, no. 8. http://theband.hiof.no/articles/modern_drummer_08_1984_lh_interview .html (accessed February 9, 2016). **129. blues tracks, or mountain music.**: Harris, "Mixing up the Medicine," *Mojo*, December 2003. **129. American popular music.**: Robert Shelton, *No Direction Home: The Life and Music of Bob Dylan* (Milwaukee, WI: Backbeat Books, 2010), p. 265. **129. And sorrow and longing.**: Paul Nelson, "Bob Dylan: The Basement Tapes," *Rolling Stone*, September 11, 1975. www.rollingstone.com/music/albumreviews/the-basement-tapes -19750911 (accessed October 18, 2016). **129. my musical career.**: Flans, "Levon Helm," *Modern Drummer*. **130. concentrated on songs.**: Sid Griffin, *Million Dollar Bash: Bob Dylan, the Band, and the Basement Tapes* (London: Jawbone Press, 2007), p. 155. **130. brand new experience.**: Harris, "Mixing up the Medicine," *Mojo*, December 2003. **130. Richard and Robbie especially.**: Andy Gill, "Dylan and the Band: Obviously Five Believers," *Q Magazine's Maximum BOB!* issue, October 2000. http://theband.hiof.no/articles/Obviously_Five_Believers.html (accessed February 9, 2016). **130. song to play *you*.**: Hoskyns, *Across the Great Divide*, p. 151. **130. like a drummer.**: Barney Hoskyns, "Levon Helm." http://theband.hiof. no/articles/hoskyns_lh_interview_2000.html (accessed February 9, 2016). **131. you're playing with.**: Jeff Potter, "Levon Helm: May 26, 1940–April 19, 2012," *Modern Drummer* 36.11 (November 2012), pp. 50–57, 59–61. **131. no weak places.**: Levon Helm, "The Music," *Razor*. **131. magical about the feel.**: Ken Sharp, "Across the Great Divide: Robbie Robertson Remembers the Band," *Goldmine* 32.5 (March 3, 2006), pp. 14–17. **132. practice the harmonies.**: Harris, "Mixing up the Medicine," *Mojo*, December 2003. **132. our recording technique.**: Ibid. **132. trying to get a balance.**: Hoskyns, "Levon Helm." **133. the Civil War.**: John Simon, *Truth, Lies and Heresay: A Memoir of a Musical Life in and out of Rock and Roll* (self-published, 2018), p. 249. **133. my musical tastes.**: Nick Deriso, "John Simon on the Band, fixing *The Last Waltz* and Taking Credit: Something Else! Interview," *Something Else!*, January 29, 2014. somethingelsereviews.com/2014/01/29/something-else-interview-the-band -producer-john-simon (accessed August 15, 2018). **133. coming up next.**: Simon, *Truth, Lies and Hearsay*, p. 133. **134. harmonies on our songs.**: *Classic Albums: The Band* (DVD), directed by Bob Smeaton, Isis Production in association with Daniel Television, 1997. **134. becomes**

second-nature.: Stephan S. Nigohosian, "Drumming and Singing: Double Skills Make You Doubly Valuable," *Modern Drummer*, September 2002. http://theband.hiof.no/articles/modern _drummer_09-2002.html (accessed November 21, 2016). **135. it all changes.":** Flans, "Levon Helm," *Modern Drummer*. **135. forth with you.":** Hoskyns, *Across the Great Divide*, p. 152. **135. less like making tracks.":** *Classic Albums: The Band*. **135. kind of album,":** Levon Helm with Stephen Davis, *This Wheel's on Fire: Levon Helm and the Story of the Band*, updated edition (Chicago: A Capella Books, 2013), p. 166. **135. impact was Motown.":** Matt Thompson, "The Jubilant Levon Helm," *Flagpole*, April 2000. http://theband.hiof.no/articles/jubilanat_levon _helm.html (accessed February 9, 2016). **135. some things we wouldn't.":** Max Weinberg, "Levon Helm," *The Big Beat: Conversations with Rock's Great Drummers* (Chicago: Contemporary Books, 1984). http://theband.hiof.no/articles/the_big_beat_lh.html (accessed February 9, 2016). **136. performances of all time,":** "100 Greatest Singers of All Time," *Rolling Stone*, December 2, 2010. www.rollingstone.com/music/lists/100-greatest-singers-of-all-time -19691231 (accessed October 20, 2016). **136. Bob tore it up!":** Craig Harris, *The Band: Pioneers of Americana Music* (Lanham, MD: Rowman and Littlefield, 2014), p. 77. **137. side of things.":** Happy Traum, interview with author, October 12, 2018. **137. feast for the ears.":** Happy Traum, "A Conversation with Levon Helm and Larry Campbell for *Acoustic Guitar Magazine*," September 18, 2015. www.happytraum.com/blog/a-conversation-with-levon-helm -and-larry-campbell-for-acoustic-guitar-magazine (accessed June 19, 2018). **137. Simon as "beautiful dirt.":** Simon, *Truth, Lies and Hearsay*, p. 140. **139. gracious to me also.":** Simon Harper, "Elliott Landy Shooting the Band," *Clash*, June 3, 2016. www.clashmusic.com/features /elliott-landy-shooting-the-band (accessed October 26, 2016). **139. how bright, how dumb.":** Hoskyns, *Across the Great Divide*, p. 164. **139. there was no boss.":** Elliott Landy, interview by Julie Motz, *Art's Desire*, KWMR Radio [Marin County, CA], April 21, 2016. https:// elliottlandy.com/interviews (accessed July 12, 2018). **139. the other guys.":** Harper, "Elliott Landy," *Clash*. **139. sense of the word.":** Suzanne Cadgene, "Levon Helm," *Elmore*, March/ April 2013. www.onlinedigitalpubs.com/article/Levon+Helm/1324071/0/article.html (accessed July 1, 2018). **139. who we are today.'":** Pat Thomas, "Organic Americana: Night Flight's Exclusive Interview with Elliott Landy About the Band and His New Photography Book," *Night Flight*, December 18, 2015. http://nightflight.com/organic-americana-night -flights-exclusive-interview-with-elliott-landy-about-the-band-and-his-new-photography -book (accessed October 26, 2016). **140. doing the wrong thing.":** "Eric Clapton—The Band's Influence" (video), www.biography.com/people/eric-clapton-9249026/videos/eric-clapton-the -bands-influence-2080111524 (accessed October 20, 2016). **140. ideas to toss around.":** Al Kooper, "The Band: *Music from Big Pink*," *Rolling Stone*, August 10, 1968. www.rollingstone. com/music/albumreviews/music-from-big-pink-19680810 (accessed October 26, 2016). **140. meant to rock.":** Charles P. Pierce, "Whip to Grave: Levon Helm, the Real Voice of America," *Esquire*, April 18, 2012. www.esquire.com/news-politics/politics/a13733/levon-helm-america -8173059/#ixzz1sWCJbIBW (accessed January 21, 2019). **140. world on its head.":** Robbie Robertson, *Testimony* (Toronto: Alfred A. Knopf Canada, 2016), p. 351. **140. deeply, deeply, deeply.":** Tom Pinnock, "The Band, Bob Dylan and Music from Big Pink—the Full Story," *Uncut*, July 31, 2015. www.uncut.co.uk/features/the-band-bob-dylan-and-music-from-big -pink-the-full-story-69989 (accessed October 20, 2016). **140. Levon Helm singing it.":** Timothy White, "George Harrison: 'All Things' in Good Time," *Billboard*, January 8, 2001. www .billboard.com/articles/news/80788/george-harrison-all-things-in-good-time (accessed July 7, 2016). **141. how much they contributed.:** David Clayton-Thomas, interview with author, April 5, 2017. **141. never intended it that way.":** Helm with Davis, *This Wheel's on Fire*, p. 174.

Chapter 8: "The Only Drummer That Can Make You Cry"

143. for God's sake!": Levon Helm with Stephen Davis, *This Wheel's on Fire: Levon Helm and the Story of the Band*, updated edition (Chicago: A Cappella Books, 2013), p. 179. **143. police and the ambulance.:** Bill Avis, interview with author, March 18, 2017. **145. history of the universe.":** "Inside the Spiritual Genesis of Richard Manuel's 'George Harrison-type Song'

That Is *Music from Big Pink*'s 'In a Station,'" Don't Forget the Songs – 365, November 13, 2016. https://dontforgetthesongs365.wordpress.com/ (accessed December 19, 2016). **145. outgoing and friendly he was.":** John Harris, "Mixing up the Medicine: Robbie and Levon on the Basement Tapes," *Mojo*, December 2003. http://theband.hiof.no/articles/john_harris_rr_lh _mojo_2003.html (accessed February 9, 2016). **145. little intimidating at first.:** Happy Traum, "A Conversation with Levon Helm and Larry Campbell for *Acoustic Guitar Magazine*," September 18, 2015. www.happytraum.com/blog/a-conversation-with-levon-helm-and-larry-campbell -for-acoustic-guitar-magazine (accessed June 19, 2018). **146. in fact, all my kids do.":** Happy Traum, interview with author, October 12, 2018. **146. compliment a lot.":** Harris, "Mixing up the Medicine," *Mojo*, December 2003. **146. personalities out of it,":** Barney Hoskyns, *Across the Great Divide: The Band and America* (London: Viking Pimlico, 2003), p. 174. **146. try to fuck you.":** Robbie Robertson, *Testimony* (Toronto: Alfred A. Knopf, 2016), p. 356. **146. away from it that quick.":** Levon Helm, interview with David Bianculli, "Levon Helm: The 2007 *Fresh Air* Interview," *Fresh Air*, NPR Music, April 29, 2012. www.npr.org/2012/04/20 /150886425/levon-helm-the-2007-fresh-air-interview (accessed July 20, 2018). **147. you play rim shots.":** Ken Micallef, "The Great Levon Helm: Playing for the Song—And More," *Modern Drummer*, February 16, 2008) www.moderndrummer.com/site/2008/02/levon-helm/ (accessed November 9, 2016). **147. different countries.":** AarCanadah, "The Band Documentary 1995 (Part 4 of 6)," May 6, 2012. www.youtube.com/watch?v=JI7C1l_Xyzc (accessed March 31, 2018). **148. more soulful voice.:** Jim Keltner, interview with author, December 19, 2019. **148. he had there.:** Ibid. **149. all started with Levon.":** Ibid. **149. be avoided, if possible.":** Ibid. **149. beauty of his playing.":** Ibid. **149. Levon's feel when I played.":** Jim Keltner, "interview with Jake D. Feinberg, "Trade All My Chops," Powertalk internet broadcast network, [n.d.]. https://forums.stevehoffman.tv/threads/jim-keltner-on-levon-helm.631066 (accessed December 14, 2018). **149. seems to me—Virgil.":** Jim Keltner, interview with author, December 19, 2019. **150. although we traded.":** Hoskyns, *Across the Great Divide*, p. 180. **150. able to express.":** Ibid., p. 179. **150. kit sounding right.":** Robyn Flans, "Levon Helm," *Modern Drummer*, August 1984, vol. 8, no. 8. http://theband.hiof.no/articles/modern_drummer_08 _1984_lh_interview.html (accessed February 9, 2016). **150. it so complicated.":** Barney Hoskyns, *Small Town Talk: Bob Dylan, the Band, Van Morrison, Janis Joplin, Jimi Hendrix and Friends in the Wild Years of Woodstock* (Philadelphia: DaCapo Press, 2013), p. 131. **150. Playing live is more fun.":** Flans, "Levon Helm," *Modern Drummer*. **151. I'd want Levon.":** Hoskyns, *Across the Great Divide*, p. 182. **151. always humble, never haughty.":** John Simon, *Truth, Lies and Hearsay: A Memoir of a Musical Life in and out of Rock and Roll* (self-published: 2018), p. 189. **151. taking place inside.":** David Hepworth, "Levon Helm 1940–2012: Master Musician, True Leader of the Band," *The Word* (June 2012), pp. 46–47 (accessed online February 10, 2016). **151. amazingly soulful singing.":** Ken Micallef, "Playing for the Song—And More: Steve Jordan Interviews the Great Levon Helm," *Modern Drummer* 32.4 (April 2008), pp. 52–58, 60–64, 66, 68. **152. It was just awesome.":** Jim Keltner, interview with author, December 19, 2019. **152. keep it working.":** Micallef, "Playing for the Song," *Modern Drummer*. **152. would fit the song.:** Simon, *Truth, Lies and Hearsay*, pp. 189–90. **153. your toes all the time.":** Russell Hall, "Levon Helm Exclusive Interview: *Gibson.com*'s Tribute to a Legend," Gibson Guitar, April 20, 2012. www.gibson.com/news-lifestyle/features/en-us/levon-helm-exclusive -interview-0420-2012.aspx (accessed July 5, 2018). **153. change the rhythm pattern.":** Simon, *Truth, Lies and Hearsay*, p. 193. **153. cymbal and so on.":** Flans, "Levon Helm," *Modern Drummer*. **153. the whole thing.":** Steve Jordan, interview with author, November 26, 2018. **154. bad as we did.":** Helm with Davis, *This Wheel's on Fire*, p. 192. **154. no extraneous cymbals.":** Greil Marcus, "We Can Talk About It Now: The Band at Winterland," in Barney Hoskyns (ed.) *The Sound and the Fury: A Rock's Backpages Reader* (London: Bloomsbury, 2003), p. 308. **154. I thought next.":** Ralph J. Gleason, "The Band," *Rolling Stone*, May 17, 1969. http://theband.hiof.no/history/The_Band_in_Concert_1969.pdf (accessed February 1. 2019). **154. crowd that way.":** Hoskyns, *Across the Great Divide*, p. 201. **155. essence of their music.":** Jack Batten, "The Band Hits a Genuine Apogee of Rock," *Toronto Daily Star*, May 12, 1969, p. 28. **156. the wooden rims.":** Micallef, "Playing for the Song," *Modern Drummer*. **156. It**

makes it even freakier.": Jeff Potter, "Levon Helm: May 26, 1940–April 19, 2012," *Modern Drummer* 36.11 (November 2012), pp. 50–57, 59–61. **156. that it's my favorite.":** Steve Jordan, interview with author, November 26, 2018. **158. We were off.":** Mike Evans and Paul Kingsbury (eds.), *Woodstock: Three Days That Rocked the World* (New York: Sterling Publishing Co. Ltd., 2009), p. 194. **158. out of there.":** David Clayton-Thomas, interview with author, April 5, 2017. **159. back to Woodstock.":** Evans and Kingsbury, *Woodstock*, p. 194. **159. syncopations and timing changes.":** Susan Lydon, "The Band: Their Theme Is Acceptance of Life," *The New York Times*, October 12, 1969, p. D31. **160. before they left his mouth.":** Craig Harris, *The Band: Pioneers of Americana Music* (Lanham, MD: Rowman and Littlefield, 2014), p. 80. **160. can make you cry.":** Allen St. John, "A Drummer Who Could Make You Cry: The Genius of The Band's Levon Helm (1940–2012)," *Forbes*, April 17, 2012. http://www.forbes.com/sites/allenstjohn/2012/04/17/a-drummer-who-could-make-you-cry-the-genius-of-the-bands-levon-helm-1940-2012/#6f87f3585f0a (accessed December 29, 2016). **160. I've ever rated one.":** Robert Christgau, "In Memory of the Dave Clark Five," *Village Voice*, December 1969. http://www.robertchristgau.com/xg/bk-aow/dcfive.php (accessed December 26, 2016). **160. a lot of greed, actually.":** Kevin Ransom, "The Band," *Guitar Player*, May 1995. http://theband.hiof.no/articles/interview_robbie_rick_guitar_player_may_95.html (accessed November 11, 2016). **160. J.R. Robertson.":** Levon Helm, "The Music," *Razor*, February 2004. http://theband.hiof.no/articles/the_music_razor_february_2004.html (accessed February 9, 2016). **160. all contributing ideas?":** Scott Spencer, "Levon Helm Returns to Blues and Tries to Put the Past to Rest," *Rolling Stone*, April 27, 2000. www.rollingstone.com/music/news/levon-helm-returns-to-blues-and-tries-to-put-the-past-to-rest-20120419 (accessed February 9, 2016). **160. He's a writer.":** C.W. Gatlin, interview with author, April 26, 2018. **161. hashed out the songs.":** David Clayton-Thomas, interview with author, April 5, 2017. **161. Levon wrong for sure.:** Jeff Carter, interview with author, September 6, 2018. **161. along for the ride.":** Hoskyns, *Across the Great Divide*, p. 147. **161. screwed by Robbie.":** Hoskyns, *Small Town Talk*, pp. 213–14. **161. I was working.":** Happy Traum, interview with author, October 12, 2018. **162. your fucking job.":** Spencer, "Levon Helm Returns to Blues," *Rolling Stone*, April 27, 2000. **162. new places musically,":** Robert Hilburn, "Robbie Robertson Resigned to Rift in the Band," *Los Angeles Times*, reprinted in the *Edmonton Journal*, January 20, 1994, p. D4. **162. didn't want to push it.":** Robertson, *Testimony*, p. 331. **162. one word, nothing.":** Greg Kot, "*Waltz* Bittersweet for Many, But Not Robbie Robertson," *The Chicago Tribune*, April 7, 2002. http://articles.chicagotribune.com/2002-04-07/news/0204070306_1_waltz-rock-n-roll-band-today (accessed November 8, 2016). **162. helped write it.":** Ransom, "The Band," *Guitar Player*, May 1995. **162. Robbie and Albert.":** Harris, *The Band*, p. 88. **163. kind of circumstance.":** Helm, interview with Bianculli, "Levon Helm," *Fresh Air*. **163. obligation to do so.:** Robertson, *Testimony*, p. 332. **163. unfairness or shortcoming.":** Helm, "The Music," *Razor*. http://theband.hiof.no/articles/the_music_razor_february_2004.html (accessed February 9, 2016). **164. who can you trust?":** Helm, "The Music," *Razor*. **164. controlling thing on my part.":** Hilburn, "Robbie Robertson Resigned to Rift," *Los Angeles Times*. **164. as the band did.":** Helm with Davis, *This Wheel's on Fire*, p. 210. **164. give him the opportunity,":** Matthew Lewis, "The Band's Rick Danko Revs Up Legendary Career," *Variety*, March 1997. http://theband.hiof.no/articles/interview_rick_march_97.html (accessed November 11, 2016). **164. the wrong trail.":** David Howell, "The Band Plays on - for a New Generation," *Edmonton Journal*, July 17, 1994, p. C1. **164. was terribly wrong.":** Helm, "The Music," *Razor*. **165. jazzman Max Roach.":** Carl Bernstein, "The Band," *Washington Post Times Herald*, October 28, 1969. http://theband.hiof.no/articles/bernstein_the_band.html (accessed November 11, 2016). **165. sensation for youngsters,":** "The Band on *The Ed Sullivan Show*," *The Ed Sullivan Show* website. http://www.edsullivan.com/the-band-on-the-ed-sullivan-show (accessed December 16, 2016). **165. trend with that.":** C.W. Gatlin, interview with author, April 26, 2018. **166. unparalleled subtlety and restraint.":** Jay Cocks, "Down to Old Dixie and Back," *Time*, January 12, 1970. http://theband.hiof.no/articles/time_1970.html (accessed November 7, 2016). **166. His Mountaineers did years ago.":** Ibid. **166. truly profound music.":** Jack Batten, "Perfect Band Concert Made Time Stand Still," *Toronto Daily Star*, January 19, 1970, p. 22. **166.**

to play for *people*.": Martin Knelman, "Home Again, the Band Does It Right," *The Globe and Mail*, January 19, 1970, p. 17. **166. so we were best friends.**": Ezra Titus, "A Miraculous Recovery." www.ezratitus.com/2012/04/23/a-miraculous-recovery (accessed December 21, 2016). **167. just devastate you.**": Hoskyns, *Small Town Talk*, p. 132. **167. souls on the planet.**": Ibid., p. 132. **167. I ignored them.**": Hoskyns, *Across the Great Divide*, p. 212. **167. almost *too* nice,**": Ibid., p. 231. **167. away from publicity.**": Harold Kudlets, interview with author, June 3, 2016. **167. rest of my life.**": Max Weinberg, "Levon Helm," *The Big Beat: Conversations with Rock's Great Drummers* (Chicago: Contemporary Books, 1984). http://theband.hiof.no/articles /the_big_beat_lh.html (accessed February 9, 2016). **167. TVs out the windows.**": "Levon Helm Works Hard to Find Golden Touch," *The Toronto Star*, May 20, 1978, p. D5. **167. room for more songs.**": Weinberg, *The Big Beat*. **168. Levon to heroin.**": Hoskyns, *Small Town Talk*, p. 208. **168. without falling off.**": Ransom, "The Band," *Guitar Player*, May 1995. **168. them up in the end.**": Ronnie Hawkins, interview with author, May 19, 2016.

Chapter 9: "The Shape I'm In"

169. he lost everything.": Bill Avis, interview with author, March 18, 2017. **169. tab for everybody.**": Ronnie Hawkins, interview with author, May 19, 2016. **169. got to his hotel room.**": Jeff Mahoney, "Book 'em Harold – Oh, He Did," *The Hamilton Spectator*, March 11, 2015. www.thespec.com/opinion-story/4569796-mahoney-book-em-oh-he-did (accessed April 26, 2015). **169. 'Eh, let 'em have it.'**": Jeff Carter, interview with author, September 6, 2018. **170. gotta keep it flowing.**": Steve Thomson, interview with author, January 24, 2017. **170. He was a typical Southerner.**": Harold Kudlets, interview with author, June 3, 2016. **170. Levon was very generous.**": Bill Avis, interview with author, May 1, 2017. **170. generous person, completely generous.**: Morse Gist, interview with Scott Lunsford, "Helena, Arkansas, Project," October 25, 2012, courtesy of the Pryor Center for Arkansas Oral and Visual History, University of Arkansas. **170. versus the rest of the band.**": Aaron Howard, "The Rock of Aged: Former Band Drummer Levon Helm Lends His Experience to the Youthful Barn Burners," Houston Press Online, January 25, 2001. http://theband.hiof.no/articles/barn _burners_mucky_duck_houston_press.html (accessed February 9, 2016). **171. there was conflict there.**": Kevin Ransom, "The Band," *Guitar Player*, May 1995. http://theband.hiof.no /articles/interview_robbie_rick_guitar_player_may_95.html (accessed November 11, 2016). **171. bruises you in your soul.**": Ibid. **171. about half of *Stage Fright*.**": Russell Hall, "Levon Helm Exclusive Interview: *Gibson.com*'s Tribute to a Legend," Gibson Guitar, April 20, 2012. www.gibson.com/news-lifestyle/features/en-us/levon-helm-exclusive-interview-0420-2012. aspx (accessed July 5, 2018). **171. but it grew deeper.**: Robbie Robertson, interview with Shelagh Rogers, "Robbie Robertson on His Storytelling Roots," *The Next Chapter*, CBC Radio, January 23, 2017. www.cbc.ca/radio/thenextchapter/robbie-robertson-on-the-storytelling-roots -of-his-new-memoir-poet-sylvia-legris-on-the-pull-of-the-body-1.3944459 (accessed January 23, 2017). **171. best band in the world.**": Ronnie Hawkins, interview with Steve Dawson, "Episode 42: Ronnie Hawkins," The Henhouse Studio, July 12, 2017. www.stevedawson .ca/makersandshakers/episode-42-ronnie-hawkins (accessed July 12, 2017). **172. some people don't.**": Lynne Margolis, "Levon Helm and Songwriting: Larry Campbell and Robbie Robertson Weigh In," *American Songwriter*, September 11, 2012. https://americansongwriter .com/2012/09/levon-helm-and-songwriting-larry-campbell-and-robbie-robertson-weigh -in/2 (accessed December 13, 2016). **173. rock and roll.**": John Burks, "Stage Fright," *Rolling Stone*, September 17, 1970. www.rollingstone.com/music/music-album-reviews/stage-fright -115961 (accessed November 17, 2018). **173. shuffling a deck of cards.**": Ibid. **174. stuff in on top.**": "The Band," *The Road* [television series], 1995. www.youtube.com/watch?v=GD1 wouCyuBU (accessed June 19, 2018). **174. made music, sparks flew.**": Robbie Robertson, *Testimony* (Toronto: Alfred A. Knopf Canada, 2016), pp. 379–80. **174. his major contributions.**": Jimmy Karstein, interview with author, December 12, 2018. **174. I was writing that.**": Margolis, "Levon Helm and Songwriting," *American Songwriter*. **175. things in rock altogether.**": Jon Landau, "*Cahoots*," *Rolling Stone*, November 11, 1971. www.rollingstone.com

/music/music-album-reviews/cahoots-102781 (accessed November 19, 2018). **176. work out that a-way.":** Baker Rorick, "Levon Helm of the Band: Way Back Up in the Woods," *Home Recording*, October 1999. http://theband.hiof.no/articles/levons_studio.html (accessed February 9, 2016). **176. even back then.":** Nick Deriso, "Garth Hudson on the Band's Influences, *Basement Tapes*, Tragic Losses," *Something Else!*, August 2, 2015. http://somethingelsereviews. com/2015/08/02/garth-hudson-band-interview-birthday/ (accessed February 8, 2018). **176. Got heat in '73.:** Rorick, "Levon Helm of the Band," *Home Recording*. **176. hog with too l'il a knife.'":** Barney Hoskyns, "The Rock's Backpages Rewind: At Home with Levon Helm in 2009," April 20, 2012. www.yahoo.com/entertainment/bp/rock-backpages-rewind-home -levon-helm-2009-102148260.html (accessed June 19,2018). **177. I've ever heard in rock.":** "The Band Comes Back to California," *Los Angeles Times*, November 30, 1971. http://theband .hiof.no/articles/the_band_comes_back_to_california.html (accessed November 11, 2016). **177. brother as you could want.":** Howard Johnson, interview with author, August 16, 2018. **177. used to say.":** Ibid. **177. he got a conversion.":** Ibid. **177. sounds to my ear.":** Robyn Flans, "Levon Helm," *Modern Drummer*, August 1984, vol.8, no. 8. http://theband.hiof.no /articles/modern_drummer_08_1984_lh_interview.html (accessed February 9, 2016). **178. brings to the equation.":** Mitch Lopate, "He Shall Be Levon ... The Band's Levon Helm Is Rocking Harder Than Ever with the Barnburners," *Gritz*, fall 2002. http://theband.hiof.no /articles/lh_interview_gritz_fall_2002.html (accessed November 11, 2016). **178. lot of Coca Cola.":** Bill Avis, interview with author, March 18, 2017. **178. down, you're set.":** Emmett Grogan, "The Band's Perfect Goodbye: A Behind-the-Scenes Report," *Oui*, 1976/77. http:// theband.hiof.no/articles/lw_oui_grogan.html (accessed November. 15, 2016). **179. He even read some books.":** Barney Hoskyns, *Small Town Talk: Bob Dylan, the Band, Van Morrison, Janis Joplin, Jimi Hendrix and Friends in the Wild Years of Woodstock* (Philadelphia: DaCapo Press, 2013), p. 270. **179. across the room.:** Ezra Titus, "Driving." www.ezratitus.com/2012/03/26 /driving (accessed December 21, 2016). **179. no more music.":** Lopate, "He Shall Be Levon," *Gritz*. **179. first three records.":** Scott Jordan, "Levon Helm," *Offbeat*, December 1, 1998. www.offbeat.com/articles/levon-helm (accessed July 6, 2018). **180. something to do with it.":** Lopate, "He Shall Be Levon," *Gritz*. **180. home of the Midnight Rambles.":** Ezra Titus, "A Miraculous Recovery." www.ezratitus.com/2012/04/23/a-miraculous-recovery (accessed December 21, 2016). **181. much public interest.":** Robert Shelton, *No Direction Home: The Life and Music of Bob Dylan* (Milwaukee, WI: Backbeat Books, 2011), p. 294. **181. extravagant in my life.":** Craig Harris, "Rick Danko Rides On," *Dirty Linen*, issue 41, August/September 1992. http:theband.hiof.no/articles/rick_danko_rides_again_dl_92.html (accessed November 10, 2016). **181. we're little stars.":** Paul Berry, interview with author, April 22, 2018. **182. so sad and pathetic.":** Hoskyns, *Small Town Talk*, p. 273. **182. onstage and out in front of it.":** Greil Marcus, "Heavy Breathing," *Cream*, May 1974, in *Bob Dylan by Greil Marcus: Writings 1968–2010* (New York: PublicAffairs, 2010), p. 45. **182. I've ever heard.":** Paul Berry, interview with author, April 22, 2018. **182. I was really enjoying it.":** Lopate, "He Shall Be Levon," *Gritz*. **182. destined to be scarred.":** Barney Hoskyns, *Across the Great Divide: The Band and America* (London: Viking Pimlico, 2003), p. 302. **182. Levon could spend with their child.:** Bill Avis, interview with author, May 1, 2017. **183. your musical education,":** Steve Dougherty, "Amy Helm Talks About Her Debut Solo Album, *Didn't It Rain*," *The Wall Street Journal*, July 21, 2015. www.wsj.com/articles/amy-helm-talks-about-her-debut-solo -album-didn't-it-rain-1437492624 (accessed November 29, 2016). **183. with [my daughter] Jenni.":** Hoskyns, *Small Town Talk*, p. 132. **183. remain relatively sober.":** Titus, "Miraculous Recovery." **184. advantage of him.":** Randy Stratton, email to author, July 7, 2018. **185. "Life changed instantly,":** Randy Stratton, interview with author, April 19, 2018. **186. feel like one of the guys.:** Ibid. **186. It was fantastic.":** Levon Helm, interview with author, July 3, 1996. **186. he was pulling off.":** Ibid. **187. just that much fun.:** Ibid. **187. go on, you know.":** Ibid. **187. I sure did enjoy.:** Ibid.

Chapter 10: Out of Step with the Last Waltz

189. some of the breaks.": Earl Cate, interview with Scott Lunsford, Bob Cochran, and Eric Johnson. "Arkansas Memories Project." April 2010, courtesy of the Pryor Center for Arkansas Oral and Visual History, University of Arkansas. **189. loyal to people.":** Randy Stratton, interview with author, April 19, 2018. **189. one of the family.":** Ibid. **190. it might be,":** Terry Cagle, interview with author, April 19, 2018. **190. ride in the car.":** Mary Vaiden, interview with author, May 1, 2018. **190. a memory like an elephant.":** Anna Lee Amsden, interview with author, April 24, 2018. **190. meaning "good health.":** John Donabie, interview with author, March 30, 2017. **191. there was to see.:** Ezra Titus, "A Miraculous Recovery." www .ezratitus.com/2012/04/23/a-miraculous-recovery (accessed December 21, 2016). **192. reflects the man's personality.":** David Clayton-Thomas, interview with author, April 5, 2017. **192. where we are.":** Matthew Lewis, "Rick Danko—Too Long in Exile," *Big O*, May 1997. http://theband.hiof.no/articles/rd_interview_bigo_may_1997.html (accessed November 11, 2016). **192. was a lot of bitching.":** Barney Hoskyns, *Across the Great Divide: The Band and America* (London: Viking Pimlico, 2003), p. 326. **193. destabilize its musical existence.:** Charlie McCollum, "The Band Is Just the Same Old …," *The Washington Star*, July 19, 1976, C4. **193. rock 'n' roll band.":** Jon Marlowe, "The Last Waltz," *The Miami News*, May 19, 1978. http://theband.hiof.no/history/The_Band_in_Concert_1976.pdf (accessed December 16, 2018). **194. without falling off.":** Kevin Ransom, "The Band," *Guitar Player*, May 1995. http:// theband.hiof.no/articles/interview_robbie_rick_guitar_player_may_95.html (accessed November 11, 2016). **194. sake of a final payday.":** Levon Helm, "Do It, Puke and Get Out," *The Independent* [U.K.], April 10, 1994. http://jonimitchell.com/library/view.cfm?id=1217 (accessed July 28, 2018). **194. decision to stop touring.":** Peter Goddard, "We Knew We'd Come to the End," *The Toronto Star*, November 13, 1976, F3. **194. going to stop playing.":** Tom Harrison, "Band's on Fire Again: Just in Time for Woodstock, 25 Years Later," *The Province* [Vancouver, B.C.], July 20, 1994, B3. **194. love it so much.":** Levon Helm, "The Music," *Razor* magazine, February 2004. http://theband.hiof.no/articles/the_music_razor_february_2004. html (accessed February 9, 2016). **195. why it was happening.":** Howard Johnson, interview with author, August 16, 2018. **195. it sort of got killed off.":** Vicki Mabry, "Comeback Kid: After a Year When the Music Came Back," *Nightline* (ABC-TV program), December 30, 2005. http://theband.hiof.no/articles/lh_nightline_12-30-2005.html (accessed February 9, 2016). **195. called it "the last lie":** Helm, "The Music," *Razor*. **195. "the last rip-off.":** Scott Spencer, "Levon Helm Returns to Blues and Tries to Put the Past to Rest," *Rolling Stone*, April 27, 2000. www.rollingstone.com/music/news/levon-helm-returns-to-blues-and-tries-to-put-the -past-to-rest-20120419 (accessed February 9, 2016). **195. public execution of the Band.":** Paul Berry, interview with author, April 22, 2018. **195. set right with me.":** Levon Helm, interview with David Bianculli, "Levon Helm: The 2007 *Fresh Air* Interview," *Fresh Air*, NPR Music, April 29, 2012. www.npr.org/2012/04/20/150886425/levon-helm-the-2007-fresh-air -interview (accessed July 20, 2018). **196. That all came later.":** Carol Caffin, "An Interview with Jonathan Taplin," BandBites, vol. I, no. 9, September 1, 2007. http://theband.hiof.no /articles/JonathanTaplinBandBite9.html (accessed November 21, 2016). **196. happy about that.":** Happy Traum, interview with author, October 12, 2018. **196. with not much notice.":** Randy Stratton, interview with author, April 19, 2018. **196. music they made.":** John Donabie, interview with author, March 30, 2017. **196. show with us.":** Levon Helm, interview with author, July 3, 1996. **196. me and Muddy Waters.":** Ian Wallis, *The Hawk: The Story of Ronnie Hawkins and the Hawks* (Kingston, ON: Quarry Press, 1996), p. 176. **197. wanted to play 'em.":** Ronnie Hawkins, interview with Steve Dawson, "Episode 42: Ronnie Hawkins," The Henhouse Studio, July 12, 2017. www.stevedawson.ca/makersandshakers/episode-42-ronnie -hawkins (accessed July 12, 2017). **197. musicians in any context.":** Bob Girouard, "Levon Helm: The Classic Drummer Interview," *Classic Drummer*, August 2008. www.levonhelm .com/articles/CLASSIC_DRUMMER_8_08.pdf (accessed November 9, 2016). **198. one fell swoop.":** Helm, "The Music," *Razor*. **198. a man—Muddy Waters!":** Martin Scorsese [director], *The Last Waltz* [movie], A Martin Scorsese Film, United Artists, 1978. **198. way too**

quick.": Levon Helm, interview with author, July 3, 1996. **198. minutes to recover.":** Janet Maslin, "Film: Scorsese and the Band: Final Fling," *The New York Times*, April 26, 1978. www.nytimes.com/1978/04/26/archives/film-scorsese-and-the-bandfinal-fling.html (accessed January 18, 2019). **199. money was ate up.:** Bill Avis, interview with author, March 18, 2017. **199. he had to wait.":** Helm, "Do It, Puke and Get Out," *The Independent*. **199. that'll be remembered.":** "Levon Helm Works Hard to Find Golden Touch," *The Toronto Star*, May 20, 1978, D5. **200. end of the Last Waltz.":** Helm, "Do It, Puke and Get Out," *The Independent*. **200. theatrical and being directed.":** Harold Wieties, interview with author, October 25, 2018. **200. straight to Levon,":** Jessica Edwards [director], *Mavis!* A Film First Production, 2015. **200. same as us.":** Sean Clancy, "Singer Mavis Staples to Christen New Auditorium," *Arkansas Democrat-Gazette*, February 4, 2016. www.pressreader.com/.../arkansas-democrat-gazette/20160204/283059823415994 (accessed January 23, 2019). **200. took off the saddle.":** Levon Helm with Stephen Davis, *This Wheel's on Fire: Levon Helm and the Story of the Band* (Chicago: A Cappella Books, 2013), p. 271. **201. and get out.":** Helm, "Do It, Puke and Get Out," *The Independent*. **202. things he never done.":** Spencer, "Levon Helm Returns to Blues," *Rolling Stone*. **202. members of the group.:** Stephen E. Severn, "Robbie Robertson's Big Break: A Reevaluation of Martin Scorsese's *The Last Waltz*," *Film Quarterly*, vol. 56, no. 2 (Winter 2002), pp. 25–31. www.jstor.org/stable/10.1525/fq.2002.56.2.25 (accessed November 6, 2016). **202. I'm just old-fashioned.:** Dave Marsh, "Schlock Around the Rock," *Film Comment*, July/August 1978, p. 7. **203. were going to make.":** Kay Roybal, "'Waltz' Among Best Rock Flicks," *Albuquerque Journal*, December 6, 2002. https://business.highbeam.com/2872/article-1G1-95387360/waltz-among-best-rock-flicks (accessed November 11, 2016). **203. most moving songs.":** Helm, "The Music," *Razor*. **203. have worked with Levon.":** Davis Inman and Rob Birdsong, "10 Goodbyes to Levon Helm," *American Songwriter*, April 23, 2012. http://americansongwriter.com/2012/04/10-goodbyes-to-levon-helm (accessed August 8, 2018). **203. still get paid, I guess.":** Spencer, "Levon Helm Returns to Blues," *Rolling Stone*. **203. do with color.":** Robert Wilonsky, "Do Look Back: The Band Dances *The Last Waltz*, But Can Time Heal Old Wounds?" *Cleveland Scene*, April 18, 2002. www.clevescene.com/cleveland/do-look-back/Content?oid=1479293# (accessed November 9, 2016). **203. Rick and Richard.":** Helm, "The Music," *Razor*. **203. all the money went.":** Bill Avis, interview with author, March 18, 2017.

Chapter 11: Restoring the Rhythm

205. I'm not going on.": Jeff Carter, interview with author, September 6, 2018. **206. main guidance system.":** Scott Jordan, "Backtalk with Levon Helm," *Offbeat*, December 1998. www.offbeat.com/articles/levon-helm/ (accessed November 10, 2016). **206. sweet spot to be.":** Levon Helm, *Levon Helm Teaches Classic Rock, Country and Blues Drumming* [DVD], Homespun Tapes, Ltd., 1992, 2005. **206. hell of a time together.":** Lahri Bond, "Recordings—Levon Helm: *Levon Helm & the RCO All-Stars/American Son*; Levon Helm & the RCO All-Stars: *Live at the Palladium NYC New Year's Eve 1977*," *Dirty Linen*, June 2008, p. 53, 55. **206. only as sexy.:** Mikal Gilmore, "*Levon Helm & the RCO All-Stars*," *Down Beat*, March 23, 1978. https://scottkfish.com/2017/02/21/levon-helm-the-possibilities-of-the-blues-1977 (accessed August 5, 2018). **207. 'em put together.":** "Levon Helm Works Hard to Find Golden Touch," *The Toronto Star*, May 20, 1978, D5. **207. runnin' at it too hard.":** Ibid. **208. going to play forever.":** "Band's Helm Takes a New Step with the All-Stars," *The Globe and Mail*, January 2, 1978, p. 13. **208. pleasure to be around.":** Russ Corey, "Local Musicians: Levon Helm Was 'Coolest Man Alive,'" *Times Daily* [Florence, AL], April 20, 2012. www.timesdaily.com/archives/local-musicians-levon-helm-was-coolest-man-alive/article_83dda8d5-680f-545b-a4e2-dc62730f5a28.html (accessed July 4, 2018). **209. Washington, D.C., politicians.:** Butch Dener, interview with author, March 21, 2017. **209. than the town dog,":** Cutler Durkee, "Levon Helm's Rock Lead to a Role: Loretta's Coal Miner Daddy in the Movie," *People*, vol. 13, no. 20, May 19, 1980. http://people.com/archive/levon-helms-rock-led-to-a-role-lorettas-coal-miner-daddy-in-the-movie-vol-13-no-20/ (accessed February 9, 2016).

209. major control of.: Paul Berry, interview with author, April 22, 2018. **210. in a way.":** Bruce Blackadar, "Levon Helm at 40: Music Is Still the Key," *Toronto Star*, June 22, 1980, D9. **210. you were dealt.":** Durkee, "Levon Helm's Rock Lead to a Role," *People*. **210. is getting lost.":** Blackadar, "Levon Helm at 40" *Toronto Star*. **210. heart and soul.":** Robyn Flans, "Levon Helm," *Modern Drummer*, August 1984, vol. 8, no. 8. http://theband.hiof.no/articles /modern_drummer_08_1984_lh_interview.html (accessed February 9, 2016). **210. and very moving.":** Davis Inman and Rob Birdsong, "10 Goodbyes to Levon Helm," *American Songwriter*, April 23, 2012. http://americansongwriter.com/2012/04/10-goodbyes-to-levon-helm (accessed August 8, 2018). **210. anchors the film.":** Rob Nixon, "Behind the Camera on *Coal Miner's Daughter*," Turner Classic Movies: Film Article, [n.d.]. http://www.tcm.com/this -month/article/962158%7C0/Behind-the-Camera-Coal-Miner-s-Daughter.html (accessed July 20, 2018). **211. fun to make,":** Blackadar, "Levon Helm at 40," *Toronto Star*. **211. hang on to him.":** Alex Morris, "Women in Music: Honorees," *Billboard* 127.37, December 12, 2015, pp. 72–78, 80–82, 84–86, 88, 90. **211. I did it anyway.":** Joshua Baer, "The Band: The Robbie Robertson Interview," *Musician—Guitar Special*, no. 43, May 1982, pp. 58–71. http://theband .hiof.no/articles/1982_interview_band_rr_musician.html (accessed November 9, 2016). **212. That's my son.":** Anna Lee Amsden, interview with Scott Lunsford, "Helena, Arkansas, Project," October 9, 2015, courtesy of the Pryor Center for Arkansas Oral and Visual History, University of Arkansas. **213. here and there unnecessarily.:** Jeff Carter, interview with author, September 6, 2018. **213. courteous and humble.":** Terry Cagle, interview with author, April 19, 2018. **213. comin' to a gig.:** Earl Cate, interview with Scott Lunsford, Bob Cochran, and Eric Johnson. "Arkansas Memories Project." April 2010, courtesy of the Pryor Center for Arkansas Oral and Visual History, University of Arkansas. **214. fixed his stand.":** Terry Cagle, interview with author, April 19, 2018. **214. lucky to be here.":** Blackadar, "Levon Helm at 40," *Toronto Star*. **214. got us through.":** Scott Jordan, "Backtalk with Levon Helm," *Offbeat*, December 1998. www.offbeat.com/articles/levon-helm/ (accessed November 10, 2016). **214. with the rest.":** Max Weinberg, "Conversations with Rock's Great Drummers: Levon Helm," *The Big Beat: Conversations with Rock's Great Drummers*" (Chicago: Contemporary Books, 1984). http://theband.hiof.no/articles/the_big_beat_lh.html (accessed February 9, 2016). **214. becoming a better player.":** Vicki Mabry [interviewer], "Comeback Kid: After a Year When the Music Came Back," *Nightline* [ABC-TV program], December 30, 2005. http://theband.hiof.no/articles/lh_nightline_12-30-2005.html (accessed February 9, 2016). **214. publishing and all that.":** Earl Cate, interview with author, April 19, 2018. **215. country singer alive.":** Jim Kelton, "Save the Last Waltz for Sonny Boy," *Blues Revue*, issue no. 72, November 2001. http://theband.hiof.no/articles/blues_revue_lw.html (accessed November 8, 2016). **215. wait to try it.":** Blackadar, "Levon Helm at 40," *Toronto Star*. **216. It really was.:** Bill Avis, interview with author, March 18, 2017. **217. play catch with.":** Weinberg, *The Big Beat*. **217. through the set.":** Bruce Blackadar, "Levon and Danko Show They Can Still Carry the Weight," *Toronto Star*, April 3, 1983. **218. true grit and spiritual fire.":** "Pop: Levon Helm and Blues Band," *The New York Times*, July 18, 1984, C19. www.nytimes.com/1984/07/18 /arts/pop-levon-helm-and-blues-band.html (accessed July 8, 2018). **218. such an education.":** Cindy Cashdollar, interview with Steve Dawson, "Episode 10: Cindy Cashdollar," The Henhouse Studio, May 18, 2016. www.stevedawson.ca/podcast-2/2016/4/23/episode-19-cindy -cashdollar (accessed July 8, 2018).

Chapter 12: And the Band Played On

219. Woodstock to rehearse.": Harold Kudlets, interview with author, June 3, 2016. **219. fun and it is.":** Robyn Flans, "Levon Helm," *Modern Drummer*, August 1984, vol. 8, no. 8. http:// theband.hiof.no/articles/modern_drummer_08_1984_lh_interview.html (accessed February 9, 2016). **219. Band broke up.":** Ronnie Hawkins and Peter Goddard, *Ronnie Hawkins: Last of the Good Ol' Boys* (Toronto: Stoddart Publishing, 1989), p. 135. **220. 100-percent musician.":** Harold Kudlets, interview with author, June 3, 2016. **221. I don't write well.":** Flans, "Levon Helm," *Modern Drummer*. **221. usually take it.:** Ibid. **222. straight with you.":** Jerome Avis, interview with author, March 26, 2017. **222. going to exhale.**: Ibid. **223. take they got it.**: Bill Avis, interview with author, March 18, 2017. **223. meet each other.**: Levon Helm, interview with author, July 3, 1996. **224. all those guys.**: Jim Weider, interview with author, September 19, 2018. **224. in** *this* **Band."**: Paul Berry, interview with author, April 22, 2018. **224. who inspired him."**: Walter Tunis, "The Band Picks Up Beat for '90s: Legendary Group Keeps the Faith with New Lineup," *Lexington Herald-Leader*, May 5, 1997. http://theband.hiof.no/articles /t2band.html (accessed November 9, 2016). **225. music as a band.**: Jim Weider, interview with author, September 19, 2018. **225. great band leader.**: Ibid. **225. much the leader."**: Carol Caffin, "Playing in The Band: Jim Weider Talks About the Old Days and His New Music," BandBites, vol. 1, no. 2, March 1, 2007. http://bandbites.blogspot.ca/2008/06/playing-in -band-jim-weider-talks-about.html (accessed November 16, 2016). **225. It was a cool thing.**: Ibid. **226. with the Band.**: "The Band Says Best Is Still Ahead," *Toronto Star*, November 1, 1985, D14. **226. he went to bed."**: Mary Vaiden, interview with author, May 1, 2018. **227. his own bathroom,"**: Steve Dougherty, "A Haunting Suicide Silences the Sweet, Soulful Voice of the Band's Richard Manuel," *People*, March 24, 1986. http://people.com/archive/a-haunting -suicide-silences-the-sweet-soulful-voice-of-the-bands-richard-manuel-vol-25-no-12 (accessed November 21, 2016). **227. nightmares about that."**: Paul Berry, interview with author, April 22, 2018. **227. my own about it."**: Greil Marcus, *Mystery Train: Images of America in Rock 'n' Roll Music* (New York: A Plume Book, 2015), p. 238. **227. took him home."'**: Mary Vaiden, interview with author, May 1, 2018. **227. go out and play."**: Jeff Carter, interview with author, September 6, 2018. **227. guy have it."**: Ibid. **228. knows the camera's there."**: Donald La Badie, "Levon's at the Helm of His Own Career," Scripps Howard Service, *The Windsor Star* [Windsor, ON], October 6, 1987, C7. **228. ten years younger."**: Ibid. **229. Canadian musical groups."**: "The Band," Canadian Music Hall of Fame website, [n.d.]. http://canadianmu-sichalloffame.ca/inductee/the-band (accessed January 20, 2019). **229. your prize, boy."**: Ian Wallis, *The Hawk: The Story of Ronnie Hawkins and the Hawks* (Kingston, ON: Quarry Press, 1996), p. 225. **229. deserved all that."**: Anna Lee Amsden, interview with author, April 24, 2018. **230. people in that area.**: "Levon Helm on the Delta Cultural Center at Helena—June 28, 1988," Mount Zion Memorial Fund website, April 9, 2017. http://www.mtzionmemori-alfund.org/2016/12/levon-helm-on-delta-cultural-center-at.html (accessed January 1, 2019). **230. my favorite musicians."**: Carol Caffin, "David Fishof Talks About The Band, the Ringo Starr tour, and the Columbia Records Deal," BandBites, vol. 1, no. 10, September 15, 2007. http://theband.hiof.no/articles/DavidFishofBandBite10.html (accessed November 21, 2016). **231. Levon so much."**: Jim Keltner, interview with author, December 19, 2018. **231. rough 'em up."**: Levon Helm, *Levon Helm Teaches Classic Rock, Country and Blues Drumming* [DVD], Homespun Tapes Ltd., 1992, 2005. **231. fine ol' time.**: Ibid. **231. so much fun."**: Jim Kelt-ner, interview with author, December 19, 2018. **232. would be great."**: Jeff Haden, "Startup: This Entrepreneur Makes Dreams Come True: David Fishof, Founder of Rock and Roll Fantasy Camp," Inc.com, March 16, 2017. www.inc.com/jeff-haden/this-entrepreneur-makes -dreams-come-true-david-fishof-founder-of-rock-and-roll-f.html (accessed September 15, 2018). **232. They set me up.**: Ibid. **232. liked to do stuff.**: Jim Keltner, interview with author, December 19, 2018. **232. outrageous or anything."**: Ibid. **233.** *eventually* **I woke up."**: David Fishof, interview with author, August 8, 2018. **233. hang out with ever.**: Jim Keltner, interview with author, December 19, 2018. **233. imagine how many.**: Ibid. **234. didn't like the guy.**: David Fishof, interview with author, August 8, 2018. **235. take Ronnie Hawkins."**: Steve Thomson, interview with author, March 15, 2017. **235. some funny stories."**: Jim Weider, interview with author, September 19, 2018. **235. most treasured possessions."**: Austin Scaggs, "Q&A: Roger Waters," *Rolling Stone*, June 7, 2012, p. 26.

Chapter 13: From the Ashes

237. always stay the same.": Levon Helm, *Levon Helm Teaches Classic Rock, Country and Blues Drumming* [DVD], Homespun Tapes Ltd., 1992, 2005. **237. and melodic thing."**: Jeff Potter, "Levon Helm May 26, 1940–April 19, 2012," *Modern Drummer* 36.11, November 2012, pp.

50–57, 59–61. **237. He has that charisma.**": Mark T. Gould, "Jim Weider and Randy Ciarlante: The 'Remedy' for Playing in The Band," *Sound Waves*, November 2002. http://theband .hiof.no/articles/weider_ciarlante_soundwaves_11-2002.html (accessed November 10, 2016). **238. be around him.**": Butch Dener, interview with Scott Lunsford, "Helena, Arkansas, Project," October 9, 2015, courtesy of the Pryor Center for Arkansas Oral and Visual History, University of Arkansas. **238. as real as it got.**": Butch Dener, interview with author, March 21, 2017. **238. good for a drummer.**'": Butch Dener, interview with Scott Lunsford, "Helena, Arkansas, Project," October 9, 2015, courtesy of the Pryor Center for Arkansas Oral and Visual History, University of Arkansas. **238. That's how he was.**": Butch Dener, interview with author, March 21, 2017. **239. gentle to that cat.**": Terry Cagle, interview with author, April 19, 2018. **239. his boots. That's all,**": Butch Dener, interview with author, March 21, 2017. **239. dream vision.**": Ibid. **239. people will hear it.**'": Ibid. **239. materials can deliver.**": Levon Helm, "The Music," *Razor* magazine, February 2004. http://theband.hiof.no/articles/the_music _razor_february_2004.html (accessed February 9, 2016). **240. just absorbed everything.**: Anna Lee Amsden, interview with author, April 24, 2018. **240. like an ugly beast.**": Bill Flanagan, "Rick Danko on The Band — New Albums, Old Wounds," *Musician*, December 1993, issue 182. http://theband.hiof.no/articles/musician_rd_dec_1993.html (accessed November 16, 2016). **241. He was that.**: Colin Linden, interview with author, July 12, 2018. **241. observer and listener.**: Ibid. **241. on the electronics of it.**": Baker Rorick, "Levon Helm of the Band: Way Back Up in the Woods," *Home Recording*, October 1999. http://theband.hiof.no /articles/levons_studio.html (accessed February 9, 2016). **243. rhythmic feel of everything.**: Colin Linden, interview with author, July 12, 2018. **243. Rick was just not around.**": Carol Caffin, "An Interview with Colin Linden," BandBites, volume I, no. 11, December 29, 2007. http://theband.hiof.no/articles/ColinLindenBandBite11.html (accessed November 21, 2016). **243. protective of that.**: Aaron "Professor Louie" Hurwitz, interview with author, February 7, 2019. **244. "The Caves of Jericho."**: Ibid. **244. record a lot.**": Jim Weider, interview with author, September 19, 2018. **244. 'Atlantic City' either.**": Aaron "Professor Louie" Hurwitz, interview with author, February 7, 2019. **245. That's really the key.**: Steve Jordan, interview with author, November 26, 2018. **246. drums when he plays.**": Ken Micallef, "The Great Levon Helm," *Modern Drummer*, February 16, 2008. http://www.moderndrummer.com/site/2008 /02/levon-helm/(accessed February 10, 2016). **246. for the music.**": Steve Jordan, interview with author, November 26, 2018. **246. lot of reasons.**: Ibid. **247. voice for my ears.**": Helm, *Levon Helm Teaches Drumming*. **247. explosive, so loud.**": Ibid. **247. conversations about politics.**": Anna Lee Amsden, interview with author, April 24, 2018. **247. company on to the very top.**": Butch Dener, interview with author, March 21, 2017. **247. real good gut instincts.**": Butch Dener, www.youtube.com/watch?v=yYOK6b5YvLI (accessed March 14, 2017). **248. it really meant something.**: Butch Dener, interview with author, March 21, 2018. **248. 'checks from God.'**": Butch Dener and Joe Lore, interview by Don Kerr, "Levon Helm and New Paltz," *Slice of New Paltz*, episode 57 [n.d.]. https://vimeo.com/100000510 (accessed June 23, 2018). **248. quite a few of them.**": Aaron "Professor Louie" Hurwitz, interview with author, February 7, 2019. **248. the way he was.**": Jim Weider, interview with author, September 19, 2018. **248. community pretty personally.**": George Lembesis, interview with author, February 7, 2019. **249. work with Stalin.**": Suzanne Cadgene, "Levon Helm," *Elmore*, March/April 2013. http://www.onlinedigitalpubs.com/article/Levon+Helm/1324071/0/article.html (accessed July 1, 2018). **249. didn't talk about.**: Paul Berry, interview with author, April 22, 2018. **249. was out looking.**: Butch Dener, interview with author, March 21, 2018. **250. excellence and artistry.**": Helm, "The Music," *Razor*. **250. really makes me feel.**": Larry McMahan, "The Band Plans to Rock Knoxvillians with Their Legendary Celestial Sounds," *The Daily Beacon*, June 14, 1994, vol. 66, no. 4, p. 6. http://theband.hiof.no/articles/theband.4a.html (accessed November 8, 2016). **250. was and still is.**": Steve Thomson [director], *Let It Rock: At the Crossroads of Rock 'n' Roll* [DVD], Backstage Productions International and Eagle Rock Entertainment, 2005. **251. everybody went along.**": Ron Rainey, interview with author, October 15, 2018. **251. a powerful personality.**": Ibid. **251. being on the road.**": Dener and Lore, "Levon Helm and New Paltz," *Slice of New Paltz*. **251. when he was a kid.**: Anna Lee Amsden, interview with author, April 24, 2018. 252. lot at that time.": Aaron "Professor Louie" Hurwitz, interview with author, February 7, 2019. 252. way of life.": Marjorie Kaufman, "An Interview with Rick Danko," *On the Tracks*, August 16, 1996. http://theband.hiof.no/articles/on_the _tracks_danko_interview.html (accessed November 11, 2016). 252. little to fit our style,": Adam Budofsky, "The Band's Levon Helm and Randy Ciarlante," *Modern Drummer*, October 1996, p. 12. www.moderndrummer.com/site/wp-content/uploads/2016/05/md203.pdf (accessed November 9, 2016). 253. some great people.: Scott Jordan, "Backtalk with Levon Helm," *Offbeat*, December 1, 1998. www.offbeat.com/articles/levon-helm (accessed July 6, 2018). 253. when I came in.": Ron Rainey, interview with author, October 15, 2018. 254. path of least resistance.: George Lembesis, interview with author, February 7, 2019. 254. New York, Boston, Pittsburgh.: Ibid. 255. rock 'n' roll history,": Patrick Doyle, "Flashback: Keith Richards, Elvis' Sidemen and the Band Hit the Studio in 1996," *Rolling Stone*, November 28, 2018. www.rollingstone.com/music/music-news/flashback-keith-richards-elvis-sidemen-the -band-1996-758566 (accessed December 31, 2018). 255. do you think, Pop?": George Lembesis, interview with author, February 7, 2019. 256. compare equipment or whatever.": Ibid. 256. Helm dueled on their kits.": Scotty Moore, "Deuce and a Quarter," Scotty Moore website, December 1996. http://www.scottymoore.net/duece25.html (accessed December 31, 2018). 256. about being in a band.": Budofsky, "The Band's Levon Helm and Randy Ciarlante," *Modern Drummer*. 256. all the way through.": Lee Gabites, "A Conversation with Levon Helm, *Band fanzine*, October 1996. http://theband.hiof.no/articles/interview_levon_oct _96.html (accessed November 10, 2016). 257. him a lot of money,": Pat O'Shea, interview with author, February 4, 2019. 257. did cause problems.: Aaron "Professor Louie" Hurwitz, interview with author, February 7, 2019. 257. everything about it,": George Lembesis, interview with author, February 7, 2019. 257. about the whole situation.": Ibid. 258. guitars and jam.": Marilyn Beck and Stacy Jenel Smith, "Seagal's Strummin'," *The Province* [Vancouver, BC], October 2, 1996, B5. 258. off in a minute.": Mary Vaiden, interview with author, May 1, 2018. 258. did they want him?": Anna Lee Amsden, interview with author, April 24, 2018. 258. coughing up blood.'": George Lembesis, interview with author, February 7, 2019. 258. just need some rest.": Mary Vaiden, interview with author, May 1, 2018. 259. gonna be here.'": Bubba Sullivan, interview with author, April 26, 2018. 259. want to admit it.": Doug Blackburn, "The Beat Goes On: A Bout with Throat Cancer Hasn't Hurt Legendary Rock Musician Levon Helm's Desire to Perform," *Albany Times Union*, January 16, 2000. Capital Newspapers Division of The Hearst Corporation, Albany, N.Y. http://theband.hiof.no/articles /beat_goes_on_helm_albany.html (accessed February 9, 2016). 259. guys co-writing.": Aaron "Professor Louie" Hurwitz, interview with author, February 7, 2019. 259. way of doing stuff.": Jordan, "Backtalk with Levon Helm," *Offbeat*. 259. things with each other.": Ibid. 260. very good co-writer.": Aaron "Professor Louie" Hurwitz, interview with author, February 7, 2019. 260. supposed to do.": John Metzger, "The Band: *Jubilation*," *The Music Box*, October 1998, vol. 5, no. 10. www.musicbox-online.com/band-jub.html#axzz5dx5tzeWf (accessed January 28, 2019). 260. bit of rest from it.": Jordan, "Backtalk with Levon Helm," *Offbeat*. 260. make this record.'": Aaron "Professor Louie" Hurwitz, interview with author, February 7, 2019. 261. fuck outta here!": Butch Dener, interview with author, March 21, 2017. 261. And she came.": Ibid. 262. she got out of school.": Levon Helm, interview with David Bianculli, "Levon Helm: The 2007 *Fresh Air* Interview," *Fresh Air*, NPR Music, April 29, 2012. www.npr .org/2012/04/20/150886425/levon-helm-the-2007-fresh-air-interview (accessed July 20, 2018). 262. him in the dark days.": Mary Vaiden, interview with author, May 1, 2018. 262. whisper or write a note.": "Innovators in Music: Levon Helm," Bravo! Canada TV, January 14, 2010. http://www.levonhelm.com/Innovators_in_Music.htm (accessed December 1, 2016). 263. saved his life.: Butch Dener, interview with author, March 21, 2017. 263. entirely grateful for.": Blackburn, "The Beat Goes On," *Albany Times Union*. 263. acted like I wasn't.": Scott Spencer, "Levon Helm Returns to Blues and Tries to Put the Past to Rest," *Rolling Stone*, April 27, 2000. www.rollingstone.com/music/news/levon-helm-returns-to -blues-and-tries-to-put-the-past-to-rest-20120419 (accessed February 9, 2016). 263. seen before, a hero.": Ibid.

Chapter 14: "Blues Before Sunrise"

265. be a drummer.": Doug Blackburn, "The Beat Goes On: A Bout with Throat Cancer Hasn't Hurt Legendary Rock Musician Levon Helm's Desire to Perform," *Albany Times Union*, January 16, 2000. Capital Newspapers Division of The Hearst Corporation, Albany, N.Y. http://theband.hiof.no/articles/beat_goes_on_helm_albany.html (accessed February 9, 2016). 265. a better Levon.'": Steven Karras, "Levon Helm's Loved Ones Honor His Legacy," *HuffPost*, October 4, 2012. www.huffingtonpost.com/steve-karras/levon-helm-rambles_b _1937488.html (accessed December 18, 2018). 266. a blues band.": Aaron "Professor Louie" Hurwitz, interview with author, February 7, 2019. 267. would lead to.: Pat O'Shea, interview with author, July 31, 2018. 267. It was hysterically funny.": Ibid. 267. join your band.": Ibid. 268. four years old.: Ibid. 268. owe that man everything.": Chris O'Leary, interview with Don Wilcock, "Helena, Arkansas, Project," October 5, 2017, courtesy of the Pryor Center for Arkansas Oral and Visual History, University of Arkansas. 268. you can hear everything.": Ibid. 268. he played became his.: Pat O'Shea, interview with author, July 31, 2018. 269. That was the trouble.": C.W. Gatlin, interview with author, April 26, 2018. 269. close the club down.": Carmen Marotta, interview with author, July 22, 2018. 269. away with the money.: Ibid. 270. out of that mindset.: Pat O'Shea, interview with author, February 4, 2019. 270. take it or leave it.'": George Lembesis, interview with author, February 7, 2019. 270. took it for granted.": Bob Girouard, "Levon Helm: The Classic Drummer Interview," *Classic Drummer*, August 2008. www.levonhelm.com/articles/CLASSIC_DRUMMER_8_08.pdf (accessed November. 9, 2016). 271. could talk or not.": Butch Dener, interview with author, March 21, 2017. 271. music for the people.": Ibid. 271. all right with me.": Scott Spencer, "Levon Helm Returns to Blues and Tries to Put the Past to Rest," *Rolling Stone*, April 27, 2000. www.rollingstone .com/music/news/levon-helm-returns-to-blues-and-tries-to-put-the-past-to-rest-20120419 (accessed February 9, 2016). 271. He *loved* that stuff.": George Lembesis, interview with author, February 7, 2019. 271. *would* show up!": Ibid. 271. and to the beat.": Ibid. 272. smile ear to ear.": Blackburn, "The Beat Goes On," *Albany Times Union*. 272. I could see it.: Butch Dener, interview with Scott Lunsford, "Helena, Arkansas, Project," October 9, 2015, courtesy of the Pryor Center for Arkansas Oral and Visual History, University of Arkansas. 272. having him there.": Pat O'Shea, interview with author, July 31, 2018. 273. funny to watch.: George Lembesis, interview with author, February 7, 2019. 273. and I miss him.": Pat O'Shea, interview with author, July 31, 2018. 273. all understood it.": Pat O'Shea, interview with author, February 4, 2019. 273. in rough shape.": Mark T. Gould, "Jim Weider and Randy Ciarlante: The 'Remedy' for Playing in The Band," *Sound Waves*, November 2002. http://theband. hiof.no/articles/weider_ciarlante_soundwaves_11-2002.html (accessed November 10, 2016). 273. was not forthcoming.": Bill Avis, interview with author, May 1, 2017. 274. boy, he did.": Jim Weider, interview with author, September 19, 2018. 274. steal your money.": Spencer, "Levon Helm Returns to Blues," *Rolling Stone*. 274. words you sang.": Ibid. 274. every goddamn day.": Lee Gabites, "Nothing But the Blues for Levon Helm (Relix Revisited)," *Relix*, December 13, 2011. www.relix.com/articles/detail/nothing-but-the-blues-for-levon-helm -relix-revisited (accessed November 10, 2016). 275. the road out.: Pat O'Shea, interview with author, July 31, 2018. 275. same room as Levon.": Harold Wieties, interview with author, October 25, 2018. 275. very down to earth.": Ibid. 275. Nobody's going to care.'": Ibid. 276. face on it or whatever.": Ibid. 276. happy-go-lucky guy.": Ibid. 276. on the poor farm.: Andy Gill, "Back to the Land," *Mojo*, November 2000. http://theband.hiof.no/articles/back_to_the _land.html (accessed November 8, 2016). 277. time to play music.": Kay Roybal, "*Waltz* Among Best Rock Flicks," *Albuquerque Journal*, December 6, 2002. https://business.high-beam.com/2872/article-1G1-95387360/waltz-among-best-rock-flicks (accessed November 11, 2016). 277. sorry for himself.": Kerry Gold, "Robertson Digs Deeply into His Native Roots: On His Third Solo Project, the Former Band Member Mixes Experimental with Traditional Styles and Sounds," *The Vancouver Sun*, March 28, 1998, B4. 277. kept doing that.": Karen Schoemer, "The Soul of Woodstock: Levon Helm, the Coolest Singing Drummer of All Time, Keeps the Spirit of an Age and a Place Alive," *New York*, 40.38, October 29, 2007,

pp. 134–35. **278. He loved Levon.":** Pat O'Shea, interview with author, July 31, 2018. **278. always comes across.":** Ryan Weber, interview with author, February 11, 2017. **278. meant so much.":** Sam Weber, interview with author, February 11, 2017. **278. he never had.":** Pat O'Shea, interview with author, July 31, 2018. **279. solely for the money.:** Pat O'Shea, interview with author, February 4, 2019. **279. blessing for us.:** Steve Jordan, interview with author, November 26, 2018. **280. along with myself.":** Ibid. **280. something magical about him,":** David Fishof, interview with author, August 8, 2018. **280. great for both of them.":** Ibid. **281. part of his personality.:** Happy Traum, interview with author, October 12, 2018. **281. heavy with the pedal.:** Butch Dener and Joe Lore, interview by Don Kerr, "Levon Helm and New Paltz," *Slice of New Paltz*, episode 57 [n.d.]. https://vimeo.com/100000510 (accessed June 23, 2018). **281. two or three hours.":** Butch Dener, interview with author, March 21, 2017. **282. we could be home.":** George Lembesis, interview with author, February 7, 2019. **282. It just had to be said.":** Chris O'Leary, interview with Don Wilcock, "Helena, Arkansas, Project," October 5, 2017, courtesy of the Pryor Center for Arkansas Oral and Visual History, University of Arkansas. **283. maybe a rumba beat.:** Pat O'Shea, interview with author, July 31, 2018. **283. away from that.":** Jerome Avis, interview with author, March 26, 2017. **283. them would still bleed,":** Ibid. **283. glove, no love!'":** Pat O'Shea, interview with author, July 31, 2018. **283. smoked at that point.":** Pat O'Shea, interview with author, February 4, 2019. **285. seen many times before.:** Ibid. **285. he would speak to us.":** Ibid. **285. soul with the blues.:** George Lembesis, interview with author, February 7, 2019. **285. be a fucking jingle,":** David Griner, "5 Songs That Musicians Sued to Keep Out of Ads," *AdWeek*, June 25, 2012. www.adweek.com /brand-marketing/5-songs-musicians-sued-keep-out-ads-141438/ (accessed January 25, 2019). **286. Richard and Rick's tombstones.":** "Levon Helm Sues to Take a Load Off Ad Firm's Profits," Stereogum, March 13, 2007, www.stereogum.com/4827/levon_helm_sues_to_take _a_load_off_ad_firms_profit/news (accessed August 17, 2016). **286. to declare bankruptcy.":** Schoemer, "The Soul of Woodstock," *New York*, p. 135. **286. go out with a bang.":** Ibid. **286. set and get paid.":** Pat O'Shea, interview with author, February 4, 2019. **287. Thank God for that.":** Levon Helm, interview with Marco Werman, *Sound Tracks: Quick Hits* [series], the Talbot Players in association with PBS Arts, February 2012. www.youtube.com/watch ?v=KVey5eGRZqk (accessed June 27, 2018). **287. just return their friendship.":** Schoemer, "The Soul of Woodstock," *New York*, p. 135. **287. It was quite something.:** Steve Jordan, interview with author, November 26, 2018. **287. persona non grata.":** George Lembesis, interview with author, February 7, 2019. **287. the Barn Burners.":** Pat O'Shea, interview with author, February 4, 2019. **288. pretense in any of it.":** Daniel Berman [director], "Levon Helm," *Innovators in Music*, produced in association with Bravo! TV, 2008. www.youtube.com /watch?v=43YYkCLUGwI (accessed January 31, 2019). **288. music you enjoyed playing.":** Steven Karras, "Levon Helm's Loved Ones Honor His Legacy," *HuffPost*, October 4, 2012. www.huffingtonpost.com/steve-karras/levon-helm-rambles_b_1937488.html (accessed December 18, 2018). **288. musically and otherwise,":** Peter Aaron, "Ramble on Levon Helm: Profile of Country Music Gem and Local Legend Levon Helm," January 25, 2008. http:// levonhelm.com/articles/Chromogram_january_08.htm (accessed November 29, 2016). **288. much less work with him.":** "Backstory: Live from the Cutting Room with Larry Campbell and Teresa Williams," [n.d.]. www.youtube.com/watch?v=pWa8Pw0cocQ (accessed January 7, 2019). **288. I thought I could.:** Girouard, "Levon Helm," *Classic Drummer*, August 2008, p. 37. **289. what a blessing.":** Austin Scaggs, "Profile: Up All Night with Levon Helm," *Rolling Stone*, August 6, 2009, pp. 26, 28. **289. staring at him, wide-eyed.":** Suzanne Cadgene, "Levon Helm,"*Elmore*,March/April 2013.www.onlinedigitalpubs.com/article/Levon+Helm/1324071 /0/article.html (accessed July 1, 2018). **289. He loved to party.":** Mark Burger, "Levon's Place Was the Place to Be: *Ain't in it for My Health*: Spending Quality Time with the Legendary Levon," *Yes! Weekly*, June 5, 2013. http://yesweekly.com/Ain8217t-In-It-for-My-Health -Spending-quality-time-with-the-legendary-Levon-a20013 (accessed August 18, 2018). **289. don't want a contact high.":** Scaggs, "Up All Night with Levon Helm," *Rolling Stone*. **290. a little more in order.":** Cadgene, "Levon Helm," *Elmore*. **290. it's a wonderful life.":** Vicki Mabry [interviewer], "Comeback Kid: After a Year When the Music Came Back," *Nightline*

(ABC-TV program), December 30, 2005. http://theband.hiof.no/articles/lh_nightline_12-30
-2005.html (accessed February 9, 2016). **290. amazing, just amazing.**": David Schultz, "Larry
Campbell: Rock 'n' Roll's Right Hand Man," April 22, 2007. http://levonhelm.com/articles
/Larry%20Campbell%20Rock%20N%20Rolls%20Right%20Hand%20Man.htm (accessed
November 29, 2016). **290. had high expectations.**": Stephen Deusner, "Catching Up With…
Amy Helm," *Paste*, January 14, 2008. www.pastemagazine.com/articles/2008/01/catching-up
-with-amy-helm.html (accessed March 2, 2019). **290. celebration for me.**": Mark Guarino,
"Up on Cripple Creek: A Legend Rediscovers His Voice," *Paste*, November 2006. http://
theband.hiof.no/articles/a_legend_rediscovers_his_voice.html (accessed November 16, 2016).

Chapter 15: "God Wasn't Through with You"

291. sit in and participate.": Vicki Mabry, [interviewer], "Comeback Kid: After a Year When
the Music Came Back," *Nightline* (ABC-TV program), December 30, 2005. http://theband.
hiof.no/articles/lh_nightline_12-30-2005.html (accessed February 9, 2016). **292. good time
and celebrate music.**": Ibid. **292. for the evening.**": "Mourners Flock to Helm's Wake," *Edmonton Journal*, April 27, 2012, C7. **292. things can come back.**": Brian Hollander, "The Survivor: Levon Lives to Ramble On," *Woodstock Times*, July 2, 2008. http://levonhelm.com/articles
/The%20survivor.htm (accessed November 29, 2016). **292. take my boots off.**": Levon Helm,
interview with Greg Gattine and Carmel Holt, WDST Radio Woodstock, October 24, 2008.
http://levonhelm.com/video/DSTLevonHelmEDIT102408.mp3 (accessed December 1,
2016). **292. seem out of place.**": Kay Cordtz, "The Midnight Ramble Lives On," Blues Wax,
July 2007. http://theband.hiof.no/articles/RambleBW2.html (accessed November 12, 2016).
292. egos flying around.": Larry Campbell and Teresa Williams, "Remembering Levon Helm
and the Midnight Rambles, *Acoustic Guitar Sessions*, String Letter Publishing, 2016. http://
acousticguitar.com/larry-campbell-teresa-williams-remember-levon-helm-the-midnight
-ramble-video (accessed July 5, 2018). **293. He just never did.**": Howard Johnson, interview
with author, August 16, 2018. **293. we were a lock.**": Kay Cordtz, "Howard Johnson's Hornspiration: There's Always Room for Something New," *Roll Magazine*, [n.d.] 2017. www
.rollmagazine.com/howard-johnson's-hornspiration-theres-always-room-for-something
-new (accessed August 5, 2018). **293. play anything in there.**": Anne Margaret Daniel, "Al
Kooper, Jimmy Vivino Celebrate Mike Bloomfield at Levon Helm's, October 4," *No Depression: The Journal of Roots Music*, August 27, 2014. http://nodepression.com/article/al-kooper-
jimmy-vivino-celebrate-mike-bloomfield-levon-helms-october-4-0 (accessed January 23,
2019). **293. opportunity to be part of.**": Levon Helm, interview with David Bianculli, "Levon
Helm: The 2007 *Fresh Air* Interview," *Fresh Air*, NPR Music, April 29, 2012. www.npr
.org/2012/04/20/150886425/levon-helm-the-2007-fresh-air-interview (accessed July 20,
2018). **294. cops so much, but he did.**": Butch Dener and Joe Lore, interview by Don Kerr,
"Levon Helm and New Paltz," *Slice of New Paltz*, episode 57 [n.d.]. https://vimeo
.com/100000510 (accessed June 23, 2018). **294. part to make it happen.**": Kay Cordtz, "Read-
ing, Writing and Rhythm: Levon Helm, One Time Drummer for The Band, Now Devotes
His Time to Bringing Music to the Classroom at Local Schools," *Hudson Valley Magazine*,
August 22, 2006. www.hvmag.com/core/pagetools.php?pageid=6054&url=%2FHudson-Valley
-Magazine%2FAugust-2006%2FReading-Writing-Rythym%2F&mode=print (accessed February 9, 2016). **294. much as we did.**": Cordtz, "Reading, Writing and Rhythm," *Hudson Valley
Magazine*. **295. our great teachers.**": Cordtz, "The Midnight Ramble Lives On," Blues Wax.
295. watching those kids.": Cordtz, "Reading, Writing and Rhythm," *Hudson Valley Magazine*. **295. me feel any better.**": Lee Gabites, "Nothing But the Blues for Levon Helm (Relix
Revisited)," *Relix*, December 13, 2011. www.relix.com/articles/detail/nothing-but-the-blues
-for-levon-helm-relix-revisited (accessed November 10, 2016). **295. he gave us a chance.**":
Alexis P. Suter, interview with author, August 17, 2018. **295. path crossed his path.**": Ibid. **296.
industry was like him.**": Ibid. **296. He never complained.**: Ibid. **296. It was like a circus.**: Ibid.
297. he was our biggest fan.": Ibid. **297. from beginning to end.**": David Schultz, "Larry
Campbell: Rock 'n' Roll's Right Hand Man," April 22, 2007. http://levonhelm.com/articles

/Larry%20Campbell%20Rock%20N%20Rolls%20Right%20Hand%20Man.htm (accessed November 29, 2016). **297. standing the whole show.":** Don Imus and Lou Ruffino, *Imus in the Morning*, MSNBC, March 19, 2007. http://levonhelm.com/video/rock_the_beacon.htm (accessed December. 1, 2016). **297. reminds me of home.'":** Alexis P. Suter, interview with author, August 17, 2018. **297. He loved my mother.:** Ibid. **298. phoniness in the world.":** Jacques Steinberg, "New Generation Hops the Mystery Train," *The New York Times*, July 9, 2007. www.nytimes.com/2007/07/09/arts/music/09levo.html. (accessed November 29, 2016). **298. people in the world.":** Bob Girouard, "Levon Helm: The Classic Drummer Interview," *Classic Drummer*, August 2008, p. 38. www.levonhelm.com/articles/CLASSIC_DRUMMER_8_08. pdf (accessed November 9, 2016). **298. "You are an American treasure.":** Calvin Gilbert, "Levon Helm Joined by Crow, Hiatt and Harris in Nashville," *CMT News*, July 19, 2007. http:// www.cmt.com/news/1565143/levon-helm-joined-by-crow-hiatt-and-harris-in-nashville (accessed August 2, 2018). **298. "Thank God for music.":** Andy Greene, "Levon Helm Finds His Voice," *Rolling Stone*, November 1, 2007, p. 26. **298. good as it's ever been,":** Brian Hollander, "The Survivor: Levon Lives to Ramble On," *Woodstock Times*, July 2, 2008. http:// levonhelm.com/articles/The%20survivor.htm (accessed November 29, 2016). **299. they were coming up.:** Levon Helm, interview with John Donabie, Newstalk Radio 1010, Toronto, [n.d.]. http://www.levonhelm.com/video/Levon_Helm_Interview_lofi.mp3. (accessed December 1, 2016). **299. I love 'em that much.:** Girouard, "Levon Helm," *Classic Drummer*, August 2008, p. 38. **299. passed along and shared.":** Deusner, "Catching Up With…Amy Helm," *Paste*. **300. music used to have.":** Peter Aaron, "Ramble on Levon Helm: Profile of Country Music Gem and Local Legend Levon Helm," January 25, 2008. http://levonhelm.com/articles/Chromogram_january_08.htm (accessed November 29, 2016). **300. comfort in today's age.":** "Levon Helm: Rambling on the Roots," *PBS Newshour*, February 2, 2009. www.pbs .org/newshour/art/levon-helm-rambling-on-the-roots (accessed December 1, 2016). **300. best out of everybody.":** Campbell and Williams, "Remembering Levon Helm and the Midnight Rambles," *Acoustic Guitar Sessions*. **300. this man was doing.":** Deusner, "Catching Up With…Amy Helm," *Paste*. **300. beauty of the music.":** Cordtz, "The Midnight Ramble Lives On," *Blues Wax*. **300. manufactured about it.":** Happy Traum, "A Conversation with Levon Helm and Larry Campbell for *Acoustic Guitar Magazine*," September 18, 2015. www .happytraum.com/blog/a-conversation-with-levon-helm-and-larry-campbell-for-acoustic -guitar-magazine (accessed June 19, 2018). **300. them with the sticks.":** Girouard, "Levon Helm," *Classic Drummer*, August 2008, p. 38. **300. Amy and Teresa's harmonies.":** Levon Helm, interview with David Bianculli, "Levon Helm," *Fresh Air*. **301. hearing him sing that.":** Deusner, "Catching Up With…Amy Helm," *Paste*. **301. your sorrows and joys.":** Girouard, "Levon Helm," *Classic Drummer*, August 2008, p. 38. **301. away with another one.":** Schoemer, "The Soul of Woodstock," *New York*, p. 134. **301. his miraculous recovery.":** Winter Miller, "Voices of Genuine Originals, Chosen by One Who Should Know," *The New York Times*, June 29, 2008. www.nytimes.com/2008/06/29/arts/music/29play.html (accessed August 2, 2018). **302. adversity of immense proportions.":** Joel Selvin, "CD Reviews / Levon Helm," *SFGate*, November 11, 2007. www.sfgate.com/music/article/CD-REVIEWS-LEVON -HELM-3236540.php (accessed January 21, 2019). **302. happened in my little life.":** Daniel Berman [director], "Levon Helm," *Innovators in Music*, produced in association with Bravo! TV, 2008. www.youtube.com/watch?v=43YYkCLUGwI (accessed January 31, 2019). **302. American music royalty.":** Arlen Roth, "Goodbye Levon: *Gibson.com*'s Arlen Roth Remembers a Musical Great," Gibson Guitar, April 20, 2012. www.gibson.com/news-lifestyle/news /en-us/arlen-roth-remembers-levon-helm-0420-2012.aspx (accessed July 5, 2018). **303. right on the money!:** Ibid. **303. bantamweight fighter,":** J. Freedom du Lac, "Playing to Beat the Band," *The Washington Post*, April 26, 2008. www.washingtonpost.com/wp-dyn/content/article /2008/04/25/AR2008042503792.html (accessed January 20, 2019). **303. like his granddad.":** Helm, interview with Gattine and Holt, WDST Radio Woodstock. **303. corn once in a while.":** Lynne Margolis, "No False Bones: The Legacy of Levon Helm," *American Songwriter*, August 30, 2012. https://americansongwriter.com/2012/08/no-false-bones-the-legacy -of-levon-helm/2/ (accessed July 5, 2018). **303. this to ourselves, right.'":** Jerome Avis, interview with author, March 26, 2018. **304. lasting communal joy.**": Nick Deriso, "Levon Helm's *Ramble at the Ryman* Underscored a Sweeping Importance," *Something Else!*, May 17, 2015. http://somethingelsereviews.com/2015/05/17/levon-helm-ramble-at-the-ryman (accessed January 10, 2019). **304. America ever put out.**": "2008 All for the Hall New York," Country Music Hall of Fame and Museum Nashville, October 15, 2008. https://countrymusichalloff-ame.org/index.php/newsandupdates/posts/all-for-the-hall-new-york-2008 (accessed January 20, 2019). **304. yet remaining unmovable.**": "100 Greatest Singers of All Time," *Rolling Stone*, December 3, 2010. www.rollingstone.com/music/music-lists/100-greatest-singers-of-all-time -147019/annie-lennox-2-36569 (accessed January 19, 2019). **304. role of the dead General.**": Jonathan Romney, "*In the Electric Mist*," *Screen Daily*, February 7, 2009. www.screendaily.com /in-the-electric-mist/4042979.article (accessed January 26, 2019). **304. help him give it,**": "Levon Helm: The Making of *Electric Dirt*," promotional video, 2009. www.youtube.com /watch?v=JZDCGCtloQ4 (accessed March 6, 2019). **305. voice left to do it.**": Austin Scaggs, "Profile: Up All Night with Levon Helm," *Rolling Stone* (August 6, 2009): pp. 26, 28. **305. real want and a *need*.**": Barney Hoskyns, "The Rock's Backpages Rewind: At Home with Levon Helm in 2009," April 20, 2012. www.yahoo.com/entertainment/bp/rock-backpages-rewind -home-levon-helm-2009-102148260.html (accessed June 19, 2018). **305. color or tone to it.**": Traum, "A Conversation for *Acoustic Guitar* magazine." **306. New Orleans thing.**": Ibid. **306. try and do it.**": Levon Helm, interview with John Donabie, Newstalk Radio 1010. **306. should be loving.**: Traum, "A Conversation for *Acoustic Guitar* magazine." **307. every earthly travail.**": Jon Pareles, "Critics' Choice; New CDs," *The New York Times*, June 29, 2009. https://archive .nytimes.com/query.nytimes.com/gst/fullpage-9902EFD61731F93AA15755C0A96F 9C8B63.html (accessed January 25, 2019). **307. he was with this band.**": Jim Weider, interview with author, September 19, 2018. **308. Turkey Scratch, Ark.**: The Spin, "Levon Helm's Ramble at The Ryman, 4/21/10," *Nashville Scene*, April 22, 2010. www.nashvillescene.com /music/article/13033677/levon-helms-ramble-at-the-ryman-42110 (accessed January 22, 2019). **308. It's called Levon Helm.**": Sandy Tomcho, "Celebrities Offer Birthday Wishes to Levon Helm," *Times Herald-Record* [Middletown, NY], May 24, 2010. www.recordonline .com/article/20100524/ENTERTAIN/100529978 (accessed January 22, 2019). **309. mortgage on that place.**: Jerome Avis, interview with author, March 26, 2017. **309. forgot about Willie.**": "Concert Review: Willie Nelson, Levon Helm at CMAC," Willie Nelson and Family, July 30, 2010. http://clubluck.willienelson.com/story/concert-review-willie-nelson-levon -helm-at-cmac (accessed July 5, 2018). **310. hurting like that.**": Jim Keltner, interview with author, December 19, 2018. **310. happy to have him.**": Bob Mersereau, "Concert Review: Levon Helm—Harvest Jazz and Blues Festival, Sept. 15/11," CBC New Brunswick, September 16, 2011. www.cbc.ca/nb/mt/east-coast-music/2011/09/concert-review-levon-helm—harvest -jazz-and-blues-festival-sept-1511.html (accessed January 23, 2019). **310. do that I'm great.**": Levon Helm, interview with Marco Werman, *Sound Tracks: Quick Hits* [series], the Talbot Players in association with PBS Arts, February 2012. www.youtube.com/watch?v=KVey 5eGRZqk (accessed June 27, 2018). **310. pride in his eyes.**": Steven Karras, "Levon Helm's Loved Ones Honor His Legacy," *HuffPost*, October 4, 2012. www.huffingtonpost.com/steve -karras/levon-helm-rambles_b_1937488.html (accessed December 18, 2018). **311. there with him.**": Mike Greenhaus, "Jim Weider Lends His Weight to The Band's Legacy," Jambands .com, April 7, 2015. https://jambands.com/features/2015/04/07/jim-weider-lends-his-weight -to-the-band-s-legacy (accessed December 27, 2018). **311. greatly for it.**": Mary Vaiden, interview with author, May 1, 2018. **311. it had consequences.**": Howard Johnson, interview with author, August 16, 2018. **311. rasp or anything.**: Steve Jordan, interview with author, November 26, 2018. **312. Helm inspires the lot.**": Robin Tolleson, "Levon Helm Ramble at the Ryman," *Modern Drummer* 36.4, April 2012, p. 90. **312. through with you.**": Anna Lee Amsden, interview with author, April 26, 2018. **312. deserved the rewards,**": Anna Lee Amsden, interview with Scott Lunsford, "Helena, Arkansas, Project," October 9, 2015, courtesy of the Pryor Center for Arkansas Oral and Visual History, University of Arkansas. **312. sitting on the soap dish.**": Mary Vaiden, interview with author, May 1, 2018. **312. I was very honored.**": Jim Weider, interview with author, September 19, 2018. **312. treasure he was.**": Chris

O'Leary, interview with Don Wilcock, "Helena, Arkansas, Project," October 5, 2017, courtesy of the Pryor Center for Arkansas Oral and Visual History, University of Arkansas. **313. quintessential band component.**: Jeff Potter, "Levon Helm May 26, 1940–April 19, 2012," *Modern Drummer* 36.11 (November 2012): pp. 50–57, 59–61. **313. free ride for me.":** Helm, interview with Werman, *Sound Tracks: Quick Hits*. **313. done without it.":** Ibid. **313. could** *he* **last?":** Janine Schaults, "Larry Campbell and Teresa Williams Talk Bob Dylan, Levon Helm and *Contraband Love*," *Chicago Tribune*, October 24, 2017. www.chicagotribune.com/entertainment /music/ct-ott-larry-campbell-teresa-williams-contraband-love-20171023-story.html (accessed August 2, 2018). **313. more years of life.":** Cordtz, "Howard Johnson's Hornspiration," *Roll Magazine*. **314. all, too: music.":** Greenhaus, "Jim Weider," Jambands.com, April 7, 2015. **314. voice was so fragile.":** Campbell and Williams, "Remembering Levon Helm and the Midnight Rambles, *Acoustic Guitar Sessions*. **314. be okay again.":** Ibid. **315. unbelievably powerful performance.:** Nick Deriso, "Steve Berlin, of Los Lobos: *Something Else!* Interview," *Something Else!*, October 30, 2013. http://somethingelsereviews.com/2013/10/30/something-else -interview-steve-berlin-of-los-lobos (accessed September 26, 2018). **315. more time, you know.":** Jim Weider, interview with author, September 19, 2018. **315. "Keep it goin',":** Karras, "Levon Helm's Loved Ones," *HuffPost*. **315. Amy, and wife Sandy:** Carrie Batten, "Levon Helm in Final Stages of Cancer," *Pitchfork*, April 17, 2012. https://pitchfork.com/news/46190 -levon-helm-in-final-stages-of-cancer (accessed January 25, 2019). **316. done and the laughs we'd had.":** Anna Lee Amsden, interview with Scott Lunsford, "Helena, Arkansas, Project," October 9, 2015, courtesy of the Pryor Center for Arkansas Oral and Visual History, University of Arkansas. **316. we loved him.":** David Browne, "Levon Helm, Drummer and Singer of the Band, Dead at 71," *Rolling Stone,* April 19, 2012. www.rollingstone.com/music/news/levon -helm-drummer-and-singer-of-the-band-dies-at-71-20120419 (accessed February 6, 2016). **316. I'm proud of you.":** Davis Inman and Rob Birdsong, "10 Goodbyes to Levon Helm," *American Songwriter*, April 23, 2012. http://americansongwriter.com/2012/04/10-goodbyes -to-levon-helm (accessed August 8, 2018). **317. will live on forever.:** Rep. Maurice Hinchey, tribute to Levon Helm in the U.S. House of Representatives, April 25, 2012, C-Span. www .youtube.com/watch?v=0fWDjS1JEyA (accessed January 26, 2019). **317. be a part of it.":** "Mourners Flock to Helm's Wake," *Edmonton Journal*, April 27, 2012, C7. **317. love in the building.":** Anna Lee Amsden, interview with Scott Lunsford, "Helena, Arkansas, Project," October 9, 2015, courtesy of the Pryor Center for Arkansas Oral and Visual History, University of Arkansas. **318. Very powerful.:** Jerome Avis, interview with author, March 26, 2017. **318. he was your best friend.'":** John Donabie, interview with author, March 30, 2017. **318. hear all the applause.":** Ibid. **318. crowd that turned out.":** Anna Lee Amsden, interview with Scott Lunsford, "Helena, Arkansas, Project," October 9, 2015, courtesy of the Pryor Center for Arkansas Oral and Visual History, University of Arkansas. **318. heck out of that.":** Ibid. **318. corps they could find.":** John Donabie, interview with author, March 30, 2017. **319. It was very fitting.":** Ibid. **320. BOB DYLAN:** "Bob Dylan Responds to Death of Levon Helm," *Rolling Stone*, April 20, 2012. www.rollingstone.com/music/music-news/bob-dylan -responds-to-death-of-levon-helm-246672 (accessed August 5, 2018).

Index

About the Author

S andra B. Tooze garnered worldwide acclaim for her book *Muddy Waters: The Mojo Man*. Eric Clapton wrote the foreword, and Levon Helm and Mick Jagger both endorsed it with back-cover quotes. The reviewer for America's preeminent blues magazine, *Living Blues*, called it a "first rate biography…An illumination and a joy, it deserves a place on our shelves as a loving and earnest tribute to one of the greats of American music." On Britain's BBC radio, her book was described as "terrific…and absolutely great." And in the U.K.'s premier music magazine, *Mojo*, it was praised as "a vivid, brilliantly researched portrait." Sandra spent most of her life living in Toronto and now lives on the West Coast of Canada.